Living The Letters

"Written with characteristic wit, theological creativity, and ethical seriousness, as well as all the linguistic dexterities of a Hebrew speaker, Michael Marmur's Elements of a Jewish Theology is fully situated in the revelatory space between Jewry's historical moment and its eternity. Meriting the attention of a general and scholarly readership, this original book looks set to be a new classic in the field."
—Melissa Raphael, Professor Emerita, Jewish Theology,
University of Gloucestershire and Leo Baeck College, London

"Is it possible to craft a Jewish theology that is both rigorous and readable, traditional and contemporary, coherent and altogether creative? With this volume, Michael Marmur, one of our generation's preeminent thinkers, answers with a resounding YES! Building on those who came before, Marmur's volume provides the living script for all future drafts of Jewish theology."
—Elliot Cosgrove - Rabbi, Park Avenue Synagogue. Author,
For Such a Time as This: On Being Jewish Today

Michael Marmur

Living The Letters

An Alphabet of Emerging Jewish Thought

Michael Marmur
Hebrew Union College
Jerusalem, Israel

David & Vera Levi Medical Research Memorial Fund

ISBN 978-3-031-81040-4   ISBN 978-3-031-81041-1 (eBook)
https://doi.org/10.1007/978-3-031-81041-1

© The Editor(s) (if applicable) and The Author(s) 2025. This book is an open access publication.

Open Access This book is licensed under the terms of the Creative Commons Attribution 4.0 International License (http://creativecommons.org/licenses/by/4.0/), which permits use, sharing, adaptation, distribution and reproduction in any medium or format, as long as you give appropriate credit to the original author(s) and the source, provide a link to the Creative Commons license and indicate if changes were made.
The images or other third party material in this book are included in the book's Creative Commons license, unless indicated otherwise in a credit line to the material. If material is not included in the book's Creative Commons license and your intended use is not permitted by statutory regulation or exceeds the permitted use, you will need to obtain permission directly from the copyright holder.
The use of general descriptive names, registered names, trademarks, service marks, etc. in this publication does not imply, even in the absence of a specific statement, that such names are exempt from the relevant protective laws and regulations and therefore free for general use.
The publisher, the authors and the editors are safe to assume that the advice and information in this book are believed to be true and accurate at the date of publication. Neither the publisher nor the authors or the editors give a warranty, expressed or implied, with respect to the material contained herein or for any errors or omissions that may have been made. The publisher remains neutral with regard to jurisdictional claims in published maps and institutional affiliations.

Cover art: ALEPH-BET, art marker and acrylic pen on paper, Elizabeth Marmur, www.marmur.co.uk

This Palgrave Macmillan imprint is published by the registered company Springer Nature Switzerland AG.
The registered company address is: Gewerbestrasse 11, 6330 Cham, Switzerland

If disposing of this product, please recycle the paper.

*For Miriam & Ben, Nadav & Amit, Gabrielle & Shahaf
With Boundless Love*

SPONSORSHIP

The publication of this work in an open access format was made possible by the generosity of the David and Vera Levi Medical Research Memorial Fund and the Florence G. Roswell Fund for Library Programs of the Hebrew Union College–Jewish Institute of Religion.

Acknowledgments

Throughout this book's long gestation, the Hebrew Union College–Jewish Institute of Religion has been my professional, intellectual, and spiritual home. This is true of all our locations and most particularly of our Jerusalem campus. Thanks for support and collegiality are due to the current president and provost of HUC-JIR, Andrew Rehfeld and Andrea Weiss, and for unflagging encouragement and friendship to the former dean of the Jerusalem school, Naamah Kelman. I also want to mention with appreciation and affection the late Aaron Panken, a former president of HUC-JIR. Several members of the staff, administration, faculty, and student body have provided invaluable assistance. Writing a work such as this depends on extensive reading, and the librarians working across our multi-campus library system have been a source of unstinting support, in particular the director of our Jerusalem library, Tamar Duvdevani.

Significant financial support has been provided by the David & Vera Levi Medical Research Memorial Fund. My thanks are due to the fund's trustees, Andrew Moss and Mark Bernstein, for a subvention which has helped make this book available in electronic form without cost to anyone interested in reading it. David and Vera Levi were the grandparents of my wife, Sarah Bernstein, and I am grateful for this opportunity to honor their memory. Similarly, thanks are due to Provost Andrea Weiss for devoting funds for this purpose from the Florence G. Roswell Fund for Library Programs of the Hebrew Union College–Jewish Institute of Religion.

Over recent years I have had opportunities to try out some of these ideas as scholar-in-residence at a number of Reform congregations around North America and Israel. Thanks are due to the colleagues who have invited me and to the congregants I have met. They have taught me much.

Some individuals have read or discussed sections of this book and provided important suggestions. I would like to thank by name Naamah Dafni (who also workshopped some chapters with members of Or Hadash Congregation in Haifa), Arthur Green, Michal Muszkat-Barkan, Andrew Rehfeld, Rachel Sabath Beit-Halachmi, and Danny Schiff. Some of these ideas have been influenced by my involvement with Rabbis for Human Rights, and a word of thanks is due to its executive director, Avi Dabush.

Daniel Taub and Jan Katzew have been extremely helpful at important stages in the development of this project. Three people read this book chapter by chapter from its beginning, and it is sad to note that two of them did not live to see it come to fruition. My father, Dow Marmur, has been without a doubt the most significant intellectual and religious influence on my life, exemplifying the engaged Reform Jewish approach I have tried to perpetuate and develop. David Ellenson was like a big brother to me, in our professional activities in the administration of HUC-JIR, in our intellectual explorations, and in countless expressions of friendship. I miss Dow and David beyond words. The third member of this reading circle is Daniel Jackson, to whom great thanks are due. His enthusiasm, acuity, and sensitivity have been truly invaluable.

Nikki Littman is an excellent literary editor. I am grateful for her close reading of this "crunchy" text and for her help in making it a little smoother. Working with her is invariably enlightening as well as fun. The team at Palgrave Macmillan has been unfailingly supportive.

Thanks are due to my family: my mother, Fredzia Marmur, who continues to exemplify grace and wisdom, and my sisters, Viveca and Elizabeth. Elizabeth's art adorns the cover of this book, and for this I am particularly grateful. My wife, Sarah Bernstein, is an endless source of love and support and, indeed, of wonder. She exemplifies what living out the alphabet of one's values can look like.

The book is dedicated with love and respect to our children: Miriam and her husband Ben Tofach, Nadav and his partner Amit Zilberberg, and Gabrielle and her partner Shahaf Yinnone. I presented the concept of this book to them some years ago and have kept them updated sporadically. I hope they know that the motivation behind this work is not to tell them what to think but to give them a sense of what I think and believe and care about and why. I trust them to continue to live the letters in new ways in the years to come. The dedication to them with boundless love is itself a quotation, since this is the way my father would sign his letters to us. The love is carried from generation to generation.

These words were written in my home in Jerusalem at a time of great uncertainty and pain. Hostages are in captivity, whole neighborhoods in ruins, and communities displaced. Lives have been shattered: thousands have died and thousands more have been injured. The prospect of peace between Israelis and Palestinians seems distant. The deepening humanitarian crisis is of enormous proportions, and the risk of war throughout the Middle East is palpable. Set against this grim backdrop, it is hard to imagine that books and ideas can make a difference in the world.

Nevertheless, it is a privilege to spend my life studying, teaching, and propagating Torah as I understand it. This is an unmistakably Jewish work, but my hope is that readers from other cultures and faith traditions might find within it a basis for creative dialogue. Perhaps this lexicon can help promote innovative ways of grappling with seemingly intractable questions. Books and ideas have always mattered, perhaps even more in times of crisis than in periods of stability. Living a life of deep engagement with a tradition offers life to those who taste it, to paraphrase a phrase from an alphabetical liturgical poem. I hope this book can offer a taste of life. Writing it has certainly given increased flavor to mine.

Contents

Introduction	1
Aspaklaria: Prophecy and Pluralism	53
Bi: Spirituality and Responsibility	67
Gader: Borders and Boundaries	79
Dovev: Quotation and Education	93
Hogenet: Decency and Society	107
Vegoralenu: Peoplehood and Chosenness	121
Zeman Nakat: History and Change	135
Chai Vekayam: The Existence and Insistence of God	147
Tefachim: A Torah of Tension	161
Yetzer Lev Ha'adam: On Human Nature	173
Kosot Yeshu'ah: Frameworks of Jewish Thought	185

Lehaniach: The Assumption of Ritual	199
Masoret: Tradition!	211
Neder: Vows and Commitments	223
Safek: The Benefit of Doubt	237
Azazel: Gaza and Expulsion	249
Pi Yagid: Prayer and Language	263
Tzechok: Judaism and Humor	277
Kehillah: Community	289
Reshit: The Flowering of Our Redemption?	301
Sha'at Hamefazrim: Judaism Thick and Thin	315
Taluy: Dependence and Independence	327
The Twenty-Third Letter	339
Works Mentioned	349
Author Index	395
Work Index	399
Subject Index	403

Introduction

I was in prison when I decided to write this book. It was the early 1990s, and I was serving as perhaps Israel's least significant soldier, a military policeman stationed at Megiddo Jail. The prison was then serving as a detention center for Palestinians detained in Jenin, neighboring villages, and other locations on the West Bank. Location of famous battles from 3500 years ago to the First World War, the site is also known as Armageddon.

In search of distraction, I had brought with me a copy of Eugene Borowitz's *Renewing the Covenant*.[1] I spent my free hours reading this important work on the possibilities for Jewish commitment in a non-Orthodox context: what he calls "a postliberal theory of Jewish duty."[2] My favored location for reading was the synagogue, selected less for its air of sanctity than for its air conditioner. Reading Borowitz's theology of Jewish duty in an Israeli military jail convinced me to write something of my own. This is the book I first imagined writing in the synagogue in Armageddon.

Living the Letters comprises this long introduction followed by twenty-two shorter chapters. Each one proposes a Hebrew word or phrase beginning with the letters of the Hebrew alphabet in order. A twenty-third chapter, based on the tradition of a letter still unrevealed, strikes the book's closing chord. It is an example of what I describe below as crunchy theology. It is not designed to be spread evenly or to answer every question systematically. It is intended ideally to be read in order, and if you read it all through you will be afforded a sense of my theological lexicon. However, the chapters can also be read out of sequence. If you choose to skip the introduction, you will have less of a sense of what I mean when I say "Jewish theology," but the choice, of course, is yours to make.

The five sections of this introduction relate to the motivation, structure, and ambition of *Living the Letters*. In the first, I argue that no book of this kind is undertaken without anxiety, nor can it be completed without hope. In the second section I explain the distinction between crunchy and smooth Jewish theology. The third section relates to this book's alphabetical structure. The fourth ponders Moses Mendelssohn's notion of Judaism as a living script, and in the fifth, I look to the example of the Masoretes, vocalizers of the letters of the Hebrew Bible.

ANXIETY AND HOPE

Anxiety

Revisiting the classic Jewish theological themes of God, Israel, and Torah in *Renewing the Covenant*, Borowitz offered a strident critique of a naïve faith in the promise of modernity and developed his notion of covenant theology. He asked: once you have rejected the metaphysical assumptions of traditional authority claims, can a foundation be established or a rationale argued for perpetuating Jewish fidelity and practice?

Borowitz was not much concerned with state power and sovereignty, topics which were very much on my mind as I read his work in the synagogue of Megiddo Jail. His emphasis was on the Jewish self, rejecting both the certainties of orthodoxy and the Pollyannaish optimism of liberalism. He described himself as "one of the postliberal/post-orthodox community because I live from a Jewish faith that my personhood derives from God who commands me yet also dignifies me with independent personal responsibility."[3]

Eugene Borowitz was motivated in his work by one of the perennial catalysts of Jewish theological creativity: anxiety. He gave voice to some of his explicit anxieties in the course of his work. In *Renewing the Covenant*, for example, he spoke of being "more anxious about the corporate than the personal aspect of Jewish selfhood."[4] Some of his anxieties are implicit, but no less prominent. In the book's final paragraphs, Borowitz concentrated on one instance of a contemporary Jewish dilemma, employing his notion of covenant theology to explain why he was not prepared to officiate at marriage ceremonies involving a Jew and a non-Jew but why he respected the integrity of those whose opinion differs from his own. This generosity of spirit did not extend to those willing to co-officiate at inter-religious ceremonies, for such an act "clearly constitutes a threat to the survival of the Jewish people and its Covenant and exceeds my liberally capacious pluralism."[5]

Borowitz was one of a long line of Jewish worriers. In Jewish civilization, anxiety is a spur to creativity. The Jews have been felicitously described as the ever-dying people,[6] perennially convinced that their generation may be the last, warding off Armageddon by constantly imagining it. When it comes to the history of Jewish anxiety, the lines between political, theological, and existential concerns have often been blurred.

In 38 CE Philo of Alexandria undertook a trip to Rome as part of a delegation. In his account of that mission, Philo tells of King Agrippa, who arrives in Rome and discovers that his erstwhile friend the Emperor Gaius Caligula (famed for paranoia and narcissism) suspects the Jewish nation of disloyalty and is minded to have a statue of himself erected in the Temple in Jerusalem. In Philo's version Agrippa prepared a letter for Caligula and was then overcome by "agony, confusion, and disorder, and anxiety, as to what was the best way of approaching and addressing the emperor."[7] He was conscious that the way he presented the Jews' case would have grave implications for Jews around the world. The sense of dread lest the intervention fail, the fear that all may be lost—these have been constant Jewish preoccupations long before Agrippa's night of torment and ever since.

Almost two millennia later, Jonathan Sacks wrote a book entitled *Will We Have Jewish Grandchildren?*[8] In the title and content of that work, the author gives voice to a question preoccupying contemporary Jews. It is, likewise, implicit in the book I read in Megiddo Jail, in which Borowitz frets about the viability of the encounter between modern notions of autonomy and traditional concepts of covenant. In the ancient example, the fear is that a capricious and unstable emperor imbued with great personal power will do untold harm to the Jews. In the modern case, the prompt is not the fear of imperial disfavor but rather the sense that the welcoming embrace of the non-Jewish world may undermine Jewish continuity. In ancient Alexandria as in contemporary London, Jews set quill to papyrus, pen to paper, or finger to keyboard in response to anxiety and fear.

Jews over the centuries have found the threat of doom to be not only debilitating but also stimulating.[9] In "the first of the great medieval Jewish philosophical treatises,"[10] Saadia Gaon described his work as a response to the prevalence of doubt and error:

> I saw in this age of mine many believers whose belief was not pure ... I saw, furthermore, men who were sunk, as it were in seas of doubt ... and there was no diver to bring them up from the depths ... I thought that it was my duty to help them therewith and my obligation to the direct them to the truth.[11]

The first great work of Jewish philosophy was thus motivated by the anxiety that the temptations of Islam, on the one hand, and the Karaite movement, on the other, may entice or confuse members of the mainstream Jewish community.

Our anxieties are many and various. In one of his Talmudic discourses, Emmanuel Levinas offers a characteristically playful and insightful reading of the ten spies described in the Book of Numbers (those other than Joshua and Caleb sent by Moses to bring a report of Canaan), so often vilified or overlooked.[12] He asks what those who counseled against attempting the conquest of the land saw. He goes on to list three fears, three core anxieties, and to remind his audience that these should be acknowledged even if not accepted.

First, he suggests, the spies were afraid of defeat, death, and injury, namely, old-fashioned fears of impending harm. Second, he adds with ahistorical whimsy, the spies were perhaps gifted with foresight and struggled to recognize tomorrow's *Sabras*, native-born Israelis of Jewish origin, as their own progeny. This second fear is that the creation of Israel may have engendered an unbreachable rupture between a diasporic sensibility and these bold, unironic new creatures. Levinas' third anxiety is moral in nature: the ten spies in his reading were concerned about the acts of destruction that would be necessary for the conquest to succeed: what right allows us to dispossess those already present in the land?

Here are three anxieties of the first order. Will we survive? Will the Jewish future after entering the Land be recognizable and desirable? And is the moral price of sovereignty too high? My approach to anxieties can be termed "bear hunt" stoicism:[13] we cannot pass over these challenges, nor can we float above them. We will have to work through them, perhaps comforted in the knowledge that this is what Jews have done for as long as there have been Jews.

It seems appropriate to list the key anxieties that motivated me to write this book. There are the big global ones, of course. Will impending climate catastrophe render all the rest of our concerns moot? Will the endless race for domination and the insatiable appetite for consumption lead to global destruction? Will the coming years bring an epidemic of pandemics, deepening intolerance, and widening inequity? Is an era of relative stability to be replaced by a period of global upheaval?

At the other extreme of the anxiety scale are concerns relating to this particular project. Articulating ideas complex enough to be worth stating and clear enough to be understood is a tall order. I am afraid that I will not be able to express my own heartfelt commitments, that turns of phrase and abstractions will obstruct true expression. I am also concerned that what I say or omit to say will cause offense or harm.

Somewhere between the angst of global meltdown and the pique of authorial self-doubt, two major Jewish anxieties inform much of this work.

Can Modern Judaism Work?
The idea of melding modernity to Judaism, the animating story of my life, may, in time, come unstuck. I doubt little that the concept of a moderate, reasonable Judaism is *right*—defensible, plausible, and sound—but worry much that it may not be *true*—resonant, capable of inducing passionate commitment, and teachable. Postmodern alternatives to naïve modernist optimism carry their own risks. Sophistication and suspicion may be the death of spontaneity and simplicity. Being ironic and knowing and clever may get in the way of direct and intense experiences. Contemporary Judaism is tied to two chariots, each pulling in opposite directions: one leads to the dissolution of Judaism in the name of a homogenized global human soup; the other surges toward chauvinism and bigotry. I am concerned that many Jews who share my vision for society and the world see scant reason to perpetuate Jewish life. In my anxiety I see them steering toward the Scylla of Jewish oblivion, giving up the Jewish story after thirty centuries because they can and because they see no good reason not to do so. And I am just as concerned that many who share my passion for thick Jewish engagement have set a course for the Charybdis of myopic parochialism.

Some assure us that all will be well, that the Jewish community is being enriched more than it is being compromised, that positive energy outstrips decay and decline. I hope they are right but cannot say that my anxieties are allayed. I remain afraid that the Judaism we profess, the one expressed in our institutions and public statements, will not keep pace with the changes overwhelming our assumptions and capacities at an unprecedented velocity.

A cautiously enthusiastic modernist. I am delighted that benighted and obscurantist views have been found wanting when held up to the cold light of reason and so rejected. I am concerned, however, on at least two fronts: first, that the cold light of reason does not generate enough warmth and passion to give us the energy we will all need to be equal to our challenges; and second, that in clearing away the debris of outdated beliefs and practices, we stop believing that distinct identities and rich vocabularies matter. If we let the flavors and fragrances of the great traditions of the world disappear or lose interest in them, I fear we will be left with little more than mediocrity, while purveyors of certainties flourish.

One iteration of the more general anxiety about modern Judaism concerns our capacity to educate, inculcate, and perpetuate. I am afraid that the kind of Judaism I profess and promote may fail to pass on robust practices, experiences, and modes of learning. It must be judicious and balanced. It cannot afford to be tepid.

I am afraid that many modern Jews know too little about the wellsprings of creativity and depth to be found within its three millennia of expression. To be sure, many contemporary Jews have access to worlds of knowledge and possibility that their forebears could not even have imagined. Some are beginning their journeys, to use Rosenzweig's apt image, from the periphery and moving toward the center of Jewish learning.[14] I remind myself that the relationship between knowledge and ignorance is not captured by a simple binary.

Doling out verdicts on who is and who is not knowledgeable is usually a power play designed to assert authority. Nevertheless, there *is* a palpable dearth of Jewish literacy in liberal circles (in Orthodox circles too, but that is less my concern here). Much of what passes for Jewish learning is superficial and trite, more likely to stir emotions than to point the way to new possibilities. Jewish learning at its finest warms the heart as it fires the imagination.

To be an heir to Jewish tradition should mean to feel affinity with and have some degree of access to the Hebrew Bible and the literature of the Second Temple period, the Mishnah, Talmud, Midrash, Geonic literature, medieval philosophy and Kabbalah, and the Jewish encounter with modernity. It should involve a geographical sweep that includes Baghdad and Berlin, Bombay and Buenos Aires. It should mean that anthropology and musicology, poetry and responsa, amulets and prayer shawls, that indeed everything human is an object of curiosity, particularly when seen through the prism of the Jewish story. It should mean more than chuckling at predictable Jewish jokes, sharing predictable concerns, or consuming predictable foodstuffs.

I am not suggesting a crude essentialism whereby you have to pass an exam or meet some externally established criterion in order to be allowed into the Jewish conversation. No such criterion exists, and whoever commits to the conversation is part of it. My anxiety, as someone who has been involved in Jewish education for their entire adult life, is that we have done a poor job in educating Jews to be consumed with the curiosity to learn and that many Jews lack the literacy that would bring them into the conversation as empowered participants.

Liberal Jews are occasionally criticized for over-emphasizing the universal ethical aspects of Judaism.[15] Plumbing tradition in search of that which most resonates with contemporary standards and sensibilities is, in fact, a highly traditional thing to do. My anxiety is that the process of reinterpreting the tradition is being undertaken too often not through close reading but through excision of anything deemed to cause discomfort. In order to ground the universal and ethical within our Judaism, we need to face the discomfort head on.

The project of modern Judaism is threatened not only by a crisis of education but also by a crisis of pluralism. Without more robust ways of standing up for values and convictions while celebrating diversity of opinions and orientations, my anxiety is that a Torah of moderation and complexity may be swept away by a torrent of fundamentalist certainties. Finding ways for Jews of radically different orientations to engage in Judaism as a common enterprise is an increasingly fraught activity. As Menachem Kellner noted with reference to the book by Jonathan Sacks mentioned above, "the critical question we face ... is not whether we will have Jewish grandchildren, but how many different sorts of mutually exclusive and mutually intolerant Judaisms our grandchildren will face."[16]

Can Israel Live Up to Its Promise?
I am afraid that the establishment of the State of Israel may prove to be not only the most consequential Jewish event in over a millennium but also a challenge to which we may not be equal. There is an existential dimension to this fear: the professed aims of a number of groups, militias, and states in the Middle East are not to be dismissed as hyperbole. This

fear is real and should be acknowledged, along with the knowledge that this fear has itself become an obstacle to overcoming our current impasse. Israel is threatened by implacable adversaries and also compromised internally by the lack of a workable vision of how Jews and Palestinians may live with or alongside each other in security and dignity.

There are other profound concerns too regarding the State of Israel. While patriotic politicians and apologists style Israel an instinctive democracy, pointing to both our institutions and our argumentative natures, they ignore the palpable erosion of democratic norms which has characterized Israeli society for decades. An astounding number of Jewish Israeli citizens seem to be prepared to countenance continued inequalities between Jews and Arabs and to espouse a systematic policy of disenfranchisement or conditional citizenship. So it goes, too, for the degree of economic inequity within Israel that most Israelis seem prepared or even happy to allow.

Perhaps these two defining anxieties are in fact two aspects of one central question since the State of Israel itself represents an encounter between the Jews and modernity. In Israel and the Diaspora, in all of the denominations and ideologies of modern Jewish life, this encounter is profoundly challenging.

However debilitating these anxieties may appear, I do not seek to deny them. There are people who insist that they have found some secret allowing them to rise above mundane concerns and leave anxiety behind. I wish them well, but I find it hard to take their insouciance at face value. Philosophies of life offering insights into our behavior and relationships matter a great deal. They cannot, however, take the place of engagement with the world. At their finest, they can help us engage more deeply with it. To be self-satisfied in the face of the challenges faced by humanity may bespeak self-delusion more than spiritual excellence.

No formula of words can make all these concerns evaporate. The lesson to be learned from the finest of our tradition is that we must face up to our fears, confront them, and stare them down. Like the bear hunt mentioned above, we cannot rise above these fears and we cannot burrow beneath them: we will have to band together and work through them.

Anxieties and fears may motivate this book, but alone they cannot generate a compelling response. For that, hope is called for.

Hope

In modern Hebrew the word for hope is *tikvah*. Two distinct root meanings for the term can be adduced. While the first implies a line, a thread, a link, the second relates to a pool or reservoir. The first of these finds its echo in the second chapter of the Book of Joshua where Rahab is instructed to hang a scarlet cord from her window, and the term employed is *tikvat chut hashani*—the *tikvah* of the scarlet thread.

Moses Haim Luzzatto, the Italian mystic and poet born 300 years ago, composed a brief sermon on the theme of hope. In his explication, hope is understood as providing a line or link capable of penetrating directly to the higher reaches. Hope will bring a person out even from hell itself since it provides a lifeline to the future.[17]

In a 1968 essay entitled "Hope Jewish and Hope Secular," Eugene Borowitz suggested a common thread between Jewish conceptions of hope and the ethos of modernity:

> Both [religion and the contemporary secular spirit] are discontent with the present situation of the individual and society. They know things are not what they ought to be and that it is critical for man to devote himself to making them better. Secularists propose to do so by what we may call horizontal transcendence. By projecting human creativity forward through time they hope to overcome the present problems .... Thus, even in secular hope there is also a certain measure of faith, a commitment that goes beyond the present evidence and is strong enough to build one's life upon.
>
> Here those who are religious and those of a secular temper can meet, for this horizontal conception of hope is clearly to be seen in the Bible. The major Hebrew term for hope, *k-v-h*, means in the Bible not just a state of soul but an expectation in time.[18]

This notion of hope as a thread linking worlds and leading to a possible future is not the only image to be found within Jewish tradition. Jeremiah (14.8 and 17.13) describes God as *Mikveh Yisrael*, which is usually translated as the Hope of Israel. Given the extremely well-developed sense of wordplay and ambiguity in our tradition, it should come as no surprise that the sages linked this word to the identical term *mikveh*, meaning sacred pool or bath. The root *k-v-h* also relates to the process of gathering, particularly as it applies to water. Rabbi Akiva played on this dual meaning and commented thus on Jeremiah's *Mikveh* of Israel: "Just as a *mikveh* purifies the impure, so does the Holy One of Blessing purify Israel."[19]

This possible meaning of pooling and gathering offers further insight into the meaning of hope. If hope is about the thin red line, the thread attaching us to the future, it is also about the comforting pool, providing us with solace, purification, and regeneration.

The word hope in all its iterations is nowhere more prominent in the Hebrew Bible than in the Book of Job. Tellingly, however, it almost invariably appears there in a negative context. Hope is a delusion, an impossibility. In one highly suggestive passage in Chapter 14, Job has recourse to a metaphor from nature. The tree has *tikvah* because, unlike an individual person, it can return from a state of desiccation and live.

The life of an individual person is such that the promise of regeneration can, Job suggests, hold little consolation. In Jewish tradition it is precisely this consolation that is offered by the family, the community, and the people Israel. Hope takes me beyond myself and places me in a communal context. It implies, as the old Jewish tale has it, that there is good reason for the old to plant saplings in the full knowledge that they will not live to see the fruit of their labors. In our tradition, hope and community are irrevocably linked. I may not live to see the withered stump renewed, but I know that, as one ring on the tree, I am part of something which will yet live again. It is interesting to note that the Hebrew Bible does not know of "those who hope for God" (Isaiah 40.31, 49.23, Psalms 37.9) in the singular form; they only appear in the plural.

Hope is thus not only a thin line. It is also a nourishing pool. It is that which links person to person, generation to generation. Hope is life itself: the Talmud has its own version of the adage that where there is life, there is hope.[20] The activist and entrepreneur Maoz Inon, whose parents were murdered on October 7 2023, teaches that "hope is not a feeling that I wait for. I make hope. Hope is a communal endeavor, something we create together."[21] The thread must be woven. The pool must be dug.

In good Jewish tradition, this work has been sparked by anxiety. In equally typical fashion, it draws upon resources of hope and strives to find a thread, a lead, a clue. Anxiety is a drain, while hope is a wellspring. Anxiety insists. Hope inspires.

Theology: Crunchy and Smooth

What Is Jewish Theology?

Beyond substantive debates between Jewish theologians, Jewish theology itself is a contested category.[22] Some reject it as a clumsy contradiction in terms, arguing that theology has its roots in classical Greece, grew strong in the soil of Christianity, and is fundamentally foreign to Judaism. Shai Cherry has summarized the ambivalent role afforded to theology in Jewish tradition, noting:

> Rabbinic religiosity did not foreground theology; no single theology was universally accepted when Jews did begin writing theology; theology, as a discrete discipline, was not a distinct category for Jews until modernity; and the gap between studying traditional texts and writing Jewish theology has still not been bridged.[23]

Throughout Jewish history, an insistent voice of suspicion and opposition has been raised in response to attempts to explain Jewish practice and harmonize Jewish belief. During the Middle Ages a debate raged between Jewish thinkers concerning the intelligibility and explicability of the *mitzvot*, the commandments which Jews are enjoined to observe. Maimonides was firmly ensconced in the rationalist camp, convinced that each of the commandments had a rational basis. In his *Guide* he describes the opposing camp: "There is a group of human beings who consider it a grievous thing that causes should be given for any law; what would please them most is that the intellect would not find meaning for the commandments and prohibitions."[24]

Maimonides' ridicule notwithstanding, opposition to the quest for intelligible reasons for the commandments has a venerable pedigree in Judaism. If Maimonides took the extreme position that the logic behind every commandment could be adduced, contrary voices held that none of them could since all were shrouded in an impenetrable divine mystery.[25]

While Maimonides was in favor of offering explanations for the commandments, he opposed proposing positive descriptions of God. Such an activity was derided by him and others for being impossible and futile (the usual categories of physical description are inadequate to the task), trivial (speculation about the Divine is less serious than hardcore study of the Talmud),[26] arrogant (it would take God to understand God),[27] or dangerous (speculation can serve as a gateway to doubt). This antitheological position suggests that the quest for understanding undermines the mystery and unconditional imperative which are at the heart of Judaism. To explicate one's deepest beliefs is, so this argument goes, to domesticate them and thus weaken their hold. A characteristically robust objection to theological speculation was offered by Menahem Mendel Morgensztern, the Kotzker Rebbe. Heschel quotes him as saying: "A God whom any Tom, Dick, and Harry could comprehend, I would not believe in."[28]

While Maimonides' view that the commandments are intelligible could be seen as theological, there is another strand of anti-theological thinking within modern Judaism which recruits Maimonides to its ranks. The argument proposed by thinkers as different in their approach as Yeshayahu Leibowitz and Emmanuel Levinas is in essence this: Judaism is a religion of action, antithetical to the notion of abstracted theorizing about one's personal belief.[29]

Maimonides' emphasis on the life of action was important for the Lithuanian French Levinas as it was for the Latvian Israeli Leibowitz. Hence Levinas' claim that "we know since Maimonides that all that is said of God in Judaism *signifies* through human *praxis*"[30] and Leibowitz's assertion that "*Emunah* is not a system of opinions predicated on other, prior opinion, but a mental quality, and like all mental qualities, as held by Maimonides, it is acquired from a person's experience in day-to-day praxis."[31]

Anti-theological arguments include the claim that Jewish theology is not authentically Jewish or not authentic theology, that it is to be replaced by engagement with halakhic observance or with responses to a great ethical imperative. These positions, however, are not devoid of theological suppositions of their own. Those whose religious life is predicated on the axiom that God's commandments are to be followed categorically with the minimum of speculation may keep their theological speculation brief. But a "just do it" theology is a theology nonetheless. Avowedly secular and certainly post-secular understandings of Judaism can similarly be said to have Jewish theology woven into them.[32]

Such objections notwithstanding, Jewish theology in one form or another has long been part of Jewish life and literature. Rationalists have pondered God's essence, existence, authority, will, and agency. Mystics have described creative processes playing out within God. In a minimalist reading, Jewish theology means: committed Jews engaged in sustained reflection about God. According to this approach, anything which is not clearly engaged Jewish God-talk is something other than Jewish theology, namely, philosophy, intellectual history, sociology, politics, current affairs, and the like.

At the other extreme, there is a maximalist position predicated on the assumption that in a sense "everything is theological."[33] The maximalist argues that Jewish theology is not to be seen exclusively as Jewish God-talk but rather as discourse regarding matters of ultimate concern from a Jewish perspective. Theology is seen as an engagement with all that matters.[34] God is not just another topic, a circumscribed object of inquiry, examined like an artifact. To speak and think about God is to relate to God's demands and God's world, not simply to ponder abstruse notions of God's essence.[35] The maximalist position enables a much looser employment of the term theology.

Nine centuries ago, Anselm of Canterbury offered a definition of theology as precise as it is concise: *fides quaerens intellectum*, faith seeking understanding.[36] The term "faith" often provokes an uneasy response in Jewish circles. Emmanuel Levinas' understanding of a story he heard from Hannah Arendt is instructive here:

> The Christians attach great importance to what they call faith, mystery, sacrament. Here is an anecdote on that subject. Hannah Arendt ... told the following story on French radio. When she was a child in her native Konigsberg, one day she said to the rabbi who was teaching her religion: "You know, I have lost my faith." And the rabbi responded: "Who's asking you for it?" The response was typical. What matters is not "faith," but "doing." Doing, which means moral behavior, of course, but also the performance of ritual .... What the rabbi meant was: "Doing good is the act of belief itself."[37]

In Anselm's formulation, it is faith that inquires after itself in search of understanding. Perhaps, then, a more recognizably Jewish version of theology would be less about the search of faith for understanding and more about a praxis in search of meaning. Faith, like the Israeli aphorism about hope quoted above, is not seen here as something one feels or acquires. It is something we do.

In an important essay on her decision to live as a Reform Jew, Martha Nussbaum quotes with approval Moses Mendelssohn's observation in *Jerusalem*:

> Among all the prescriptions and ordinances of the moral law, there is not a single one which says: *You shall believe or not believe.* They all say: *You shall do or not do.* Faith is not commanded, for it accepts no other commands than those that come to it by way of conviction.[38]

The statement is liable to mislead. To deny articles of faith, such as the resurrection of the dead or the divine provenance of the Torah, is to forfeit a place in the world to come according to the Mishnah.[39] However this and other rabbinic teachings are understood, it would be disingenuous to suggest that questions of believing have been ignored throughout Jewish history. Nonetheless, Jews from earliest times have conceived of these questions differently from their Christian counterparts, and attempts to squeeze Jewish theology into Christian categories usually yield unsatisfactory results. My candidates for the quintessential moments of Jewish theology are described in the Books of Exodus, Deuteronomy, and Joshua. They are not characterized by faith examining itself but rather by a parent challenged by their child to provide an explanation for their behavior. Consider four variations on this theme:

> Should your children say to you "What do you mean by this rite?," you shall say "It is the Passover sacrifice to Adonai, Who passed over the houses of the Israelites in Egypt but saved our houses." (Exodus 12:26-27)
>
> Should your child ask you in time to come "What is this?," you shall reply, "It was with a mighty hand that the Lord brought us out from Egypt, the house of bondage." (Exodus 13.14)
>
> When, in time to come, your children ask you "What mean the decrees, laws and rules that Adonai our God has enjoined upon you?", you shall say to your children, "We were slaves to Pharaoh in Egypt and Adonai freed us from Egypt with a mighty hand. Adonai wrought before our eyes marvelous and destructive signs and portents in Egypt, against Pharaoh and all his household; and Adonai freed us from there, that He might take us and give us the land that He had promised to our ancestors. Then Adonai commanded us to observe all these laws, to revere Adonai our God, for our lasting good and for our survival, as is now the case. It will be therefore to our merit before Adonai our God to observe faithfully this whole instruction, as He has commanded us. (Deuteronomy 6:20-25)
>
> This shall serve as a symbol among you: in time to come, should your children ask: "What is the meaning of these stones for you?," you shall tell them: "The waters of the Jordan were cut off because of the Ark of the Lord's Covenant; when it passed through the Jordan, the waters of the

Jordan were cut off." And so these stones shall serve as a memorial for all time. (Joshua 4.6)⁴⁰

Over the centuries, this question of meaning has often been asked by normative children (of all ages) well-schooled in the languages and rituals of their ancestors. But there have been times in Jewish history, none more than in the modern period, when the question has been posed by individuals situated at the periphery of Jewish life, more acquainted with intellectual and cultural trends in the non-Jewish society they inhabit yet motivated (for some reason) to turn again to something Jewish, sometimes little more than an amorphous sense of identity, and to ask that most resonant of Jewish theological questions: what is this?

Both for the acculturated and for the alienated, the passage of time and the shift between generations leaves space for a question of meaning: what do these stones, these commandments, "this" in general mean to you? It is hard not to discern the shadow of another question here: does your understanding of what Jews do satisfy me? Can I adopt it without demurral, or must I search for an understanding of my own? Jewish theology has been greatly enriched by responses to questions from insiders and outsiders and all the gradations between those extremes. The moment described in these biblical passages combines the question "what does this mean to you?" with the corollary "what must it mean for me?"

Theology as articulated by Jews seeking understanding for their Jewish commitments faces the past, the present, and the future simultaneously.⁴¹ It is sparked by a future challenge to a present commitment imbued with a historical consciousness. In each of the biblical examples cited above, the response is not purely descriptive. If I am asked, "What is the combination of foliage and fruit that you are shaking in all directions during the festival of Sukkot?" and my answer is strictly botanical, I have not engaged in Jewish theology, nor have I addressed the real intention of the question. Embedded in the "what" question, there is a "why" question.

Various attempts have been offered to set out the parameters of modern Jewish theology and the criteria by which it should be judged. David Blumenthal, for example, suggests that to be a theologian is to speak for Judaism, for God, for humanity, and from within one's prior commitments.⁴² Byron Sherwin claims that "the four criteria that characterize a valid Jewish theology are identical to those of any valid theology. These are authenticity, coherence, contemporaneity and communal acceptance."⁴³ Jewish theological work, he argues, should be soaked in Jewish sources and a commitment to Jewish life, couched in comprehensible terms, resonant with contemporary modes of thought (yet not subjugated to their dictates)—and it should also find an audience.[44]

Jewish theology at its most compelling is an act of testimony. Reflecting on the words of Isaiah 43 "you are my witnesses, declares Adonai, and I am God,"[45] an early midrash cites Rabbi Simeon bar Yochai offering a daring reading: "When you are my witnesses, then I am Adonai. But if you are not my witnesses, I am not Adonai."[46]

To testify to the reality of God is to realize God, so the midrash would have it, and many who have practiced Jewish theology have sought not only to explain their faith commitments but to instantiate them through expressing them.

Personal testimony will not suffice. Jewish theology should be rooted in learning and curiosity, informed by critical methodology, framed in an engaging way, and offer new insights capable of sparking innovation and action. But in my reading of the biblical child's question, as of every theological prompt since, response calls for personal engagement.

In the course of this book, I engage in Jewish theology as a response of testimony to an imagined question by following generations. The question is posed not only in admiration but also in accusation. In a period of malaise, the inquiry of future generations sounds like: what does this ancient practice have to say to individuals searching for meaning and purpose? At times of crisis, I hear the question as: what is this Judaism you are living, and how can it possibly be equal to the challenges faced by a world of tumult and turmoil?

Liberal Theology

What kind of theology is expressed in these pages? I am a Reform rabbi, son of a Reform rabbi, raised in an intellectual milieu of liberal Jewish theology. My father's teacher Ignaz Maybaum studied at the Hochschule für die Wissenschaft des Judentums in Berlin and was a disciple of Franz Rosenzweig.[47] My father studied at a seminary named in honor of Leo Baeck, one of the greatest figures of Liberal Judaism.[48] I studied at the Hebrew Union College, once the bastion of Classical Reform Judaism, founded on the liberal theology of the likes of Kaufmann Kohler.

So my theological pedigree is liberal. What does that mean? In a Christian context, Garry Dorrien describes liberal theology as:

> A theology based on reason and experience, not external authority, which offers a third way between orthodox authority religion and secular disbelief.... Liberal theology conceives the meaning of Christianity in the light of modern knowledge and ethical values. It is reformist in spirit and substance. It is deeply shaped by modern science, humanism, and historical criticism, and it is committed to making Christianity credible and socially relevant.[49]

I am heir to a Jewish version of this liberal theological tradition, and I both identify with it and critique it.

The primary function of Orthodox Jewish theology is to demonstrate the truth or, at least, to argue for the coherence of traditional Jewish beliefs and practices.[50] This is the version of the child's question described in the biblical verses above which means: I know that I will continue to perform the rituals and follow the ways set down in tradition, and I am looking for ways to defend and explain these ways. To some degree, liberal theology mirrors its orthodox counterpart, offering an explanation or apologia for this or that non-Orthodox articulation of Judaism. It is remarkable how orthodox it is possible to be about aspects of liberal theology and practice.

Beyond apologetics, however, the key question asked by liberal Jewish theology is: what can I say and believe about Judaism in light of new understandings wrought by science and history?[51] The term "liberal" has political and economic connotations which can be traced onto the theological domain. Liberalism here implies a laissez-faire approach which allows everyone the freedom to make their own decisions and plot their own course.

Orthodox theology typically claims that an emphasis on individualism is fundamentally at odds with the essence of Judaism. In response to this claim, liberals tend to employ one of two defenses. The first is to assert that a judicious reading of Judaism shows a far greater degree of choice and change than is commonly held. The second is to argue that modernity has so changed the playing field that a new Judaism is now called for. These and other ideas will be rehearsed in various chapters of this book.

Given my skepticism about some of the more naïve claims often found in liberal thought, it is also possible to characterize my position as postliberal, although it is at this point that my interest in the use of signifiers begins to wane. If the only liberal option is the version popular in the early twentieth century, according to which science and progress and informed choice would make everything succeed, I am postliberal.[52]

Jewish feminist thought, or a dominant trend within that burgeoning field, is often identified with postliberal theology.[53] Rachel Adler, for example, has offered an excoriating critique of the liberal tendency to offer women the status of honorary men, unable or unwilling to acknowledge the more profound shift of consciousness necessary for the engendering of Judaism. Platitudinous declarations of equality are not equal to the task of recognizing difference and uncovering structural injustice. Here, as in other areas, it is necessary to look beyond the liberal horizon.

The events of the twentieth century have done much to erode the unbridled confidence in progress which so typified liberal theology in the nineteenth century. As will become clear in this book, I am critical of Pollyannaish faith in reason and democracy to carry the day and very interested in aspects of tradition which were largely eschewed by the classical Reformers while remaining passionately committed to reason, democracy, historical perspective, scientific rigor, political moderation, universalism, and many other core characteristics of liberal theology.[54]

Postmodern, Radical, and Other Kinds of Theology

The advent of modernity might have been expected to herald the demise of theology. The replacement of religious doctrines by scientific methods might have led to a general undermining of the theological realm. As the secular world became disenchanted, faith's search for understanding might have been abandoned. However, some chose to link their modernist orientations with their theological urge. Classical Reform Jewish theology, as exemplified by such works as Kaufmann Kohler's *Jewish Theology*, was a profoundly modern enterprise. It was predicated on the optimistic axiom that truth can be discovered through the judicious use of reason and research. The orthodoxies it overturned had become untenable considering recent advances, and the classical Reformers maintained that they must therefore be replaced with more plausible notions.[55]

Broadly speaking, a postmodern sensibility substitutes irony for optimism and indeterminacy for certainty. It challenges the claim that the arc of history bends inexorably toward justice and improvement and undermines the claims to objectivity made on behalf of science and rationality. The local and embodied is rediscovered, while the generalized and homogenized is regarded with suspicion.[56]

Indeed, both modernity and postmodernity have been perceived as dealing mortal blows to the project of theology, but neither has stopped people from theologizing and each has had a profound impact on theology itself.

John Caputo made a useful distinction between strong and weak theology which can be linked to the modern–postmodern distinction and to my proposed axis of smooth and crunchy, explained in the next section. In strong theology one's faith disposition becomes a defensible position. Premodern theology was usually strong, and the moderns inherited the predilection for this kind of thinking, announcing the Truth in all its magnificent certainty. In Caputo's reading, weak theology has no such aim. It has its own kind of strength, which is:

> To adhere strictly to the demands of the matter to be thought and spoken, adhering not to an object, constituted by a proposition but to the things themselves, *die Sache selbst*, the matters of deepest concern, which precede propositions. It is a false rigor to demand that everything be exact, that everything submit to the requirements of objectifying thinking.[57]

We can align what is termed here strong theology with modern and systematic theological exploration, while the weak version shows affinity with postmodern and interpretive trends in theology.

Some other terms for types of theological discourse appear from time to time in this book. Take, for example, the distinction made between positive and realist theology, on the one hand, and negative and instrumentalist theology, on the other.[58] Negative theology has been described as consisting of "a critical negation of all affirmations which can be made about God, followed by an equally critical negation of our negations."[59] While positive theology dwells on what *can* be said about God's reality, revelation, law, ritual, and tradition, the negative variant is preoccupied with the impossibility of such assertions. The realist holds that God is really there, independent of our efforts to grasp God. The instrumentalist finds that the language of being and existence is inadequate or inappropriate when used in relation to God. What matters to them more is what I mean by God or what happens when God is invoked.

The distinction between moderate and radical positions is well known in a political context. The moderates speak for incremental change, look for opportunities to further consensus-based policies, and embrace the notion that the best should not be the enemy of the good. Radicals, on the other hand, strike at the roots of the problem and are interested in shaking up the system rather than maintaining equilibrium.

The term "radical theology" gained currency in the 1960s in the wake of the "death of God" movement prevalent in some circles of Christian thought. According to one explanation, radical theology "recognizes God as a formulation of extremity that gets *at the root* of thought and opens up pathways for a thinking that *knows no bounds*."[60] Often the radical nature of radical theology takes a political and social turn since it tends to involve a critique of power structures and accepted truths. Some Jewish thinkers have used the term "radical" to describe their own work,[61] usually to set it apart from more conventional and predictable modes of Jewish theological discourse.

Radical thought of all kinds has a built-in advantage over its moderate counterparts. It shows a willingness to ask searching questions and to peer behind the veil of accepted conventions. It gets to the root of things. It casts a relentless gaze on the structures which underpin our everyday conventions, exposing their hypocrisies and inadequacies. All this notwithstanding, this book makes a case for moderation and argues that it does not have to imply mediocrity and intellectual compromise. Rather, moderation can denote an acknowledgment of tensions which must be lived rather than resolved.

I want to finish this section on Jewish theology by underlining its creative potential. This was well expressed by David Blumenthal:

> To "do theology" is to reflect and share one's thoughts about, and one's experiences of, God, tradition, community, and meaning. All such theology is confessional, though not in a sectarian sense. It is teaching about God—as embedded in the particular theologian who is, in turn, embedded in his or her tradition and community. To do theology is to create a dialogue between forebear, teacher, and listener. It is to talk from the intertextuality of the traditions, the collective readings of the traditions, the selves of the theologians, the persons of the hearers, and the presence(s) of the divine. Theology flows from the confluence of these "texts." Theology is the intertextual forming of these elements into an interpersonal medium; it is creation. To be a theologian is to create—in the midst, and on the boundaries.[62]

On Peanut Butter and Theology

There are many adjectives affixed to the noun theology, often in the minimalist sense of discourse about God. Their role is to qualify, classify, and clarify the kind of theology being practiced. This book proposes a novel terminology and distinguishes between smooth theology and crunchy theology. This smooth and crunchy distinction, commonly used to market peanut butter,[63] may be helpful in characterizing different kinds of theological activity. In my understanding, smooth theology grinds down narratives, laws, doctrines, and traditions into a singular consistency, while the crunchy variety retains chunks of these ingredients within the discourse. Smooth theology has the advantage of clarity but may read as generic and abstracted. Crunchy theology is demonstrably linked to the tradition on which it draws, but that can make it harder to digest.

Smooth theology answers the question of the Bible's inquisitive child with certainty and consistency. It spreads easily. Crunchy theology, on the other hand, will have more texts to unpack, more tangents and digressions; it is less homogenized than its smooth counterpart, but it may offer more to get your teeth into.

For readers not familiar with traditional Jewish practices of quotation and allusion,[64] most Jewish religious works read as crunchy: there are allusions, hints, and digressions. However, there are some works, often more philosophical than esoteric, which read more smoothly. One such example is Joseph Albo's fifteenth-century *Sefer Ikkarim*. In the introduction, Albo explains that knowing the fundamental principles on which the laws are based is both simple and difficult: simple because everyone should clearly have at least a rudimentary understanding of the laws in order to believe in them; and difficult because of the disagreements between sages in how they present and understand these principles:

> I, Joseph Albo, residing here in the city of Soria, led hither by the providence of the Prime Mover, having in my humility realized the high importance and great value of the substance of investigation, and seeing the great confusion in the minds of those who have speculated concerning it ... I undertook to make an adequate investigation of the general principles of divine law.[65]

Albo's work is substantial and contains chunks of insight, interpretation, and innovation.[66] In scope, intention and style, however, it is smooth.

This book aims for a balance between the crunchy and the smooth. Its structure is crunchy—twenty-two short chapters on a wide variety of themes, with terminology gleaned from many sources. The endnotes provide readers in search of more roughage with references and additional comments. Even for readers who have no need for or interest in the notes, this is not a smooth read; it includes chunks of materials gleaned from

Jewish tradition and discussed in what is intended to be a comprehensible manner.

Linked to the smooth–crunchy distinction is the difference between systematic and narrative theology. Systematic theology attempts to set out the core claims of a religious tradition in an orderly fashion.[67] It is a response to the question: what does Islam say about this? What is the Christian position on that? The limitations of such an enterprise are clear, but so too are its advantages, particularly in a polemical context.[68] In contrast to the proposition that Jewish theology can tell you what Judaism says definitively on a number of core topics, a narrative approach suggests that Judaism can best be understood by immersion in its modes of discourse.[69] The conversation is no less theological even according to the minimalist understanding of the term, but the question at hand becomes how do Judaisms speak of God rather than what does Judaism say about God. A systematic theology is top-down; an interpretive or narrative theology is bottom-up. The former strives for symmetry. The latter thrives on the bumps and fissures of the particular.

The Jewish theology you will encounter in this book is crunchy in the sense that it is comprised of chunks and nuggets from across a broad range of Jewish sources and employs a range of theological voices. Some are analytical in tone, suggesting rubrics for understanding contrasting positions. Others speak to underlying characteristics of my own theological approach, such as doubt, humor, and a particular understanding of human nature. Some of the chapters engage in theology in the original sense of the term, namely, discourse about God, while others address aspects of traditional Jewish belief and practice. In my expansive understanding of what constitutes theology, some of these chapters engage with urgent moral and political questions. All of these kinds of discussion are found here and help give my theology its crunch.

Alphabets in Jewish Culture[70]

Like every other genre and discipline, Jewish theology is also concerned with questions of form.[71] Some of the greatest works of Jewish theology have structures which are themselves reflective, explicitly or in a less obvious way, of their author's intentions.[72] Writers of Jewish theology think a great deal about the way in which their ideas should be ordered.[73] I have chosen an alphabetic structure for this book. As I demonstrate below, there is a tradition of mining the Hebrew alphabet and employing it as a framework. I hope to be part of that tradition. Such an approach is more like a periodic table than a flow chart or road map, pointing to elements from which a new chapter in Judaism may yet emerge.

The alphabet is surely one of the most remarkable inventions in human history.[74] Not only the circumstances of its invention or promulgation but also the conditions which caused the innovation to spread are debated hotly by scholars from a variety of disciplines.[75] Research into the ways in which the human brain came up with such a system and its impact on the human brain is ongoing.[76] The relationship between alphabetic and non-alphabetic systems is a topic of contention. While some are convinced that alphabetic writing (and indeed thinking) is superior to all other systems, others point out the cultural prejudices inherent in any such assumption.[77]

I am drawn to the link between letters and elements. Indeed, one attractive possible explanation for the etymology of the word "element" links it to the "l," "m," and "n" at the heart of the alphabet itself.[78] The alphabet serves as a kind of periodic table of core elements, compounds of which create all that is and points to all that is yet to be created.

Hebrew civilization is profoundly alphabetic in nature; indeed, the story of the Semitic tribes from which the Jewish people emerged and the story of the earliest abecedaries from which the alphabet emerged are inextricably linked. It has been noted, however:

> Outside of a very small circle of scholars in Jewish Studies interested in language and mysticism, the role of the alefbet in Hebrew exegesis and its importance in Jewish religion and culture is either not recognized or is poorly understood.[79]

More research on the impact of the alphabet on Jewish culture remains to be undertaken. This book looks to focus on three dimensions of this rich and largely unexplored field: the use of alphabetic structure; the valuing and interpretation of individual letters of the alphabet; and the connection between alphabet and revelation.

Alphabetic Structure

Alphabetic order is employed on a number of occasions in the Hebrew Bible: the first chapter of Nahum, eight or nine psalms, Chapter 31 of Proverbs, much of Lamentations, and perhaps more.[80] It evokes totality and comprehensiveness. In Adele Berlin's words relating to one of the alphabetic psalms,

> The entire alphabet, the source of all words, is marshalled in praise of God. One cannot actually use all of the words in a language, but by using the alphabet one uses all potential words. So the form is made to serve the message.[81]

That a number of the alphabetical psalms are incomplete in one way or another has sometimes been seen as the result of textual corruption. For example, Psalm 145, perhaps the most famous example of this phenomenon in the Masoretic canon, does exist in ancient versions with the *nun* verse intact. Another reading, however, suggests that the inclusion of an element of incompleteness within the totalizing model of the alphabetical form is no accident. Rather, it is intended to serve as a teaching, a reminder that however much we may strive for an all-encompassing rubric, our own experience is necessarily limited and incomplete. The inclusion of this psalm into the daily liturgy, indeed its repetition three times each day, means that a Jew attuned to the rhythms of the classical liturgy regularly recites a flawed litany.

Not only does Psalm 34 have an alphabetic structure in which one letter is missing, but the original author or a later redactor has also taken pains to spell out the letter "aleph" in the first verse and across the psalm as a whole.[82] The twenty-three verses of this psalm are replete with alphabetic consciousness. Following a method that seeks out key words in order to discern intent,[83] the psalm reads as an extended reflection on completeness and lack, on everything and nothing, as these words in bold should illustrate:

> 2 I will bless Adonai, **always, at every time**
> 5 he delivered me from **all my fears**
> 7 he saved him out of **all his troubles**
> 10 there is **no lack** to those that fear Adonai
> 11 those who seek Adonai **will lack no good thing**
> 17 to **erase their name from the earth**
> 18 Adonai delivers them **from all their troubles**
> 20 Adonai delivers them **from them all**

The last three verses bring these motifs of all and none, everything and nothing, to a climax:

21 He protects **all his bones, not one of them will be broken**
22 Evil will slay the wicked; the foes of the righteous will be condemned
23 Adonai will rescue the lives of His servants, **no one who takes refuge in Adonai will be condemned**

In this reading, the psalm speaks of completeness and its structure reflects its theme. All the letters in the alphabet, just like all the bones in the human body, are marshaled in service of the psalm's teaching.

Evidence from Qumran shows that the composition of alphabetical hymns continued into the post-biblical period, and thereafter it grew in prevalence and versatility of usage.[84] It appears that in the early centuries of the Common Era, the composition of alphabetical verse was well known. In at least one rabbinic source, alphabetical songs are connected to frivolity. Under the influence of food and drink, some of the great men of Jerusalem start singing songs and others *alphabetrin*, alphabetic acrostics.[85] A midrashic source, perhaps from the fifth or sixth century CE, describes the proficiency of King Solomon in the composition of alphabetical verse, suggesting a cultural reality in which such creativity was well known.[86]

Within Jewish liturgy, the alphabetic acrostic form is ubiquitous. Through it, liturgical poets are presented with a challenge to their artistry and originality, while gesturing to tradition (this is the format used by King David and King Solomon or, at least, by those whose work is attributed to them), to totality (these are the letters denoting the basis from which all permutations arise), and to ultimacy (these are the tools by which all that is came originally into being). The siddur, the Jewish prayerbook as it has evolved with its variations based on ideology and geography since the early Middle Ages, is replete with alphabetic acrostics. During the High Holyday period and at other festivals, the prevalence of the alphabetic form is all the more pronounced.[87]

A thorough examination of the provenance, prevalence, function, and significance of alphabetical structure in Hebrew liturgical poetry has yet to be written. Unlike in secular poetry of the Jewish Middle Ages where the alphabetical acrostic is rare, in sacred poetry from perhaps the sixth century CE it is much loved and often employed. For the present purpose of showing how significant it has been, it may help to quote two sources. The first is the original alphabetic confession known as *vidui zuta*, a central feature of the penitential liturgy since the ninth century:

Ashamnu – we have trespassed; *Bagadnu* – we have dealt treacherously; *Gazalnu* – we have robbed; *Dibarnu dofi* – we have spoken slander; *He'evinu* – we have acted perversely; *V'hirshanu* – we have done wrong; *Zadnu* – we have acted presumptuously; *Chamasnu* – we have done violence; *Tafalnu sheker* – we have practiced deceit; *Ya'atsnu ra* – we have counseled evil; *Kizavnu* – we have spoken falsehood; *Latsnu* – we have scoffed; *Maradnu* – we have revolted; *Ni'atsnu* – we have blasphemed; *Sararnu* – we have rebelled; *Avinu* – we have committed iniquity; *Pashanu* – we have transgressed; *Tsararnu* – we have oppressed; *Kishinu oref* – we have been stiff necked; *Rashanu* – we have acted wickedly; *Shichatnu* – we have dealt corruptly; *Tiavnu* – we have committed abomination; *Tainu* – we have gone astray; *Ti'tanu* – we have led others astray.[88]

The second is a twenty-first-century Hebrew poem by Sivan Har-Shefi called "With Hand on Heart":

Ahavnu – we have loved: *Bagarnu* – and matured; *Gadalnu* – we have grown; *Dibarnu Yofi* – we have spoken of beauty. *Hevenu Vehishpanu* – we have brought and influenced. *Zikinu* – we have acquitted. *Chilinu* – we have sweetened. *Tavalnu Emet* – we have immersed in truth. *Yaatznu Tov* – we have given good advice. *Kasafnu* – we have yearned. *Lamadnu* – we have learned. *Maadnu Nafalnu?* Did we slip and fall? *Samachnu Alecha* – we relied on you. *Paalnu, Tzipinu. Kivinu Orcha* – we acted, expected, hoped for Your light. *Rashamnu Shehivtachta* – we noted that You promised. *Shelcha Tamid, Temimecha* – ever Yours, Your innocents.[89]

Har-Shefi makes ingenious use of the alphabetical confession, and with minimal changes to the words she turns the confession into a defense of human striving and a gentle reminder of divine promises still to be fulfilled. The totality of the alphabet remains.

Thus, over the centuries, the Hebrew alphabet has continued to provide structure for creativity, offering a sense of finitude yet of boundless possibility.[90] However, at stake here is not only an issue of form.

Valuing and Interpretation of Letters

By the first centuries of the Common Era, what might be called an alphabetic sensibility and theology of letters is discernible: the letters contend before God to win pride of place as the first letter in the creation account,[91] and the biblical acrostics are discussed and explanations offered.[92]

According to the bold approach inherent in this nascent theology of the alphabet, letters have personality and the interaction between them takes on metaphysical significance.

Jews have long given expression to the notion that the letters of the alphabet are fundamental building blocks of existence. They are comprised of points generated by sublime processes within divinity itself. Far from being understood as humanly contrived conventions of communication, in some works of esoteric literature the letters comprise the seed from which the sefirotic emanations came to be, constitute the vestments through which the ineffable name is woven, and offer signposts that lead from the revealed to the concealed.[93]

In Gershom Scholem's formulation, already in the Talmud there is evidence of a worldview according to which "the letters of the divine language are what lie at the basis of all creation by way of their combination."[94] The letters themselves are the building blocks of existence, and sanctity is even attributed to their order within the alphabet.[95]

Sefer Yetzirah (the Book of Creation or the Book of Formation), a foundational work of the Jewish esoteric tradition, presents the letters of the alphabet as tools by which the universe was brought into being: the "thirty-two most occult and wonderful paths of wisdom" employed by God in order to engrave the divine name comprise the ten *sefirot* (understood as either numbers or divine emanations) and the twenty-two letters of the alphabet, formed from spirit or wind and divided into categories. Great significance continued to be attached to the letters of the Hebrew alphabet later in the Middle Ages[96] and in Hasidism.[97] In this metaphysics of the twenty-two letters, they are seen as the nexus between human ingenuity and divine creativity. Letters are written and read, pondered and prayed.[98] Nothing is more human than language, but it is employed to strive for that which lies beyond human understanding.[99]

Alongside its other claims to significance, the alphabet can also be regarded as a pedagogic tool of the first order. The promulgation of a manageable number of symbols has worked in two directions as an educational technique: as a way of inducting infants into a system at an early age and as a way of connecting literacy to ethics. To learn the alphabet is to learn a world of values and insights connected to it.[100]

One Talmudic source gives pride of place to the pedagogic aspects of the alphabet, blending literacy education with ethical instruction. Predicated on the notion that orality, morality, and literacy are intimately intertwined, it begins with a conversation between some anonymous sages and Rabbi Joshua ben Levi, a great Palestinian rabbi of the third century CE.[101] They tell him of a remarkable teaching method developed not by teachers but by young students in the house of study. This source, found in Tractate Shabbat 104a of the Babylonian Talmud, is perhaps that voluminous work's "only complete discussion" of the alphabet.[102] It presents a method by which the order and morphology of the Hebrew alphabet (not the earlier script but the post-exilic version) may be learned, combining mnemonic methods with ethical insights:

> The Rabbis told Rabbi Joshua ben Levi: Some children have come to the study hall today, and have said things whose equal was not said even in the days of Joshua ben Nun, They said: *Aleph Bet* stands for *Aluph Bina*, learn understanding;[103] *Gimel Dalet* stands for *G'mol Dalim*, give to the poor. Why is the foot of the *gimel* stretched out to the *dalet*? – because it is proper for those who do kindness to run after the needy. And why is the foot of the *dalet* stretched toward the *gimel*? – because the poor person should make himself available to him. And why is the *dalet*'s face turned away from the *gimel* ? – because one should give discreetly, to avoid the feeling of shame. *Hey, Vav* – this is the is name of the Holy One of Blessing.

The next six letters are adduced to show that to all who fulfill the ethical practices outlined so far, God will: sustain, show favor, do good, provide a heritage, and bind a crown for the world to come. The text continues:

> The open *mem* and the closed *mem*[104] represent revealed teaching and closed teaching. The bent *nun* and straight *nun* teach that if a faithful person [*neeman*] is humble, he will become an upstanding faithful person [in the world to come]. *Samech* and *ayin* teach that one should support the poor [*smoch aniim*]. Another version is that one should devise memory aids [*simanim aseh*] in the study of Torah in order to acquire it.[105]
>
> The bent *peh* and the straight *peh* allude to an open mouth and a closed mouth.[106] The bent *tzadi* and the straight *tzadi* teach that if a righteous person [*tzadik*] is humble, he will become upright.

Following a digression on humility, the Talmud continues:

> *Kuf* stands for the Holy One [*kadosh*]. *Resh* stands for a wicked person [*rasha*]. Why is the face of the *kuf* turned aware from the *resh*? – the Holy One of Blessing says, "I cannot bear to look at the wicked one." And why

does the crown of the *kuf* turn toward the *resh?* – the Holy One of Blessing says, "If he repents, I will bind upon him a crown like My Own."

Following another interpolation on the means accessible to the wicked to attain purification, the teaching moves to the final letters of the alphabet:

Shin stands for falsehood [*sheker*]. *Tav* stands for truth [*emet*].[107] Why are the letters for falsehood juxtaposed in the alphabet[108] while the letters of truth are spread out? – because falsehood is common, and truth is rare. And why do the letters of falsehood stand on one foot[109] while the letters of truth have brick-like solidity? – because truth stands firm while falsehood does not stand firm.

I have quoted this source extensively because of what it demonstrates: young students in the house of study who create a device for learning which brings literacy and ethics together. To learn *alef bet* is to learn the elements of a life worth living.

Two more iterations of alphabet as curriculum deserve mention. *The Alphabet of Ben Sira* is one of the most controversial and even scandalous works of Jewish literature.[110] My interest in it is less for its status as satire or parody or for its salacious content but more for its employment of alphabetic acrostics, both in Aramaic and in Hebrew, some of which are presented in a context of learning. Proverbs organized in alphabetical order are used in the process of moral formation. A millennium later, the renaissance of Hebrew called for the development of methods for teaching the alphabet. In Naomi Shemer's alphabet song, the words she attaches to each letter of the alphabet speak to a different set of values, rooted in an appreciation of the natural world.[111] In her version the letters reveal an emphasis on the joys of simple living in nature. Same alphabet, different teaching.

Alphabet and Revelation

In a 1726 essay, Daniel Defoe advanced the theory that the origin of the alphabet was the divine revelation of writing to Moses on Sinai.[112] The historical assumptions that informed Defoe's idea have not stood the test of time. Today's scholarship demonstrates that writing systems of different kinds appeared in different places around the ancient world, some of them many centuries earlier than the thirteenth century BCE.[113]

While I am not advancing the belief that God's hand revealed the mysteries of writing to Moses on Sinai, I am intrigued by a more modest yet highly suggestive possibility. At least one version of the story of how the West Semitic alphabet came into existence speaks of Canaanite slaves in the Sinai desert proposing a simplification of Egyptian writing systems through the use of Semitic words: *alef* as bull, *bet* as house, and so on. Semites returning from the Sinai Peninsula between perhaps 1850 and 1300 BCE[114] with a revelatory technology capable of opening up entire new worlds of possibility constitutes an intriguing reading of the Sinai theophany. In the words of a modern author, "perhaps the transforming event that transpired so long ago at the foot of Mount Sinai was the invention of the alphabet."[115]

Some cultural theorists have argued that the alphabet as engine of Western culture is on the wane due, in no small measure, to the new possibilities offered by rapid technological change. They look beyond the alphabet to a new day.[116] This claim is not only based on a reading of current digital trends but also on an ambition to overthrow notions of rationality deeply imbedded in alphabetic literacy.

I have no such ambition. The hyper-literal character of Jewish culture is unlikely to disappear, although the balance between literacy and orality may well change significantly in response to monumental changes in technology and communication. Rather than see in the centrality of the alphabet evidence of hierarchical thinking, José Faur argued that Hebrew thought is informed by "horizontal dialectics," insisting that the alphabetic mind recognizes the other as free and equal.[117] His suggestion (polemical to be sure) is that the use of a small range of symbols denoting core elements promotes a broad horizon of imagination. Might we imagine Moses in the desert, struck by the infinite creative possibilities of this most elemental of human techniques?

A theology of revelation is being sketched here. The great revelation to the people Israel (distinct in its particular manifestation but not exclusive) is of the potentialities—intellectual, ethical, sacred and creative—inherent in literacy. Torah is an unfolding process of bringing life to the letters. It is in that process that the human and the divine realms meet.

Judaism as a Living Script

Moses Mendelssohn, arguably the first modern Jewish thinker, was fascinated by the historical origins and religious significance of the alphabet and other writing systems. In the second part of his 1783 work *Jerusalem*, Mendelssohn constructs an ingenious yet opaque argument concerning hieroglyphics, the alphabet, idolatry, and the ceremonial law. The claim seems to be based on the rabbinic distinction between the Written and the Oral Law. He notes that only with reluctance was the Oral Law ever written down and that the ceremonial law is essentially oral: "The ceremonial law itself is a kind of living script, rousing the heart and mind, full of meaning, never ceasing to inspire contemplation and to provide the occasion and opportunity for oral instruction."[118]

Written words are, he claims, "rigid forms, into which we cannot force our concepts without disfiguring them."[119] It is the performance of distinctively Jewish acts that is bound to provoke the purest form of instruction, whereby the ethical heft and contemporary resonances of the tradition are imparted to the younger generation. Through the performance of ritual acts mandated by tradition, he argues, the circumstances are created which allow for instruction and explanation. Such justifications will certainly change over time. By employing the living text of the ritual commandments, underlying values can be inculcated and the possibility of finding new and relevant explanations is maintained.

Mendelssohn's notion of Judaism's living script has been the subject of significant scholarly inquiry since the 1990s.[120] The steady rise of interest in questions of language, ritual, meaning, and chosenness has brought readers back to what was previously dismissed as little more than a curious digression.

Mendelssohn's interest in aspects of language is at the nexus of his Jewish and general philosophical concerns. In *Jerusalem* Mendelssohn presents a theory of the historical development of alphabets which owes much to contemporary research into what would be called today anthropology and linguistics. He argues that before alphabets there were hieroglyphic systems, and before them pictorial representations from nature (often of animals). These pre-alphabetic systems suffered from a propensity to confuse the symbol with the object represented. The next phase of the development of writing systems represents a leap, "and the leap seems to have required more than ordinary human powers."[121] The use of a limited number of symbols, rooted in the hieroglyphic system as they were, constitute in Mendelssohn's view "one of the most glorious discoveries of the human spirit; one sees at any rate how men may have been led, step by step, without any flight of inventiveness, to think of the immeasurable as measurable."[122]

Mendelssohn's account of the transition from the hieroglyphic to the alphabetic is intriguing yet difficult to understand.[123] He links it to an analysis of idolatry and mythology since images of animals and the like were thought to be not symbols but the things themselves. Hieroglyphic script offered a stylized version of these images which should have militated against the slide into idolatry but instead spawned superstition, inventions and fables. Even the attempt to sidestep this risk by focusing on numbers did not prove effective; here too, people began to seek secret power in the numbers themselves. Mendelssohn is describing a constant tension between the undoubted benefits of graphic notation and the inherent risk of idolatry.

The following passage from *Jerusalem* relates to the crux of the argument:

> We have seen how difficult it is to preserve the abstract ideas of religion among men by means of permanent signs. Images and hieroglyphics lead to superstition and idolatry, and our alphabetical script makes man too speculative. It displays the symbolic knowledge of things and their relations too openly on the surface; it spares us the effort of penetrating and searching and creates too wide a division between doctrine and life. In order to remedy these defects the lawgiver of this nation gave the *ceremonial law*.[124]

In Mendelssohn's reading, the creation of the alphabetic system mitigates against the corrosive impact of superstition and idolatry, which are a necessary by-product of the images and hieroglyphs which preceded it. However, alphabets bear the risk of falling prey to unmoored abstraction. The alphabetical script is not to be discarded, but it needs to be supplemented by the ceremonial script as the performance of ritual acts is not, in his view, mired in permanence:

> Man's actions are transitory; there is nothing lasting, nothing enduring about them, like hieroglyphic script, could lead to idolatry through abuse or misunderstanding. But they also have the advantage over alphabetical signs of not isolating man, of not making him to be a solitary creature, poring over writings and books.[125]

It is hard to agree with Mendelssohn's assertion that an emphasis on the performative is an effective protection against the perils of imprisonment within dogma. If religious observance is designed to enhance ethical sensitivity, there is ample evidence that it often fails to do so. Indifference and even brutality are not at odds with attention to detail. His second claim, however, that ritual is an antidote to isolation, is much easier to substantiate.

During the discussion, Mendelssohn quotes an English work about Indian mythology to demonstrate that misunderstanding another's culture can lead to errors in interpretation. His warning can still serve anyone striving to understand another religion or culture:

> In judging the religious ideas of a nation that is otherwise still unknown, one must, for the same reason, take care not to regard everything from one's own *parochial* point of view, lest one should call idolatry what, in reality, is perhaps only *script*.[126]

Generations later, the kernel of this pluralistic approach was to be expanded by some to make the claim that any categorization of a foreign belief as idolatrous is no more than an admission of our incapacity to read the script. The imagery and beliefs of other religions, even when they embrace views which seem antithetical to our own, are not graven images to be smashed, as expressed persuasively by Naomi Janowitz:

> Every religion has some objects that are understood to represent divinity formally; that is, every group interprets some signs as being iconic forms of representation. Religious texts may attempt to regiment these modes of representation by establishing whose interpretation is most authentic, but it is in fact impossible to fix the meaning of a symbol unless it is dead. On this understanding, idolatry is the claim that other people have the wrong way of interpreting their images, which is by definition, an impossible case to make.[127]

Employing the image of a script serves as an invitation to consider the relationship between the local and parochial, on the one hand, and the universal, on the other. It is part of an implicit ideology of pluralism at the foundation of Mendelssohn's approach.

Mendelssohn's thoughts on hieroglyphics, numbers, and alphabets bear the traces of contemporary theories of language, with which he was well acquainted.[128] They are also imbued with traditional Jewish sources and ideas. His capacity to combine these two areas of expertise and to embody a melding of the two explains his significance as not just an exemplar of modern Jewish thought but one of its creators. Mendelssohn contends that a ritual act lives in the present and is gone. Its ephemeral nature provides a bulwark against the reification and deification which the world of hieroglyphs and symbols is prone to yield. In his remarkable theory, commitment to a prescribed set of practices offers a guarantee against submission to desiccated doctrines and gross idolatry. Keeping the embodied script alive through commitment and repetition paradoxically allows for a rich and ever-changing explanation. Mendelssohn, a Jew of great learning, employs the image of a living script to offer Jews at the cusp of modernity an approach, an alphabet, and a theology. The Jew does not follow the script. The Jew lives the script.[129]

Heirs of the Masoretes

Jakob Petuchowski, Professor of Liturgy and Theology at the Hebrew Union College in Cincinnati, entitled one of his works *Heirs of the Pharisees*.[130] His argument was that, at its finest, the project of Reform Judaism might be compared to the epoch-making efforts of the Pharisees which gave Judaism the tools required to survive the upheaval wrought by the destruction of the Temple.

It is easy to critique this kind of reading of history, whereby one compares oneself with a great hero of a bygone era. Ultra-Orthodox Jews, one can speculate, see themselves as the true heirs of the Pharisees and Reform Jews as feckless schismatics. Questions of historical accuracy are not our concern here; what matters is the nature of our self-description. Whom do we aspire to resemble? It is a dull game to look at every great Jewish figure through history and claim them for one's own team. But it is of some interest to ask, as one's eyes range over 3000 years of Jewish history: whose heirs do we think we are?

My vote goes to the Masoretes. While debates about their historical provenance are ongoing, it is generally agreed that the Masoretes were preoccupied with the question of how the biblical text should be vocalized.[131] Hebrew, after all, provided not a true alphabet but rather a list of letters, almost all fundamentally consonantal in character.[132] When placed together, the letters call out for vocalization:

The Jew searches with his eyes for inaudible roots in order to flesh them out with his breath. The Greek picks the sound from the page and searches for invisible ideas in the sounds the letters command him to make.[133]

The Masoretic text of the Hebrew Bible adds vocalization to the letters, actualizing the potential inherent in the words.[134] Two distinct theories concerning the vocalization of the Hebrew Bible have had significant currency over the centuries. One, represented by Moses Mendelssohn, argued that Moses received the Torah complete with all the appropriate grammatical notations. In his view, the essence of the Oral Law is that generation passed to generation the secret of the true way in which to enunciate the Torah. This act of transmission is intimate and verbal. It is the Oral Law that allows the Written Law to come alive. In Mendelssohn's account, it is only after some time that this most perfect arrangement comes unstuck. From around the time of Ezra the Scribe the original true version of the biblical vocalization was reconstructed by experts. By this account, the Masoretes were engaged in an act of restoration and were guardians of the truth.[135]

In the fourteenth century, Bahya ben Asher ibn Halawa offered a different understanding of the process of vocalization. In his commentary to Deuteronomy 7.2, he wrote:

> We learn from this how great is Torah, since it can be interpreted in a variety of ways, so that even one word can be understood in several ways according to the vowels. As the vowels move so the meaning changes, for the letters are the body and the vowels are the spirit ... for this reason we have been commanded not to add vowels to the Sefer Torah for the meaning of each word is defined by its vocalization. With vowels it has one meaning, but without them a person can understand many wondrous things.

If as one theory holds there is a single right answer to the question of how the text was originally vocalized, then the inclusion of vocalization is a quest for the retrieval of authenticity. If, however, the text invites multiple vocalizations, the process is more creative than conservative in nature.

These two approaches to the origin of the vowels reflect different understandings of tradition. In the first, our role is to approximate what the text has always meant. In the second, we are called on to strive to understand what the text might or must mean for us.

Some examples of the interpretive possibilities offered by this indeterminacy are in order. Moses has a theophanic encounter in the Tent of Meeting, described in the Book of Numbers using a peculiar vocalization:

וּבְבֹא מֹשֶׁה אֶל אֹהֶל מוֹעֵד לְדַבֵּר אִתּוֹ וַיִּשְׁמַע אֶת הַקּוֹל מִדַּבֵּר אֵלָיו

When Moses came to the Tent of Meeting to speak with Him, he heard the Voice speaking to him (Numbers 7.89)

The word מדבר is not vocalized in the way one would typically expect. Rashi explains the phenomenon thus: "מדבר is the same as מתדבר [mitdaber] – 'he heard the Voice uttering itself.' It is out of reverence for the Most High God that Scripture speaks thus: 'The Voice was speaking to itself,' and Moses would listen in."

The difference in vocalization has significant theological implications. Rather than God speaking to Moses, God is portrayed here speaking to God's own self. Revelation as sacred eavesdropping represents a fascinating and somewhat surprising read of a classic source.

The Masoretic version of Exodus 12.17 reads:

וּשְׁמַרְתֶּם אֶת הַמַּצּוֹת כִּי בְּעֶצֶם הַיּוֹם הַזֶּה הוֹצֵאתִי אֶת צִבְאוֹתֵיכֶם מֵאֶרֶץ מִצְרָיִם וּשְׁמַרְתֶּם אֶת הַיּוֹם הַזֶּה לְדֹרֹתֵיכֶם חֻקַּת עוֹלָם

You shall observe the Feast of Unleavened Bread/You shall preserve the Unleavened Bread, for on this very day I brought your ranks out of the land of Egypt; you shall observe this day throughout the ages as an institution for all time.

In an early midrashic work, note is made of the fact that the word מצות could be vocalized *matzot*, unleavened bread, or *mitzvot*, commandments:

Rabbi Yashya says: you should read: and you shall keep the commandments. Just as you should not miss the timing of the matzah and cause it to ferment, so you should not squander the mitzvah and let it ferment – if you have the chance to perform a mitzvah, do it immediately.[136]

Here the Rabbis propose an ingenious teaching based on the similarity between two words. Keeping *matzot* and keeping *mitzvot* are presented as parallel activities: the former a specific instance of the latter. To this day in modern Hebrew, to squander an opportunity is expressed in keeping with the ancient midrash as "to let it ferment."

Another biblical verse whose vocalization transforms its meaning is Psalm 119.126:

עֵת לַעֲשׂוֹת לַיהֹוָה הֵפֵרוּ תּוֹרָתֶךָ

It is time to act for Adonai, since they have broken / you should break Your Torah.

This verse is subject to a broad range of interpretations, many of which depend on whether the fourth word of the verse should be vocalized as *haferu* or *heferu*. Some radical readings understand the verse to be a license for overriding existing law for the sake of a pressing moral imperative.[137]

A last example is taken not from the Bible but from a modern Jewish thinker offering a surprising reading of a classic text of medieval Jewish philosophy. The opening to Maimonides' Mishneh Torah reads: "The foundation of all foundations and the pillar of wisdom consists in knowing that there [*sham*] is a being and that it is the first being."[138] Michael Fagenblat noted that, in an essay on the name of God, Emmanuel Levinas reads that word as *shem*, thus rendering: "the pillar of wisdom consists in knowing that the Name exists and that it is the first being."[139] Levinas is acting here as an heir of the Masoretes, judging how a text needs to be read and suggesting a creative misprision. Heirs of the Masoretes are thus bound to read closely yet expansively with attention and intention in roughly equal parts.

Driven by anxieties and buoyed by hope, guided by a sense of what Jewish theology might mean and how I might try to express it, inspired to embrace an alphabetical structure prevalent in Jewish culture since biblical times, challenged and stimulated by Mendelssohn's notion of Judaism as a living text, and encouraged by precedent to find tradition in interpretation, I offer twenty-two elements of a Jewish theology.

Notes

1. Borowitz, *Renewing the Covenant*.
2. This phrase is used to describe a large section of Borowitz's book. See ibid., 53–299.
3. Ibid., 30–31. For an appreciation of Borowitz among postmodern Jewish thinkers, see Ochs, "Borowitz and the Postmodern Renewal."

4. Borowitz, *Renewing the Covenant*, 294. In his *How Can a Jew*, Borowitz refers to the trust in God that contemporary believers must find in the face of secular scrutiny, adding: "It is because they trust in him that they can face the anxiety of this new open-texturedness which the secular age demands," 179.
5. Borowitz, *Renewing the Covenant*, 299. For an extensive discussion of intermarriage as a barometer in modern Jewish thought, see Rosenak, *Zehuyot Mitnagshot*. It is appropriate to note here that for much of his career Borowitz refused to recognize the legitimacy of ordaining LGBTQ persons as rabbis. His views would thus hardly meet contemporary criteria for "capacious pluralism." Late in life, Borowitz publicly stated that his previous position on ordination was in error, and he asked for forgiveness. See Adler and Podolsky, "Sexuality, Autonomy and Community," particularly 126–132, and Maimin, "Interview with Borowitz."
6. For the origin of this expression, see Rawidowicz, *Israel, Ever-Dying People*.
7. *On The Embassy to Gaius* XLII (330), in Yonge (transl.), *Works of Philo*, 787. The degree to which Philo's account is historically plausible has been debated. See Zeitlin, "Did Agrippa Write a Letter?" In *Philo of Alexandria*, Niehoff sees Agrippa in this episode as a mouthpiece for Philo's own views, noting that "Philos's Agrippa, like himself, is less concerned about politics than about the Jewish religion," 44.
8. Sacks, *Will We Have Jewish Grandchildren?*
9. Anxiety has been a preoccupation for some Christian theologians, but it tends to have a quite different valence. For foundational discussions of anxiety in modern theological discourse, see Kierkegaard, *Concept of Anxiety* and Tillich, *Courage To Be*. For anxiety in the thought of Hans Urs von Balthasar, see Cirelli, "Facing the Abyss." Theological anxiety of the kind expressed by these Christian theologians relates to the human condition. Cirelli (ibid.) describes von Balthasar's anxiety as "the experience that emerges in the … void (*Leere*) between God and man whenever one turns away from God and toward the self," 707.
10. Harvey, "Author's Haqdamah," 136.
11. Ibid., quoting the Introduction to Saadia's *Beliefs and Opinions*.
12. Levinas, "Promised Land or Permitted Land" in *Nine Talmudic Readings*, 51–69.
13. The reference here is to a refrain found in a popular children's book by Michael Rosen, *We're Going On a Bear Hunt*: "We can't go over it. We can't go under it. Oh no! We've got to go through it!"
14. See Rosenzweig, "Upon Opening Jüdisches Lehrhaus" in *On Jewish Learning*, 95–102.

15. See Ahad Ha'am's 1910 essay, "Judaism and the Gospels" (Kohn, *Nationalism and Jewish Ethics*, 289–319) and Cuddihy, *Ordeal of Civility*. For a robust statement of these Reform commitments, see Nussbaum, "Judaism and Love of Reason."
16. Kellner, *Must a Jew Believe?* 1.
17. Moses Hayim Luzzatto, "Maamar al Hakivui," *Otzarot Ramchal* (Bnei Brak, 1986), 246–247.
18. Borowitz, "Hope Jewish," 148–149. For more on the concept of hope as a thread, see Genesis 49:18; Lamentations 2:16. For use of the term to denote "end" in Second Temple and later literature, see Ben Sirah 7:17, Thanksgiving Hymns from Qumran 3:27. See also PT Nazir 1.4 51c.
19. Mishnah Yomah 8:9.
20. PT Berakhot 9.2 13b. See also Baeck, *This People Israel*, 292. Erich Fromm, *Revolution of Hope*, defines a human being as *homo esperans* (60). For a discussion of hope as a theological category see Marmur, *Star of Return*, 87–100.
21. https://www.emanuelnyc.org/2024/07/27/threads-of-hope-maoz-inon/.
22. For the distinction between Jewish thought, Jewish philosophy, and Jewish theology, see Altmann, "Encounter of Faith" and Altmann, "Do We Need?" Goldy, *Emergence of Jewish Theology*, demonstrates how influential the German tradition was in what he describes as the emergence of Jewish theology in America. There have also been significant contributions to Jewish theology in other countries. One good example of this is the British rabbi Louis Jacobs (see, e.g., Jacobs: *We Have Reason; Jewish Theology; Judaism and Theology*). Jacobs' definition of Jewish theology as "an attempt to think through consistently the implications of the Jewish religion" (*Jewish Theology*, 1) is interpreted in a conservative fashion by some. Byron Sherwin avers that "Jewish theology is a necessary vehicle for Jews who need and want to know that nature of the religion they espouse: what it affirms, what it rejects, how it differs from other religions, how its beliefs developed, and which of these beliefs can be asserted today with intellectual honesty" (*Faith Finding Meaning*, 43). In my own view, the purpose of Jewish theology is to delineate the contours of a possible Judaism not yet formed. The axiomatic constant is not the truth of Judaism but the urge to grapple with changing realities from a Jewish perspective.
23. Cherry, *Coherent Judaism*, xviii.
24. Maimonides, *Guide*, III.31. For an extremely illuminating discussion of this debate, see Lorberbaum, "Rise of Halakhic Religiosity."

25. One example among many may help illustrate this tendency. Chapter 19 of the Book of Numbers includes a description of the ritual of the red heifer, long held to be an example of a commandment not susceptible to rational explanation. Commenting on this, the Hasidic rabbi Klonimus Kalman Epstein argued that in fact none of the commandments can be explained and that even when some reason was suggested, it is impossible to understand the wonders and true reasons for any commandments, all of which are recondite from human knowledge. See Epstein, *Sefer Maor Vashemesh*, 448.

    For a systematic survey of attempts to provide reasons for the commandments, in stark contrast to the claim of such an attempt's futility, see Heinemann, *Reasons for Commandments*. The Hebrew original of Heinemann's work continues beyond the Renaissance.
26. Goldy, *Emergence of Jewish Theology* (13–14), lists four interwoven arguments traditionally given against engagement in Jewish theology: it is pie in the sky, alien to the Jewish spirit, contained in a different form in traditional literature, and lacking the rigor of other disciplines.
27. For a thorough treatment of the medieval expression "If I could know God, I would be God," see Kreisel, "Ilu Yedativ Hayyitiv." Kreisel points out that the term was employed by some Jewish thinkers, such as Joseph Albo, who themselves engaged in what could be categorized as theological speculation. Nonetheless, the expression sums up an objection to the notion of humans knowing God.
28. Heschel, *Passion for Truth*, 293.
29. What follows owes much to Fagenblat, "Lacking All Interest" and *Covenant of Creatures*, 111–139.
30. Levinas, *Nine Talmudic Readings*, 14.
31. This quotation is a translation from Leibowitz's 1954 work *Torah u-Mitzvot Bazman Hazeh*, and I quote it from Kasher, "On Yeshayahu Leibowitz's Use," 30. For a critique of Leibowitz, claiming that his position goes far beyond Maimonides and that it constitutes a danger to Orthodoxy, see Statman, "Negative Theology."
32. See: Diamond, "The Post-Secular"; Dinur, "Secular Theology as Challenge"; Goodman, *Faith of Secular Jews*; and Lahav, "Post-Secular Jewish Feminist."
33. Kosman, "My starting assumption is that 'everything is theological.' By this I mean that a human being cannot exist divorced from some connection, whether open or concealed, to something 'above him', toward which, and in the face of which, his everyday existence is directed," ("Cultural Crisis," 30).

    Kosman deliberately leaves the word "God" outside this description. It is interesting in this regard to consider the comment made by Martin Heidegger that "every philosophy is theology in the primordial and

essential sense that comprehension (*logos*) of beings as a whole asks about the ground of Being, and this ground is called *theos*, God" (*Schelling's Treatise*, 50). For a fascinating discussion of Heidegger's notion of the last gods, see Wolfson, *Heidegger and Kabbalah*, 138–155.
34. See Brody, *Martin Buber's Theopolitics*.
35. See Novak, "What is Jewish Theology?" particularly 20–24.
36. Sherwin has altered this phrase to read "faith finding meaning" in his eponymous book.
37. Quoted in Fagenblat, *Covenant of Creatures*, 141.
38. Mendelsohn, *Jerusalem*, 100. It is quoted in Nussbaum, "Judaism and Love of Reason," 14.
39. See Mishnah Sanhedrin 10.1. The meaning of this statement and the subsequent development of systematic theology in medieval Judaism is summarized and the complexity of the issue of belief in Judaism is discussed in Kellner, *Must a Jew Believe?*
40. See also Joshua 22.24.
41. Borowitz writes: "An idea of God set before Israel must ... meet the criterion of history past, present and future. It must demonstrate it as an authentic development of the Jewish past. It must be logical enough in contemporary terms and standards to make the present generation want to live by it, and its content must be such that this life is recognizably Israel's life of Torah before God. And it must be willing to stand before the judgment of the lives of generations yet to be. Past, present and future; the aggadic freedom is given – but the responsibility is great" ("The Idea of God," in Borowitz, *Studies in Meaning of Judaism*, 41).
42. Blumenthal, *Facing the Abusing God*, 3–4.
43. Sherwin, *Faith Finding Meaning*, 49. In "New Directions," an essay written in the 1990s, Arthur Green offered a definition of Jewish theology which emphasizes the communal and textual aspects of the enterprise: "Each Jewish theology is a religious attempt to help the Jewish people understand the meaning of Jewish life and Jewish existence out of the store of texts, symbols and historical experiences that are the shared inheritance of all Jews" (5).
44. Melamed, "Mihu Filosof Yehudi Moderni?," makes the controversial claim that many considered to be in the first rank of Jewish thinkers lack the grounding in rabbinic literature necessary to qualify them for such a description. He argues that Salomon Maimon is one of the very few worthy to be considered a modern Jewish thinker. Melamed's position is exaggerated, but I have long been interested in the degree to which the greatest thinkers have a command of traditional Jewish learning. Some, like Heschel and Soloveitchik, clearly did. Others, like Franz Rosenzweig at the time of the composition of his *Star of Redemption*, were highly intuitive but not profoundly learned.

45. Isaiah 43.12. See also Isaiah 43.10 and 44.8.
46. *Sifre* to Deuteronomy 346, and parallel sources. I have related to this midrash and its versatile role in modern Jewish thought in Marmur, "Are You My Witnesses?"
47. For a sample of Maybaum's thought, see Maybaum, *Ignaz Maybaum: A Reader*. For a theological statement showing a similar provenance to my own, see Bayfield, *Being Jewish Today*.
48. For a sense of Dow Marmur's key theological and other concerns, see Marmur, *Beyond Survival* and *Star of Return*.
49. Dorrien, "Crisis and Necessity," 3.
50. A new generation of philosophically sophisticated and self-aware Orthodox Jewish theology deserves serious attention. See Gellman, *Perfect Goodness*. See also Lebens, *Principles of Judaism*.
51. For an acute appreciation of the distinction between liberal and orthodox Jewish theology, see Altmann, "Do We Need?" particularly 210. Another useful resource for understanding the distinction between liberalism and orthodoxy is to be found in Blacker, *Democratic Education Stretched Thin*.
52. For an application of the postliberal theological approach of George Lindbeck and others to Judaism, see Kepnes, "Revelation as Torah."
53. Farneth, "Feminist Jewish Thought," makes the case for classifying feminist Jewish thought as a form of postliberal theology. The thinkers she mentions—Tamar Ross, Rachel Adler, Judith Plaskow—as well as a newer generation—I would highlight Mara Benjamin and Melissa Raphael in this regard—have irrevocably changed the ground of Jewish theological discourse.
54. For a discussion of liberal and postliberal trends in theology, with particular reference to reference and William Alston, see Knight, *Liberalism versus Postliberalism*.
55. See Kohler, *Jewish Theology*, 309.
56. For a review of trends in postmodern Christian theology by one of its key practitioners, see Raschke, *Postmodern Theology* and Vanhooser, *Cambridge Companion to Postmodern Theology*. Feldmann Kaye, *Jewish Theology*, offers a reading of the encounter between theology and postmodernism in a Jewish key.
57. Caputo, *Cross and Cosmos*, 109.
58. In theological literature, the terms kataphatic and apophatic will often be found instead of positive and negative theology, respectively. For a recent discussion of positive theology in a Jewish context, see Seeskin, "Can There Be?" For a profound discussion of negative theology, rooted in Jewish thought but not limited to it, see Wolfson, *Giving Beyond the Gift*.
59. Armstrong, "Negative Theology," in *Plotinian and Christian Studies*, 185. See Kenney, "Critical Value." In our time, aspects of modernity in

general have combined with a consciousness of the Holocaust in particular to strengthen interest in negative theology: for example, in the thought of Richard L. Rubenstein. A chapter on Rubenstein in a collection of essays on modern Jewish philosophies is entitled "The Encounter with Nothingness" (Kaufman, *Contemporary Jewish Philosophies*, 78–93). See also: Coward and Foshay, *Derrida and Negative Theology*; Franke, "Apophasis and the Turn"; and Lichtman, "Negative Theology." For two works which make this connection in an explicitly Jewish context, see the excellent collection of essays in Fagenblat, *Negative Theology*, which offer multiple perspectives on its theme, and Wolfson, *Heidegger and Kabbalah*, which is a sustained exploration of the parallels and resonances between two disparate approaches. Wolfson's work offers an immensely erudite, occasionally impenetrable (for this reader at least) and highly suggestive exploration of some striking commonalities. His work makes an emphatic case for the blurring of lines between theology and philosophy, between the medieval and the contemporary, between Jewish and "general" thought. For a discussion of the turn to mathematical notation in theological inquiry, see Smith, "Infinitesimal as Theological Principle." Avi Sagi describes the approach offered by Yeshayahu Leibowitz as a case of "Jewish religion without theology" since for him "Judaism shifts away from the metaphysical-theological realm and is perceived as a system of values" (*Jewish Religion After Theology*, 113.) For a recent discussion of theological realism and some alternatives to it, see Fisher, "Theological Realism." See also Gellman, "Theological Realism." The work of Jean-Luc Marion has greatly influenced this area of ontotheological discussion. See Marion, *God Without Being*.

60. Robbins, *Radical Theology*, 6. Robbins credits the postmodern theologian Charles Winquist as being the originator of the term "formulation of extremity."
61. Green, *Radical Judaism*; Rubenstein, "On Becoming."
62. Blumenthal, *Facing the Abusing God*, 4.
63. Joseph L. Rosefield took out a patent to produce smooth peanut butter in 1923 and the crunchy variety in 1932. A quintessentially modern and North American foodstuff, the Incas were grinding nuts centuries earlier. Here too, modern practices have pre-modern precedents. See Mishnah Nedarim 6:4 and Avodah Zarah 2:6 for a parallel in rabbinic literature.
64. See Marmur, "Why Jews Quote."
65. Albo, *Sefer Ha-'Ikkarim*, volume 1, 37.
66. See Weiss, *Joseph Albo* and Harvey, "Albo's Discussion of Time."
67. See Thiselton, *Systematic Theology*.
68. See Kellner, *Must a Jew Believe?*, particularly 44–51.

69. Fisher, *Contemplative Nation*, makes the case that many interpreters of Judaism have erroneously presented homiletical theology as an alternative to rigorous systematic thought. I do not share his apparently dismissive attitude to the sermonic and the homiletical, but I am compelled by his argument that an understanding of Jewish theological practice is indispensable. Another term that has been employed recently to distinguish Jewish theology from the strictures of certain Christian assumptions about theology and Judaism is "unbound theology." See Diamond, *Jewish Theology Unbound*.
70. My interest in alphabets can be traced to the publication of King's *The 22 Letters*. The novel, reflecting contemporary scholarly theories, hints at a variety of motivations for the development of this remarkable technology: religious, commercial, political, military, and more.
71. See Borowitz, "The Problem of the Form of a Jewish Theology" (Borowitz, *Studies in Meaning of Judaism*, 115–131), which opened up the question of the form of Jewish theology for me and is in fact an excellent introduction to a certain strand within modern Jewish theology.
72. Kellner, "Maimonides' 'Thirteen Principles,'" argues that the structure of Maimonides' *Guide* can be understood with reference to his Thirteen Principles, which appear to be absent from the *Guide* but are, if Kellner's suggestion is to be accepted, at the heart of its tripartite form. For an excellent discussion of a modern work whose structure is clearly of great importance, see Batnitzky, "Philosophical Import."
73. To take just one example, consider the remarkable attempt by J. David Bleich, *With Perfect Faith*, to organize his exposition of Jewish belief around Maimonides' Thirteen Principles.
74. An understanding of the emergence of alphabet systems should rest on an appreciation of the phenomenon of writing in general. An earlier generation of research, exemplified by Diringer, *Writing*, and Gelb, *Study of Writing*, has been both challenged and enhanced by works such as Daniel and Bright, *World's Writing Systems* and Houston, *First Writing*. For a more concise introduction to this topic, see Robinson, *Story of Writing*. For a good summary and excellent bibliography of how the earliest alphabets came into being, see Bowes and Steele, *Understanding Relations*; the editors' introductory chapter is particularly helpful. See also Haring, "Ancient Egypt" in that volume. A foundational work for understanding the global significance of the alphabet, now decades old and still invaluable, is Diringer, *Alphabet*. Despite great changes in the field since then, this work continues to be of great value. Regarding West Semitic epigraphy, see Hamilton, *Origins of West Semitic* and Naveh, *Early History*. From among Benjamin Sass' several works in this field spread over decades, see *Alphabet at Turn* and "Emergence." In "West Semitic

Alphabet Inscriptions" Finkelstein and Sass propose a chronology for the spread of the alphabet from its earliest stirrings in the thirteenth century BCE (other scholars suggest a significantly earlier starting date) to its ubiquity by the seventh. They argue, for example, that in light of what is currently known, "the events of much of the ninth century described in the Book of Kings were transmitted orally and first put in writing some two generations later," 202. They also hypothesize that it was in a part of the Land of Israel known as the Shephelah that "the alphabet was reduced from 29-27 to 22 graphemes in the 13th century," 201. Theories concerning the development of alphabets abound. Kermani, *Sonic Soma*, offers a cross-cultural reading of the origins of the alphabet with an emphasis on the human body and the goddess in mythology. Israeli performance artist Victoria Hanna has created a remarkable performance relating to the physicality of the alphabet, discussed in Pressman, "The Hebrew Alphabet." The work of Orly Goldwasser (see, e.g., "How the Alphabet," "Advantage of Cultural Periphery," and "Invention of the Alphabet") is important in advancing a compelling thesis about the origin of the alphabet. The cultural significance of the alphabet for the contemporary West is surveyed in Drucker, *Alphabetic Labyrinth*. For examples of contemporary uses of the alphabet, see Ardam, "ABCs of Conceptual Writing" and Stout, "Experimenting with Letters."

75. For an account of the spread of the alphabet into Greece from an economic perspective, see Pappa, "Poster Boys." See also Brown, "Proverb-Book." An alternative view, according to which "to record the hexameters of dedications was the initial motive that called the Greek alphabet into existence" (8) is propounded in Robb, *Literacy and Paideia*. For yet another approach emphasizing the private nature of the earliest uses of the Greek alphabet and "the striking omission of any public or economic matters" (248) see Bourougiannis, "Transmission of the Alphabet." On the educational aspect of this remarkable story, see West, "Learning the Alphabet." For an approach to the question of origins and dissemination employing linguistics, epigraphy, and archaeology, see Mertzani, "Interdisciplinarity."

76. See, for example, de Kerckhove and Lumsden, *Alphabet and Brain*. In that volume, see in particular Lafont, "Relationships Speech and Writing." For a strident rejection of the notion that alphabetic systems are superior to non-alphabetic systems from a linguistics perspective, see Baroni, "Alphabet vs. Non-Alphabetic Writing." For the case of Chinese, see Zhong, *Chinese Grammatology*. For a robust presentation of the argument that the alphabet has had a profound impact on Western culture, see de Looze, *Letter and Cosmos*. Remarkably, the Jewish dimension of this impact is not to be found in de Looze's book.

77. See, for example, de Kerckhove and Lumsden, *Alphabet and Brain*. In that volume, see in particular Lafont, "Relationships." For a strident rejection of the notion that alphabetic systems are superior to non-alphabetic systems from a linguistics perspective, see Baroni, "Alphabet vs. Non-Alphabetic Writing."

    The case of Chinese is a particularly significant one, and a fascinating account of the encounter between Western concepts and modern China can be found in Zhong, *Chinese Grammatology*. For a robust presentation of the argument that the alphabet has had a profound impact on Western culture, see de Looze, *Letter and Cosmos*. Remarkably, the Jewish dimension of this impact is not to be found in de Looze's book.

78. For the possible etymology of the word "element," see Strugnell and Eshel, "It's Elementary." In his analysis of the development of the Greek language, Porter claims that "the idea that language comprises a system and is made up of primary constituents seems to have originated in the latter half of the fifth [pre-Christian] century" ("Language as a System," 514). In "Plato's Use" De Simone argues that the primary meaning of the term *stoicheion* is "letter of the alphabet." See also Acevedo, *Alphanumeric Cosmology* and Coogan, "Alphabets and Elements." In a number of important studies, Tzahi Weiss has shown that "the creation of the world from alphabetic letters is a well-known myth whose earliest literary descriptions can be found in Jewish, Samaritan, Christian and Gnostic sources" ("On Matter of Language," 101). Weiss distinguishes between different versions of this tradition: some have portrayed the creation of the world through the letters of the Divine Name, while others have suggested that the entire alphabet (and in some cases some further letters) were involved. See also Weiss, *Otiot Shenivrau*. In "Rashi on Creation" Warren Zev Harvey makes the playful claim that the medieval Jewish commentator Rashi "held that the world was created out of a primordial matter called '*tohu*,' which is insubstantial and intangible, and made of the Hebrew letters of the Torah, which are nothing but 'mere speech and word.' With this imaginative argument, Rashi may have gone a bar's length beyond Plato and Derrida," 47.

79. Katz, "Letter as Essence," 133. In my judgment the single most significant attempt to appreciate the Jewish preoccupation with the alphabetic is Faur, *Horizontal Society*. This work, however, is not a measured and systematic account of the subject; rather, it provides a sprawling canvas upon which Faur sketches his own tendentious understanding of Judaism.

80. Eshel and Strugnell, "Alphabetic Acrostics." Two papers by David Noel Freedman relate to this same phenomenon: "Acrostics and Metrics" and "Acrostic Poems." See Benun, "Evil and Disruption" on the psalms. Benun is convinced that the "acrostics in Psalms are part of a sophisticated literary system which creates a series of signposts intended to guide

the reader to each psalm's embedded message," 2. However, the evidence for this thesis is far from conclusive. See also Ho, "Macrostructural Logic" and Kimelman, "Psalm 145." Regarding the Book of Lamentations, see Assis, "Alphabetic Acrostic." For an article considering both Psalms and Lamentations with reference to grammar, see Giffone," 'Perfect' Poem." On Proverbs, see Hurowitz, "Often Overlooked." For a comparison between biblical alphabetic acrostics and Babylonian parallels, see Soll, "Babylonian and Biblical Acrostics."
81. Berlin, "Rhetoric of Psalm 145," 18.
82. See: Botha, "Psalm 34"; Ceresko, "ABCs of Wisdom"; and Ceresko, "Endings and Beginnings."
83. This method is employed with regard to Psalms 34 and 145 in Liebreich, "Psalms 34 and 145 ." While my emphases are different than his, it was his reading that alerted me to this possibility.
84. See Eshel and Strugnell, "Alphabetic Acrostics" and Henderson, "Structure and Allusion."
85. Ruth Rabbah 6.4. The event is reported to have taken place at the circumcision ceremony of Elisha ben Abuys, and two great sages present there, Rabbi Eliezer and Rabbi Joshua, contrast the frivolity of the guests with the serious business of Torah study.
86. Ecclesiastes Rabbah 1.13.
87. See: Elizur," Limkoram Shel Piyutei Selichot"; Lieber, "Confessing from A-Z"; and Schirmann, "Hebrew Liturgical Poetry."
88. For an issue relating to the translation of the confession, see Holtz, "Hatav Hakemutzah."
89. Har-Shefi, "Im Yad al Halev" in Cohen, *Shevarim Neesafim*, 60. The translation is mine.
90. I am grateful to Arthur Green to directing my attention to a small Hasidic work by Rabbi Zvi Hirsch of Nadworna entitled *Alpha Beta* (I saw the 1878 Warsaw edition of this work). The book offers a number of words for each letter of the alphabet, which when read together suggest a program for ethical living. Aleph, for example, includes Emet (Truth), Emunah (Faith), Ahavah (Love), Erech Ruach (Patience, Tolerance), and Achilah (Eating). For recent examples of alphabetical works in Hebrew, see Calderon, *Alfa Beta Talmudi* and Tsalka, *Sefer Haalef Bet*. This latter work has a particularly ingenious structure, building autobiographical and literary reflections around the alphabet. For examples of English works exploring the letters of the Hebrew alphabet for mystical insights, see: Ginsburgh, *The Alef-Beit*; Kushner, *Sefer Otiyot*; Haralick, *Inner Meaning*; and Munk, *Wisdom in Hebrew Alphabet*.
91. United States Bureau of Education, *The Letters of Rabbi Akiba*. See also Dan, "Otiot Derabbi Akiva."

92. See, for example, Lamentations Rabbah 1.20, where Rabbi Judah and Rabbi Nehemiah offer contrasting explanations for the alphabetic structure of the Book of Lamentations.
93. Lipiner, *Chazon Haotiot*, offers a remarkable description of what he terms the metaphysics of the Hebrew alphabet, drawing mainly on sources from within the Jewish esoteric tradition. Another invaluable work yet to be translated into English is Weiss, *Otiot Shenivrau*, which focuses on approaches to letters of the alphabet in late antiquity and employs a very different methodology from that of Lipiner. Weiss' more recent English work builds on much of this scholarship. See Weiss, *Sefer Yesira*, particularly 1–75. For an important and highly suggestive Hebrew article offering an extended reflection on the letters of the alphabet in the Zohar, see Oron, "Sipur Haotiot."
94. Scholem, "Name of God," 71. For insightful re-readings of this classic essay by Scholem, see Ben-Sasson, " 'Name of God'" and Wolosky, "'Gershom Scholem's Linguistic Theory."
95. See Dan, "Language of Creation" and Dan, "Language of the Mystics," 14.
96. See: Idel, "Perush Nosaf Le-Alef Bet"; Langermann, "From My Notebooks"; Sviri, "Words of Power." For a fascinating insight on the influence of Sefer HaTemunah on Christian Kabbalah, see Copenhaver and Kokin, "Egidio da Viterbo's Book." See also Thon, "Power of (Hebrew) Language."
97. For a particularly thorough, original, and engaging account of the linguistic theology of one of the giants of early Hasidism, see Mayse, *Speaking Infinities*. See also Idel, "Models of Cleaving."
98. Traditions have been attached both to Rabbi Isaac Luria and to the Baal Shem Tov, the founding figures of Safed mysticism and the Hasidic movement, respectively, in which simple worshippers recite the alphabet to great effect. See Munk, *Wisdom in Hebrew Alphabet*, 37–38. I am grateful to David Assaf and Zeev Kitsis for locating the origin of the Hasidic tale which, in fact, appears in two variations. See Dov Ber Ehrmann, *Dvarim Arevim* (Munkacz: Kahn et Fried, 1903), vol.1, 10a, and Aaron Walden, *Kehal Hasidim* (Lemberg, 1866), 5d. The first of these versions was set to music and sung by Hava Alberstein under the title "Tefillot Hadashot" (New Prayers).
99. See Marmur, "God of Language."
100. Demsky, "Interface of Oral and Written," relates to the possibility that the particular order of the alphabet can be explained in terms of pedagogic mnemonic considerations. This thesis was advanced by Tur-Sinai: "Origin of the Alphabet I"; "Origin of the Alphabet II"; and "The Origin of the Alphabet: B)."

101. See van der Heide, " 'Mem and Samekh.'"
102. Munk, *Wisdom of Hebrew Alphabet*, 39. The translation which follows is taken from that work with a few emendations (39–41). For Greek parallels to this kind of educational approach, see West, "Learning the Alphabet," which includes Greek examples from as early as the fifth century BCE and also Goldin, "Several Sidelights," particularly 181. For an early medieval Latin Christian text with some parallels, see Wright and Pelle, "Alphabet of Words."
103. In order for this teaching to work it is necessary to shift easily between Aramaic and Hebrew. This ability to transition between languages seems to be an important aspect of the story of alphabetic systems in general. From their inception alphabets have relied (at least for their development) on a degree of familiarity with more than one language. Alphabet purists and chauvinists have—in this as in so many other realms—little upon which their theories can rely.
104. Those letters which have two orthographies depending on whether they appear in the body of a word or at its end are known as double letters and from each of them a double lesson is adduced.
105. It is most likely that the alternative reading offered here is provided since the first possibility is very similar to the teaching for *gimel* and *dalet*.
106. The implication here is that there is a time to speak and a time to refrain from speaking.
107. Note that here the letter is not the first but the last of the word in question, as if to emphasize the journey from the first to very last. It also opens the way to this ingenious reflection on the word *emet*, truth.
108. The letters of the word *sheker* are adjacent. More precisely still, the order is *kuf, resh, shin*, but the point here is that the letters are in close proximity, unlike the word for truth, which comprises the letters most distant from each other in the alphabet.
109. In the current orthography, the letter ק stands on one leg, unlike the letters of the word אמת, *emet*, each of which stands, as it were, on a solid foundation.
110. See Stern, "Alphabet of Ben Sira," for a judicious survey of scholarship on this work.
111. For the lyrics to this song: https://www.hebrewsongs.com/?song=alefbeit.
112. This excerpt from Defoe's "Essay On Literature" is quoted in Hudson, *Writing and European Thought*, 77.
113. For an excellent survey of recent scholarship, see Houston, *The First Writing*.
114. See Haring, "Ancient Egypt," for an up-to-date survey of theories of provenance.
115. Shlain, *Alphabet Versus Goddess*, 71.

116. Two works which make this case with great conviction are Flusser, *Does Writing?*, and Rotman, *Becoming Beside Ourselves*. In an earlier work, Rotman ("Thinking Dia-Grams," particularly 389) decries what he terms alphabeticism.
117. Faur, *Horizontal Society*, 220.
118. Mendelssohn, *Jerusalem*, 102–103.
119. Ibid., 102.
120. Most of the books and articles listed here, all of which offer insightful readings of this section of *Jerusalem*, have been published since 2000, demonstrating the degree to which Mendelssohn's concerns resonate with contemporary areas of interest. See: Almog, *Secularism and Hermeneutics*, 82–106; Batnitzky, *Idolatry and Representation*, particularly 33–40; Braiterman, "Emergence of Modern Religion"; Breuer, "Rabbinic Law and Spirituality"; Eisen, "Divine Legislation"; Eisen, *Rethinking Modern Judaism*, particularly 79–104; Fenves, *Arresting Language*, particularly 80–97; Freudenthal, "Remedy to Linguistic Skepticism"; Freudenthal, *No Religion Without Idolatry*; Freudenthal, "Idolatry Everywhere, Idolaters Nowhere"; Hilfritch, "Making Writing Readable Again"; Jospe, "Superiority of Oral over Written"; Lifschitz, "Natural Yet Providential Tongue"; Pollok, "Power of Rituals"; Rosenstock, *Philosophy and the Jewish Question*, particularly 28–78; Sacks, *Mendelssohn's Living Script*; Weber, "Fending Off Idolatry."
121. Mendelssohn, *Jerusalem*, 108.
122. Ibid., 109.
123. Altmann, *Moses Mendelssohn*, refers to the digression on writing and idolatry as "the least substantiated of all theories he ever advanced," 546. However, in his notes to Mendelssohn, *Jerusalem* (220–224) Altmann offers a number of important insights, drawing parallels between Mendelssohn's theories and the work of Herder, Warburton, and others.
124. Mendelssohn, *Jerusalem*, 118.
125. Ibid., 119.
126. Ibid., 113.
127. Janowitz, "Good Jews Don't," 251.
128. See Hudson, *Writing and European Thought*.
129. Fisher, "Jewish religious life is a decision to live in the language of the oral and written Torah ... this is a living in 'living language'; that is, a series of textual forms and modes of expression that demand the active intellectual and personal engagement of the practitioner" ("Jewish Philosophy," 85).
130. Petuchowski, *Heirs of the Pharisees*. One of the dedicatees of Petuchowski's work is Leo Baeck, who himself wrote an essay on the Pharisees in 1927 which was published in 1934 as a booklet, *The Pharisees*. See also Finkelstein, *The Pharisees* and Schiffman, "Pharisees Revisited."

131. See Himmelfarb, "Identity of First Masoretes."
132. See Goody, *Interface*, 40–58.
133. Ilich and Sanders, *ABC*, 13.
134. For an illustration of vocalization as an interpretive practice in the Hebrew Bible, in this case regarding some chapters from Isaiah, see Tiemeyer, "Vocalization and Interpretation."
135. Moses Mendelssohn, *Or Lenetiva* (Berlin, 1783), 10.
136. Mekhilta Bo, 9.
137. For a survey of some of the main interpretive possibilities, see Heschel, *Heavenly Torah*, 736–739.
138. *Yesodei* Torah 1.1. That is the way in which the word is read in the Mamre vocalized edition of the text.
139. Fagenblat, *Covenant of Creatures*, 128. Levinas' reading can be found in Levinas, *Beyond The Verse*, 11.

Open Access This chapter is licensed under the terms of the Creative Commons Attribution 4.0 International License (http://creativecommons.org/licenses/by/4.0/), which permits use, sharing, adaptation, distribution and reproduction in any medium or format, as long as you give appropriate credit to the original author(s) and the source, provide a link to the Creative Commons license and indicate if changes were made.

The images or other third party material in this chapter are included in the chapter's Creative Commons license, unless indicated otherwise in a credit line to the material. If material is not included in the chapter's Creative Commons license and your intended use is not permitted by statutory regulation or exceeds the permitted use, you will need to obtain permission directly from the copyright holder.

Aspaklaria: Prophecy and Pluralism

"I am a Jew. Hath not a Jew eyes?"

Shylock's speech in Shakespeare's *Merchant of Venice* is intended to humanize the Jew. Of course, Jews have eyes as other humans do (which means that some Jews have trouble seeing or have lost an eye or two). The rhetorical question goes beyond physiology and speaks to questions of truth, interpretation, pluralism, individuality, and culture.

How to understand being Jewish? Is it a religion, a civilization, a community of memory, an ethnic group, an ethical imperative, an accident of birth, a joy, a blight?[1] I see it is as an alphabet, building blocks of meaning which prompt the formation of vocabularies and modes of discourse; for me, it is an instrument of perception, a way of seeing.[2] It does not follow from this that Jews pronounce the same words or see the same realities as each other. Indeed, there has never been a time in which the question of what being Jewish implies and demands has been subject to such wide and often contradictory interpretations. One of the motivations for this book is the unnerving possibility that the gulf between Jewish self-understandings will become unbridgeable. Against this backdrop, the first letter in my proposed alphabet relates to a pervasive optical metaphor.[3]

I am a Jew. This fact represents my primary marker of identity, the strongest of the multiple lenses through which I perceive and process the world.

I am a Jew. Here are my eyes.

Aspaklaria: One Lens or Many?

The Mishnah records a disagreement between the House of Shammai and the House of Hillel concerning the blessing recited over the candle lit at the end of Shabbat.[4] The House of Shammai proposes a version blessing God "who created the flame of the fire"; the House of Hillel suggests "who creates the flame of the fire." Both schools look at the same combustion, but what they see is different. One view calls to mind the primordial flame, singular in essence, perfected, and past. The other celebrates the unfolding present and sees countless shades of possibility and difference dancing within the flame. This disagreement represents a local iteration of a well-established trope: the one and the many, epitomized in the Greek world by Plato and Aristotle, respectively. At the dawn of the twentieth century William James proposed the distinction between the all-form and the each-form of thinking. The former, practiced by monists, tends toward the unity of all things, while the latter, favored by pluralists, is always inclined to notice particular differentiating details.[5]

Aspaklaria, sometimes translated as speculum, is a term employed in rabbinic literature to explain a distinction between the prophecy of Moses, on the one hand, and all the other biblical prophets, on the other.[6] This tradition offers, I suggest, a particular instance of the each/all distinction, centered not on that which is observed but rather on the equipment employed to do the observing. While the prophets saw through a speculum that was cloudy or speckled or dull, Moses saw through a speculum that shines and is clear and pure. In yet another iteration, the prophets saw through multiple *aspaklariot*; Moses saw through only one. The version of this tradition found in Leviticus Rabbah warrants quotation here:

> How is Moses to be distinguished from the other prophets? There is a response to this question in the name of Rabbi Judah son of Rabbi Ilai, and one in the name of our Rabbis. Rabbi Judah says: the prophets saw through nine *aspaklariot* as it is written: "The vision I saw was like the vision I had seen ..." (Ezekiel 43:3),[7] while Moses saw through only one *aspaklaria*, as it is written: "... clearly and not in riddles" (Numbers 12:8). Our Rabbis teach: all the other prophets saw through a dirty *aspaklaria*, which is as it is written: "I spoke to the prophets, gave them many visions, and told parables through them" (Hosea 9:10),[8] Moses saw through a polished *aspaklaria*, and this is as it is written: "... he sees the form of the Lord." (Numbers 12:8)[9]

The speculum employed in these rabbinic traditions is a kind of optical aid, a lens through which the Divine is encountered and perceived. The tendency of this midrash and its parallels is to privilege Moses' single *aspaklaria* over those of the prophets. However, I am less sure. In my reading, the two ways of seeing epitomized here represent two versions of vision: the univocal and the multifocal, the all and the each. One approach offers immediacy and clarity, the other nuance and depth.

Some medieval commentators suggest that Moses' clarity of vision allowed him to see that there was nothing to see and that in this sense his vision was clearest.[10] The urge to see through as uncorrupted a lens as possible, to encounter things as they really are, is common to biblical protagonists and pioneers of modernity alike. Moses, our biblical exemplar, yearns to look directly—in wonder (at the Burning Bush), in solidarity (at the plight of people dehumanized by slavery), and in search of the Divine. I want to compare the figure of Moses with that of Baruch Spinoza some thirty centuries later. Spinoza was a lens grinder by profession, and the search for unblemished truth is a feature of his philosophy. Analyzing the words of the prophets of the Bible, he concluded that they should not be looked to for scientific accuracy or philosophical clarity. He asserted:

> God adapted revelations to the understanding and opinions of the prophets, and ... in matters of theory ... the prophets could be, and, in fact, were, ignorant, and held conflicting opinions. It therefore follows that we must by no means go to the prophets for knowledge, either of natural or of spiritual phenomena.[11]

If, as Spinoza claims, these traditional sources of wisdom had been discredited, how was wisdom to be found? "Demonstrations are the eyes of the mind, whereby it sees and observes things."[12] A new spirit of science and empiricism was intended to replace illusion with reason, doctrine with experiment, and flights of fancy with the cold hard truth.

The clear lenses of Moses and of Spinoza have much in common: a search for truth, a love of text, and an eye for detail along with a thirst for the grand panoramic sweep. They represent an ideal to be found in old-fashioned religion as in new-fangled science: the belief that under the right conditions, come the glorious day, we will be able to see no longer as through a glass darkly but with pellucid clarity.[13]

There is another ideal, epitomized by the other biblical prophets in our midrash and articulated by generations of rabbis, sages, therapists, and thinkers. Lens is layered upon lens and the appropriate aggregation yields the best vision. It is not the blinding realization of a singular truth that takes pride of place but the optimal combination, namely, the blend of *aspaklariot*.

SCREENS AND MIRRORS

It is most appropriate for a word employed in a discussion of difference that *aspaklaria* can be translated in a number of contrasting ways. Along with the sense of a lens through which one looks, others have also been suggested: screen, mirror, and perspective, among others.

Both Rashi and Maimonides, giants of medieval Judaism, translated *aspaklaria* to mean a barrier, separating humans from the divine presence.[14] For Maimonides, these screens are barriers to prophetic perfection. Moses' clear *aspaklaria* represents the pinnacle of human moral achievement whereby almost nothing separates human perfection from divine reality. Every strong cultural grounding, every prism through which reality is perceived, necessarily includes barriers and blind spots. Both our capacity for insight and our myopia often have a common origin. At its finest, concern for one's people's unique pathway to fulfillment and redemption should not be at odds with an appreciation of universal concerns. Too often, however, our Jewish *aspaklaria* is not only a prism refining vision but a barrier rendering the other invisible. At a time when particularism is giving way to chauvinism, that lesson should not be forgotten.

Another translation of the term presents the *aspaklaria* not as a window looking out to that which is beyond but as a mirror, reflecting back to the viewer a version of themselves. The twelfth chapter of the Book of Numbers provides the basis for the notion that Moses had a distinct way of perceiving the divine presence:

> When there is a prophet among you,
>   I, the LORD, reveal myself to them in visions,
>   I speak to them in dreams.
> But this is not true of my servant Moses;
>   he is faithful in all my house.
> With him I speak face to face,
>   clearly and not in riddles;
>   he sees the form of the LORD.[15]

The Hebrew word describing the other prophets' mode of seeing and Moses' mode of seeing is comprised of the same letters, but the standard Masoretic text vocalizes them differently. The word rendered in this translation as "visions" appears in the original Hebrew as *mar'ah*, a mirror.[16] In Tractate Kelim in the Mishnah the word *aspaklaria* refers to "a glass mirror with which a woman looks at her face" or a metal equivalent.[17] A glass mirror comprises a combination of transparent and reflective ingredients: different kinds of *aspaklaria*.[18]

To modern ears, the notion that a prophet is in fact gazing at a reflection of themselves sounds like an admission of fraud or perhaps a psychological commentary: to attempt to see is always a version of the attempt to see oneself. This, it might be argued, is the risk inherent in religions and philosophies. I believe I am looking out on the universe but am in fact gazing at a reflection of myself. Solipsism, narcissism, and delusion are bound to follow. But it is not all bad news. The mirror is not only a symbol of vanity but also a gateway to self-reflection and self-understanding. [19] Our impression of the world outside ourselves is inevitably imprinted with our self-understanding. By acknowledging that a mirror is part of our perceptual equipment, we understand that even when we are looking out beyond ourselves, we are looking at ourselves as well. When Feuerbach commented that if birds wrote theology, God would have wings, he was making this same point, subsequently taken up by feminist theologians.[20] None of us is as objective as we would like to think we are. We see reflections of ourselves and call them God and truth.

However, the mirror represents more than self-absorption and self-deception. One remarkable eighteenth-century commentary on the *aspaklaria* traditions by Rabbi Shneur Zalman of Liadi suggests that at least in one way the non-luminous speculum had an advantage over the speculum that shines: it includes a mirror.[21] Reflectiveness, attentiveness, self-awareness—these are invaluable aids to perception and not shameful obstructions.

Perspective

Samuel Lebens chose to open his work *A Guide for the Jewish Undecided*, whose title is adorned by the descriptor "A philosopher makes the case for Orthodox Judaism," with the statement: "Every human being looks upon the world from their own unique perspective."[22] Perspective is positional; it explains what we see in terms of where we are. Each generation is bound to experience and understand the Torah differently. The term *aspaklaria* was used extensively in this sense by Abraham Joshua Heschel, whose monumental Hebrew work was entitled *Heavenly Torah Through the Aspaklaria of the Generations*.[23] Heschel also took a term known from esoteric texts—the upper *aspaklaria*[24]—and added the parallel notion of a lower *aspaklaria*. He argued that while Rabbi Akiva often strove to contemplate questions from a celestial or other-worldly perspective, Rabbi Ishmael adopted a world's-eye view, looking at persons and their problems in a more pragmatic and practical way.

Most of us see with two eyes and manage to hold more than one perspective in mind. Furthermore, an awareness of the multiplicity of perspectives encourages a generosity of spirit and a tolerance of diversity: it is not that I see what is really there and you are deluded, but rather that we start out from different vantage points and consequently see differently. Seeing with two eyes, each offering a different perspective, allows for depth of vision.

Heschel coined the expression "the *aspaklaria* of the generations," suggesting that each era is in need of a lens suited to the times. The Torah from heaven is regarded in different ways as the generations pass, not because the further away from Sinai we are the less we see but because different historical eras bring different possibilities to light. In the 1940s, Heschel expressed this view with a degree of impatience:

> Not through our own eyes but through lenses ground by our intellectual ancestry do we look at the world. But our eyes are strained and tired of staring through spectacles worn by another generation. We are tired of overlooking entities, of squinting at their relations to other things. We want to face reality as it is.[25]

Unlike Spinoza, Heschel did not deem it necessary to debunk the claims of tradition; he preferred to view them in a new light. When he wrote in 1960, "Perhaps it is the will of God that in this eon there should be diversity in our forms of devotion and commitment to Him. In this eon, diversity of religions is the will of God,"[26] attention should be paid to his repeated emphasis of "this eon." Truth is to be perceived through a clear lens, but the truth will change over time. Different aspects of the truth become visible from different vantage points.

A Talmudic principle of judicial practice determines that "the judge only has what their eyes can see."[27] The Talmudic authors found a proof text for this idea from a source which appears to say the very opposite. The second book of Chronicles tells the story of a judicial reform purportedly enacted by King Jehoshaphat of Judah in the ninth century BCE. The king offers a charge to the judges: "Observe what you are doing, for you do not charge on behalf of human beings, but on behalf of Adonai, who is with you when you pass judgment."[28] The king is aware of the risk that the judge will consider the case from a limited human perspective, whether that be through the prism of personal experience and bias or (more crudely) in return for blandishments offered by unscrupulous transgressors. Remember, he tells them, you are supposed to be considering the case from God's perspective not your own. In a similar vein, the prophet Isaiah, imagining a future king, avers that "he shall sense the truth by his reverence for Adonai: he shall not judge by what his eyes behold, nor decide by what his ears perceive."[29]

The advice offered in these biblical examples to judges and kings is addressed to all of us, prompted every day to make decisions, be they consequential or trivial. Should I give money to this cause or that? Should I privilege my wish to consume resources over the planet's need to preserve them? Is this leader or that philosophy worthy of my support? Should I move beyond my comfort zone or stay with what I know? Should I embrace the cultures and assumptions in which I have been raised, or should I reject them, ignore them, or seek to give them new expression?

Jehoshaphat and Isaiah both employ optical metaphors. Each assumes that I see with my own eyes, defined by my body, experiences, historical setting, and physical location. Yet, because I strive to see clearly, I appreciate that there is another perspective, purer and clearer than my own. My own perceptual equipment encourages me to appreciate its own inadequacy.

This awareness of two points of view speaks, I believe, to one of the most significant and pervasive aspects of the human condition. Thomas Nagel's 1988 work, *The View from Nowhere*, opens:

> This book is about a single problem: how to combine the perspective of a particular person inside the world with an objective view of the same world, the person and his viewpoint included. It is a problem that faces every creature with the impulse and capacity to transcend its particular point of view and to conceive of the world as a whole.[30]

Nagel asserts that this "is the most fundamental issue about morality, knowledge, freedom, the self, and the relation of mind to the physical world."³¹ Two apparently irreconcilable insights are at the heart of this problem: first, there is more in heaven and earth than that which I perceive; and second, it is only by means of my perceptual equipment that I can understand anything. Chronicles, the Talmud, contemporary thought, all point to this paradoxical and challenging truth: I see (whether the seeing is physical or metaphorical) clearly enough to understand that there is much that I fail to see. The process of human maturation includes this capacity to distinguish between my own line of vision and an all-embracing, panoramic understanding. All I have is what my eyes can register, but I know that there is more in heaven and earth than I can take in. The proliferation of narcissism, naivety, and arrogance in our social discourse is, in part, due to our neglect of this apparently simple question: when I look, what am I seeing?

Change of perspective is a necessary condition of consequential change. To cite an example relating to environmental crisis, Jasmine Ulmer uses the medium of photography to encourage a reconsideration of the place of human beings in the wider context of the planet, expressing the hope that such an approach "can help us perceive ourselves from the perspective of the earth, in which we are smaller parts of a larger, interconnected whole."³²

The aspiration to see the world as objectively as possible is a key feature of modernity. Baruch Spinoza, no doubt influenced by his own professional expertise, spoke of the possibility of perceiving *sub specie aeternitatis*, from the perspective of eternity. Spinoza distanced himself (and was distanced) from the parochial perspectives of the Jewish community into which he was born, and his striving for a more universal point of view is one of the foundations of Western modernity. All disciplines have been influenced by the imperative of perspective. Hence, for example, "a view of theology as the presentation of a perspective calls attention … to its formal character as something relative to its cultural position, historically conditioned and continually developing."³³

Like the judge in the Talmud, each of us only has what our eyes can see. Like the judge, we should be conscious of our particular perspective and strive to see beyond it. The judge's dilemma—how to be aware of one's own embodied specificity while striving for a view that outstrips the particular—is the Jew's dilemma too.

Judaism as an *Aspaklaria*

Pliny recounts that Nero was in the habit of viewing the duels of gladiators *in smaragdo*, through a precious stone, presumably in order to render the colors more vivid and the experience more lurid or as an aid to eyesight.[34] Not all the lenses we use are like sunglasses or kaleidoscopes; some are built in. Consider the expression "cultural lens": it implies that for better and for worse each of us faces reality employing a range of perceptual and interpretive tools by which we see and make sense of what we see.

The *aspaklaria* applies on the broad cultural level as well as the personal, individual one: the way we see is informed by our background and influences as well as by our personality and idiosyncrasies. Indeed, a person may be described as being an *aspaklaria*.[35] A mystical tradition compares the exceptional human being to glass, constituted from sand and purified into clarity.[36] The term has come to mean both the means by which a person perceives and the perceiver themselves. We use *aspaklariot*, the various prisms presented to us through family, education, and experience. At the same time, we also are *aspaklariot*, lenses through which the world "out there" is filtered and understood "in here." We are encouraged to make speculums of ourselves.

Human experience is inescapably grounded and specific. We cannot attain the view from nowhere.[37] Jews in modernity have often trodden a path originating in specificity, directed at universal abstraction. Some have found the Jewish spectacles unsatisfactory and thrown them away. For me, these Jewish spectacles, adapted to my needs and capacities, are the way I try to make sense of the world.

There can be few better examples of modernity's challenge to traditional modes of thought than Spinoza's attack on the prophets of ancient Israel. He quoted numerous scriptural illustrations of his assertion that the rich and varied imagery they employed is evidence not of revelation but of auto-suggestion. The Babylonian Talmud notes that no two of them prophesied in the same style without assuming that this fact impugned their claim to be experiencing a revelation from God.[38] Spinoza's reading of the prophetic tradition was more damning, and even Moses did not escape his critique. His suggestion that what was portrayed as prophecy is better understood as illusion became a mainstay of modern critiques of religion. Later in modernity, another kind of criticism gained more traction. It is not only that the prophets were delusional, deficient, or charlatanical. Thinkers like Richard Rorty have gone even further, arguing that the assumptions underlying the metaphor—namely, that the world contains Truth whose meaning can be unlocked through the mind, the mirror of nature—are unfounded.[39] Truth is not to be glimpsed by use of our optical devices because there is no essential external Truth. Rather, we can use our reason and our language to construct more or less useful understandings of the relations between processes.[40]

A sad result of our polarized times is that we accuse anyone with a perspective different from our own of delusion or deception. It is harder to consider the possibility that when they look in good faith, they see something different than we do. I gaze upon Jerusalem and see an ancient hope reborn; poverty and social inequity; cultural and intellectual flowering; intolerance and obscurantism. Rather than deride anyone who sees with different lenses from ourselves, it behooves us to consider the multiple *aspaklariot* we all employ.

Opponents of this approach argue that to acknowledge the possibility of multiple viewpoints is to give up on moral clarity. I have become convinced that it is not. There remain opinions and behaviors to which I am opposed and against which I feel compelled to act. The prophets of Israel, so the rabbis teach, viewed reality through multiple prisms, yet managed to articulate compelling visions. There are, occasionally, moments of clarity during which it becomes clear that attitudes or actions are unacceptable and need to be opposed. To give up on such a possibility is to hand a victory to every unscrupulous party keen to keep us docile for the sake of market share or the perpetuation of power. The Moses paradigm, according to which the truth is experienced through one shining *aspaklaria*, is just as risky. We are better off embracing the path of multiple *aspaklariot*, which offers lenses and mirrors, doubts and revelations, blind spots and perspectives. All any of us can do is employ this approach in service of the truth. When the lens is distorted by bigotry or limited by self-infatuation, the *aspaklaria* is more of an obstruction than an aid. However, when it offers perspective and insight, the *aspaklaria* can allow us to see further than we ever could alone. Knowing that I am both limited and empowered by my *aspaklaria* might make me more willing to empathize with those I love, those I oppose, and those I have never even met.

A Jew hath eyes, including those whose physical capacity to see is limited. The imperative is to lift them up, to see, and then to act.

NOTES

1. In *Insecurity of Freedom*, Heschel offers a blistering attack on the tendency to focus on the question: "Are the Jews a race, a people, a religion, a cultural entity, a historic group, a linguistic unity? As if the only important question concerning Judaism and Jewish life were the sociological category to which it belongs!" 223. Writing in 1953, Heschel was speaking out against the sociological trend in post-war Jewish life in America. There is little doubt he would have found my framing of a similar question to be reprehensible. This book as a whole, however, could hardly be said to privilege the sociological over the theological and ethical.
2. I do not mean by this term the physical mechanics of seeing. In *Totality and Infinity*, Levinas coins the memorable assertion that "ethics is an optics" but immediately notes that he is referring to "a vision without image, bereft of the synoptic and totalizing objectifying virtues of vision" (23). My image is not intended to suggest that a physical visual impairment is an impediment to looking through the *aspaklaria*.
3. For more on the historical construction and cultural significance of vision, see: Berger, *Ways of Seeing*; Crary, *Techniques of the Observer*; Foster, *Vision and Visuality*; Lindberg, *Theories of Vision*; and Nelson, *Visuality Before and Beyond*. For penetrating discussions of vision in Jewish contexts, see: Boyarin, "Eye in the Torah"; Neis, *Sense of Sight*; and, above all, Wolfson, *Through a Speculum*. This chapter would not have been conceived if not for Wolfson's remarkable work.
4. Mishnah Berakhot 8:5. See also BT Berakhot 52b.
5. See James, *Pluralistic Universe*, particularly 30–48.
6. For more on the origin of this term, see Löw, "Aspaklaria" in *Fauna und Mineralien der Juden*, 175–181 and Brand, "Aspaklaria."
7. The verb root *r-a-h* implying vision can be found nine times in this verse.
8. The reading here implies blurriness of vision.
9. See Leviticus Rabbah 1:14 and, for a version of that tradition without use of the word *aspaklaria*, Lekah Tov to Numbers, Beha'alotcha 104a; BT Yebamot 49b.
10. See Harvey, Rashi on creation.
11. Spinoza, *Tractatus*, Chapter 2, 40.
12. This translation from Part 5 Section 23 of *Ethics* is suggested in Carriero, "Descartes (and Spinoza)," 22. The article compares Spinoza's optic insights with Descartes' notion of being struck by the overwhelming truth of a pro position. For Solomon Maimon's account of having his eyes opened when he first read works of optics and physics, see Maimon, *Autobiography of Solomon Maimon*, 107.

13. See 1 Corinthians 13:12 for a New Testament parallel to the rabbinic tradition.
14. See Rashi to BT Sukkah 45b, Maimonides Commentary to Mishnah Kelim 30:2, and particularly Maimonides Eight Chapters, at the beginning of Chap. 7, where in the search for moral perfection the prophet removes as many *aspaklariot*, representing ignorance, list, avarice, and the like, as possible.
15. Numbers 12:6-8.
16. See Abarvanel and Alshech to these verses where the link with *aspaklaria* is made explicit; Shnei Luchot Haberit, Shavuot, Torah Or, 228.
17. Ovadiah of Bertinoro to Mishnah Kelim 30:2.
18. See, for example, Horowitz, *Shnei Luchot Haberit* (Warsaw, 1930), vols. 1–2, Tractate Shevuot, Torah Or, 41c.
19. See Nolan, *Now Through a Glass Darkly*, for dimensions of this image in Roman and medieval contexts.
20. See Feuerbach, *Essence of Christianity*, 17. In *Religion, Feminism and Idoloclasm*, Melissa Raphael notes the influence of Feuerbach's theory of projection on feminist theorists including de Beauvoir, Firestone, Lenk, Irigaray, and Daly (25) and employs the image of the mirror, noting, for example, that "even before Feuerbach had pointed out that the idea of God is to be a magnifying mirror to man, Wollstonecraft understood that feminine artifice and weakness is the result of being trapped in a claustrophobic world of the reverse mirror image,"29.
21. Shneur Zalman of Liadi, *Torah Or*, 33a.
22. Lebens, *Guide*, xvii.
23. This is my translation of the original Hebrew title. Heschel gave the book the English title *Theology of Ancient Judaism*. The English translation of the work, published in 2006 long after Heschel's death, was named *Heavenly Torah as Refracted Through the Generations*.
24. See, for example, *Zohar Hadash*)Munkacs, 1911), 28b.
25. Heschel, "The Holy Dimension," 118.
26. Heschel, "No Religion Is an Island," 126.
27. BT Sanhedrin 6b. See also Baba Batra 131a.
28. 2 Chronicles 19.6. See Jackson, "Law in 9th Century?"
29. Isaiah 11.3.
30. Nagel, *View from Nowhere*, 3.
31. Ibid.
32. Ulmer, "Refocusing the Anthropocenic Gaze," 242.
33. Jones, "Gordon Kaufman's Perspectival Language," 90.
34. See Plantzos, "Crystals and Lenses."
35. See, for example, *Tikkunei Zohar* 40a, relating to Moses; sages are frequently described as being an *aspaklaria* in introductions to and

recommendations of their work. For an example of this in Hasidic literature, see *Beit Aharon*, (Brody, 1875), title page.
36. See *Kedushat Levi* (Jerusalem: 1958), 312b.
37. In *Of Time and Lamentation*, Tallis offers an extended critique of the notion of the observerless or objectively perceived universe.
38. BT Sanhedrin 89a.
39. See Rorty, *Philosophy and Mirror*.
40. See Stone, "Truth and Illusion."

Open Access This chapter is licensed under the terms of the Creative Commons Attribution 4.0 International License (http://creativecommons.org/licenses/by/4.0/), which permits use, sharing, adaptation, distribution and reproduction in any medium or format, as long as you give appropriate credit to the original author(s) and the source, provide a link to the Creative Commons license and indicate if changes were made.

The images or other third party material in this chapter are included in the chapter's Creative Commons license, unless indicated otherwise in a credit line to the material. If material is not included in the chapter's Creative Commons license and your intended use is not permitted by statutory regulation or exceeds the permitted use, you will need to obtain permission directly from the copyright holder.

Bi: Spirituality and Responsibility

Judaism is an *aspaklaria*, one trained on the world around us, on the generations before us, on God beyond us, and on the self within. According to Roger Kneebone, "in physics, total internal reflection is a phenomenon whereby light is reflected from the surface of a liquid without penetrating it. A goldfish in a goldfish tank therefore can see clearly only within the water he swims in."[1] Because of this physical effect, it would be necessary for the goldfish to get out of the bowl to see what is happening outside. Total internal reflection creates in this case a blind spot and thus the scientific term offers an important insight: sometimes it is necessary to escape an environment and a set of expectations in order to achieve a clearer view.

This book makes no claim to expertise in scientific matters, but the irony of total internal reflection limiting one's capacity to see goes beyond physics. It speaks to the human condition. This chapter employs one short word, *bi*, in an attempt to delineate some parameters of the self without getting lost in all-engulfing self-reflection.

The Elusive Self

"Man is only a recent invention, a figure not yet two centuries old, a new wrinkle in our knowledge, and … he will disappear again as soon as that knowledge has discovered a new form."[2] When he made this mischievous comment, Michel Foucault was not suggesting that human beings only came into existence at the time of the Enlightenment. Rather, he was arguing that many of our current assumptions about the self—that we have will, choice, and agency, that we have inner lives worthy of exploration—are informed by a particular set of cultural assumptions.

Reform Judaism is predicated on this modern Western notion of humanity, arguing that it has its roots in the Hebrew Bible and in later manifestations of Judaism. Informed choice is one of its slogans, implying that each of us devote our intellects and channel our predispositions to making moral judgments and personal decisions about what to believe and how to live. Kaufmann Kohler wrote in his Reform theological treatise:

> Judaism holds that the soul of man came forth pure from the hand of its Maker, endowed with freedom, unsullied by any inherent evil or inherited sin. Thus man is, by the exercise of his own free will, capable of attaining to an ever higher degree his mental, moral, and spiritual powers in the course of history.[3]

Judaism has long had much to say about the nature of the self and the soul.[4] The Judaism of recent centuries has emphasized the individual more than most pre-modern Jewish movements and thinkers.[5] I believe that the wellsprings of Jewish creativity and wisdom may offer succor to the contemporary self which is, in Christopher Lasch's formulation, under multiple assault:

> Our growing dependence on technologies no one seems to understand or control has given rise to feelings of powerlessness and victimization. We find it more and more difficult to achieve a sense of continuity, permanence, or connection with the world around us. Relationships with others are notably fragile; goods are made to be used up and discarded; reality is experienced as an unstable environment of flickering images. Everything conspires to encourage escapist solutions to the psychological problems of dependence, separation, and individuation, and to discourage the moral realism that makes it possible for human beings to come to terms with existential constraints on their power and freedom.[6]

Famously, the instruction "know thyself" is a mainstay of classical Greece. No such instruction is to be found in the Hebrew Bible; rather, the expression "I did not know myself" appears twice: once at the height of ecstasy (Song of Songs 6:12) and once in the pit of despondency (Job 9:21). Nonetheless, self-knowledge is valued in Jewish tradition. In a Zoharic text, for example, self-knowledge is listed as one of the kinds of wisdom to be sought alongside knowledge of God, of one's own body, of this world, and of the supernal realm:

> To consider and know the secrets of one's soul: what is this soul inside him? From where does it come? And for what purpose has this body come, formed of a drop of semen, here today and tomorrow in the grave?[7]

This text employs some of the vocabulary of inner architecture known since the days of the Bible, including the words *ruach, neshamah, nefesh*—instantiations of inner life force which are often contrasted with *sechel*, the intellect charged with the task of channeling these energies and imbuing them with purpose.[8]

The self is pervasive and elusive. It is as incorporeal as the most abstruse abstraction and as immediate and palpable as anything can be. When a website asks you to affirm that you are not a robot, it is requesting confirmation that you possess a self. To judge from the prophesies associated with the imminent rise of artificial intelligence, the meaning of that term and its distinction from the non- or post-human realm is likely to become immensely complex in the decades to come.[9]

What is the self? When I speak to myself, to whom I am speaking? What is the nature of this self? Does it strive for the good, thrusting toward its own fulfillment regardless of moral qualms? Is there a self there at all, or is this simply another story I tell myself? The question is beyond me, not only because of my limitations but because the self is rarely seen. Various disciplines offer new clues as to its whereabouts, and yet it resists capture.[10]

Self and Soul

Some 4000 years lie between the composition of Papyrus Berlin 3024 and the publication of a poem by W.B. Yeats. Both texts describe a conversation between the self and the soul.[11] Much has changed in the understanding of the inner life between antiquity and modernity—much but not everything. One part of "me" considers some other inner part, and some exchange between the two then ensues. While metaphysical assumptions and cultural lenses differ hugely, the notion that my self and my soul catch sight of each other is older than the pyramids and as recent as today's news.

For me, the connection between these inner dimensions is usually far less articulate than a conversation. It is closer to the sentiment expressed in an Israeli song by Yehuda Gur Arie[12] which makes extensive use of the Hebrew word *bi*, "within me":

> Someone is crying within me
> Someone is happy within me
> Someone is going within me
> Without knowing where
>
> Someone is groaning
> Someone exults
> A person within me weeps
> A person within me rejoices
>
> Someone within me is a child
> Someone within me is old
> Someone within me turns their eyes to the sky
>
> Something quietly stirs within me and waits
> And I know
> And I don't understand.

The song describes a reality familiar (I assume) to everyone reading this book who is not a robot. It speaks to the sense that somewhere within there are processes at play of which I am aware but which I observe through a cloudy *aspaklaria*, as through a glass, darkly. I know and I do not understand. How to explain this experience of inner layers of the self about which my conscious self has only a vague understanding? One approach can be described as a non-essentialist position. It is not that within me lies a self or a soul with an essence but rather "a bundle or collection of different perceptions."[13] The "someone" I sense inside me is simply the rattle of the bundle as it moves about—the interplay of my various perceptions. Such a materialist or non-essentialist views is typically employed against traditional religious doctrines and is part of a general demystifying trend. There is no soul, just as there are no ghosts, no tooth fairy, no man in the moon, and no such place as Hogwarts. There is no "there" there but rather a kaleidoscope of perceptions and emotions which come to expression. We mythologize and personalize, but that is our weakness not reality.

This philosophical rejection of the idea of "something in there" has been bolstered by other modern disciplines, such as the psychological theory positing a perpetual drama being played out within each of us: ego, id, and superego locked in conflictual embrace. The bafflement professed in the song can be alleviated, if not obviated, through attention and therapy. I have a chance not of attaining unalloyed happiness but at least of being better acquainted with the "someones" and "somethings" within me. More recently, neuroscience has begun to understand what happens within our brains as these various voices are heard and as our sense of self is enacted. It has become possible, so we are told, to point to where the self lives in the brain. Thus philosophy, psychology, and brain science along with other disciplines combine to demystify the self and domesticate the soul.[14]

I find much compelling in the materialist approach. It is practical and realistic. It eschews pomposity and keeps naivety at bay (although it is sometimes accompanied by its own form of arrogance). It is not demonstrably wrong, but I do find it to be insufficient. The notion that if one kind of explanation is true, every other perspective must be false is unnecessarily reductive. To be sure, there are incommensurable truth claims: either the crowd at President Trump's inauguration was the largest ever or it was not.[15] The question of what lives within me, however, is not reducible to this level of discourse. It is rich and deep enough to warrant different expressions. The reductive minimalism of the materialists offers an important *aspaklaria* through which the self can be observed. But there are other perspectives not to be missed. If it is explained to me that the movement I perceive at the screening of a movie is illusory and I am, in fact, watching still photographs shown to me at speed, I may find the explanation illuminating. But I still want to watch the film. To demystify everything is to miss the point that once all the little mysteries have been solved, much more consequential ones are bound to remain. When Emmanuel Levinas asserted that "Judaism is a religion for adults,"[16] it was this kind of position he was adopting. He held (and I agree) that it offers ways of grappling with realities not reducible to simplistic coin-toss possibilities.

What is this inner life I experience and what are its implications? What to do with these someones and somethings that dwell *bi*, within me?

Within Me, On Me, To Me, Through Me

The word *bi* offers a window into Jewish conceptions of self and soul. A central prayer of the daily morning service, the first words to be uttered upon waking according to the Babylonian Talmud, begins thus:

> My God, the soul which You bestowed in me (*bi*) is pure. You created it, You formed it, You breathed it into me and Your preserve it within me. You will eventually take it from me, and restore it to me in the time to come.[17]

The sentence which came to replace this prayer as the opening liturgy of every day, *Modeh Ani,* expresses thanks to God who has restored my soul within me (*bi*).

The soul, *neshamah,* is understood to be a divine gift, housed and preserved within me. Some distinction, then, is assumed to pertain between "me," on the one hand, and that part within me which houses the divine gift or alien emissary, "my soul," on the other. I may turn to my soul and address it as another. The 103rd psalm opens with a call made by the psalmist to his soul:

> Bless Adonai, O my soul;
> And all that is within me, bless God's holy name.[18]

The soul has been planted within us and yearns for contact with its maker. A millennium ago, Bahya ibn Paquda explained it thus:

> It is proper, brother, for you to know that our devotion in prayer is nothing but the soul's longing for God, humbling itself in His presence, exalting its Creator, offering praises and thanksgiving to His name, casting all burdens upon Him.[19]

That popular trope of contemporary culture, the alien who wishes to report back to its mother planet, to phone home, is a secularized version of a mainstay of Jewish spirituality: the soul situated within the human frame like a majestic bird in a cage yearning for its home.[20]

At its most sublime, the image of a self, a soul situated *bi* (inside me), a personality within my person which experiences change and growth, is transformative:

> I will give you a new heart and put a new spirit in you; I will remove from you your heart of stone and give you a heart of flesh.
> And I will put my spirit in you and move you to follow my decrees and be careful to keep my laws. (Ezekiel 36: 26-7)

I interpret the prophet's words to relate to the process whereby a petrified version of myself is overcome[21] and replaced by a selfhood which calls me to social responsibility. If the journey of the self leads to unthinking obedience and conformity, it will not be long before the heart calcifies once more. The heart of flesh lives in its specificity and individuality and yet is bound to something beyond itself.

Bi carries several meanings. The God of the Hebrew Bible uses it more frequently than does any human character, often pointing to the wrong perpetrated by backsliders.[22] God swears by Godself, averring the formula *bi nishba'ti*, "I take an oath on myself."[23] A number of characters in the Hebrew Bible turn to the Divine and say בי אדוני, vocalized in this context as *bi Adonai*. Others, addressing human interlocutors, use the term in a way vocalized to read *bi adoni*.[24] In most of the biblical contexts, it means something like "begging my lord's (or my Lord's) pardon," "excuse me" rather than "within me." Nonetheless, some choose to read the expression as an assertion of the belief that the soul within contains a piece of the Divine.[25]

In the case of Abigail in 1 Samuel 25, the phrase is clearly employed to convey the acceptance of responsibility. The words added to the *bi adoni* formula transform the meaning to something like "upon me, my lord, be the guilt."[26] In the topography of the self that is delineated in the Hebrew Bible, responsibility is as central a notion as inner spiritual resonance. The continued resonance of Yom Kippur, the Day of Atonement, in the lives of some Jews otherwise estranged from Jewish practice or thought attests to the abiding call of personal responsibility. In order to know better the someones and somethings within me, I must ask myself what I am responsible for: not only what is in me but also what is on me.

Elazar Ben Dordaya figures in a tale told in the Babylonian Talmud. The whole bawdy story can be found in Avodah Zarah 17a. For our purposes here it is sufficient to quote his words after he has turned to the greats wonders of nature (including the mountains, the heavens, the sun, and the stars) to request their intervention on his behalf after he sins. After they all refuse, he reaches his nadir. He says: "this matter is dependent entirely on me (*bi*)." He places his head between his knees and cries until his soul leaves his body. This capacity to acknowledge responsibility for one's actions is a key component of the self.

Alongside what is in me and what is on me, I want to highlight two further dimensions of the biblical usage of *bi* which help establish the parameters of our discussion of self and soul: anxiety and purpose. For the first of them, let us consider Saul and the Philistines. Twice in the account in 1 Samuel, Saul expresses his profound anxiety at what the despised foes will do to him. Saul explains to Samuel (1 Samuel 28:15): "I am exceedingly distressed – the Philistines are waging battle against me (*bi*), and God has turned away from me." Later, at the end of his life (31:4), he implores his weapons bearer to run him through with his sword so that the enemy does not abuse and toy with him, employing the word *bi* once again.[27] In this usage, the focus on the self within magnifies existential anxieties.

Another use of *bi* in the Bible speaks to another aspect of the self. Here the prophet Zechariah serves as a fitting exemplar since, on several occasions, he refers to "the angel who speaks through me (*bi*),"[28] suggesting that he is a sounding board, a vehicle through which the will of God can be expressed. In my reading, this sense of the self speaks to the question of meaning. What am I here for? What do I hope to achieve? The notion that something can be achieved through my life, that my life may have a purpose even if its details are unclear, is a transformative concept.

Tamar Rudavsky has ventured the sweeping observation that "Jewish theology presents no clearly elaborated views either on the relationship between body and mind, or on the nature of the soul."[29] This lack of elaboration is due in part to a common preoccupation with action rather than speculation and a general suspicion of metaphysical maps and detailed descriptions. There is a great advantage to this lack of detail, as noted in a different context by Judith Butler: "If the subject is opaque to itself, not fully translucent and knowable to itself, it is not thereby licensed to do what it wants or to ignore its obligations to others."[30] I do not know myself, let alone the soul of the other. This ignorance should provide the basis for a moral posture of abiding respect for the selfness of every other. A sense of humanity is rooted in a lack of certainty and a shortage of clarity. Unable to hear clearly the someones and somethings within me, I ought to develop sympathy and empathy with my fellow humans as we all stumble on.

I have mentioned four aspects of personality all alluded to by a simple Hebrew word. I may not be able to say what my self is or offer a sketch of my soul, but here I am proposing four dimensions which help us get closer to their location. Look within, to a soul which our tradition says bears a trace of the Divine.[31] Look to the way in which I face up to responsibility. Look to what I have experienced in the course of my life. And look to that which I sense moving through me, motivating me to act. Each of these dimensions has a dark side. Concern with the soul within can lead to self-absorption or self-aggrandizement. There is a thin line separating the shouldering of responsibility from paralysis by guilt and shame. Life's experiences may include not only growth and discovery but also trauma and struggle. And the consciousness of being an instrument of some higher purpose can easily turn into unchecked messianism or unbridled narcissism. All of these risks exist, and I know of no remedy guaranteed to prevent them.

My spirituality is more messy than messianic and more ironic than serene. Total self-reflection is not an option. I know that many approach the soul through work *bi*, in their embodied corporeality, through meditative techniques and other disciplines. I fully appreciate and celebrate the fact that the dialogue between the self and the soul takes place in different ways. As for myself, I catch glimpses of myself when I look inside, face up to my actions and motivations with honesty, consider that which has impacted me, and ask myself what good I may be called upon to effect in the world.

My prayer life directs me to that which is beyond me as I turn to that which is within me. Each morning I recite a formula thanking God for having mercifully placed yet again my soul "*bi*." As each day unfolds, I employ a variety of tactics regarding this inner personality, in turn hiding from and seeking it, deflecting and reflecting upon it, distracting and nourishing it. Sometimes this self within is like someone too young or too old to be exposed to the stark realities of life "out there," and sometimes that inner voice is telling me something I contrive not to hear.

Either because of my own personality or because of my Jewish commitments, I cannot help thinking about the inner dynamic in wider terms: the personal in light of the political. In the 1940s, Karen Horney suggested, in relation to other selves, that three key dynamics emerge in the neurotic behavior of troubled children and, by extension, in all of us. We are either moving toward, moving against, or moving away from others. The vulnerabilities driving these behaviors are helplessness, hostility, and isolation respectively.[32] Beyond the diagnosis of neurotic disorders, these three responses apply to the interactions between one *bi* and another. I reach out; I define myself in contrast; I disengage.

The search for spiritual fulfillment is not fundamentally separate from the quest for social improvement or the need for significant relationship. In each of these dimensions:

>   Something quietly stirs within me and waits
>   And I know
>   And I don't understand.

Notes

1. Kneebone, "Total Internal Reflection," 516.
2. Foucault, *The Order of Things*, xxiii.
3. Kohler, *Jewish Theology*, 26.
4. For important explorations of Jewish approaches to individuality, choice, the self, the soul, and much more, see: Margolin, *Inner Religion*; Mittleman, *Human Nature*; and Persico, *Adam B'Tzelem Elohim*.
5. For a statement on how Hasidism can provide the basis for a contemporary Jewish religiosity with an approach which acknowledges the centrality of the self but aims beyond it, see Green, "A Neo-Hasidic Life".
6. Lasch, *Culture of Narcissism*, 248–249. These words were first published in the late 1970s. The fact they sound so contemporary decades later makes them all the more poignant.
7. *Zohar Hadash* 9d, Song of Songs.
8. See Genesis Rabbah 14:9 where five names are listed—*nefesh, ruach, neshamah, yechidah,* and *chaya*.
9. For a description of this complexity and its implications for Judaism in the twenty-first century, see Schiff, *Judaism in a Digital Age*.
10. For particularly suggestive treatments of the self and personality in general discourse, see Edwardes, *Origins of Self* and Hofstadter and Dennett, *The Mind's I*. For a treatment of biblical sources, see Olyan, "Search for the Elusive Self."
11. See Assmann, "Dialogue Between Self and Soul," and Yeats' 1933 poem, "A Dialogue of Self and Soul," in Yeats, *Collected Poems*, 162–163. For musings on the soul in medieval Jewish poetry, see Ibn Gabirol, *Vulture in a Cage*, particularly 83, and Scheindlin, *The Gazelle*. For dialogues in which the soul is an active participant, see Part 3 of Bahya ibn Paquda's *Duties of the Heart*, where the Soul and the Intellect are engaged in a protracted discussion and Moses Hayim Luzzatto's *Da'at Tevunot*, where the same protagonists are engaged in a debate some seven centuries later. In the fourteenth century, a dialogue between a living person and a disembodied soul is described in the fifth part of Isaac Polgar's *Ezer Hadat* (Hughes, *Art of Dialogue*, 88). A century earlier, employing a different genre, the allegory, Jacob ben Eliezer mused upon the complex interrelationship between the soul, the body, the intellect, and "me." For an explication of this thirteenth-century text, see Rosen, "Meshal Sechel Alei Ahav."
12. The lyrics to the song were composed in 1967 and can be found in the original at:
    https://www.nli.org.il/he/items/NNL_MUSIC_AL990030216000205171/NLI.
13. Hume, *Treatise of Human Nature*, 277.

14. The work on the self which has most influenced my understanding of this topic is Taylor, *Sources of the Self*. For a recent discussion through a psychological prism, see Kashima et al., "Connectionism and the Self." For a summary of recent developments in neuroscience, see Deleniv, "The 'Me' Illusion." Other modern disciplines are also engaged in this investigation. For an anthropological perspective, see Edwardes, *Origins of Self*.
15. See McIntyre, *Post-Truth* and Zierler and Garroway, *These Truths We Hold*.
16. Levinas, *Difficult Freedom*, 11–23.
17. BT Berakhot 60b. See *Siftei Cohen* to Deuteronomy 7:6. Hacohen states that the formula asserting that the soul within us is pure is intended to underline that our souls are not our own property, but rather it has been planted within us for the purpose of divine service.
18. Urbach asserts in *The Sages* that "in the Bible a monistic view prevails," arguing that there is no distinction to be found between "body and soul or flesh and spirit" (214). Nonetheless, this expression implies a distance between me and my soul. Urbach is well aware of the rabbinic sources brought in this chapter, many of which are to be found in his work. See BT Berakhot 19a, where the five occurrences of the psalmist's call "bless, oh my soul" are linked to five stages in the life cycle. See Job 27:3.
19. Bahya ibn Paquda, *Duties of the Heart* (Moses Hyamson, transl.) (Jerusalem: Feldheim), Heshbon Hanefesh, 211. For one description of the roles played by the mother, the father, and God in the creation of the person, see PT Kilayim 8:4, 31c.
20. See Ibn Gabirol, *Vulture in a Cage*.
21. See Marmur, "On Petrification."
22. See, for example, Leviticus 26:40; Isaiah 66:24; Jeremiah 2:5, 8, and 29; Ezekiel 20:8,13, 21, and 27; and Zephaniah 3:11.
23. Genesis 22:16; Isaiah 45:23; and Jeremiah 22:5 and 49:13. The notion of God's inwardness is discussed in *Od Yosef Hai* by Yosef Hayim ben Eliyahu of Baghdad to Vayeshev, where he connects it to the tradition in BT Berakhot 7a according to which God offers a prayer in which God says: "May it be my will."
24. The full list comprises Joseph's brothers to Joseph in Genesis 43:20 and Judah to Joseph in 44:18; Moses to God in Exodus 4:10 and 4:13; Aaron to Moses in Numbers 12:11; Joshua to God in 7:8; Gideon to the angel and then to God in Judges 6:13 and 6:15; Manoach to God in Judges 13:8; Hannah to Eli in 1 Samuel 1:26 and Abigail to David in 1 Samuel 25:24; and one of the women asserting maternity over a contested baby to Solomon in 1 Kings 3:17 and 3:26. See also the competing interpretations of the word *bi* in Genesis 43:20 by Rashi and Nachmanides, respectively.
25. See Jacob Joseph of Ostraha, *Rav Yeivi* (Slavuti: 1792), Vayigash, 10a.

26. Genesis 22:16; Isaiah 45:23; and Jeremiah 22:5 and 49:13. The notion of God's inwardness is discussed in *Od Yosef Hai* by Yosef Hayim ben Eliyahu of Baghdad to Vayeshev, where he connects it to the tradition in BT Berakhot 7a according to which God offers a prayer in which God says: "may it be my will."
27. For other examples of *bi* used in the context of personal harm or umbrage, see Genesis 31:7 (relating to Jacob), Genesis 39:17 (Potiphar's wife), Numbers 20:18 (Balaam), Judges 15:12 (Samson), Judges 16:10 and twice more in that chapter regarding Delilah, and 1 Kings 3:7 (Yehoram).
28. See Zechariah 1:9, 1:14, 2:2, 2:7, 4:1, 4:4, 5:5, 5:10, and 6:4.
29. Rudavsky, *Jewish Philosophy*, 208.
30. Butler, *Giving an Account*, 19–20.
31. Mordecai Kaplan, *Future of American Jew*, offers a naturalistic take on the soul which still fits into this model: "What is most distinctive about himself is termed 'soul,' and what is most distinctive about the Power or powers upon whom he depends is termed 'God' ... As men ... learn to think of the soul as independent of the body, they also learn to conceive an over-soul, or super-ego, or God as independent reality," 171.
32. Horney, *Our Inner Conflicts*, particularly 42–44.

Open Access This chapter is licensed under the terms of the Creative Commons Attribution 4.0 International License (http://creativecommons.org/licenses/by/4.0/), which permits use, sharing, adaptation, distribution and reproduction in any medium or format, as long as you give appropriate credit to the original author(s) and the source, provide a link to the Creative Commons license and indicate if changes were made.

The images or other third party material in this chapter are included in the chapter's Creative Commons license, unless indicated otherwise in a credit line to the material. If material is not included in the chapter's Creative Commons license and your intended use is not permitted by statutory regulation or exceeds the permitted use, you will need to obtain permission directly from the copyright holder.

Gader: Borders and Boundaries

Balaam and his ass are on a journey. One of the passengers is a much-lauded declarer of visions, the other a mute beast. En route, an angel is set to meet them. Why is the angel, as recounted in the Chapter 22 of the Book of Numbers, described as standing *gader mizeh ugader mizeh*, with a fence on either side? The most immediate explanation is that by being placed there, the angel was bound to be encountered either by the human being or by the means of his transportation. Indeed, the ass squeezed Balaam against the wall of the path since it could see the angel blocking their progress, while the professional seer was incapable of seeing. Various ingenious interpretations and allegorical readings have been offered over the years regarding the angel's position between two barriers.[1] My suggestion is that revelation is being described here not as falling out of the sky at the whim of the Divine but rather as engendered within boundaries. We need the fences in order to encounter the angel. New possibilities become apparent when we come up against limitations and are forced to search for alternatives. This is true even when sophisticated viewers cannot see what is in front of them.

As the animal and the angels teach in this biblical tale, to be human is to be caught between a rock and a hard place, between Scylla and Charybdis, between a fence on one side and a fence on the other. Jewish experience has been molded by this sense of creative constraint. Some of these boundaries have been defined from within; indeed, Halakhah represents an intricate system of definitions and restrictions. Through much of our history, limits have also been imposed from outside, defining where and how Jews are allowed to live their lives. We are not unique in this, of course, but we have certainly made walls and boundaries central to our self-understanding.

In this chapter I want to consider the *gader*, the fence, wall, or boundary, which has for so long been such a central part of the Jewish experience, and what happens to it and to us at a time when boundaries are being redrawn and, in many cases, removed. Where does the angel dwell when the *gader* is gone? What happens to Jewish creativity if it is not pushing up against a barrier? Many Jews grapple with this challenge as it applies to barriers of social separation, but it applies on many levels. What does Jewish practice, Jewish faith, and Jewish education look like without commonly acknowledged boundaries?

Do Fence Me In

Twice confronted with the prospect of confinement, Wildcat Kelley sings a paean to the glories of the outdoor life, self-reliance, and freedom in the 1934 song "Don't Fence Me In" by Robert Fletcher and Cole Porter. The joke at the heart of the song is that on the first occasion it is incarceration in a jail cell which threatens to curtail Kelley's wanderlust and on the second his sweetheart's wish to settle down. True to its time, and still popular in ours, the song's explicit content is imbued with a kind of whimsical misogyny: commitment is a prison, marriage is jail time, to be avoided for as long as possible in favor of untrammeled roaming in the great outdoors. The song also pays homage to a dream born of modernity, agency and territory, particularly potent in America: the idea that the individual can disappear into the sunset with no commitments.

> I want to ride to the ridge where the west commences
> Gaze at the moon till I lose my senses
> I can't look at hobbles and I can't stand fences
> Don't fence me in.

Judaism's liberation myths tend to look different. The Children of Israel emerge from Egypt (it has often been pointed out that its Hebrew name *Mitzrayim* can be read as "narrow places") out of the straits of bondage, but the journey through the wilds of the desert leads to Sinai, where liberation is complemented by revelation and, thence, to the Land.

It is a journey reenacted each year in the process leading from Passover to Shavuot, from exodus to theophany, from the promise of spring to the bounty of harvest. Being free is not the ultimate goal of this story, although it is a necessary part of it.

In most of its manifestations Judaism has sung a version of a chorus at odds with Fletcher and Porter. It calls out: *do* fence me in, within a particular context, a people, a story, a destiny; *do* fence me in with a set of practices designed to inform my journey from dusk to dawn, from spring to winter, from birth to death. Liberation from enslavement is cherished as a precious prerequisite on the road to redemption, but freedom from all responsibility is not celebrated as a laudable aim. The Mishnah famously reminds the individual that "while you are not required to complete the task, you are not free to desist from undertaking it."[2] God alone, so the medieval philosophers asserted, is beyond definition and, in this sense, truly free.[3] We humans live a necessarily bounded existence.

A midrash tells of Israel's transition "from the iron yoke to the yoke of Torah, from slavery to freedom ... from oppression to redemption."[4] The implication here is that a yoke of one kind or another will have to be borne because release from everything is not an option. Enlightenment and responsibility is to be preferred over enslavement and alienation.

The notion that human beings are always in bondage to something inspired this couplet by Rabbi Yehudah Halevi:

> Servants of time – the slaves of slaves are they;
> The Lord's servant, he alone is free.[5]

Boundlessness, the poet implies, is an illusion. Human beings are inevitably constrained by the limits of mortality, capacity, imagination, opportunity, and more.

The English word "definition" comes to its present meaning through a parallel process to its Hebrew equivalent, *hagdarah*. The root of this word is *gader*, one of the several terms indicating borders and divisions which the Hebrew language has accumulated over the many centuries of its development.[6] Its original sense is a low barrier constructed of stone or wood, used in agricultural contexts and for the demarcation of boundaries. Over time it has come to be one of the most versatile and resonant of the many boundary words in Hebrew culture: the security fence in the West Bank is a *gader*; the Hebrew word for gender, *migdar*, is, ingeniously, derived from *gader*; a person who loses their way or their mind is said to leave their *gader*.[7]

If the *gader* is to be found in discourse about society and identity, its classic role relates to the system of laws promulgated by the ancient rabbis. Like the Aramaic word *siyag*, also meaning a fence, *gader* describes the function played by the thick network of practices and abstinences which characterize rabbinic Judaism. Nissim of Gerona, a Catalonian talmudist of the fourteenth century, provides an example of the use of the term in this halakhic context which links the word to its original agricultural setting:

> Rabbinic ordinances and their restrictions (*gader*) are the basis of being God-fearing. They provide a margin of distance to keep the human hand from touching a biblical prohibition, like the owner of a field who makes a fence (*gader*) for their field ... by virtue of the protections (*gader*) they have established against transgression, fear of God will dawn on a person's soul.[8]

Attention to the specifics of restrictions is already present in sections of Leviticus and other biblical books, but the sages of the early centuries of the Common Era turn this propensity into a preoccupation. To read the Mishnah, the foundational work of post-biblical Judaism is to see how meaning is derived from the construction of fences distinguishing between *mutar* (permitted) and *asur* (forbidden). From among the hundreds of examples to be found of this *gader*-building activity, I want to mention one which relates explicitly to the construction of a *gader* in its original sense. One of the most significant innovations of rabbinic Judaism is the creation of different categories of Shabbat space: inside an enclosed area it is permissible to carry, while outside, in the world at large, it is not. This distinction works well for people settled in a fixed home, but how should travelers define an enclosed Sabbath space?

> If a caravan camped in a valley (an open space not enclosed by walls), and the travelers enclosed their camp with partitions made of the animals' equipment (such as saddles and the like), one may carry inside the enclosed area, provided that the partition will be a *gader* ten handbreadths high, and that there will not be breaches greater than the built segment. Any breach that is approximately ten cubits wide is permitted, because it is considered like an entrance.[9]

The Mishnah sets out criteria by which piles of equipment taken from the backs of pack animals can be deemed a *gader*. A fence is a fence when the system deems it to be so.

In one section of his *Kuzari*, Judah Halevi considers the significance of the *gader*, the fence around the law constructed by the rabbis of the Mishnah and the Talmud. He defends their achievement and takes issue with the Karaites, a Jewish sect opposed to rabbinism and the entire edifice of the Oral Law. In the third chapter of his work, Halevi asserts that "every law has certain limits fixed with scientific accuracy, though in practice they may appear illogical."[10] He recommends his readers not to be guided by their own taste nor by opinion or reasoning but rather to embrace the strictures set down by tradition. In his view, these boundaries can only be maintained if individuals forego the temptation to let their reason take them where it will.

A thousand years later, the temptation to test the stability and the validity of the *gader* is stronger than ever. Some resist or ignore this temptation and continue to observe traditional restrictions with enthusiasm. Some eschew the very concept of the *gader*. Some of us find neither of these positions palatable or even possible and are looking for another approach to the *gader*.

Moving Boundaries, Blurring Boundaries

The great changes which have overtaken the Western world since the seventeenth century have involved shifting traditional boundaries. For many enthusiasts of modernity, a new set of fences were called for since the old ones were no longer fit for purpose. Reason was now to trump revelation. Science would determine the boundaries since religion no longer can, while laws passed by democratic governments were to stand in for divine legislation: "Modernity has its own traditions of tearing down boundaries and erecting new ones at the same time."[11]

Classical Reform Judaism was founded on the notion that the old *gader* ought to come down and that new criteria would now prevail. Consider Samuel Holdheim's 1845 assertion that "the Talmud speaks out of the consciousness of its age and for its time *it* was right. I speak out of the higher consciousness of my age and for my time *I* am right."[12] Underlying this declaration is the assumption that the wisdom of the rabbis was produced in an era in which parameters of law, morality, authority, and evidence were understood in a way which has since been superseded. As the *gader* shifts, so does our understanding of how best to behave. Modernity proposed replacing outdated myths with new-fangled truths and the boundaries of tradition with the bounds of reason.

As a modern Jew, I identify with Balaam's ass, caught between two fences: the unfolding traditions of Judaism on one side and the dictates of modernity on the other. Here is an example of being caught between two fences. I believe my children know that I want them to see themselves as links in a chain that starts with Abraham and stretches beyond them. They also know that I do not want them to take on this yoke out of guilt or inertia. The Torah of life that I want more than anything to impart can only be received by them on their terms, at their pace, with their will. It is a yoke to be borne by choice. The assertion that personal freedom is bounded practically and ethically should not be confused for undervaluing that freedom. It is precious and to be guarded vigilantly. I reject any theology of Jewish commitment which bypasses individual personal liberty. The price for this value is the awareness that my children might choose to abandon all vestiges of Jewish life. While that prospect fills me with dismay and despair, I acknowledge that this is indeed the case. Their right to decide is not an unfortunate accident but a hard-won prize. The *gader* of personal freedom is as tangible as the *gader* of Jewish continuity. I believe that caught between two barriers, revelation (or at least innovation) becomes possible.

Modernity thus proposes new boundaries. Recent decades have seen the rise of a yet more unsettling (and exciting) development: the blurring of the very notion of boundaries. The anthropologist Clifford Geertz was right to suggest that "what we are seeing is not just another redrawing of the cultural map – the moving of a few disputed borders ... but an alteration of the principles of mapping."[13] The notion that absolute boundaries set clear distinctions between genders, genres, disciplines, norms of behavior, types of reality, and many other domains has been brought into doubt.[14]

Regarding gender, Judith Butler gives voice to the position that questions the validity of these categories:

> To assume that gender always and exclusively means the matrix of the "masculine" and "feminine" is precisely to miss the critical point that the production of that coherent binary is contingent, that it comes at a cost, and that those permutations of gender which do not fit the binary are as much part of gender as its most normative instance.[15]

Never before has such a passionate and informed case for the abandonment of traditional binary categories been made. The ferocity of the response and the concomitant need to ascribe ultimate status to traditional boundaries is a result of a reaction to new boundary-busting trends. It is surely no coincidence that the same era which has seen the questioning of gender distinctions has also seen the rise of the gender reveal party, made possible by ultrasound technology, in which cascades of pink or blue balloons are used to announce to which of the two possible of gender the fetus belongs. The old *gader* seems to offer comfort just as the very concept of *gader* is undermined. The resurgence of fundamentalisms around the world is to be understood as a reaction to the terror of being left undefined, unfenced, and undefended.

I want to suggest a distinction between the term *gader*, denoting a fence wrought by human hands, a humanly generated distinction, and an even more prevalent biblical term, *gevul*, denoting "both a demarcated area ... and the boundary by which the territory is limited."[16] In its etymology, *gevul* relates to something "out there" in the extant world, a physical feature which comes to express a boundary, while a *gader* is something constructed, not originally part of the landscape. To use a geographical example, Israel is bounded to its west by a *gevul*, the Mediterranean Sea. To its east there is also a natural *gevul*, the Jordan river, but also by a *gader*, a wall intended to define and confine.

This might seem obvious: surely the distinction between a boundary existing in nature and one wrought by human artifice is clear. In our day, however, the distinction between the natural border (*gevul*) and the humanly constructed fence (*gader*) is highly contested. Recent trends in philosophy and various branches of science have made the obvious anything but obvious. Distinctions thought to be incontrovertible and unchanging may now be understood as a construct or a narrative. Each *gader* and every *gevul* is radically challenged. While I am intrigued, challenged and stimulated by new challenges to banal binaries, I am slow to give up on the existence of certain fundamental boundaries, even as I acknowledge how difficult it is to know precisely where they lie. To cite the name of one of Israel's protest organizations, *Yesh Gevul* [There Is a Boundary], there is a limit to what kinds of behavior should be tolerated and explained away as a competing narrative. There *is* a difference between nobility of spirit and selfless devotion, on the one hand, and cynical self-serving manipulation, on the other. *Yesh gevul*. When postmodern critique of established boundaries becomes an excuse for indifference or a gateway to paralysis, I part company from it.[17] While the critique of human-made distinctions is compelling, ironic detachment will only take us so far.

At the same time, I am not able to embrace many traditional boundaries with unquestioning faith, perhaps because I cannot muster the credulity required to do so. I do not believe that to be a believing Jew one need to leave one's critical faculties at the door. Nonetheless, I embrace a Judaism of boundaries. I reject the notion, to cite an example, that by effecting a legal fiction, the whiskey I keep in my storeroom during the Passover festival (whiskey is leaven and clearly not permissible for consumption or ownership) is acceptable because I have temporarily sold it. It is not my conclusion, however, that the distinction between Passover and the rest of the year should be abandoned. In the days leading up to Passover I seek out leaven, destroy it, give it away, or, when all else fails, put it out of my mind. I doubt that there is some intrinsic difference (under a microscope or in genetic terms) between what was deemed leaven by my ancestors and what was not. But I am not prepared to conclude that Passover is to be rejected as a falsehood or an error. Spiritualizing or symbolizing the festival so that it is only the leaven in my heart that I remove is a nice try, but you will still find me two days before Seder night trying to get into the difficult corner behind the sofa in search of the elusive crumb. I acknowledge that the *gader* is a human construct, but I resist the temptation to demolish it. This *gader* has been a spur to meaning. I do not want to lose the possibility of encountering an angel situated between the boundaries. It is a fence I accept with love.

Feminism Redefines Judaism

The categories by which Judaism is understood have been profoundly transformed by feminism. Describing the most sublime moments which a pious Jew could hope to experience, Judah Halevi in the eleventh century noted that after each purifying uplift of the thrice-daily cycle of prayers, his soul is forced to endure the company of "youths, women, or wicked people."[18] It is self-evident to him that the pious person is a pious man and that women constitute a challenge to the maintenance of this higher spiritual plane. Boundaries legislating the separation of women and emphasizing their profound otherness have played a fundamental role in every stage of Judaism's development.

Modernity sought to change this paradigm, although the success of this attempt and even its integrity can be called into question. A strident assertion of the modernist position has been made by Martha Nussbaum in an essay explaining her decision to live her life as a Reform Jew. She highlights a number of key concepts she finds in the writings of Reform's founders, which I summarize as four main points:

1. The moral has primacy. The love and pursuit of social justice, peace, and mercy are the core and purpose of living and being Jewish. Each person has not only the right but the duty to exercise their discretion in adducing what best advances these principles, and conscience has priority over any text, even when it claims to be the product of external revelation.
2. Judaism is a cosmopolitan religion. The fundamental moral mission of the people of Israel is universal in nature.
3. Our version of Judaism proposes a historical understanding of the tradition, in which the search for eternal truth must always be bound in a particular historical context. This historical perspective allows us to understand the moral imperfections of earlier ages.
4. Sex equality is written into the very heart of this Judaism, and anything that contravenes this moral principle is to be rejected.[19]

Explicating this last point, Nussbaum rejects the assertion "that Judaism is inherently or originally patriarchal, and that modern reforms are changes or reconstructions."[20] In her view, the essence of Judaism is not its foundational texts but rather the moral principles underlying and partially expressed within them:

> One should conclude that Judaism never was misogynistic or patriarchal at its core: erring human beings, blinded by habit and culture, put that construction upon it. We recall it, in this way, to its purity.[21]

In Nussbaum's reading, the categories set down in the Hebrew Bible and in the halakhic system are not to be confused with the core of Judaism. That core calls for justice and equality, and the redrawing of ancient and medieval categories to reflect this higher state of understanding is the opposite of a dilution of Judaism; it should be seen as a purification.

Postmodern feminist readings of Judaism and of the categories of morality tend to offer a more radical critique, arguing that pre-modern and modern texts alike are riddled with inescapable gendered assumptions, both explicit and implicit. They argue that the same can be said for the moral principles presented as universally valid and somehow disembodied. In light of this, traditional texts are not to be overcome so easily. Fully aware that Jewish tradition is, on the whole, phallocentric, it may nonetheless be trawled for meaning and read anew through a feminist *aspaklaria*.[22]

According to this kind of feminist critique, modern conceptions of the individual are themselves expressions of male assumptions. The body of this archetypal modern individual "is tightly enclosed within boundaries, but women's bodies are permeable, their contours change shape and they are subject to cyclical processes."[23] A feminist re-reading of the tradition thus goes far beyond allowing some women treated as honorary men to be allowed a seat at the table. It involves a reimagining of the table itself, including the legs upon which it stands. In her discussion of post-Holocaust theology Melissa Raphael asserted that "Jewish feminist theological revision … is … at the heart of Judaism and at the heart of a properly Jewish theological response to Auschwitz."[24] This statement can be expanded yet further: a Jewish theological response to any significant question that fails to note the degree to which Judaism has been redefined and reengendered in our day is inadequate to this task.

The question of when gender distinctions are to be understood as a *gevul*, a natural boundary, or as a *gader*, a human construct, provides fuel for many fierce debates. For the purposes of this discussion, suffice it to note that feminism has engendered new ways of considering the borders and boundaries separating Jews from other Jews, from their tradition, and from the non-Jewish world. In Judith Plaskow's words, one major task of Jewish feminism is "to articulate a model of community in which difference is acknowledged without being hierarchalized."[25]

Lehitgader

A preoccupation with definitions and borderlines can lead to pedantry and worse. What for some is the beating heart of the rabbinic system can seem to others to be obsession with niceties. Since the New Testament (for example in Matthew 23), the Pharisee has been associated with a kind of hypocritical pettifoggery, obsessing on legal niceties and ignoring broader ethical considerations. A recent sympathetic account of Halakhah notes that "all legal systems – Halakhah included – have the potential to become overrun by technical minutiae that can drown out the law's overarching goals and principles."[26]

Leo Baeck highlighted another danger of thought systems: their tendency to breed intolerance and self-righteousness. He contrasted this with openness to the prophetic word:

> The prophetic word, on the other hand, as a living and personal confession of faith, which cannot be circumscribed by demarcation, possesses breadth and boundlessness. It has a freedom, the extent of which cannot be anticipated, which carries within itself the seed of revival and development, and so becomes inevitably, again and again, incorporated into present and actual life.[27]

Baeck sought a way of living within a bounded system while staying open to boundless possibility. To use my terminology, he accepted the broad contours, the *gevul*, of Jewish life while doubting that obsessive attention to every *gader* was the most important Jewish virtue. In the spirit of Baeck's Judaism, I have scant interest in the fine details of halakhic decisions, but I am intrigued and inspired by the argumentation involved in reaching the opinions. There is much innovation to be found by pushing up against boundaries and seeing how far they might move.

Tractate Hullin of the Babylonian Talmud includes a phrase based on the word *gader* which speaks to the creativity found in boundary maintenance. Rabbi Judah the Prince explains a break with tradition by saying: my ancestors left me space *"lehitgader bo,"* literally, to fence myself, usually translated as to achieve prominence or take a step forward.[28]

According to this image, the limitations of tradition are not just fences; they are also springboards. Drawing lines in one generation is seen as an invitation to consider redrawing them at a later time. One definition of religion, notable for its playfulness and for the possibilities it opens up, was proposed by Thomas Tweed: "Religions are confluences of organic-cultural flows that intensify joy and confront suffering by drawing on human and suprahuman forces to make homes and cross boundaries."[29] Religion sets boundaries and offers pathways for overcoming them. The Judaism I inherited, the Judaism I want to pass on, is indeed a confluence that intensifies joy and confronts suffering. It does indeed make homes and cross boundaries.

For anyone even peripherally acquainted with Judaism, it is not difficult to see where it meets the standard for setting limits. From the account of creation at the start of the Book of Genesis, distinctions are established and their boundary lines patrolled—between time periods, territories, peoples, categories of purity, and much more. Where, though, does Judaism propose methods by which boundaries may be crossed? I am convinced that the resources offered by 3000 years of Jewish creativity include tools to grapple with blurred and contested boundaries. To be a Hebrew, according to that word's Hebrew etymology, is to be a person who goes across, occasionally a transgressor but quintessentially a transverser. The antinomian option of demolishing every fence provides the satisfaction of release and may also clear away much overdue debris. By itself, however, it is insufficient. Our challenge is to find ways to grow and move forward in conversation with the boundaries of the past.

A nuanced reading of gender and sexuality offers one area in which our generation has an opportunity to make significant advances, even if they unsettle established categories. In her *Engendering Judaism*, Rachel Adler notes that when viewed through a feminist *aspaklaria*, "power determines who draws the boundary and how and who makes the categories and for what reasons."[30] She asserts that "our sexuality marks us as both boundaried and boundary-transcending."[31] An engendered Judaism of tomorrow may find ways to make homes and cross boundaries. Balaam's ass may have dreamed of wandering to the ridge where the west commences, but instead it ambled into posterity, *gader mizeh ugader mizeh*, flanked by limiting fences, forced to look up and pay attention to the angel. While my version of Judaism is light on specific iterations of the *gader*, it is fueled by the belief that *yesh gevul*—there are limits, even when they cannot be defined. Like the ass, modern Judaism is squeezed between nihilism and fundamentalism, animated by the possibilities presented by new understandings of old distinctions. When there seems to be no way to proceed, an angel may be lurking.

Notes

1. Two medieval interpretations, quite different in emphasis, are particularly worthy of mention here. In the introduction to his 1204 translation of Maimonides' *Guide*, Samuel ibn Tibbon describes the path of translators restricted on one side by the language from which they translate and fenced in on the other by the demands of the language into which they translate. He identifies the translator not with the angel but with the humble beast of burden, caught within these two restrictions. Some 300 years later, Don Isaac Abravanel read the tale as a kind of philosophical allegory according to which one fence represents the heavenly system of preordained fate and the other divine fiat. In this reading, biblical narrative becomes a platform for philosophy.

2. Mishnah Avot 2: 16.
3. See Halevi, *Kuzari*, 4:26, 236–237; Albo, *Ikkarim*, 2:6.
4. Exodus Rabbah 15:11.
5. Halevi, *Selected Poems*, 121.
6. In an article devoted to this topic, Ruvik Rosenthal, "Gvul Im Kol Davar," lists *gvul, gader, ghetto, chomah. chayitz, kotel, metzar, siyag, sfar, kav, kor, retzu'ah* and *tchum*.
7. In Mishnah Ohalot 8:2 the term refers to that which literally reaches out beyond its enclosure. In the Middle Ages it came to refer to something beyond a particular context. Today it can also mean to go to extraordinary lengths in order to do something.
8. Rabbenu Nissim of Gerona, *Darshot HaRaN* (Jerusalem: Machon Shalem, 1977), Fifth Discourse, Second Version, 91.
9. Mishnah Eruvin 1:8.
10. Halevi, *Kuzari*, 3:49, 178.
11. Denis and Ufer, "Of Modernity's Boundaries," 211.
12. Quoted in Ellenson, "Antonimiamism and Its Responses," 271.
13. Geertz, *Local Knowledge*, 20.
14. In *Judaism Disrupted*, Michael Strassfeld includes a call to imagine Judaism beyond the domain of binary distinctions. For a fascinating discussion of boundary blurring in another context, see Jordan, "Blurring Boundaries."
15. Butler, *Undoing Gender*, 42. For some implications of these ideas in specifically Jewish contexts, see Fonrobert, "Regulating the Human Body." In a recent work, *Trans Talmud*, Max Strassfeld explores the disambiguation and re-ambiguation of gender distinctions.
16. Wazana, *All the Boundaries*, 12.
17. Rorty grapples with this question in *Philosophy and Social Hope*.
18. Judah Halevi, *The Kuzari*, 3.5, 140.
19. Nussbaum, "Judaism and the Love of Reason," particularly 18–31.
20. Ibid., 31.
21. Ibid., 31.
22. For an example of such a reading, see Pessin, "Loss, Presence, Gabirol's Desire."
23. Pateman, *Sexual Contract*, 96. This is cited and discussed in Boyarin, *Unheroic Conduct*, particularly 90.
24. Raphael, *The Female Face*, 4.
25. Plaskow, *Standing Again at Sinai*, 97.
26. Saiman, *Halakhah*, 125. The author goes on to point out that in the case of Halakhah the opposite may be true. He adds that "whether by design, effect, or some combination thereof, halakhah became the forum to explore and develop the most weighty matters of the law," 125–126. For two very different treatments of the boundaries of Jewish peoplehood and their implications, see Hartman, *Boundaries of Judaism* and Boyarin, *Border Lines*.

27. Baeck, *Essence of Judaism*, 36–37.
28. BT Hullin 6b-7a. See also BT Yoma 78a and Mekhilta d'Rabbi Simon b. Yochai, Epstein/Melamed edition, 132.
29. Tweed, *Crossing and Dwelling*, 54. See also Hughes, "Boundary Maintenance."
30. Adler, *Engendering Judaism*, 115.
31. Ibid., 118.

Open Access This chapter is licensed under the terms of the Creative Commons Attribution 4.0 International License (http://creativecommons.org/licenses/by/4.0/), which permits use, sharing, adaptation, distribution and reproduction in any medium or format, as long as you give appropriate credit to the original author(s) and the source, provide a link to the Creative Commons license and indicate if changes were made.

The images or other third party material in this chapter are included in the chapter's Creative Commons license, unless indicated otherwise in a credit line to the material. If material is not included in the chapter's Creative Commons license and your intended use is not permitted by statutory regulation or exceeds the permitted use, you will need to obtain permission directly from the copyright holder.

Dovev: Quotation and Education

Everyone quotes. Even those who insist they never do are bound to recall something a grandparent used to say or to retell a joke. To speak is to quote, namely, to re-purpose words once employed by those no longer here. Who and what you quote is significant. If your assertions are proved with recourse to biblical verses and halakhic precedents, chances are your views are substantially different from someone whose beliefs are bolstered by articles from *Nature* or the opinions section of the *New York Times*. To bolster my claim for the ubiquity of quotation, the words of Emerson seem appropriate: "All minds quote. Old and new make the warp and woof of every moment. … By necessity, by proclivity, and by delight, we all quote."[1]

Ruth Finnegan employs a compelling visual metaphor to explore what she calls "the distancing dimension inherent in quotation."[2] Her explanation deserves quoting:

> We call on text or voice *outside* the self, *beyond* the ephemeral interests of the passing moment. Here is an external voice to which the speaker or reader of the moment conjoins their own, endowing it with the aura and tone of the

other. They put another perspective on some situation—the voice of revered authority, of some universal human dilemma, of the truth in proverb, of some recollected voice—and in doing so venture to bring that outside vision to themselves.³

In the terminology of this book, quotation serves as an *aspaklaria*: a prism through which the current moment is perceived, a perspective from which it might be understood, and often a screen distancing the quoter from the immediacy of this moment.

In an article published elsewhere, I set out some key aspects of the history and functions of Jewish quotation.⁴ After touching on some of the key points of that more extensive presentation, I want to relate to one word that is part of the lexicon of Jewish quotation practice and through it to consider challenges of culture, education, and morality.

The Jewish Art of Quotation

For millennia, Jews have quoted extensively and enthusiastically, and it has helped give Jewish thought what I am terming its crunchy quality. Smooth theology, as I suggested in the Introduction, offers a consistent and digestible version of complex and elusive concepts. The crunchy variety, in contrast, includes notions and teachings that do not break down so easily. Most Jewish sources and most classic examples of Jewish oral performance too are replete with ideas and insights from the past, repeated and often recontextualized.⁵ If the only object of communication is to impart an abstract idea smoothly and clearly, the inclusion of chunks of traditional lore would make little sense. Nonetheless, the literature, language, and folklore of the Jews throughout history have included a cascade of verses, sources, and references. "Jewish culture," Moshe Idel observed, "is a cumulative culture par excellence; it assumes that the earlier is very often the better."⁶

As Jewish history unfolded, the words of the Bible came to be seen as the raw material from which any subsequent fabric may be spun.⁷ The primacy of the biblical text does not obviate the need for creativity; it is the first word, not the last. Nor is the canon of authoritative literature closed: over time, later rabbis of the Talmud come to relate to their rabbinic predecessors with almost biblical reverence.⁸ In the rabbinic ideology of quotation, a verbal tradition was to be cited as far back as possible:

Rabbi Hezekiah, Rabbi Jeremiah and Rabbi Hiyya in the name of Rabbi Yochanan: if you can link the teaching [being transmitted] all the way back to Moses, do so. If not, relate either to the originator of the tradition or to its last tradent. And how is this proven? "...and make them known to you children and to your children's children. The day you stood before the Lord your God at Horeb..." (Deuteronomy 4:9–10). Gidul said: Whoever brings a tradition in the name of its originator, should see the source of the teaching as if he were standing before him.[9]

The future validity of the tradition is affirmed through the confirmation of its Sinaitic pedigree. Citation is a kind of resuscitation as the wisdom of the past is brought to life.

Verses and sayings from tradition served to bolster, prove, anchor, and embellish. For most of Jewish history, to speak or write without them was to be unclothed.[10] Perhaps the single and most explicit reference to the act of citation in all of rabbinic literature is found in the sixth chapter of Tractate Avot (a later accretion to the tractate known as *Kinyan Torah*). At the conclusion of a catalog of forty-eight virtues through which Torah is acquired, we read:

> by being precise in transmitting what he has learned; by quoting his source. From this we learn that a person who quotes his source brings deliverance to the world, as it is written: "Esther spoke to the king in the name of Mordechai" (Esther 2:22).[11]

The rabbis also prohibit non-attribution citing Proverbs 22:22: "Never rob a helpless man because he is helpless."[12] The person in whose name wisdom is imparted may not be able to insist on their claim to posterity, but that does not give us the right to dispossess them. To quote fully and with attribution is to save the day. Not to do so is daylight robbery.

From the rabbinic period on, virtually every genre of Jewish creativity is characterized by quotations of these foundational texts. Open any work of liturgy, poetry, philosophy, esoteric speculation, legal discourse, or ethical instruction produced within Jewish circles over the last 2000 years and you are likely to encounter a dense thicket of quotations. From within the thicket, something new may be revealed.

ANIMATING AND FLOWING

The word *dovev* appears only once in the Hebrew Bible. It makes its appearance in the Song of Songs, a work whose fundamental meaning has itself always been contested. The word, then, is shrouded in indeterminacy. Being a *hapax legomenon* (the technical term for a word appearing only once), there is no clear way of fixing its meaning. In the JPS translation, verse 7:10 reads:

> And your mouth like choicest wine.
> Let it follow to my beloved as new wine
> Gliding over the lips of sleepers.

This last phrase, *dovev siftei yeshenim*, has been discussed by both classical interpreters and modern Bible scholars with suggested translations including speaking, causing to speak, gliding, flowing, dripping, and languishing.[13] In the rabbinic imagination, the fact that *yeshenim* may refer to those who now sleep in eternity helped turn the biblical phrase into the basis for a profound teaching about the posthumous citation of traditions in the name of their originators. From the eros of personal intimacy, the term has come to refer to the dynamics of intergenerational encounters.

It is both ironic and characteristic that the teaching appears in various sources attributed to different sages. One from the Palestinian Talmud can serve as an example of how *dovev* enriches the discussion of tradition and transmission:

> Rabbi Yochanan required that traditions should be reported in his name. Also David begged for mercy in this respect (Psalms 61:5), "may I dwell in Your tent forever (*olamim*)!" Rabbi Phineas, Rabbi Jeremiah in the name of Rabbi Yochanan: could David think of living forever? Rather, David meant: May I have the merit that my words will be mentioned in my name in synagogues and houses of study. What good does that do to him? Levi the son of the *Nazir* said: if someone mentions a tradition in the name of its author, the latter's lips move (*dovevot*) with him in the grave. What is the reason? "Dripping from the lips of those who sleep" (Song of Songs 7:10). Like a bunch of ripe grapes which drips by itself.[14]

The biblical King and the Talmudic Sage are plagued by the same anxiety: that with mortality will come oblivion. Both are comforted by the thought that what they teach will be repeated. Their lips will somehow be animated from the grave. English idiom speaks of someone spinning in the grave if something of which they would not have approved comes to pass. Here the intention is different: even if the contemporary teacher is using the tradition in a way that the original author could not have imagined, it is as if they recite the words. To bring the teachings of the dead is to animate and vivify them, to engage them in the continued process of growth.

Dovev implies oozing or dripping as a result of natural effulgence. Haim Nachman Bialik is reported to have described Nachman Krochmal, the great nineteenth-century philosopher and theologian, thus:

> It is as though he has digested the Hebrew Bible, the Talmud, the Kabbalah, Jewish Thought and general philosophy, and one cannot tell that all this is external to him. It all seems to derive from within him, from within his very soul. That is how it ought to be.[15]

Krochmal, like Bialik himself, was particularly prodigious in his mastery of sources, but one of the characteristics of rabbinic culture is its propagation of an educational standard of fluency with a much wider reach. Prayer, for example, is said to flow within the mouth of the accomplished worshipper.[16] Here is a vision of cultural competency that can make spontaneity and creativity possible: to be so engaged with the words of others that they become one's own words and flow as from a ripe grape.

These two senses of *dovev*, animating and flowing, help explain the Jewish culture of quotation. The first relates to the dynamics of innovation, while the second speaks to presence and authenticity. In both of these ways, Jewish tradition is perpetuated: when former and current generations animate each other, and when words, gestures, and practices that have become inculcated come to natural expression.

This interplay has characterized Jewish culture for 2000 years. In recent centuries, the practice of quoting sacred sources has changed profoundly. It is not that with the advent of modernity, quotation and citation have ceased; it is rather that its basis has been irrevocably changed.

Pre-modern, Modern, Postmodern

Harold Bloom coined the expression "anxiety of influence" to describe the process of innovation within great poetry, whereby the latest poetic voice builds on the greatness of predecessors yet also seeks to overcome them.[17] Drawing on the teachings of Sigmund Freund, one of the great voices of modernity, Bloom describes a characteristically modern struggle to break free from the shackles of the past while being tied to it.

Pre-modern Jewish culture was characterized by what has been described in another context as "the anxiety of not being influenced."[18] Even startling innovations were couched in the language of tradition and surrounded by verses and allusions. Much of pre-modern culture was concerned with deference and reference, and the Jews were usually at the epicenter of this tendency. In the Western world, adherents of modern movements as different from each other as scientific rationalism and Romanticism opposed the old practices of extravagant citation: it was better to look outside to the natural world and inside to the individual's urge for self-expression than to be swathed in the sayings of predecessors. In the modern sensibility, evidence would be provided by verifiable data, deduction, or authentic self-expression but not by canonical prooftexts. In a novel by the Israeli novelist Hayim Be'er, two non-Jewish characters are discussing the protagonist, a Hasidic rabbi, who is undergoing a crisis of faith. One of them comments that if the Renaissance painter Giuseppe Arcimboldo were to paint this rabbi's portrait, it would not be rendered in the artist's usual style by employing fruit and other foodstuffs but rather all the verses and adages and homiletical teachings used by the rabbi. The character goes on to wonder what the face of the rabbi would look like if stripped of all this artifice.[19]

In modernity, the pendulum swung away from the practice of intense quotation so prevalent in medieval and ancient Judaism. Just as the rise of the scientific method undermined the primacy of old ways of quoting and proving, some of the most acute observers of modern society, among them Jews, became fascinated by the potential offered by quotation. We can term this a postmodern turn. Today, in our hyper-modern or postmodern context, there is more "sampling," more excerpting of quotations of almost every type than ever before.[20] A significant forerunner of this return to quotation was Walter Benjamin, a pivotal figure of twentieth-century European culture. Hannah Arendt analyzed Benjamin's interest in quotation, arguing that

> Walter Benjamin knew that the break in tradition and the loss of authority which occurred in his lifetime were irreparable, and he concluded that he had to discover new ways of dealing with the past. In this he became a master when he discovered that the transmissibility of the past had been replaced by its citability.[21]

Benjamin was interested in Jewish tradition while remaining convinced that technological and social changes had created a rupture separating the contemporary person from tradition. The montage of quotations he proposed was not designed to blur the distinction between the present and the past but rather to acknowledge it.[22] If pre-modern quotation served to bolster the wisdom of the past and legitimize innovation, Benjamin's approach was deliberately disruptive. He proposed a bricolage of excerpted snippets of the past, expressing our fundamentally ruptured condition.[23] At no stage of history have Jews stopped quoting. They simply quote different materials in different ways. Our quotation practices reveal much about our attitudes concerning authority, aesthetics, and even morality.

THE MORALITY OF QUOTATION

A rabbinic aphorism presents itself as a kind of scriptural quotation. A passage in BT Sanhedrin 72a reads: "The Torah said: if someone comes to slay you, forestall them by slaying them." The Talmud purports to quote a Torah teaching, but there is, in fact, no such biblical verse. A number of commentators suggested that it is a paraphrase of a Pentateuchal teaching.[24] Elsewhere in the Talmud[25] the same teaching is presented using the formula "the Torah said" (*hatorah amrah* or *amrah hatorah*) in support of *din rodef*, the principle mandating the use of preemptive deadly force. The expression is often used to bring a quotation from the Pentateuch.[26] How then is a term denoting the quotation of a supremely authoritative and canonical text employed to cite what appears to be nothing more than a rabbinic aphorism? Clearly, there is more than one meaning to the statement "the Torah says." Here it signifies "the Torah means" or "Tradition teaches."

In later sources, when the issue of preemptive force is discussed and the teaching quoted, it appears variously in the name of the Torah,[27] the Sages,[28] and something "we" say.[29] In contemporary Israel, the Talmudic saying is used in a variety of secularized contexts. For example, the coach of the Maccabi Tel Aviv basketball team was quoted in October 2010 citing this Talmudic principle as his intended tactic ahead of the team's match against a Lithuanian opponent. The strategy proved effective.

Unsurprisingly, we find the Talmudic teaching employed in less trivial settings too. It is a commonplace of Israeli military parlance and employed to justify taking out those classified as terrorists.[30] More disturbingly, it has also been argued that the murderous acts of Baruch Goldstein, perpetrator of a mass killing in 1994, and of Yigal Amir, Yitzhak Rabin's assassin, can be justified with reference to this principle and to other biblical precedents.[31]

The Talmud cites a saying which it attributes to "the Torah." For fifteen centuries the saying has been employed in abstract theoretical discussions of Halakhah. With the Jewish return into history the teaching that one should rise early to slay the person who plans to slay you comes to express a key part of the Zionist consensus, namely, that Israel has every right to defend the life of its citizens by means of preemptive strikes.[32] It is not my intention to argue the ethics of Israel's doctrine of proactive defense. My point here is that what and how we quote and the results, intended or otherwise, of such a reference are subject to significant changes in context. It is not enough to cite a sacred source in the knowledge that it has been cited before. The new politics of the situation calls for a new ethics of citation.

By itself, of course, the fact that one tends to bring a plethora of verses and sayings into one's discourse says nothing about one's vision of the future or one's moral orientation. The devil, after all, can quote Scripture, as Shakespeare's Antonio comments in response to the Jew Shylock's biblical references.[33] A capacity to quote in prayer, study, conversation, and cultural production is an important educational aim. Without it, the chances of significant Jewish creativity are greatly reduced. Nonetheless, extensive Jewish literacy devoid of moral acuity, common sense, and self-awareness is not only inadequate; it is dangerous.

Every year on the Shabbat before Purim, a portion from the fifteenth chapter of 1 Samuel is read in synagogue. Samuel informs Saul that it is God's command to slay Amalek and his cohort, sparing no living being from his camp. The challenge is to raise a generation capable of quoting this verse while being aware of the immense danger it represents if interpreted literally. The significance of quotation changes as the context changes. In his fifteenth-century commentary on Zechariah 13, Isaac Abarvanel quoted a phrase from the traditional liturgy: "the idols shall surely be cut off" to express his opposition to the proliferation of Christian iconography in Jerusalem.[34] In 2015 this same phrase was sprayed on a wall at the Church of Multiplication of Loaves and Fishes on the Sea of Galilee after it was burned and vandalized. The former example was part of a religious polemic. The latter suggested a license for religious violence.

We all quote the sources that suit our opinions. An ethics of citation should demand that we also acknowledge the existence of traditions less conducive to our worldview. One of the failures of liberal Jewish education is that too many products of our educational frameworks are a brittle, shallow, and patchy understanding of what "the Torah" says. We need to educate for complexity and for fluency. We need chapter and verse, not just cut and paste.

What we choose to quote is a moral as well as a curricular question. What colors are included on our palettes? Is wisdom from other traditions likely to find its way into our discourse? And what about giants of contemporary science and philosophy? Among Jewish sources, are we to limit ourselves to the rabbinic canon, or will we look to a richer and more diverse range of men and women upon whose wisdom we hope to build? Who, if anyone, is beyond the pale?

Who, how, why, and what is quoted is more than an issue of literary embellishment. It involves questions of ethics, politics, and morality.

Bam

An earlier chapter of this book considered questions of spirituality and responsibility by considering the Hebrew word *bi*, meaning "on me" or "within me." In our present context we should consider also *bam*, which means "in them," "through them," or "about them." In the first paragraph of the *Shema* we read:

> These words that I command you today shall be upon your heart. Repeat them to your children, and talk about them when you stay at home and when you are away, when you lie down and when you get up.[35]

The instruction is to speak *bam*, usually understood to refer to the words of Torah which are to be repeated. In my reading, the instruction is to speak through or within our children, to encourage them to speak, to animate their lips in the cradle. In the second paragraph of the *Shema* the word appears again as we are instructed to "teach them to your children so that they should speak *bam*."[36] Here again the literal meaning would appear to be: teach your children to speak the words. They can also mean: teach your children to speak through the words of Torah. Teach them to find their own expression through the words of tradition.

To live within a Jewish culture of quotation is to be animated by—and indeed to animate—the generations preceding us and the generations still to come. It should be much more than attaching an over-used prooftext to a predictable opinion. Rather, it should provide the opportunity for expression as spontaneous as the dripping of ripe fruit, as tender as a kiss gliding over sleeping lips, and as morally responsible as an act capable of redeeming the world.

Tell me who you quote and I will tell you, fairly accurately, who you are: your cultural milieu, your religious affiliation, your age, and whether you are more easily categorized as pre-modern, modern, or postmodern. A thorough examination of what is being quoted is a more faithful indicator of educational achievement than the usual diagnostics.

To pray as a Jew is to quote. The words of the Bible feature prominently in the liturgy.[37] The rabbis' own liturgical formulations, some of them 2000 years old, are constantly cited and recited. The ideal of *dover* is particularly evocative in this context: to speak the words of others with fluency and conviction. Knowing the words by heart will not make them flow and come alive. For this to happen, they must be known in the heart.

Herein lies the broad outline of a core goal for Jewish education: to instill in each new generation the ability to quote from a broad range of sources with confidence and accuracy, the urge to fashion new Jewish expressions wrought of ancient materials, and the capacity for moral discernment. Thus, in the words of an ancient adage, may redemption be brought to the world.

Notes

1. Emerson, "Quotation and Originality," 178.
2. Finnegan, *Why Do We Quote?*, 262.
3. Ibid., 262. While Finnegan makes no mention of Gadamer in her book, his hermeneutic notion of the fusion of horizons comes to mind in this description.
4. Marmur, "Why Jews Quote."
5. In Marmur, "Why Jews Quote," I attempted to delineate some of the key contours of Jewish quotational practice. The current chapter leans heavily on some aspects of that article.
6. Idel, *Absorbing Perfections*, 5. There are significant differences in the style and density of quotation in pre-modern Jewish literature. For a comparison of the quotational styles of Rav Saadia Gaon and Abraham ibn Ezra, see Stroumsa, "Masoret Tsitut," 167–169.
7. Only very rarely does the Hebrew Bible contain an example of self-conscious quotation from an identifiable biblical source. For an outstanding example, see Jeremiah 26:18 which quotes Micah 3:12. For excellent

discussions of quotations in the Bible, see: Gordis, "Quotations"; Gordis, "Virtual Quotations"; and Savran, *Telling and Retelling*.
8. See Chernick, *A Great Voice*, particularly 33–68.
9. PT Shabbat 1:1, 3a. The source also appears in PT Kiddushin 1:7, 61a. See also Tanchuma Noach 3 for another intergenerational theme.
10. The exceptions to this rule are themselves instructive. *Sefer Yetzirah*, a foundational work of the Jewish esoteric tradition, is remarkable for its lack of intertextual references.
11. Mishnah Avot 6:5.
12. See Tanchuma Buber, Numbers 27. See Midrash Proverbs 6:16, where failure to attribute is listed as one of seven mortal sins and the Esther verse rather than the verse from Proverbs is employed.
13. See Pfenniger, "Speaking or Smouldering Lips."
14. PT Berakhot 2:1, 4b. Given the emphasis on attribution of sources, it is worth dwelling on the ways in which this teaching has been transmitted in the name of various rabbis. Two traditions, one relating to the lips moving in the grave and the other using the image of the grapes, are conflated in a variety of rabbinic sources. The former is attributed to Rabbi Shimon ben Yehotzadak in BT Sanhedrin 90b. In Midrash Tehillim to Psalm 30 and Yalkut Shimoni 431 to Isaiah 26 it is taught in the name of Rabbi Yochanan while it is Rabbi Yochanan in the name of Rabbi Shimon ben Yochai in BT Bekhorot 31b and Yalkut Shimoni 992 to the Song of Songs Chapter 7. In Yalkut Shimoni 781 to Psalm 61 that attribution reads Rabbi Yochanan in the name of Rabbi Shimon ben Levi and Song Rabbah 7:27 reads Rabbi Yochanan ben Torta. In Midrash Shmuel 19 we find the teaching in the name of Bar Nezira, which is rendered Bar Tira in PT Moed Katan 3:7 84a. As for versions of the second tradition, the names mentioned in various sources include Rabbi Yitzchak ben Zeiri or ben Zeira, Rabbi Shimon ben Zeira or Shimon Zeira, and Levi bar Zeira. Here is a source emphasizing the need for precise transmission whose own transmission is anything but an example of this practice.
15. Krochmal, *Kitvei Rabbi Nachman Krochmal*, 6.
16. For an outstanding discussion of this motif, see Naeh, "Boreh Niv Sfatayim." In "Hatefillah Hashogeret" Walfish uses the image of the scholar causing recondite sources to speak (*dovev*) in his response to Naeh's article.
17. See Bloom, *Anxiety of Influence*. Bloom's work has been the subject of great controversy. For a persuasive feminist critique, see Orr, *Intertextuality*.
18. Miner and Brady are referring here to literary language in East Asia, which, they claim, is "by definition, precedented language" (*Transmission and Authority*, x).
19. Be'er, *El Hamakom Sheharuach Holekh*, 176.

20. See Stratton, "Sampling and Jewishness."
21. Arendt, "Walter Benjamin," 38.
22. The literature on Benjamin is voluminous. The discussions of his approach to quotations and sources which I found most helpful include: Perloff, "Phantasmagorias of the Marketplace: Citational Poetics in Walter Benjamin's Arcades Project," in *Unoriginal Genius*, 24–49; Rose, "Walter Benjamin"; Sax, "Walter Benjamin's Karl Kraus"; and Sax, "Judaism, Experience." For excellent treatments of quotation and modernity, see: Knowlton, *Joyce, Joyceans* and *Rhetoric*; Sartiliot, *Citation and Modernity*; and Stern, *Quotations as Pictures* (Chapter 1).
23. For more on rupture and disruption in citation, see: Derrida, "Signature Event Context" in *Limited Inc.* 1–23; Dickinson, "Citing 'Whatever' Authority"; Garber, *Quotation Marks*.
24. Tanchuma Pinhas 3 links the teaching to Numbers 25:17 as do a number of other sources. For an example of linkage with Exodus 22:1, see Rashi to Exodus 22:1, BT Berakhot 58a, and BT Sanhedrin 72a. Deuteronomy 22:26 is also cited as a potential source of the saying.
25. BT Berakhot 58a. See also BT Berakhot 62b and BT Yoma 95b.
26. See Mishnah Hullin 12:5; Sifre Numbers 107; BT Pesachim 27b; BT Yoma 57a; BY Yebamot 25a; BT Ketubot 17a; BT Gittin 99a; BT Kiddushin 73a; BT Baba Kamma 34b; BT Baba Kamma 72b: BT Sanhedrin 9a, 25a, 27a, 72b; BT Avodah Zarah 62a; BT Zevachim 107a.
27. See, for example, *Sefer Hasidim* 45, where the behavior of David in not attacking Saul is singled out for mention despite the fact that the Torah says to kill one's putative assailants.
28. See the Derashot of ibnShu'eib to *Ki Tetze* (Cracow, 1573), 88b. See Zohar I, 138a, where an Aramaic version of the aphorism appears with the formula *taninan*, denoting a rabbinic teaching.
29. Tosafot to BT Avodah Zarah 10b. For an example of the teaching used in the context of internal spiritual struggle, see *Sefat Emet*, Balak 5661 (Jerusalem 1997), 166a.
30. For the former, see, for example, the remarks by Benjamin Netanyahu in June 2014 and repeated on other occasions according to which the Talmudic saying represents Israel's official policy: https://www.gov.il/en/pages/spokesgaza110614 (accessed April 25, 2024). For the latter, see, for example, Friedman, "Din Rodef Lemechablim!" For a classic example of the application of the general principle in the context of Israel's security, see Hayim David Halevi, *Techumin* 1 (1980), 343.
31. To cite one example, the N12 website reported on November 20, 2022, that the Kan broadcasting corporation had apologized after a caller to a radio show had justified Goldstein's acts with reference to the Talmudic principle of self-defense. See Paine, "Behind the Hebron Massacre." For

more on the use of the Talmudic principle in Israeli discourse, see Ellenson, "The Talmudic Principle."
32. A book on Israel's policy of targeted assassinations uses the Talmudic principle as its title. See Bergman, *Rise and Kill First*.
33. Shakespeare, *The Merchant of Venice*, Act 1 Scene 3.
34. Abarvanel to Zechariah 13:2.
35. Deuteronomy 6:7.
36. Deuteronomy 11:19.
37. In "Biblical Texts" Langer explores four key ways in which the Hebrew Bible is employed in rabbinic liturgy.

Open Access This chapter is licensed under the terms of the Creative Commons Attribution 4.0 International License (http://creativecommons.org/licenses/by/4.0/), which permits use, sharing, adaptation, distribution and reproduction in any medium or format, as long as you give appropriate credit to the original author(s) and the source, provide a link to the Creative Commons license and indicate if changes were made.

The images or other third party material in this chapter are included in the chapter's Creative Commons license, unless indicated otherwise in a credit line to the material. If material is not included in the chapter's Creative Commons license and your intended use is not permitted by statutory regulation or exceeds the permitted use, you will need to obtain permission directly from the copyright holder.

Hogenet: Decency and Society

In a 2019 book, the philosopher Todd May explored the concept of decency, which he situated somewhere between moral mediocrity and altruism.[1] Most current philosophical discourse about morality, he argues, fall into one of three categories: consequentialism, which focuses on the outcome of our actions; deontology, which emphasizes our intentions; and virtue ethics, which is concerned with the right way to live, namely, balancing various virtues in the spirit of Aristotelian thought. May notes that each of these kinds of moral thinking, if taken to their logical endpoints, places stringent demands on the individual. It is hard to justify the extent to which most of us prioritize our own comfort and self-fulfillment over the demands of social equity, climate justice, and animal rights. Thinkers like Peter Singer remind us that, according to the dictates of strict morality, we ought to be living according to different priorities.[2] The resources we spend treating ourselves should, in fact, be devoted to more significant purposes.

May does not suggest that these moral arguments are wrong but observes that few of us are likely to live by them. This should not imply, however, that we are devoid of a compass by which we attempt to steer our lives, and here he introduces the notion of decency. In her discussion of this topic, Elaine Sternberg differentiates what she terms "ordinary decency" from simply being nice. It consists of "fairness and honesty and refraining from coercion and physical violence, typically within the confines of the law."[3]

In this chapter, I propose a term for decency from within the classical sources of Judaism and suggest how it might be applied to the State of Israel in a morally compromised era.

Anchored in Decency

Roman historians recount that in the year 39 or 40 CE, the Emperor Caligula built a pontoon bridge across part of the Bay of Naples. Boats were anchored in a double line in the water and sand poured over them. Upon its completion, the Emperor donned a gold cloak and the breastplate of Alexander the Great and crossed the unlikely bridge on his horse.[4]

News of this account reached the Jews of Palestine[5] and clearly fueled the midrashic imagination. An ancient parable in the name of Rabbi Shimon ben Yohai reads:

> A man brought two ships, tied them to anchors [*hagunim*] and iron weights, stationed them in the middle of the sea, and built a palace upon them. As long as the two ships are tied together, the palace stands firm. Once the ships are separated, the palace cannot stand.[6]

The Caligula anecdote sheds light on what would otherwise be an obscure teaching. The Jews are called upon to leash their boats together and make common cause, not for the glorification of a human potentate with divine pretensions but rather so that a platform can be erected on the choppy waters of reality, a place in which the Divine can dwell. The midrashic reworking of Caligula's folly can also be read as a reflection on political life, striving for a degree of fixity in a sea of indeterminacy. The anchors and weights required to achieve this precarious feat include armies and taxes and realpolitik but also core values. Some heft is required to keep disparate vessels bound together.

The anchors and iron weights afford the vessels the stability they need to act as a foundation. The root *h-g-n*,[7] and sometimes *ʿa-g-n*, denotes a heavy weight, more specifically an anchor. In rabbinic Hebrew, it takes on a range of further meanings, among them balance, appropriateness, suitability, and consistency, all of which are connected in some way with the notion of being set in the right place. The root is applied to appropriate advice,[8] a suitable wife[9] or fitting suitor,[10] and a person who is up to a particular task.[11] It also has moral implications: the Talmud asks how a teacher should behave with respect to a student who is not *hagun*, namely, one who lacks integrity or piety.[12] Something not *mehugan* may be seen as unpleasant or unbecoming.[13] One Talmudic dictum holds that one who sees in another an unseemly matter, *davar she'eno hagun*, must reprimand the wrongdoer.[14]

In its various forms—*hogen, hagun, mehugan*, and more—the term occupies a semantic field relating to that which is fitting, becoming, appropriate, suited, decent. In modern Hebrew it even comes to refer to fair trade and a decent wage. A person, concept, or institution devoid of *h-g-n* may be heavy, even overbearing, but will lack gravitas and will not fit. The tannaitic midrash Sifra tells of two wealthy brothers, Lulianos and Paphos, whose Roman kidnapper assumes will be redeemed from his clutches just as Hananiah, Mishael, and Azariah were saved from the hands of Nebuchadnezzar in the Book of Daniel. In answering their captor, the brothers characterize Nebuchadnezzar as a bona fide king, *hagun,* and taunt the Roman tyrant by saying: you are not *hagun*, and no miracle will be perpetrated through you.[15]

Hebrew purists may object to linking Western terms such as fairness and decency to the Hebrew/Aramaic *h-g-n*. These purists would be wrong, however, for such a link was forged more than fifteen centuries ago. In one version of a midrash preserved in Genesis Rabbah, a Hebrew term for decency is explicitly linked with a Hellenistic concept delineating something similar. Imagining the episode in Genesis 18 where Abraham is visited by three "men" who are to predict Sarah's unlikely pregnancy, Rabbi Levi ascribes distinct ethnic appearances to each of the three: one appears as a Saracen from the East, one a Nabatean, and one an Arab. In Rabbi Levi's reconstruction of the episode, Abraham examines his three visitors to discern if their intentions are amicable or malicious:

> "If I see that the Divine Presence attends upon them, I know that they are decent (*hagunim*), and if I see that they show respect to each other, I know that they are people of virtue" (*hognosin*). As he saw them showing respect to each other, he knew them to be people of virtue.[16]

In Rabbi Levi's reading of the Abraham episode, there is a rung arguably higher than that of *hagun,* decency. It is represented by the Greek term *eugenes* (εὐγενής), implying noble birth and excellence. The two terms he employs, *hagunim* and *hognosin,* are derived from different value systems, but for the ancient rabbi, they are on the same scale, situated somewhere between basic decency and moral excellence. I read this as a deliberate blurring of the distinction between Jerusalem and Athens, between ethical discourse from both within and beyond the sources of Judaism.

Decency in Government

The expression *malkhut she'eina hogenet* is taken from the eighth chapter of Tractate Gittin in the Mishnah. It can be translated as an unworthy government, a kingdom that is not legitimate, or an inappropriate regime and features here as part of a discussion on the validity of bills of divorce. If the document shows a glaring inconsistency, its standing is brought into doubt. One such case is that of a bill of divorce written in the name of a kingdom which is not *hogenet*, meaning inappropriate, illegitimate, or unaligned.[17] Commenting on this expression, Maimonides suggests that the connotation here is a mismatch or an overreach: the king whose name is invoked does not rule in the location where the document was generated. It is as though a document read: here in Brooklyn in the reign of Queen Beatrix of the Netherlands. Something does not fit, and this renders the document suspect.

If the interpretation holds that the illegitimacy is to be found in the lack of correspondence between the claim within the text and the reality beyond it, another reading of the illegitimate kingdom suggests that there is something intrinsically worthy of reproof in the political system under discussion. "And why is it called: a kingdom that is not legitimate? Because they have neither their own script, nor their own language."[18] The Talmud, created beyond the borders of the Roman Empire, offers a critique of Roman culture as crude and derivative. The taunt seems to be: overwhelming military might and technological superiority are no guarantee of decency.

The word *hogenet* here blurs the distinction between the descriptive and the normative. It relates to the lack of correspondence between what is stated in a document and what pertains in reality and to the gulf between how a system of government ought to be and how it really is.

Some 2000 years after its first appearance, this term resonates anew in our days. For most of the intervening time, Jews have looked on at the game of thrones played by nations and empires as bystanders and commentators. Now, like it or not, we are protagonists.

Some applications of the root *h-g-n* are framed in the passive form: to be a *hagun* person is to be anchored in values and practices worthy of admiration and emulation. The form *hogenet* is all the more appropriate for my purposes here since it is couched in an active form. To be a *malkhut hogenet* is not to have achieved perfection in the conduct of society. Rather, it is to be committed to this perpetual act of anchoring. For a state or social network to be *hogenet*, it needs to be open to criticism, committed to bettering itself.

Is the State of Israel a *malkhut hogenet?* Is there a sufficient correspondence between its declared aspirations and its manifestation in reality? In the eyes of its sternest enemies, Israel is immoral by definition. For its most fervent defenders, Israel is rooted deeply in the soil of justice, and any errant weeds deserve only scant attention and occasional clearance. My uncomfortable question is aimed at those who fit into neither of these categories. As for myself, I love Israel with a passion, and for that very reason I despair daily over the prospects of it remaining, or becoming, *hogenet*. I know of no more urgent question on the agenda of contemporary Jewish life. I am not prepared to sidestep it by either assuming that Israel is a lost cause or asserting that it is a shimmering jewel of perfection.

"Decency" is usually rendered in Hebrew as *haginut*, taken from the same root as the word for anchor and its associated terms. It is a difficult notion to get excited about since it often smacks of quaint bourgeois morality or a kind of clipped mediocrity. Doing the decent thing may sometimes come at the expense of doing the morally excellent thing.[19] Rather than call for an absolute, abstract, and unattainable commitment to the Other, the dictates of decency set out plausible requirements to be fulfilled by the citizen in keeping with their social obligations.[20] Key to this concept of decency is an unwillingness to settle for the erosion of the fundamental human rights of anyone with whom one shares a civil space. Any honest assessment of even the most progressive democracies must lead to the conclusion that we do, in fact, manage to overlook the human rights of our fellows with great regularity. However, the mark of a *malkhut hogenet*, a system anchoring in decency, is that citizens can be sensitized to wrongdoing and strive to alleviate it.

Isaiah Berlin placed decency at the center of his politics and his pluralism. In a conversation held toward the end of his life, Berlin uttered these words:

> If you ask why we believe in human rights, I can say because that is the only decent, even tolerable way human beings can live with each other, and if you ask what is "decent", I can say that it is the only kind of life which we think

that humans should follow, if they are not to destroy each other. These are general truths, but this does not assume something unalterable. I can not guarantee anything against change.[21]

Berlin was not such a naïve believer in liberal democracy that he afforded it ultimate and eternal validity. He did, however, hold with a commitment to decency grounded in a recognition of human rights. It is my belief that Israel should be held to this clumsy standard of decency. Are we striving for it, and are we prepared to acknowledge when we are failing to achieve it?

This abstract term *haginut*, denoting anchored decency, was employed by Rabbi Hayyim David Halevi, Sephardic chief rabbi of Tel Aviv, in a 1985 responsum:

> The great moral to be derived by every government among the people Israel is that it possesses an obligation to conduct itself with integrity and fairness (*haginut*) towards its minorities and those who are strangers in its midst. In so doing, it will sanctify the Name of Heaven and the name of Israel in the world.[22]

This seems obvious. It seems hard to disagree with the instruction to deal decently with those with whom one shares the land. However, tiptoeing through the ideological minefield of discourse in and about Israel today, strong arguments against this version of decency are made. Three of them, mutually exclusive, have particular force. The first claims that by any plausible standard, Israel *is* decent and that failure to acknowledge this betrays the true murky agenda of those offering the criticism. The second acknowledges that aspects of Israel's behavior fail to live up to these standards because decency is an unaffordable luxury in the quest for survival. Responding to one of the greatest indecencies in human history, Jews have had to decide to abandon a strategy of relying on the kindness of strangers and adopt in its place a posture of robust self-reliance. The third condemns Israel as a fundamentally immoral enterprise: any gestures of "decency" are futile at best, and cynical at worst. On this account, structural inequality and systematized injustice cannot be alleviated by cosmetic adjustments.[23]

Jerusalem, City of Decency?

If these positions are conclusions based on grappling and research, if they emerge as a result of facing up rather than doubling down, I respect them even when I disagree with them. But even for the deniers, the excusers, and the Cassandras, the *hogenet* question ought to be relevant: what needs to happen in order for Israel to be a decent society? Scant consolation is offered by the fact that many societies around the world struggle to live up to this expectation. Even the fact that Israel has all too real security concerns and that its annihilation is wished for and planned for by some key actors in the Middle East should not exempt us from this discussion. I was writing this book in October 2023, and the war unleashed is still raging as I continue to write. The atrocity at its start and the catastrophic loss of life and displacement which has ensued make the conversation acutely difficult and particularly urgent. Rarely have the prospects for basic decency seemed so bleak.

The test case I want to mention regarding the prospects for Israel to qualify by its own criteria as a *malkhut hogenet* is not Gaza or the West Bank nor any of the other of those more regular challenges to decency, such as the poverty gap or our attitude to asylum seekers. Instead, I have chosen an example even closer to home.

Jerusalem is my home. I chose it from among all zip codes, and the thought of living anywhere else induces in me melancholy and panic. On any given day, a Jewish Studies faculty of the highest caliber could be assembled from the clientele of a host of coffee houses around the city. Torah is taught here in seventy languages and accents. Religious traditions from Ethiopia to Estonia can be discovered here. I love Jerusalem's alleys and its nooks, its follies and its books.

I will match this protestation of love with a condemnation of a moral stain at Jerusalem's heart. I am not suggesting that Jerusalem be judged by some abstracted and unattainable standard of moral purity. Such a stringent embrace, holding Jerusalem close while holding it to the highest of expectations, has characterized some of the greatest of the biblical prophets:

> Ah, Jerusalem has stumbled,
> And Judah has fallen,
> Because by word and deed
> They insult Adonai,

Defying His majestic glance.
Their partiality in judgment accuses them
They avow their sins like Sodom,
They do not conceal them.
Woe to them! For ill
Have they served themselves. (Isaiah 3:8–9)

Why is this people—Jerusalem—rebellious
With a persistent rebellion?
They cling to deceit,
They refuse to return.
I have listened and heard:
They do not speak honestly.
No one regrets his wickedness
And says, "What have I done!"
They all persist in their wayward course
Like a steed dashing forward in the fray. (Jeremiah 8:5–6)

It is not that Jerusalem is polluted or overrun by cars or sets up numerous stumbling blocks before the blind, the old, and the users of wheelchairs. All this is true, but such indignities are common in many of the great cities of the world. All this is to be regretted and resisted, but it places Jerusalem within the pale, not beyond it. If Jerusalem were only as unjust as Paris and London, as Washington DC and Stockholm, it would be replete with economic disparity and rank unfairness; the situation would be grave but unremarkable.

Some forty percent of Jerusalem's residents live in limbo. Palestinian Jerusalemites pay municipal rates and have the notional right to vote in city elections. The overwhelming majority of them are not citizens of Israel and do not vote in national elections. While significant financial resources have been allocated by the municipality and the state in order to ameliorate the conditions of Jerusalem's Palestinian residents, there is still a glaring disparity in the infrastructure provided. Land, a commodity more precious than cash, is not made available to allow residents of Palestinian neighborhoods to expand naturally and safely. An East Jerusalem resident found to have left the city risks losing their citizenship rights. The security wall constructed in the early 2000s has only rendered the situation yet more complicated, since it does not precisely follow the contours of the city limits, and there are now a couple of neighborhoods which, for lack of alternatives, have seen rapid, unsafe, and uncontrolled expansion. Tens of thousands of Palestinian residents of Jerusalem/Al Quds live in low-quality, high-risk high-rises in the heart of an earthquake zone without most of the municipal services for which they still pay rates.[24] During some months in 2024, residents of Kafr Aqab, one such neighborhood, have had to make do with twelve hours of water per week.[25] They pay municipal fees like I do.

This is an offense against decency. A city whose inhabitants are not afforded fundamental civil rights should not be held up as a shining example of unity and a foreshadowing of redemption. The reasons given for the status quo are many and varied: some compelling, some outdated, and some disingenuous. No observer of Jerusalem will tell you that the issues are all easily resolved. A growing number of Jewish Israelis are happy to keep their fellow Jerusalemites disenfranchised, and there are some (represented and legitimized in Israel's parliament) who would be happy to see these hundreds of thousands of neighbors gone from the city. Many excellent initiatives and individuals work every day to make Jerusalem more decent. Many others seek to unravel whatever decency it may currently possess.

The most pervasive rationalization of the anomalies of Jerusalem concerns temporary measures taken in the immediate aftermath of the 1967 war before most of the city's residents were born. The temporary has been made permanent, and, over time, high walls have been built, made of concrete, fear, ignorance, and prejudice. East Jerusalem residents are caught in an apparently endless anomaly.[26]

I could understand a *malkhut hogenet* which said to Jerusalem's Palestinian population: we are so intent on having a Jewish majority here that we want you to have a state of your own and we will come up with some sophisticated way of sharing sovereignty. I could understand a *malkhut hogenet* saying: we want all of you to be Israeli citizens, to enjoy the same rights, and to fulfill the same responsibilities as the Jews who live here. I find it increasingly difficult to see Israel as a *malkhut hogenet* when it intends to turn a temporary status into a permanent reality, perhaps with a few more playgrounds and a marginally improved sewage system for a few underprivileged areas.

Isaiah (1:26) predicted that the day would come when Jerusalem would be called "place of justice, faithful city." In order to realize Isaiah's prophecy, it will be necessary to pay attention to Isaiah Berlin and to anchor the city's policies and the allocation of its resources in keeping with the dictates of decency. When each group focuses on its own umbrage, rehearses its own grievances, and renders the immediate other invisible, the prophecy recedes. The State of Israel has to use its power to promote the fundamental humanity and equality of all over whom it claims authority. Anything less than this is indecent.

The *Aspaklaria* of Decency

Seen abstractly through the *aspaklaria* of morality, the notion of a *malkhut hogenet* is hardly a lofty ideal. It sets the bar low. Through the *aspaklaria* of current reality, with existential fears unaddressed and fundamental questions unresolved, striving for a decent society is perhaps as much as could plausibly be expected. For the decades awaiting Jews and Arabs in Israel and Palestine, the *aspaklaria* of decency may prove to be more useful than the prism of abstract moral excellence.

I do not pretend to know the answers to intractable questions. I am willing to be told where my own perspective is faulty. I can already hear the counterarguments, reminding me of all our trauma and justification and heroism. I am bemused when critics of a human rights agenda accuse its proponents of lacking Zionist fervor or Jewish legitimacy. I am mustering all the Zionist fervor and Jewish legitimacy I can find to say: we have to address fundamental questions of decency or we will lose our way.

This chapter has skirted round the biggest geopolitical questions relating to Israel and the Middle East. I am convinced that Israel's occupation of territories since 1967, now weighed down with anchors of inertia and vested interest, is a profound error and an existential risk. But my suggestion that *hogenet* be introduced into a contemporary Jewish lexicon is directed at those who hold very different views from my own. I hope that any fair-minded person would agree that our Palestinian neighbors must be allowed to live, vote, move about, and express themselves with at least as much dignity and security as that which is afforded to us. That needs to be an anchoring conviction. We can disagree about how we get there and fight about the details. To our shame, increasing numbers of Jewish Israelis, caught up in the local version of a global wave of populism, seem to be comfortable with an institutionalized trampling of fundamental rights. They are Caligula's heirs. Unless the rest of us resist this bigotry and uphold a sense of fundamental decency, we forfeit the possibility of constructing an improbable bridge. Our aim is not the vanity project of a deranged emperor, but a sacred platform.

Notes

1. May, *A Decent Life*. For another important discussion of this concept, see Margalit, *The Decent Society*.
2. For an early articulation of Singer's position, see Singer, "Famine, Affluence, and Morality." In "Peter Singer," Greenway considers Singer's stance on animal liberation through the prism of the thought of Emmanuel Levinas.
3. Sternberg, *Just Business*, 82.
4. For a survey of the ancient accounts, see Barrett, *Caligula*, particularly 211–213, and also Reese, "Roman Emperor Caligula."
5. Josephus recounts a version of the event, without the details of the boats but with an explicit commentary that this exemplifies the Emperor's delusional self-deification.
6. *Sifre* to Deuteronomy 346. It seems quite likely that the source of this bizarre image is the account recorded by Dio and Suetonius.
7. See Ezekiel 42.12 for a biblical usage based on this root which may be linked, although some commentators connect the word to defense (*h-g-n*) or to playing music (*n-g-n*). See also Ruth 1.13 for the sole usage of a verb whose root is '*a-g-n*. The meaning there would appear to be connected to the idea of restraint. The word *ogen* appears to have made its way into the Hebrew language from Greek, so it is unclear if these biblical usages speak to an early common root or are simply coincidental.
8. For the term *eitzah hogenet lo*, meaning some counsel suited to a person, see BT Yebamot 44a, 101b, and 106b and Sanhedrin 49b.
9. BT Baba Kama 80a. For the usage of *isha she'eina hogenet* for an unsuitable wife in the Babylonian Talmud, see also BT Yebamot 99b and 100a, Ketubot 28b, Kiddushin 70a-b, and Niddah 70b.
10. BT Ketubot 22a.
11. Esther Rabbah 5.4.
12. BT Hullin 133a. See also BT Yoma 38a and Gesundheit, "Rav Utalmid She'einam Hagunim."
13. See BT Ta'anit 22b, where it is recounted that Jeremiah saw the lips of King Josiah moving on his deathbed and thought that perhaps the king was saying something not *mehagna* (an Aramaic form of our root), meaning here something improper or inappropriate.
14. BT Berakhot 31b.
15. Sifra Emor 9.5. For a discussion of the laws relating to students and teachers deemed not to be *hogen*, where the term implies moral probity, see Gesundheit, "Rav Utalmid She'einam Hagunim."
16. Genesis Rabbah 48.2, Theodor-Albeck edition, 486.

17. See Bigman, "Katav Leshem."
18. BT Gittin 80a. To understand the provenance of this curious criticism of Rome, see also BT Avodah Zarah 10a.
19. For a discussion of the way in which settling for the decent may blunt the full force of one's moral obligation to the Other, as Levinas saw it, see Cohen, "The Movement from Ethics." In "Judaism and Revolution" (Levinas, *Nine Talmudic Readings*, 94–119), Levinas quotes a Mishnah (Baba Metzia 7:1), in which Rabbi Yochanan ben Matya insists that his son specify the conditions of laborers' employment because without such stipulation there is no limit to what is owed to a fellow Jew. For Levinas, this anecdote surfaces an ethical discussion of the greatest significance. By not stipulating a limit to the commitment to the workers, Rabbi Yochanan's son is exposed to the limitless debt owed to other human beings (for the Mishnah, the Jews, descendants of the patriarchs; for Levinas, any descendant of Adam). His father instructs him to specify that this boundless debt is to be replaced by the more limited requirement to pay a minimum wage. Reflecting on this episode through his philosophical lens, Levinas notes that adherence to the law masks the true limitless obligation of each person to each Other. In this way, decent behavior tames the full force of the other's moral claim upon us.
20. For a presentation of the thesis that bourgeois decency is one of the underpinnings of modernity, see McCloskey, *Bourgeois Dignity*.
21. Quoted in Riley, "Isaiah Berlin's Minimum," 72.
22. Ellenson, "Jewish Legal Interpretation," 20.
23. See Marmur and Ellenson, *American Jewish Thought*, 185–211, for brief excerpts from thinkers covering a broad range of positions on the fundamental legitimacy of Israel. The thinkers included are Irving Greenberg, Marc Ellis, Judith Butler, Ruth Wisse, Daniel Gordis, Daniel and Jonathan Boyarin, Peter Beinart, and the editors of *Commentary*.
24. For background on East Jerusalem, see materials available online from the Jerusalem Institute of Policy Research and Hason, *Urshalim*.
25. https://www.english.acri.org.il/post/water-supply-in-the-kfar-aqab-neighborhood-in-jerusalem
26. See Amir, "On the Border" and Hason, *Urshalim*.

Open Access This chapter is licensed under the terms of the Creative Commons Attribution 4.0 International License (http://creativecommons.org/licenses/by/4.0/), which permits use, sharing, adaptation, distribution and reproduction in any medium or format, as long as you give appropriate credit to the original author(s) and the source, provide a link to the Creative Commons license and indicate if changes were made.

The images or other third party material in this chapter are included in the chapter's Creative Commons license, unless indicated otherwise in a credit line to the material. If material is not included in the chapter's Creative Commons license and your intended use is not permitted by statutory regulation or exceeds the permitted use, you will need to obtain permission directly from the copyright holder.

Vegoralenu: Peoplehood and Chosenness

For millennia, chosenness has been both a touchstone of Jewish identity and a touch paper igniting controversy and peril. Demanding honest appraisal and serious grappling rather than bland apologetics, the concept touches upon the meaning and purpose of Jewish existence and has been described as both a scandal and a linchpin.

Scandal

The claim that God chose the Jewish people and afforded them a special standing is a scandal. A *skandalon* in the original Greek sense means a snare, a trap, or a stumbling block.[1] Ever since the thorough dismantling of the concept of Jewish Election propounded by Spinoza, modern Jews have struggled to make sense of the idea that of all the peoples of the world, God picked out the Jews, bestowing them with particular qualities or certain responsibilities which set them apart from the rest of humanity.[2] The assumptions about God, humanity, law, and nature inherent in this doctrine are scandalous, and Jewish thinkers have been stumbling over them for centuries.

In the third chapter of his *Tractatus Theologico-Politicus* of 1670, Spinoza asserts that people should enjoy the blessings bestowed upon them without recourse to the base notion that such blessings are inaccessible to others. He argues that these verses and others cannot be understood literally:

For you are a people consecrated to the Lord your God: of all the people on earth the Lord your God chose you to be God's treasured people (*am segulah*). It is not because you are the most numerous of peoples that Lord set his heart on you and chose you – indeed you are the smallest of peoples; but it was because the Lord favored you. (Deuteronomy 7:6–8)³

He suggests that the verses in Deuteronomy claiming an exalted status for the Jews can only be understood in terms of the rhetorical impact they are designed to have on their audience and not as statements of philosophical truth.

Ethics, politics, history, legal theory, group psychology, and theology are all combined in Spinoza's attempt to dismantle chosenness. In his view, to suggest that God has favorites is to misunderstand the meaning of God, since God is equivalent to nature and not a supernatural deity with preferences. Jews are no more intelligent or talented than anyone else, and divine favor can only be understood as a synonym for accidents of nature which once benefited them. Spinoza attributes the persistence of the Jews long after their fall from political power to a combination of the external pressure of Jew hatred and the internal impact of rituals.⁴ In a comment which was to attain particular significance in the twentieth century, Spinoza accepts (perhaps more in sarcasm than in earnest) that the Hebrews may yet achieve sovereignty in the future, which would mean they were elected by God once more. To be chosen means no more and no less than to thrive.⁵

Modern Jews committed to Jewish continuity have had to come up with responses to the scandal of chosenness. Some accepted much of Spinoza's critique.⁶ Mordecai Kaplan, for example, asserted plainly: "The idea of Israel as the chosen people must … be understood as belonging to a thought-world we no longer inhabit."⁷ Judith Plaskow also condemned the doctrine of Jewish Election, noting that feminist objections to the doctrine "center not just on its entanglement with external hierarchical differentiations but with internal hierarchies as well."⁸

If the Jews were not chosen, what raison d'être can be adduced for Jewish continuity? In Plaskow's view,

> Jewishness is a rich and distinctive way of being human, of linking oneself with God and other people, of finding a pattern within which to live that gives life depth and meaning. That is enough reason to be a Jew.⁹

She argued that we will have to wean ourselves off the idea of Jewish Election and settle instead for the intrinsic beauty and worth of being Jewish. Significantly, however, both Kaplan and Plaskow suggested replacement concepts for chosenness: for the former it is "distinctness,"[10] and for the latter it is "vocation."[11] It would appear that this stumbling block cannot be easily removed, even by those keen to do so.[12] How can the persistence of this scandalous doctrine be explained?

Linchpin

The election of Israel is a linchpin concept, holding together several key elements of Jewish self-understanding.[13] It provides a religious dimension to the peoplehood aspect of Judaism and a national dimension to the religious aspect. Some major thinkers have sought to downplay the centrality of the concept, but none can avoid its lure and its challenge.[14] The authors of the following three statements represent Modern Orthodox, Conservative, and Reform worldviews, but readers may be hard-pressed to discern the ideological provenance of each of these remarks:

> It is this belief, perhaps above all else, which sustained Jewish communities through the hardships of exile, persecution, and pogrom. And it may still.[15]
>
> The central point of Jewish theology and the key to an understanding of the nature of Judaism is the doctrine, "God chose Israel as His people."[16]
>
> The essence of Judaism is the affirmation that the Jews are the chosen people; all else is commentary.[17]

Philosophers may have interpreted it in widely different and even contradictory ways,[18] but before the watershed of modernity (and after it too for those who ignore it), a consciousness of being chosen was a linchpin of Jewish identity for most Jews throughout history. Even after Spinoza, despite severe challenges to the concept, it continues to exercise a significant hold on committed Jews of all stripes[19]:

> The "chosenness" of Israel, whether believed in or not, is an inescapable fact for the Jew. He cannot think or live as a Jew without in some way implying it. For better or for worse, it confronts him as a destiny which he cannot escape because he cannot escape himself and his history.[20]

To assert that chosenness is central and inescapable is not to fix its meaning. Indeed, its endurance is in part due to the fact that it has been understood in different ways. Each of them has looked to the concept's biblical roots for their inspiration, but these roots are sufficiently tangled and contested to provide a basis for a wide range of responses.[21]

One such response is a covenant-based, Torah-centered reading, according to which we are chosen to take on the yoke of the commandments. Adopted and adapted by ancient sages and by medieval thinkers of the stature of Saadia Gaon and Maimonides, such a position emphasizes the conditional nature of Election: to be so chosen is a yoke not a free pass or a hollow epithet.[22]

Judah Halevi is associated with a contrasting theory which attributes some innate qualities to the Jewish people as a collective that dictate a fundamental difference of order between the Jews and everyone else.[23] A thousand years later, Michael Wyschogrod offered an "embodied" theological reading according to which "God chose a carnal people, whose physical being in the world is a sign of existence of God."[24] The reasons for this divine choice are mysterious, but some attempts at theological and philosophical explanation have been undertaken.[25] Franz Rosenzweig understood chosenness as "constitutive both of human individuality and of Jewish existence."[26] His complex thought is situated between the non-rationalist position of Halevi on the one hand and the messianic universalism of Hermann Cohen on the other.

Cohen was one of the most articulate exponents of the theology of chosenness which has come to typify classical Reform Judaism: the Mission of Israel. A stern critic of Spinoza's reading of the Jewish condition,[27] Cohen argued that it was not a particular teaching which the Jews are charged with imparting but the very possibility of religion itself: "For the establishment of religion the people of Israel was necessary. That is what it means for Israel to be the chosen people."[28]

Many liberal Jews have understood Jewish existence in terms of some redemptive mission whereby the Jews bring a universal message to humanity.[29] The advantage of such a view in a modern context is clear. The stain of chauvinism is removed, and a defining purpose for Jewish particularity is propounded: the Jews have been chosen "to be His servant, the bearers of the highest knowledge of Him and of His way of life for mankind, unto all nations and peoples and throughout all time."[30]

Opponents of the Mission ideal argue that it misrepresents the premodern Jewish experience, encourages a sense of inflated self-importance, and fails to offer something more inspiring than a "dim cloud of general philanthropy and universalism,"[31] incapable in itself of engendering thick Jewish engagement. Such objections notwithstanding, the notion that Jews have been charged with bringing ethical monotheism to the world has remained powerful and evocative.

Another popular modern version of the classical idea is an inversion, seeing the Jews as choosing rather than being chosen. Like many notions dismissed as fanciful or foreign to Jewish tradition, its roots can be traced to that very tradition in such sources as *Sifre* to Deuteronomy 312 which, commenting on a grammatical ambiguity in Psalms 135:4, states: "we do not know whether it is God who has chosen Israel or it is Israel who has chosen God." After Spinoza, placing the emphasis on human initiative rather than mysterious divine preference sounds palatable and defensible. It moves the emphasis from some essential quality of the Jews to a historical characteristic and ethical condition: God may not have favorites, but the story of the Jews can be read as a choice on their part.

In a modern context, it is tempting to argue that "the election of Israel does not preclude the election of others."[32] Indeed, some of the most compelling treatments of chosenness in recent years have explored the possibility that "instead of being *the* chosen people, my people begin to see themselves as *a* chosen people."[33] Positions such as these make a version of the doctrine compatible with what seems humble, sensible, and constructive. Nonetheless, the "all are chosen" stance can be criticized both logically (if all are chosen, then none are) and historically: in Leo Baeck's view, for example, election "primarily expresses a historical fact: there was assigned to this people a peculiar position in the world by which it is distinguished from all other peoples."[34] Lest it be thought that only modern pluralists would countenance the idea that Israel's election is non-exclusive, it is worth noting the remarkable passage in Isaiah 19 in which the prophet looks forward to the day in which Israel will be part of a triad of nations, which God will bless, saying (verse 25): "Blessed be Egypt my people, Assyria my handiwork, and Israel my inheritance."[35]

These are just a few of the strategies which have been employed to understand what to do with the idea that the Jews are chosen, ranging from biological essentialism to universalizing evangelism. These and other ideas have been tessellated in various ways in the thought of Jews unable to avoid this tricky yet central topic.[36]

The People of Adaptation

Segulah, the biblical word at the heart of Jewish understandings of chosenness, is difficult to translate and bears several meanings.[37] One of them relates to a later Hebrew word, *histaglut*, which means "adaptation." The *am segulah*, the special or treasured nation, is a people that adapts to changing realities. Such a principle certainly applies to the doctrine of election, which has been understood differently through changing eras and circumstances.[38]

Three trends demand particular attention in the quest for a new understanding of chosenness. The first relates to peoplehood, a twentieth-century term which in the twenty-first century has become increasingly contested and attenuated in non-Orthodox circles.[39] The second, the rise of Jews to prominence and affluence in many parts of the Diaspora, and the third, the impact of the establishment of the Jewish state, both concern changes in the status of the Jews in the world in recent decades. Together, these trends have changed not only the mood of Jewish discourse about the concept of chosenness but also its moral boundaries.

The third trend, the impact of sovereignty, has implications which are only beginning to be realized. The conclusion of some is that Jews should prefer their anomalous chosen status over the banal trappings and traps of power.[40] This argument is made forcefully by Daniel Boyarin, who asserts that "to preserve the positive ethical, political value of Jewish genealogy as a mode of identity, Jews must preserve their subaltern status."[41] Before Jews had power over others, he argues, the discriminatory potential always inherent in the idea of election lay dormant. To believe that as a Jew one belongs to an elect elite is excusable as a survival technique employed by a disadvantaged minority. To elevate this belief to the level of a militant ideology when in possession of military might is a different proposition altogether.

There is an urgent need for concepts of chosenness to be adapted in light of these new realities. Failure to make these adaptations is fraught with danger. A version of Jewish election is currently being deployed in the service of a destructive theopolitics in Israel.[42] Combine Judah Halevi with kabbalistic and Hasidic theories about the intrinsic distinction between the Jew and the Other, add an army, an economy, and a narrative of David and Goliath, and you have a cocktail both intoxicating and lethal. Mordecai Kaplan feared this possibility in 1949 when he wrote that *"Judaism can certainly not afford to harbor any doctrine which is in conflict with the ethical basis of democracy.*"⁴³ Martin Buber spoke against this possibility in 1921, predicting that election may be forfeited if Israel boasts about it rather than striving to live up to the challenge of being chosen, and again in 1936, when he said:

> Israel is only chosen when it is not certain that it is chosen. But if it is certain that it has been chosen, it is famous for itself, does it benefit itself from that the fact that it has been chosen, it now thinks that it has some security and security that it has been chosen, then it is not chosen.⁴⁴

None of this would be relevant if all of us in Israel were like some idealized caricature: sensitive but strong, peace-loving but fierce, patriotic but humanistic. The reality is inevitably far more complex either than this or than its demonic negative impression. In too many cases the basic humanity of the other is forgotten, obscured, or denied. The people of adaptation are in urgent need of a way of connecting passionate particularity with human solidarity. The dramatic events which have engulfed Israel ever since the Nation-State Law in 2018 have led me to wonder whether Spinoza may have had it wrong: chosenness may only make sense when it is not allied with far-reaching military might and political agency. In view of the ways in which the concept is so often corrupted and used as fuel for bigotry, the concerns of Kaplan, Buber, and Plaskow resonate stronger than ever.

The idea that the Jews are chosen is a scandal, but it is also a linchpin. Is there some way of maintaining the concept while maintaining fundamental human values?

Vav

The letter *vav* plays a versatile role in the Hebrew language. When placed at the head of a word, for example, its function can be conjunctive, indicating "and" or "and then." In other cases, the *vav* is disjunctive, expressing a contrast between one clause and another.⁴⁵ The humble *vav* can thus denote both connection and distinction.⁴⁶

In the *Aleinu* prayer, which concludes every service, there are two paragraphs that shift from the particular to the universal. In the first paragraph, we say that it is incumbent upon us to praise the Lord of All and give honor to the Creator⁴⁷: "Who has not made us like the peoples of other lands, nor placed us like the families of the earth. Who has not made our portion like theirs, our fate like all the rest (*goralenu kechol hamonam*)." This prayer constitutes a robust assertion of distinct identity—so robust that the sections in which the faith of other nations is derided were censored in Christian Europe in the Middle Ages.[48] The second paragraph goes on to speak of a future time in which God's name will be one and the world redeemed, and the two paragraphs can be read together in the spirit of many Jewish theologies of chosenness: eventually, they argue, in some messianic future, the particularities of God's choice of Israel will redound to the benefit of all humanity.

In non-Orthodox circles, various alternatives to the traditional prayer have been offered in order to remove any whiff of triumphalism and stain of bigotry, and it is here, in the sentence of the prayer I have quoted above, that simple letter *vav* comes into play. It may be read, conjunctively, to mean not that God has made our fate separate from all others but rather that, despite all the differences, in the end, *goralenu kechol hamonam*, our fate is their fate. Read disjunctively, the *vav* suggests, in my interpretation, that we ought to praise God for the fact that we have been born into or chosen to take on a distinct path in the world, one with its own contours and challenges. All this is possible and necessary and good so long as we remember that our fate is that of all other people. We share common humanity, the same crowded planet, the same fundamental striving for security and fulfillment. We look to Abraham and Sarah our particular ancestors and through them to Adam and Eve, our shared progenitors.

Jews have long reflected on the nature of their distinction from other nations. This distinction has been warranted by theology and bolstered by history. The perpetual (and understandable) Jewish concern with survival has obscured an equally important truth: that Judaism offers a "vision of a universal fate and faith for all humanity."[49] Distinctness need not necessarily imply superiority. In Ruth Sandberg's formulation, "the goal is not for all humanity to be united in an undifferentiated homogenization without ethnic or religious differences. Inclusive universality ... sees each distinct people or community as inherently worthy."[50]

I believe that there is an urgent need for an expression of the Jewish specificity I embrace and the wider reality of which I am a part—our world, thrown off kilter by abuse and neglect, our shared humanity. There have been noble attempts to claim that the belief in a special connection between God and the Jews has no bearing on God's connection to anyone else.[51] Many of the thinkers mentioned in this chapter have posited some connection between our own unique identity and our commitment to a wider redemptive process.

The new reality of Jewish sovereignty calls for a more urgent and more explicit statement of these core convictions. To continue to repeat the narrative of chosenness as if we were an oppressed minority provides the groundwork for groundless discrimination, bigotry, and chauvinism. It makes us less worthy to be *am segulah*, a people whose self-understanding adapts as circumstances change.

Chosenness is about love, but I cannot accept those theologies, old and new, that seek to ascribe this love to a discriminating God. Instead, chosenness tells the story of our love—for the life of Torah, for the language of Jewish creativity, for a people and its extraordinary history, for the God we seek even in doubt. The election of Israel should point to empathy and solidarity with all people, all of whose fate and humanity we share. Any contemporary iteration of a chosen people theology which is used to justify acts of inhumanity has to be resisted with vigor.

Being Jewish is the *aspaklaria* by which I see the world, a multivocal and multifocal prism. I thank God every day for choosing us along with other peoples, for the dignity inherent in difference, for the distinctness of our constantly changing tradition, for providing us with ways—should we choose to explore them—by which our specificity can be a hyphen leading us to a sense of universal empathy and solidarity. I do not believe that the redemptive happy end can be achieved by skipping particular, embodied, thick ways of responding to God's call. And even if this were possible, I choose not to skip that specificity which is our life and the measure of our days.[52]

Theories of innate superiority may once have been understandable but are now unconscionable. However, dismantling specificity in all its varied permutations for the sake of a homogenized pudding of identity-in-general holds no attraction. Life in the coming decades is bound to be hyphenated as scraps of our identity are sewn into bespoke raiments, and each person works out for themselves who they choose to be in the world. I know of no finer hyphen than the *vav*, offering flexible connections between ancient beliefs and practices and contemporary responses. The *vav* which can be employed to keep us distinct from others is also the link that binds us to all others. Our particular selves are linked to the world at large by a fragile yet crucial link: the *vav*—an uncommon articulation of a common humanity.

Notes

1. For *skandalon*, see Schonfeld, "Shichchi Elohim," 351. In "Spinoza's Election," Geller describes Jewish persistence as a *skandalon*, which he translates as "stumbling block," 43. See also Herberg, "The 'Chosenness' of Israel," where he sardonically describes the doctrine as representing "a scandal and an offence" for moderns (280). Lévy, *Genius of Judaism*, describes "election" as "that scandalous, almost scabrous word on which, since Jews have been Jews, their misunderstanding with the nations hangs," 115. See also Wyschogrod, *The Body of Faith*, 176.
2. Jacobs, *God, Torah, Israel* (58f), makes a helpful distinction between qualitative and associative versions of the doctrine of election.
3. For other classic sources regarding the status of Israel in the Hebrew Bible, see: Exodus 19:3; Deuteronomy 14:2, 26:17–19; Joshua 24:22; Isaiah 43:10; and Amos 3:2.
4. See Yerushalmi, "Spinoza on the Survival."
5. For a fascinating discussion on the reception of this passage, see Geller, "Spinoza's Election." See also Harvey, "Spinoza's Counterfactual Zionism," which argues that Zionist readers from Moses Hess on failed to appreciate the sarcasm of Spinoza's remark. See also Harvey, "Idel on Spinoza." In Abraham Abulafia's *Mafteach Hara'ayon* (included in his *Sefer Hacheshek*, Jerusalem 2002, 43), the thirteenth-century kabbalist declares that the Hebrew term for nature is choice. This comment is a foreshadowing of at least one aspect of Spinoza's argument by four centuries.
6. See Wiese, "Most Powerful Comrade," in which the rejectionist position of Samuel Holdheim is contrasted with the stance of David Einhorn, who, like most Reform Jews, continued to find meaning in a modified version of the concept of election, translated into the language of mission.
7. Kaplan, *Future of the American Jew*, 211.
8. Plaskow, *Standing Again at Sinai*, 101.
9. Ibid., 103.
10. "What must replace chosenness … as the model for Jewish self-understanding is the far less dramatic 'distinctness'" (ibid., 105).
11. Kaplan, "The place previously occupied previously occupied in the Jewish consciousness by the doctrine of election will have to be fulfilled by doctrine of vocation" (*Future of the American Jew*, 229).
12. In *The Chosen People*, 73–98, Eisen offers a detailed and brilliant account of Kaplan's idea of vocation and its failure to gain traction in American Jewish thought, noting that most "chose to reconstruct the belief rather than reject it," 96. In *We Are Not Alone*, 54–62, Kellner argues that Kaplan—along with Isaac Deutscher and George Steiner—did not in fact

reject the concept but, surprisingly, "each answered with a variant of the old notion of the Jews as the chosen people," 54.
13. See Amir, "Gishot Laraayon Bechirat Yisrael," 275, for an argument that it is a linchpin concept insofar as it exposes the poverty of the usual terminology according to which Judaism is either a religious or a national category. These two spheres are unavoidably linked, and the concept of chosenness makes this apparent. A number of commentators have argued for the centrality of the chosen people concept. In *Humanity Divided*, Oliveira asserts that "it is staggering to realize how central the concept of chosenness is to Jewish self-assertion and identity," 12.
14. See Kellner, *Maimonides on Judaism*, particularly 81–95.
15. Soloveichik, "God's Beloved," 81.
16. Kohler, *Jewish Theology*, 323.
17. Arthur Hertzberg in *Condition of Jewish Belief*, 90. See also Oliveira, *Humanity Divided*, 12.
18. For a survey of the approaches of fifteen thinkers from the tenth to the twentieth centuries to this topic, see Kasher, *Elyon Al Kol Hagoyim*. For in-depth studies of some of these approaches, see: Eisen, *Gersonides on Provenance*; Kellner, "Chosenness, Not Chauvinism"; Hollander, *Exemplarity and Chosenness*; and Krinis, *God's Chosen People*.
19. In a *Commentary* symposium from 1966 (*The Condition of Jewish Belief*) the editors formulated five questions to which participants were invited to respond. The second of these was: "In what sense do you believe that the Jews are the chosen people of God? How do you answer the charge that this doctrine is the model from which various natural theories of national and racial superiority have derived?" 7.
20. Herberg, "The 'Chosenness' of Israel," 283.
21. For some outstanding explorations of chosenness in the Bible, see: Buber, "The Election of Israel"; Frymer-Kensky, "Biblical Voices on Chosenness"; Kaminsky, *Yet I Loved Jacob*, which prefaces a more conventional discussion with an analysis of rivalry stories in Genesis; Knohl, "The Election and Sanctity"; and Levenson, "Chosenness and Its Enemies," "Miscategorizing Chosenness," and "The Universal Horizon." See also Novak, *The Election of Israel*, 108–162. For chosenness in the Second Temple and Rabbinic periods, see Kaminsky, "New Testament and Rabbinic" and Simkovich, *The Making of Jewish Universalism*. See also Atlan, "Chosen People" and Kellner, *We Are Not Alone*, 42–67.
22. Abraham Joshua Heschel wrote very little on the theme of chosenness, but in one rare foray, in 1965 he published a piece in the Israeli newspaper *Ma'ariv* (Heschel, "Lo Toar Ela Ol"), the title of which declares that to be called the Chosen People is not a description but a yoke.

23. In *God's Chosen People*, Krinis exposes Halevi's reliance on Shi'i Imam doctrine and places his theory in a wider Jewish context, arguing that the *Kuzari* frames the idea "in a completely different manner from its traditional framing in the biblical and Talmudic literature," 243. That said, Krinis does note that there are precedents in rabbinical literature which can be seen as consonant with Halevi's reading. Abraham Geiger also entertains notions of the Jews' distinct national genius. See, for example, Geiger, *Judaism and Its History*, 60.
24. Wyschogrod, *The Body of Faith*, 177.
25. See Batnitsky, "Election and Affection" and Gellman, *God's Kindness*, and, for a brief outline of some of the key arguments of that important book, see "Jewish Chosenness."
26. Hollander, *Exemplarity and Chosenness*, 3.
27. See Cohen, *Spinoza on State*, for example, 27, where Cohen upbraids Spinoza for failing to appreciate the significance of God's call to Abraham to be a blessing.
28. Cohen, *Religion of Reason*, 363.
29. See Maybaum, *The Jewish Mission*, particularly 155–164. See also Eisen, *The Chosen People*, particularly 67–72.
30. Julian Morgenstern in 1945, quoted in Eisen, *The Chosen People*, 54.
31. Arendt, *The Origins of Totalitarianism*, 200. In "Transvaluation of Values," Ahad Ha'am asserted that Mission "has no foundation in actuality, and rests entirely on a metaphysical dogma … the Jewish people as a whole has always interpreted its 'mission' simply as the performance of its own duties, without regard to the external world, and has regarded its election … as the end of all else, and not as a means to the happiness of the rest of the world," 113. See Oliveira, *Humanity Divided*, particularly 365–374, and Ramon, "Tziyonut Tarbutit Kechalufa Lareforma." In *Judaism, Human Values*, Leibowitz also rejected the Mission ideal, stating that "the idea that the people of Israel has been endowed with a capacity for instructing and guiding all of humanity has no basis in authentic Jewish sources, and played no role—at least no more than a marginal one—in the consciousness of generations of Jews who assumed the yoke of the Kingdom of Heaven in the form of the yoke of Torah and Mitzvoth," 115.
32. Plaut, *Case for the Chosen People*, 145. See Immanuel Jakobovits' response in *The Condition of Jewish* Belief, 111–112.
33. Kogan, *Opening the Covenant*, 241. In *The Dignity of Difference*, Sacks offers a brilliant reframing of the chosenness idea in terms of current debates about shared society.
34. Baeck, *The Essence of Judaism*, 61. Buber's "Hebrew Humanism" (in *Israel and the World*, 240–252) includes a stirring rebuttal of the idea that the chosenness of the Jews is identical to the sense of destiny common to many peoples.
35. See Heschel, *The Insecurity of Freedom*, 166.

36. Rav Kook's thought serves as a good example of the presence of both particular and universal themes. In *Rav Kook*, Mirsky notes that "again and again Rav Kook returns to this question of election and the universal, and never really resolves it," 108. See also: Goshen-Gottstein, "A Kingdom of Priests"; Kasher, *Elyon Al Kol Hagoyim*, 198–208; Nehorai, "Halakhah, Metahalakhah, and Redemption."
37. See Bloch, "Iyun Mechudash Bemashmaut Hamunach Segulah" and Uffenheimer, "Segula." See also Marmur, "Israel, God's Chosen People?".
38. In *Jews as a Chosen People*, Gürkan makes an interesting schematic distinction with a historical element. The three sections of her study relate to chosenness as "holiness," "mission," and "survival," respectively.
39. See Pianko, *Jewish Peoplehood* and also Magid, *American Post-Judaism*, for analysis of both the twentieth- and the twenty-first-century development of these themes in American Judaism. Schweid, *Ra'ayon Ha'am Hanivchar*, particularly 15–31, offers an original and important critique in which he links the weakening of Jewish national identification with neo-liberal cultural and economic trends.
40. Rosenzweig argued that "Judaism qua Judaism is completely separate from politics" (Batnitzky, *How Judaism Became a Religion*, 86) and removed from secular history. See also Moses, *System and Revelation*, particularly 181.
41. Boyarin, *A Radical Jew*, 242.
42. For analysis of virulent versions of settler theology, see Satherley, "'The Simple Jew'" and *Unity and Opposites*. See also: Afterman, *Understanding the Theology*; Gitlin and Leibovitz, *The Chosen Peoples*, particularly 1–64; Miller, "Kvar Lo Mavdilim"; and Sharkansky, *Governing Israel*, particularly 1–26.
43. Kaplan, *Future of the American Jew*, 224. The italics are his.
44. Martin Buber's 1936 lecture, quoted in Oliveira, *Humanity Divided*, 104.
45. Two examples of the disjunctive *vav* at work highlight two different applications. The first relates to a circumstantial clause:

וַיֵּרָא אֵלָיו יְהוָה בְּאֵלֹנֵי מַמְרֵא וְהוּא יֹשֵׁב פֶּתַח הָאֹהֶל כְּחֹם הַיּוֹם:

God appeared to him at Elonei Mamre as he was sitting at the entrance to the tent in the heat of the day. (Genesis 18:1).

The *vav* before "he was sitting" is not intended to indicate a sequence or an addition but rather a temporal circumstance: this happened when Abraham was seated at the entrance to the tent. Another form of the disjunctive *vav* has a contrastive function: it highlights a distinction rather than signposting a connection. Hence, for example:

כִּי כָּל אֱלֹהֵי הָעַמִּים אֱלִילִים וַיהוָה שָׁמַיִם עָשָׂה:

For all the gods of the nations are idols, but Adonai made the heavens. (1 Chronicles 16:26)

See also Genesis 29:17, Hosea 13:1, and Psalms 1:6.

46. The letter *vav* plays a crucial role in the blessing before reading Torah, described in BT Brachot as the most excellent of blessings. See Kadari, "Asher Bachar Banu." For another reading of the blessing in the context of Election, see Jacobs, *God, Torah, Israel*, 60. The editors of the 2020 Israeli Reform Siddur opted to include alternative blessings over the Torah alongside the classic blessings. The alternative blessing before reading is taken from Tractate Soferim 13.6, and it has no mention of Election; however, the alternative blessing after reading is taken from Deuteronomy Rabbah 11.6, and it praises God for having chosen the Torah and sanctified those who follow it.
47. There is much literature on this prayer. See Bar-On and Paz, "Adon Hakol Veyotser Breshit," whose reading of the theological and ideological dimensions of the prayer is fascinating. See also Katz, "*Aleinu*"; and Langer, "Jewish Universalism?" See also a remarkable aside by Strauss, "Why We Remain Jews," 327, and Karsenti, "Si Je Me Bats."
48. This is comprehensively discussed in Langer, "The Censorship of Aleinu."
49. Neusner, *Recovering Judaism*, 5.
50. Sandberg, "Rethinking the Notion of Universality," 8.
51. See Levenson, "Miscategorizing Chosenness."
52. See Cohen, *Arthur A. Cohen Reader*, 33–40. The essay entitled "Why I Choose to Be a Jew" was originally published in 1959.

Open Access This chapter is licensed under the terms of the Creative Commons Attribution 4.0 International License (http://creativecommons.org/licenses/by/4.0/), which permits use, sharing, adaptation, distribution and reproduction in any medium or format, as long as you give appropriate credit to the original author(s) and the source, provide a link to the Creative Commons license and indicate if changes were made.

The images or other third party material in this chapter are included in the chapter's Creative Commons license, unless indicated otherwise in a credit line to the material. If material is not included in the chapter's Creative Commons license and your intended use is not permitted by statutory regulation or exceeds the permitted use, you will need to obtain permission directly from the copyright holder.

Zeman Nakat: History and Change

Jews have long employed *simanim*, mnemonic devices comprising letters which spell out a formula or list to be remembered. One of these is employed to help remember the structure of the Mishnah, the foundational work of Jewish law. Its tractates are arranged according to six sections, and the acronym employed to remember the traditional order is זמ״ן נק״ט, *Zeman Nakat*. These two words, when read not as initials for six other terms but in their own terms, have meaning. From the Hellenistic period, *zeman* has meant "time"; *nakat*, however, can be interpreted to mean several quite different things: "hold" or "take," on the one hand, "abhor" or "reject," on the other.[1]

Beyond the context of the Mishnah mnemonic, I propose to read this phrase to mean: what time does.[2] The title of Heschel's monumental work refers to heavenly Torah as perceived through "the *aspaklaria* of the generations," describing the process of history as an optic through which the timeless is translated into the language of the temporal. Bound by the circumstances of our own mortality, we encounter the world from a perspective that is formed not only by our innate natures but by cultural assumptions and historical events. A famous Talmudic tale depicts Moses miraculously attending Rabbi Akiva's House of Study. Initially perplexed, he does not understand what the Sage and his students are discussing but is comforted to hear that it is the law given to Moses on Sinai that they are debating.[3] The implication of the tale is that time changes our perception even of the Torah. Seen through the *aspaklaria* of the generations and heard after countless tellings and re-tellings, it is no longer precisely as it was. Torah may stand beyond time, but we cannot.

This chapter is about time and particularly about modernity's main contribution to Judaism's deep involvement with this theme: the methods, critique, and analysis of history. In a classic discussion of this theme, Yosef Haim Yerushalmi observed that as a modern Jewish historian, "the very mode in which I delve into the Jewish past represents a decisive break with that past."[4] History predates modernity, of course, but it is only in recent centuries that we find a "systematic distinction between past and present."[5] The past, that other country, is then investigated by means of painstaking research, designed to expose anachronisms and unsupportable myths. Studying the past in this way distances the observer from it, while for millennia Jews have been encouraged to live at no degree of separation from it, immersed in Jewish time.

A modern historical sensibility—a key feature of Reform Judaism from its inception—emphasizes the impact of time. Contrary to the rabbinic doctrine that there is no past or future in the Torah, Reform thinkers and other modernists based their understanding of Judaism on the significance of change over time. Once exposed to this sensibility, one cannot but see the difference that context makes on attitudes, actions, and events.[6] Time takes hold. *Zeman nakat.*

The Judaism I profess is imbued with a sense of history, but that does not imply that the growth of modern historical consciousness has brought only blessings in its wake. Emil Fackenheim enumerated some of its "grave spiritual effects," listing skeptical paralysis, pragmatic make-believe, and ideological fanaticism as three such pathologies.[7] In the first effect, knowing that everything is historically contingent renders one incapable of doing or believing anything deeply and therefore leads to despair. In the second effect, beliefs and practices are reduced to the level of convenient fictions and thereby robbed of their commanding power. The third grave effect is to block out all nuance and any trace of irony and insist on absolute ideological purity as a bar to the perils of relativism. The insistence that my truth obliterates all historical context is itself a response to the nagging suspicion that nothing can escape the homogenizing pull of historicism. The awareness that we are inexorably bound within the times and places we occupy leaves a complex legacy.

Jews and Time

Jews have been pondering time if not since the dawn of time, then at least since the dawn of Jews.[8] In the main, God stands beyond time, while no creature can escape it:

> Of old You established the earth; the heavens are the work of your hands
> They shall perish, but You shall endure; they shall wear out like garments;
> You change them like clothing and they pass away
> But You are the same, and Your years never end.[9]

A Hasidic teaching by Moshe Teitelbaum complicates this absolute distinction between a God out of time, on the one hand, and the rest of creation fixed within it, on the other. Commenting on Exodus 6, where God says to Moses: I appeared to the first patriarchs as El Shaddai but not as Adonai,[10] Teitelbaum sees these two names for God as denoting two aspects of divinity. El Shaddai implies manifestations of God that exist *within* time; Adonai, however, speaks to the sublime essence of being, beyond all temporal differentiation.[11] Adonai is beyond time. The ways in which we search for the ultimate and express that search live within time.

Discussions of time are mired in paradox. Physicists, philosophers, psychologists, and mystics have all sought to understand its pervasiveness and elusiveness. As physical beings we are bounded by temporality, aware of its passage, beneficiaries of its gifts, and prey to its ravages. At the same time our capacity to reflect on time places us, or an aspect of us, beyond it.[12] Medieval kabbalists and modern philosophers alike have spoken about this paradox, channeling (in Teitelbaum's terminology) both El Shaddai, rootedness in time, and Adonai, surpassing it.[13]

Coterminous with the creation of the world in the Genesis account is the introduction of a system of time divisions and distinctions as either a by-product or a necessary condition of creation: "God then said, 'Let there be lights in the expanse of the sky, to separate day from night, to be markers for sacred seasons, for days and years.'"[14] These sacred seasons and special days offer a matrix within which Jewish life has been conducted for millennia. While medieval thinkers wrestled with the essence of time in abstract terms, Jewish law and lore provided encounters with time on multiple levels. The Mishnah also opens with a discussion of time. Its first tractate opens not with the beginnings of the universe but with a prosaic question: from when does one recite the Shema in the evening?[15]

In rabbinic Judaism, a thick network of time-related practices was developed, comprising diurnal rhythms, Shabbat, and the festivals pinned to the natural year and rehearsing a sacred narrative, the sabbatical cycle, and more. The prayers I recite, the songs I sing, the texts I read, the moments marked in the life cycle, the year cycle, the sun's daily course—all these are invitations to dwell intentionally within time and take hold of it rather than let it simply pass.

Between the extremes of philosophical abstraction and practical application, Jewish sources are replete with reflections on time in a variety of tenors and dimensions.[16] Seated at the Seder table, Jews from infancy to dotage engage in the imparting of collective memory and group identity. We are enjoined to read the story in the first person plural and to see ourselves as if we had come out of Egypt.[17] Indeed, the passage of time in the course of our own lives has preoccupied Jews for millennia.[18] Psalm 90 reminds us that in the morning we flourish but by the evening we are cut down.[19] Our years, even if they reach seventy or eighty, fly by. Verse 12 reads:

> Teach us to count our days rightly,
> That we may obtain a wise heart.

The psalm ends by looking to the time when divine grace will be witnessed and the generations renewed. It shifts from mortality to messiah—to a future state of redemption. Prophets and sages, rabbis, and revolutionaries have placed this dimension of time at the forefront of their consciousness.

Time and Jewish Modernity

The rise of the historical-critical method in recent centuries is no doubt linked to the process of secularization and the disenchantment of the world, but the creation of a modern Jewish historical consciousness can be read as a profoundly religious process. In 1897, Gotthard Deutsch, professor of Bible at the Hebrew Union College in Cincinnati, published his *Philosophy of Jewish History* in which he presented two contrasting historical orientations. Materialists, to use his terminology, deny the possibility of discerning a tendency toward a certain goal, while teleologists promote the notion of a purpose and a direction in history. Deutsch himself clearly believed that historical insights could help clear the path toward a better future.

Materialist and teleological aspects of the modern project of history continue to live in uneasy relation to each other. The former is gradual, specific, painstaking, skeptical of grand claims and totalizing theories. The latter is stirring and inspiring, telling a compelling tale of a nation's manifest destiny, a religion's rise to greatness, and a political ideology's growth to maturity. The former analyzes a process; the latter proclaims progress. While some of the teleologies disavow religion, they are all fueled by some kind of faith.[20]

The legacy of the Masoretes, a theme to which I have referred in the introduction to this book, plays a role in Deutsch's thesis. He illustrates his belief that Jewish history can be understood in terms of its "drift towards the goal of humanity" by mentioning *Masoret Hamasoret*, a sixteenth-century work by the grammarian Elijah Levita which discredited the claim that the system of vowel points was ancient. Through painstaking perusal of the textual evidence, Levita demonstrated that this system could not have existed before the seventh century CE:

> To the average reader of historical works this may seem an insignificant detail in the history of Hebrew script, but in the light of philosophical contemplation it is a stepping stone on the way towards the liberation of mankind from blind acceptance of traditional opinions, without examining, whether or not they are born out by scientific research.[21]

Deutsch regarded the fact that close reading had uncovered a deviation from the traditional presentation of Judaism not as a disaster but rather as "a mile-post on the highroad to human destiny."[22] Accordingly, history is not a wrecking ball but a means by which the arc of progress is revealed. Myth will thus give way to Truth. Far from being seen as a threat to the true God of History, the historical method is regarded as a way of bringing God into clearer view.

A decade after Deutsch's work was published, Walter Rauschenbusch, a leading theologian and Baptist pastor, argued that history contributes to systematic theology such blessings as "freshness of perspective, human sympathy with its thinkers, biological comprehension of its origins, self-reformatory impulses, and the training of the critical faculty."[23] Similar benefits were to be found regarding other theological spheres. Rauschenbusch, a major figure in the Social Gospel movement, was also keen to argue that "the study of history is a profound incentive to action."[24] Rather than be paralyzed by an awareness that all our efforts may be washed away within a few short years, we should be galvanized by the sense that windows of opportunity, when opened, should not be squandered.

Reform Judaism embraced this historicist turn with enthusiasm. Institutions, doctrines, and practices were now to be held up to historical scrutiny.[25] In 1844, however, the Jewish historian Leopold Zunz issued a stern rebuke to Samuel Holdheim and others on the radical wing of the emergent Reform movement. The nature of Zunz's criticism was remarkable given his standing as one of the founders of the modern scientific study of Jewish history. He predicted that the demolition of Jewish ritual practice in the name of historical authenticity would lay waste to much of the lived experience of Jewish life: "Before the goddess of history, whom these Reformers set over the God of Abraham, the symbols of Judaism will not long find much grace."[26]

Zunz, the historian, believed that a Jew should not deify history. The historical method was to be a servant of the truth and a tool for the progress of the Jewish people in the world. But it was not to be adored to the point where it undermined that which it sought to understand. To return to Teitelbaum's terminology, Zunz saw history as a servant of El Shaddai but not as a goddess to be worshipped. Some of the most significant developments in modern Judaism have been sparked by something similar to Zunz's critique of radical Reform: a rejection of the worship of the goddess of history.[27] Heirs of those early Reformers should ask themselves to what degree Zunz was right: do we cut ourselves off from Jewish symbols and practices when we make them objects of inquiry rather than "our lives and the measure of our days"?

Savior or Downfall?

History—its methods, insights, and implications—has been regarded by some as the savior of modern Judaism and by others as its downfall. The growth of a historical consciousness has been one of the key characteristics and primary engines of Jewish modernity.[28] History is pressed into the service of various ideologies, all keen to argue that everything that happened before was preparing the way for Zionist fulfillment/the socialist paradise/Orthodox hegemony/Reform redemption and all the other great modern ideologies. While some see this abuse as evidence of the uselessness of history and promote immediacy, authenticity, or spirituality as alternatives, I believe that the best response to Bad History and to No History is: more history, more curiosity, more humanity, more critical thinking.

Learning Jewish history is not primarily about dissection and deconstruction, although it can involve both. More essentially, it is about striving to meet persons, communities, and concepts in as intimate way as possible. When I read a note from the late 1190s describing a visit to the home of Maimonides and see that his ten-year-old son, Abraham, was present and that lemon cakes were consumed, one of the greatest figures of Jewish history is humanized.[29] When I read the introduction to an 1863 work in which the author says that he knows that the Talmud is not always the best interpreter of the Mishnah but he chooses to adopt a more conservative view so as not to start a wildfire of controversy and disbelief, I see both the lure and the threat of new understandings of Jewish religious development at play.[30] When I learn how women were barred from access to medieval Jewish mystical practices through the adoption of practices originating in the Temple cult relating to menstruation, I cannot help but think of all those unheard voices, all that lost Torah.[31]

Technological and cultural shifts are creating new experiences of time,[32] and the Judaism of tomorrow will be impacted by this radical change. Given the rate of change we are currently experiencing, we should not have long to wait before finding out what new dimensions of time await us. For now, I search for the God of History within history, questioning certainties and motivations but not rejecting any of the other Jewish engagements with time in its many forms. Cosmic and calendar time, memory, mortality, and messianic time—all these have been integral to the fabric of Jewish life for three thousand years. A viable and vigorous Judaism of the future will need them all.

Yerushalmi ends an essay on a history of Jewish hope with words that speak to the consolation and inspiration I find in the addition of history to the retinue of El Shaddai:

> Why a history of hope? To assuage our loneliness. To realize that we are not the first to whom despair was not alien, hope a gratuitous gift, and that by the same token we are not necessarily the last. And that, perhaps, may be a small and modest step toward hope itself.

Notes

1. Mine is not the first attempt to search the expression for meaning beyond its mnemonic function. See the preface to Landau, *Tziyon Lenefesh Chaya* (Slavuta, 1856), where the expression is interpreted as underlining the validity and sanctity of the Oral Law. Without it, Landau argues, it would not be possible to pin down the dates and details concerning the calendar. It is only by means of the wisdom epitomized by the Mishnah that one can get a grip on the times set out in the Written Torah. Hebraists will note that the root of this verb *n-k-t* may, in particular contexts, bear a quite different meaning; "despise time" or "time has dispensed with" are also possible readings.
2. It resonates with the title of a short poem by John Bowring entitled "Changes Wrought by Time," an optimistic affirmation of the capacity of time to rectify past wrongs and omissions (*Memorial Volume*, 4).
3. BT Menachot 29b.
4. Yerushalmi, *Zakhor*, 81.
5. Schiffman, *Birth of the Past*, 204. Some of the implications of this book are developed further in Schiffman, "Historicizing History."
6. Rather than list the voluminous literature on the historical-critical approach to the formation of the Bible, I mention just two works. The first, Heschel, *Heavenly Torah* (published in Hebrew), is not a work of history in any conventional sense. Nonetheless, the aim of its second part is to undermine the notion that the only approach to the provenance of the Bible is the doctrine of heavenly origin. Heschel marshals sources from within rabbinic tradition to make his claim. In treating such questions as the authorship of the final verses of Deuteronomy, Heschel opens up the notion that human agency was at work in the formation of the Pentateuch. The full title of the work reveals its intention: the doctrine of heavenly Torah is seen refracted through the generation. It exists in history. The second, Brettler, *How to Read*, makes a similar point but uses quite different tools—the methods of contemporary Bible scholarship—to argue that in order for the Bible to be understood, it must be read in context.
7. Fackenheim, *Metaphysics and History*, 2.
8. For a brief overview of time divisions in ancient Judaism, see Ratson, "Counting the Hours." Brin, *Concept of Time*, offers a systematic presentation of terms and concepts relating to time in the Hebrew Bible and the Dead Sea Scrolls. Stern, *Time and Process*, presents a thesis about early conceptions of time. For a contrasting approach, see Ben-Dov, "Apocalyptic Temporality" and Ben-Dov, "Time and Natural Law." Gribetz, *Time and Difference*, and Kaye, *Time in the Babylonian Talmud*, are both important contributions to an understanding of the conception of time in rabbinic

literature. Herr, "Tefisat Hahistoria Etzel Chazal," is more dated but offers an important perspective. For important research on time in medieval Jewish philosophy, see Rudavsky, "Crescas on Time" and *Time Matters*. An insight into time in the thought of Abraham Ibn Ezra is offered by Levin, in "Various Times." For the esoteric tradition in this context, see Wolfson, *Suffering Time*, and for a study of an aspect of this question regarding Hasidism, see Tworek, *Eternity Now*.

9. Psalm 102: 26–28. It is quoted in this context in Ellenson, "Eternity and Time," 189. As an example of Jewish theological approaches to the non-temporality of God, I mention a comment found in *Meshekh Chokhmah* by Meir Simchah Hacohen of Dvinsk. In his commentary to Numbers 23:21, he notes that according to Maimonides and others, God is beyond time. Unlike human beings, time brings no new knowledge to God, for whom time is simply one more creation. God created time out of nothingness, and for God all time is in the immediate present. He is commenting here on the surprising order of the formula in the morning prayer service (God rules, God ruled, God will rule) and uses the opportunity to provide an extended reflection on divinity and temporality. See also Exodus Rabbah 3.6; BT Berakhot 9b and Nahmanides to Exodus 3:14.

10. The reference here is to the Tetragrammaton, written YHVH but pronounced quite differently in order to highlight the sanctity of the word. Modern biblical scholarship often seeks to demystify, and the word YHVH is bandied about freely so as to demonstrate that one cannot utter it without fear of immediate divine sanction. I do not harbor that fear, but I am heir to a tradition which is slow to utter the word itself.

11. Moshe Teitelbaum, *Yismach Moshe*, 131a-b. While YHVH relates to a God before creation in which past, present, and future are combined, El Shaddai is planted in time, dependent on time (both expressions are employed). The implication here is that aspects of divinity are experienced within the dimension of time.

12. For a highly stimulating and articulate expression of this view in an atheistic tenor, see Tallis, *Time and Lamentation*. For a reflection on the paradoxes of history and memory in modern Jewish life, see Ellenson, "History, Memory and Relationship."

13. For a remarkable example of this parallel, see Wolfson, *Heidegger and Kabbalah*.

14. Genesis 1:14. For a reading of this account as a description of time itself, see Bar-Ilan, "Hazman Lesugav BeBreshit Aleph," particularly 1–2. For a discussion of some of the issues relating to the first word of Genesis in the context of the creation of time itself, see Sasson, "Genesis of Time." Yovel, "Creation of Language," offers a fascinating reading of creation through language before the creation of time. Perhaps the most extensive discus-

sion of the significance of the Genesis account for an understanding of the nature of time can be found in Book 6 of Gersonides' *Wars of the Lord*. For Menachem Mendel Schneerson's direct statement that when God created the world, God created time, see *Derekh Mitzvotekha*, 57a.
15. M Berakhot 1:1. The question "when" in the form *eimatai* (when?) or *me'eimati* (from when?) appears over eighty times in the Mishnah and is the first word of another tractate, Ta'anit. It is interesting to note that the word appears twice in the very last chapter of the final tractate in all of the Mishnah—perhaps the end of the work is gesturing back to its beginning.
16. See Idel, "Some Concepts" and "Sabbath" for other categories. In the former, Idel proposes a tripartite distinction between microchronic, rectilinear, and macrochronic, while in the latter he outlines cosmogonic, cosmological, and ritualistic approaches.
17. For a fascinating perspective on this theme, see Raz-Krakotzkin, "Jewish Memory."
18. BT Berakhot 5b includes a tale of Rabbi Yohanan and Rabbi Elazar weeping over the fleeting nature of beauty, fated to decompose in the earth. A remarkable twentieth-century parallel to this reflection on mortality and time can be found in Simmel, *View of Life*, written in light of Simmel's consciousness of his approaching demise. See Jalbert, "Time, Death and History," and Molseed, "Problem of Temporality."
19. See Pinker, "Famous but Difficult," Turner, "Reading of Psalm 90," and Witczyk, "Eternal God's Response."
20. Much has been written about the theological underpinnings of various modernist conceptions of historical progress. In *The Poverty of Historicism*, Karl Popper dedicated his famous critique of these notions to the "memory of the countless men and women of all creeds or nations or race who fell victims to the fascist and communist belief in Inexorable Laws of Historical Destiny" (iv). For a recent consideration of the ideas of Karl Löwith, Jacob Taubes, and others, see Bielik-Robson, "God of Myth."
21. Deutsch, *Philosophy of Jewish History*, 6–7.
22. Ibid., 7. In "Two Persistent Tensions," Meyer notes that "for all of its novelty and even iconoclasm, Wissenschaft des Judentums for most of its history was to varying degrees and in very different ways predominantly a religious enterprise" (74). This is true not only because many of its practitioners were in seminary settings but also because this act of probing for the truth and aiming for amelioration was religious in nature.
23. Rauschenbusch, "Influence of Historical Studies," 120.
24. Ibid., 125.
25. It is no longer the case that Reform and Conservative Jews hold the monopoly on the historical method (indeed, its standing within these movements has slipped discernibly). The rise of a modern Orthodox schol-

arship which is fully engaged in the historical-critical approach has been one of the most remarkable developments of recent decades.
26. Quoted in Schorsch, *Leopold Zunz*, 121.
27. This is brilliantly chronicled in Myers, *Resisting History*. For the question of Rosenzweig's approach to history, see Altmann, "Frank Rosenzweig on History," and Funkenstein, "Escape from History"; for a more recent treatment of this perennially interesting theme, see Hollander, *Exemplarity and Chosenness*, particularly 159–183.
28. For accounts of Wissenschaft des Judentums, see Feiner, *Haskalah and History*, and Schorsch, *From Text to Context*.
29. See Fenton, "A Meeting with Maimonides."
30. Pineles, *Darkah Shel Torah* (Vienna, 1863), 19. This and other works are elucidated in Gafni, *Pshuta Shel Mishnah*.
31. See Koren, *Forsaken*, a remarkable study of this aspect of the Jewish esoteric tradition. One of the great strengths of the study is the comparison of the Jewish material with Muslim and Christian parallels.
32. The fact that Bauman, *Liquid Times*, is in some respects already outdated is in fact evidence of the strength of its central claim.

Open Access This chapter is licensed under the terms of the Creative Commons Attribution 4.0 International License (http://creativecommons.org/licenses/by/4.0/), which permits use, sharing, adaptation, distribution and reproduction in any medium or format, as long as you give appropriate credit to the original author(s) and the source, provide a link to the Creative Commons license and indicate if changes were made.

The images or other third party material in this chapter are included in the chapter's Creative Commons license, unless indicated otherwise in a credit line to the material. If material is not included in the chapter's Creative Commons license and your intended use is not permitted by statutory regulation or exceeds the permitted use, you will need to obtain permission directly from the copyright holder.

Chai Vekayam: The Existence and Insistence of God

> I called to you—is it because of your existence
> Or from fear of being without you?
> I heard you speak—is it because you answered
> Or the desert's desire—to hear!…
>
> The voice we invented is the voice that answered!
> It is that voice you asked:
> Do you exist?
> And you answered.
>
> And you answered:
> You exist!
> Because I called to you.[1]

Grappling with the question of God's existence or non-existence is a feature of the modern condition. The Israeli poet Avraham Shlonsky captures something of the challenge associated with this search for confirmation.

This chapter is prompted by my strong sense that a simple either/or is not equal to the greatest questions. If God is either "really there" or not "really there" like a physical thing in the world, the conversation about God will be reduced to discourse about verification, like the Loch Ness monster or a politician's promise. Surely the God question should allow for a higher order of complexity, at least as much as that afforded to a discussion of love or aesthetics or quantum theory.

Old-fashioned believers are often offended by the doubt expressed by Shlonsky and so many others since the Enlightenment. Offense, however, is not a winning argument or even a generous sentiment. Taking umbrage on God's behalf implies that in some way God is threatened by human speculation, thus casting God as an insecure human. A more fruitful approach to this kind of speculation is encapsulated in the Talmudic dictum, "impudence (*chutzpah*) is effective even when it is directed toward Heaven."[2]

In order to approach God's existence, we begin with a famously flawed human ruler.

King David Lives

A midrash tells of a moment of resurrection for King David when his son Solomon invokes his name. The reason for Solomon's desperation is one familiar to anyone who has experienced complications when doing home renovations but on a grander and more consequential scale. Solomon constructs an ark ten cubits wide, and it is only when he brings it to the Temple that he realizes that the entrance is the same width; there was no way that the ark along with those who were bearing it could fit through the door. Solomon pleads with God and, for maximum persuasiveness, he brings the coffin of his father, David, and prostrates himself before it while imploring God to bend the rules of physics and allow the ark to get through the door:

> Rabbi Berechiah declared in the name of Rabbi Helbo: "At that time David came to life, as you may understand for yourself from David's own words: 'O Lord, Your brought up my soul from the netherworld; You kept me alive, that I should not go down to the pit' " (Psalms 30:4). Solomon said: "Master of the Universe, make it go in for his sake: 'Remember the good deeds of David Your servant' " (2 Chronicles 6:42). And his prayers were answered immediately.[3]

The tactic is effective, and the ark is installed. At the moment described here, a parent is brought to life when his child brings up his memory (and, in this case, his coffin) and invokes it for a constructive purpose. Faced with an apparently intractable problem, Solomon, in his wisdom and his desperation, turns to the living God with the assistance of his dead father.

As a result, David participates posthumously in the building of the Temple, something not granted to him in his lifetime. In this sense, David lives.

In 1993, the archeological team of the Hebrew Union College discovered fragments of a stele (a monumental declaration engraved on stone) at Tel Dan in the north of Israel.[4] What generated international interest was the mention in the stele, reliably dated to the ninth century BCE, of the House of David.[5] While a traditional reader of the Hebrew Bible would have no doubt that David existed, neither he nor Solomon is mentioned in contemporary extra-biblical sources. The stele, according to most well-supported readings, provides such evidence. It does not demonstrate that the biblical account of David—musical, passionate, effective, philandering—is historically accurate. More modestly, the Tel Dan find shows that some decades after David is thought to have lived, the House of David was an acknowledged political reality. In this sense, it seems reasonable to conclude that David lived.

In Jewish tradition another question has been asked: not the historical-philological-archeological question, Did King David exist?, but rather the existential-political-messianic question, Is King David alive? Such a question could be asked concerning any of the patriarchs (Joseph asked it concerning Jacob, for example[6]), but in the case of David, it came to have a particular resonance. At the Jewish primary school I attended in London, we often sung the five-word song *David Melekh Yisrael Chai Vekayam*—David, King of Israel, is alive and endures. The tune was catchy, but the lyrics were somewhat mysterious to me. Something significant was intended by this enthusiastic repetition, but we nine-year-olds had little idea what that significance might be.

While the phrase relates to a biblical hero, its first appearance is in the Babylonian Talmud in the context of a discussion about the sanctification of the new moon. In ancient times the decision concerning the date of a new month was subject to the testimony of reliable witnesses and the upholding of authoritative rulings. The Talmud (BT Rosh Hashanah 25a) relates that Rabbi Judah the Prince,[7] a sage of the second and third centuries who combined scholarly eminence with political influence, instructed Rabbi Chiyya to go to a particular place and declare that the new month had begun. The message used to convey that the will of the Patriarch had been carried out consisted of a five-word slogan, still sung by uncomprehending children almost 2000 years later.

Why would Rabbi Judah the Prince request that this particular motto be employed? The slogan served as a code,[8] asserting the right of the

Patriarch to decide when the new month was to be declared. Rabbi Judah's evocation of King David reveals something of his own sense of mission. He traced his lineage back to David and had messianic ambitions.[9] Over the course of Jewish history, Davidic lineage has been claimed for a number of key figures, bolstering each of their respective claims to legitimacy. A partial list of those presented as the living embodiment of King David's line would include Jesus of Nazareth in the first century of the millennium named for him,[10] Sabbatai Zevi in the seventeenth century, and Menachem Mendel Schneerson in the twentieth. Devotees of each of these figures and others besides have declared that David, the King of Israel, lives within them.

The use of this imagery in the sanctification of the new month is also redolent with symbolic significance. There is a long-attested connection between the figure of King David and the moon, linking it back to his lineage from Peretz, son of Judah, brother of Zerach. Those two sons have come to symbolize the moon and sun respectively, with the house of King David symbolized by the moon.[11] While the sun's appearance is predictable on a daily basis, the moon becomes visible cyclically and is not always recognized. By employing this cipher, Rabbi Judah the Prince was indicating his belief that the conditions may pertain in his day for the reinstatement of Jewish sovereignty.

To ask whether King David existed is to search for demonstrable proof that the tales of the Hebrew Bible concerning this historical personage have a factual basis. To declare that King David is alive and endures (*chai vekayam*) is something different. By stating it, present consciousness and future aspiration are framed within a traditional context. Singing the Talmudic slogan some twenty years after the establishment of Israel was intended to place the tumultuous events of the twentieth century in a wider perspective. Glimpsing the nascent moon, we were declaring: David lives and will yet endure.

Even in its most secularized versions, there has long been a messianic drive at the heart of Zionism. In the thought of such figures as Rabbi Abraham Isaac Kook, this drive is made explicit, but it was present in its least creedal and most original manifestations. At the First Zionist Congress in Basle in 1897, the Zionist writer known as Ben Ami[12] wrote about Theodor Herzl:

> The two-thousand-year dream of our people seemed to be approaching fulfilment; it was as if the Messiah, the son of David, stood before us. A

powerful desire seized me to shout through this tempestuous sea of joy: *Yechi Ha-melech!* Long live the King.[13]

In virtually all of its manifestations and across its internal ideological debates, Zionism can be seen as a modern messianism, translating the promise of the imminent moon of David into modern terms.[14]

The question of David's existence has been posed in different ways. In the midrash, he lives beyond the grave when his name is invoked. At Tel Dan, evidence comes to life supporting the belief that he actually lived and was not simply the stuff of legend. And in the repetition of a Talmudic slogan, the possibility of national rebirth and messianic innovation is declared. There is more than one way of being alive.

God as King

A sentence recited upon waking up has found its way into Jewish practice in recent centuries. It precedes any of the formal morning liturgy. Translated, it reads: "I thank you, *melekh chai vekayam*, living and enduring Sovereign, for returning my soul to me (*bi*) in compassion, great is your faithfulness."[15] The similarity to the Talmudic reference to the new moon and the old king is striking. In both cases mention is made of a monarch, *chai vekayam*, alive and enduring. It may seem somehow blasphemous to speak of a living God with the same terminology as that used to describe a living person. Surely, God and David live in fundamentally different ways. Nevertheless, we are bound to employ terminology also applied to humans when attempting to say something about the Divine.[16] The impossibility of reaching beyond our own frame of reference to consider that which lies beyond it was expressed by Ludwig Feuerbach:

> If God were an object to the bird, he would be a winged being: the bird knows nothing higher, nothing more blissful, than the winged condition. ... To ask whether God is in himself what he is for me, is to ask whether God is God, is to lift oneself above one's God.[17]

All we human beings have at our disposal in our clumsy attempts to describe what lies beyond our horizon are the tools provided to us by our language, our experience, and our imagination. In a tradition forbidding pictorial representation of the Divine, the creation of any graven image is forbidden, but the poetry of the Bible is replete with images:

God is praised as warrior and judge, shepherd and potter, husband and mother. What the sculptors were denied, the poets celebrated. Thus the biblical record is a clear model for human conduct: the theological assertion that God is wholly other meets the human hope that a likeness exists between Creator and creature. Often the human hope wins the day.[18]

Metaphor is at the heart of all languages. I cannot attempt to talk about God without resorting to metaphor.[19] The process by which metaphors are formed should be constantly changing, responsive to new understandings of society and identity. Reading Marcia Falk on God language in the 1980s and Mara Benjamin in the 2020s gives powerful testimony to the significance of these evolving metaphors.[20] Their work convinces me that to limit one's God imagery to a few tired expressions redolent with the assumptions of male hegemony is to leave our spiritual vocabulary greatly impoverished. To insist on restricting our metaphorical range to fathers and kings is unwarranted and unconscionable. I have not given up grappling with the idea of Rosh Hashanah, the Jewish New Year, as a moment in which God is crowned monarch; but I see no reason, traditional or otherwise, to be limited to this image.

In 2023, Paul Simon released a record in which he describes "The Lord" (the God he describes is still firmly "The Lord") using a remarkable array of images:

> The Lord is my engineer
> The Lord is the earth I ran on
> The Lord is a face in the atmosphere
> The path I'll slip and slide on
>
> The Lord is a virgin forest
> The Lord is a forest ranger
> The Lord is a meal for the poorest of the poor
> A welcome door to the stranger[21]

Simon makes no claims to be a theologian and has no truck with conventional religion. But his lyrics can be seen in terms of a long Jewish tradition of searching for God through metaphor. Is God a forest ranger? Can the image convey a truth without recourse to empirical evidence?

In interviews Paul Simon has said that the songs on that record came to him in dreams.[22] They can be seen as part of a long tradition, one explored by Jews considering the validity of a visual encounter through various kinds of *aspaklaria*. In the fifteenth century Joseph Albo asked: "How is it possible that one should see what does not exist and yet acquire truth by means of it?... the prophet understands that there is no such form in reality as he sees, though he sees it."[23]

The morning formula rehearses the familiar metaphor of God as king. As I recite it, I concentrate on the first three words: *modeh ani lefanecha*. Since words in Hebrew usually bear more than one meaning, this phrase, usually taken to mean "I thank you," can also be understood as "I thank your facets, your multiple faces." The prayer book I use offers four alternatives to the king image alongside the original: mother of all life, living source, live spirit, creator (using the feminine term) of all that lives.[24] I give thanks to the God who lives and endures in variety and possibility.

God Who Insists

In recent decades, a genre of anti-God literature has become popular in the West.[25] Given the political and ideological backdrop, this is no surprise. I read some of these works with intermittent responses of appreciation, fascination, annoyance, and discomfort. Anyone interested in thinking about God is well advised to read the best of this kind of work not in order to come up with rebuttals, but rather to think more deeply about what God means through encounter with those who argue convincingly that God means nothing.

The question of God's existence has been a preoccupation not only of critics but also of believers.[26] My own sense is that framing the question in terms of a banal yes or no is unsatisfactory, because "existence is an inappropriate concept to apply to God."[27] Reducing the God conversation to the level of existence or non-existence impoverishes the register of possible theological understandings. It turns the conversation into a version of the famous scene in *The Wizard of Oz* when it transpires that the great and mighty wizard does not exist and is in fact nothing more than an illusion operated by a little man behind a screen. According to this reading, either God exists and does all the things God is believed to be able to do or God does not exist, in which case a great hoax has been perpetrated upon us.

John Caputo has made an ingenious counter-suggestion. God does not exist, he states provocatively, God insists:

> To speak of the insistence of God is to say that God is a *problema*, a provocation, an insistent disturbance, a solicitation, a visitation by a stranger, like a

call knowing I know not what, or an insistent knock on our door in the middle of the night.

...the insistence of God means the insistent problem, task, challenge, obstacle, hurdle, question and barrier that goes under the name of "event", an idea I keep coming back to, circling around, refining and defining, but without trying to be too confining. The name of God... is the name of the chance of an event, a chance for grace, but that spells trouble, a problem, to which the world, and our being-in-the-world, are a series of shaky solutions.[28]

To read Caputo's striving for a radical postmodern Christian theology is to be reminded of Abraham Joshua Heschel's theology, despite all that separates these two thinkers. In his formulation, God's pathos in responding to the world is sent out to humanity in the form of untranslatable pulses or prompts, inviting a response:

The ultimate question, bursting forth in our souls, is too startling, too heavily laden with unutterable wonder to be an academic question, to be equally suspended between yes and no. We can no longer ask: Is there a God? In humility and contrition we realize the presumption of such asking. The more deeply we meditate, the more clearly we realize the question we are being asked: that *man's question about God is God's question of man.*[29]

Heschel drew on the image of a voice calling out daily from the mountain, posing this question to each person at each moment.[30] Here the emphasis is not on the abstraction of existence but on the reality of insistence. Heschel and Caputo espouse different metaphysical assumptions and employ different religious vocabularies, but both respond to the question, "Does God exist?" in a way I find to be more interesting than Wizard of Oz theology.

The expression *chai vekayam* can be seen to refer to distinct approaches to God. The living God is a personal God who makes specific demands, expresses preferences, offers support and consolation, and rewards pious adherence. The enduring God denoted by *kayam*, on the other hand, is a God who occupies a different register of existence. This God has been described as the ground of being, the fundamental unifying principle of all that is. In my interpretation of the expression *chai vekayam*, the first word relates to a relatable, personal God, a God who relates with pathos to that which is taking place in the earthly realm—a God who notices and reciprocates. The second word speaks to God as the linchpin of reason and morality or, in some versions, as the ceaseless flow of nature and reality. It is important that the two be held together because God perceived exclusively through one of these images is either limited or dangerous or both.

Some argue that liberal agonizing over God's existence is beside the point. The relevant question should be: does this living and loving God do things in the world? If not, so goes the argument, then you are welcome to call your beliefs whatever you like but they are of little consequence. Here is a point upon which fundamentalists and atheists often agree. Liberals try to have their cake and eat it too, it is suggested, and should be seen as hypocrites or as wishful thinkers. They affirm God with no consequences for their affirmation. It would indeed be neater if all believers were credulous fundamentalists and all deniers were crude materialists; luckily, the spectrum of deeply held opinions is far more complex. The greatest contributions to our God-talk have been made by people who relate (in vastly different ways) both to the *chai* of a living, personal God, and to the *kayam*, the grounding foundational God. Non-fundamentalist understandings of God do not deny the existence of imperatives. They often take issue with the ways in which divine imperatives are understood and regulated.

It is possible, indeed necessary, to consider the plausibility of various claims made for God's agency and efficacy. If God has healed the sick person, then presumably, for inscrutable reasons, God has caused the other sick person to die. If God stands behind a particular government policy, then by the same logic it can be adduced that God would vote against the opposing policy. But these are questions relating not to God's existence but rather to the capacity of an individual or an institution to know God's will. I believe that beyond manipulation and projection, beyond the apparently limitless capacity of human beings to turn the sublime into the crass, God lives. To declare that God has died means simply that a particular version of God is no longer possible for a particular community. When this or that version of God becomes impossible, I do not conclude that we are done with God. Rather, I thank God's many faces and look for one I may yet be able to glimpse.

The God I encounter lives and endures. I have nothing to say about this God as an object of inquiry but instead testify to the reality of God's insistence. I have great respect for those whose God discourse demands a creedal text-based affirmation and for those who insist on a firm rebuttal of all theological claims. While each of these paths is understandable to me, neither is possible if I am to be honest. I am stuck with a God who insists and with the question: what is God insisting that I do?

It is easier to pose the question than formulate the response. The experience of God goes beyond theological prescriptions. The God of existence and vitality even renders the category God unnecessary. Dorothy Allison has questioned the distinctions we tend to place on our ultimate concerns:

> Some things never change. There is a place where we are always alone with our own mortality, where we must simply have something greater than ourselves to hold onto—God or history or politics or literature or a belief in the healing power of love, or even righteous anger. Sometimes I think they are all the same. A reason to believe, a way to take the world by the throat and insist that there is more to this life than we have ever imagined.[31]

Allison is quoted by Richard Rorty, who links her words with William James' statement that "the divine can mean no single quality, it must mean a group of qualities, by being champion of which in alternation, different men may all find worthy missions."[32]

Statements such as this are open to criticism from adherents of traditional monotheistic religions. The God affirmed in them, they claim, is little more than a bland synonym or a generic term for an assortment of qualities. If it makes no difference, if the something we are holding onto is God or anger or literature, then why speak of God? If God is anything then God is nothing. Opponents of the Allison/James axis insist on a God more demanding than a ubiquitous metaphor. Liberal religion is often pilloried from the left and the right for flirting with a God idea so all-inclusive that it has become redundant.

I understand the criticism, but prefer to be in this conversation than in any other I know. Both Allison and James offer a call to action, a way of taking life by the throat, a worthy mission. Aware of the pitfalls, walking with uncertainty, I call to God in the desert. I live in the presence of God who lives and endures beyond my lifespan and beyond my capacity. I express this in the words of the book attributed to David who, however differently, also lives and endures: "By day Adonai directs their love, by night their song is with me, a prayer to the God of my life."[33]

Notes

1. Shlonsky, "Karati Elekha" (my translation). For an examination of the theological underpinnings of Shlonsky's poetry, see Jaeger, *Avraham Hama'amin Ha'ivri*. For a study of other leading Hebrew poets in this context, see Rechnitzer, *Ars Poetica*.
2. BT Sanhedrin 105a.
3. Tanchuma Vaera 7.
4. The team was led by Avraham Biran and the actual discovery made by Gila Cook.
5. For this scholarly debate, see Athas, "Setting the Record Straight," and Finkelstein and Silberman, *David and Solomon*, 261–266.
6. Genesis 45.3.
7. This nomenclature is confusing, since he was not a prince but a patriarch, but this is how his Hebrew title is usually rendered.
8. The phrase is indeed a code word, since the numerical value of the letters in the phrase is equal to that of the term *rosh chodesh*, new month. See Menachem Munisch Heilpern, *Menachem Meshiv Nefesh*, 3 (Brody, 1907), 46, where the tradition is attributed to the eighteenth-century kabbalist Yitzchak Isaac Hacohen of Koretz.
9. See Baumgarten, "Rabbi Judah I."
10. See Matthew 1:1.
11. See, for example, Nachmanides to Genesis 38:29.
12. This was the pseudonym of Mark (Mordechai) Iakovlevich Rabinovich.
13. This is quoted in Wistrich, "Theodor Herzl," 31.
14. See: Biale, *Power and Powerlessness*; Luz, *Wrestling with an Angel*; Ohana, *Modernism and Zionism*, particularly 80–121; and Ratzabi, "Religious Thinkers." Other Jewish modernisms, among them Reform and Socialism, have also identified a nascent transformative change—they are messianisms too.
15. For a number of interesting essays exploring aspects of this formula, see Birnbaum and Cohen, *Modeh Ani*. See Daniel 6:27 for an Aramaic version of the expression denoting a living and enduring king.
16. It is worth noting Heidegger's use of the archaic form *Seyn* distinct from the more regular *Sein*, often rendered in English versions of his thought as *Beyng* and *Being* respectively. What Heidegger means precisely by this distinction is beyond the scope of this chapter (and the capacity of this author). What matters here is that the wish to push language to its capacity in contemplating Being comes to expression. See Harries, *Antinomy of Being*, 13–17.

17. Feuerbach, *Essence of Christianity*, 17. Reference to this comment is also made in the first chapter, *Aspaklaria*.
18. Ramshaw, *God Beyond Gender*, 93.
19. For important discussions of metaphor in a biblical context, see: Avis, *God and Creative Imagination*; Brettler, *God Is King*; and Weiss, *Figurative Language*, particularly 1–34. Masson, *Without Metaphor*, relates to this topic through the prism of cognitive linguistics.
20. Falk, "Notes on Composing"; Benjamin, *Obligated Self*.
21. https://genius.com/Paul-simon-the-lord-lyrics
22. See, for example, https://www.bigissue.com/culture/music/paul-simon-in-conversation-with-paul-muldoon/
23. Albo, *Ikkarim*, 3.9, volume 3, 81. See Heschel, *God in Search*, 277, note 23.
24. Marx and Lisitsa, *Tefillat Ha'adam*, 57.
25. In his *Reason, Faith, and Revolution*, Terry Eagleton conflates the work of Richard Dawkins and Christopher Hitchens and refers to them irreverently as Ditchkins. Along with them I would add the names of Daniel Dennett and Sam Harris.
26. For an outstanding example, see Küng, *Does God Exist?*
27. Beiser, *Hermann Cohen*, 358, explicating Cohen's position. Buber, "Love of God," offers an interpretation of Hermann Cohen's conception of God as an idea and his love of God. See also Nahme, "God Is the Reason." For important insights into Cohen's understanding of God, including Rosenzweig's controversial essay on this topic, see Cohen, *Writings on Neo-Kantianism*.
28. Caputo, *Insistence of God*, 28–29.
29. Heschel, *God in Search*, 132.
30. See, for example, Heschel, *God in Search*, 145–151.
31. Allison, *Skin*, 181.
32. James, *Varieties of Religious Experience*, 384. See Rorty, *Philosophy and Social Hope*, 161–162.
33. Psalms 42.8.

Open Access This chapter is licensed under the terms of the Creative Commons Attribution 4.0 International License (http://creativecommons.org/licenses/by/4.0/), which permits use, sharing, adaptation, distribution and reproduction in any medium or format, as long as you give appropriate credit to the original author(s) and the source, provide a link to the Creative Commons license and indicate if changes were made.

The images or other third party material in this chapter are included in the chapter's Creative Commons license, unless indicated otherwise in a credit line to the material. If material is not included in the chapter's Creative Commons license and your intended use is not permitted by statutory regulation or exceeds the permitted use, you will need to obtain permission directly from the copyright holder.

Tefachim: A Torah of Tension

There is a ritual common to synagogues that cuts across differences of denomination and provenance. Whenever the Torah is read (customs differ as to whether this takes place before or after the reading), the scroll is held up and a biblical verse is recited: "This is the Torah which Moses presented before the children of Israel."[1] It is not only the altitude at which the Torah is held; it should also be opened up so that three columns can be seen.[2] In many Sephardi communities, the scroll is encased in a container, while the Ashkenazi scroll is typically wound around two wooden poles. It is therefore not surprising that some enthusiastic Ashkenazi practitioners of Torah lifting hold that two poles as wide apart as the span of their arms will allow. The honor of lifting up the Torah is usually reserved for a person fit enough to undertake it without risk or discomfort. When I perform this task, it is not only the weight of the physical object or its shape to which I pay attention but also the tension produced by the parchment stretched between two poles.

The Torah is a physical object: the Pentateuch copied onto parchment. It is also much more. In this chapter I examine what Torah means to me, paying attention not only to the height at which it is held (its sanctity and centrality) but also the breadth of its span (its range and capacity). Holding it up to examination provides an opportunity to consider the tension at the heart of Torah.

Torah

"Turn it and turn it for all is in it."³ This ancient adage relates to the study of the Torah, and something similar can be said of the word "Torah" itself.⁴ It can refer to a particular set of laws within the biblical corpus, to the first five books of the Hebrew Bible, or to the entire biblical canon. The latter constitute the Written Torah, alongside which the Pharisees and their heirs posited an Oral Torah, originally revealed to Moses and then passed on by word of mouth from generation to generation. More widely still, Torah can mean a praxis, lived experience imparted from teacher to student. The Talmud records how students risked impropriety in order to learn appropriate behaviors in the bathroom and the bedroom from their teachers, explaining their willingness to do so with the explanation: this is Torah, and I need to learn.⁵ In modern Hebrew, we speak of Darwin's Torah of evolution and of quantum Torah, meaning theory and philosophy. Michael Fishbane has suggested another category, *torah kelulah*, which "denotes absolute reality, and comprises the totality of existence and world-being." It is "the inherent datum and ground of all world-happening."⁶

Torah, then, is a book, a process, a theory, a reality, a practice, a passion, a discipline, an *aspaklaria*, and more. Turn it and turn it, and it can mean everything that is. Most of these usages share two significant features: they describe something engrossing and something of divine provenance. "How I love your Torah, it is my discourse all day long!," declares the psalmist (119:97). While poor educational practices have often rendered Torah a burden, to be engaged in Torah is never meant to be a chore; indeed a characteristic of Torah is "to carry those who carry it."⁷

The eighth of Maimonides' Thirteen Principles of Faith reads: "I believe with complete faith that the entire Torah which is now in our possession is the very one which was given to our teacher Moses, may he rest in peace."⁸ According to the Mishnah, a person who has the temerity to state that the Torah does not originate in Heaven has no place in the world to come.⁹ It might be assumed from these examples that here is an article of faith to be accepted by the pious and rejected by the rest. Surely, Torah can be Torah only for those who accept these theological assumptions up front.

I disagree. There is no dogma in Judaism which defies reinterpretation. I do not believe that the Torah—every verse, jot, and tittle—originated in the heavens and was dictated to Moses at one sitting; luckily, it is not necessary to do so, even from a traditional Jewish point of view. In a monumental work, Abraham Joshua Heschel trawled thousands of classical Jewish sources in order to demonstrate that the concept of *Torah min Hashamayim*, Heavenly Torah, has been understood within the classical Jewish interpretive tradition in a broad variety of ways.[10] More recently, Benjamin Sommer has made the remarkable claim that within the Hebrew Bible itself we can find traces of more than one idea concerning revelation. He describes the familiar version as stenographic: God speaks and Moses takes down dictation. In contrast to this approach, he identifies a version of revelation seen as collaborative and participatory, forged in the human response to divine prompts.

The thought of a modern Orthodox thinker such as Tamar Ross demonstrates that today there are many thoughtful Jews who follow the strictures of traditional Jewish law to the letter who cannot (or see no need to) accept the axiom that God spoke to Moses on a particular day and imparted a particular freight of meaning. Her notion of cumulative revelation offers a way for Jews to reconcile traditional ritual and communal commitments with intellectual integrity.[11]

I want to employ an evocative metaphor from the Jewish exegetical tradition to say something about what I mean when I say Torah. My views certainly do not fit within Orthodox Judaism, nor do they strive to be accepted as such. I believe they do fit into a broader Jewish process by which the Torah is turned and turned again for meaning. Here is an extra rotation.

The Proportions of Torah

Some rabbinic traditions relate to the Torah, meaning, in this case, not the primordial metaphysical one[12] but the tablets upon which Torah (however that term is understood) was inscribed, which Moses took to hand, and which were subsequently broken:[13] "The tablets were God's work, and the writing was God's writing, incised upon the tablets" (Exodus 32:16).

There is one rabbinic tradition, referenced in a number of authoritative sources, which relates to the physical proportions of the tablets. Some versions of it suggest that they were square in form, six handbreadths by six handbreadths (*tefachim*);[14] alternative readings suggest that they were rectangular, six handbreadths in length but only three in width.[15] Some of these sources go further and suggest that the tablets of the law were divided into what might be termed zones of influence:

The length of the tablets was six handbreadths; two were—could we but speak thus!—in the hands of He who called the world into being. Two handbreadths were in the hands of Moses. And two handbreadths separated the two hands.[16]

This version of revelation at Sinai is far from the image of a passive human recipient of divine grace. Rather, the representative of humanity, Moses, is one part of a three-part process involving God and a mediating substance, namely, the tablets themselves. This is a Torah of tension, a Torah only experienced through the pull of the different parties.

This midrashic account of revelation brings to mind Michelangelo's description of the creation of Adam on the ceiling of the Sistine Chapel in the Vatican. Two hands, the human and the divine, come close to touching each other, and the eye is held by the gap separating them. If the two hands had been made to meet on the ceiling, the painting would not make the profound impression it does. So too the midrash describes a Torah of tension and participation. Moses cannot hold the hand of God, but he has the opportunity to hold on, as it were, to what God is holding.

The tripartite distinction in the midrash also evokes a modern Jewish association. In his *Star of Return*, Franz Rosenzweig describes a star comprising one triangle superimposed on another. The first triad is comprised of three disaggregated core constituents of existence which cannot be reduced to an all-encompassing One. God, the World, and Humanity are basic elements, and the encounter between them yields the second triad of creation, revelation, and redemption. Whether or not Rosenzweig knew the midrash and was hinting at it, the parallel is hard to ignore. The three-thirds of the tablets correspond to these three domains of existence. In order for the model to hold, all three aspects must be distinct from each other, and they must be present. This portrayal of the Sinai moment does not present a one-sided or hierarchical delivery from donor to recipient. It implies a more complex dynamic, according to which God, humanity, and the world must be present in order for revelation to occur.

The midrash in Exodus Rabbah goes on to describe Moses ascending beyond the earthly realm and taking the Torah captive, to the chagrin of the angels who resent this human interloper.[17] Rather than presenting Moses as a heroic Prometheus figure, boldly stealing the heavenly treasure, it proposes an ambiguous picture: "Lest you think that because he captured it, he took it for free … it was given to him for a price. Lest you think that he actually paid in money … it was given to him as a gift."[18]

The Torah is given and received.[19]

Rays of Glory

One risk of adopting a maximalist approach to understanding Torah is that it is tempting to conclude that everything and anything is Torah. If I busy myself with sports statistics or entertainment trivia, can that be considered Torah? Without pretending to know where exactly these lines are to be drawn, I would argue that any interest, any area of research or engagement, any attempt to deepen and discover can be Torah so long as the three-thirds are present in the activity. In my reading of the midrashic image, I have a sense of engaging in Torah in a true sense when I am aware of the tension exerted by three partners: myself within (*bi*, to employ another term in this lexicon), the world of which I am a part, and God beyond me.

"So Moses came down from Mount Sinai. And as Moses came down from the mountain bearing the two tablets of the Pact, Moses was not aware that the skin of his face was radiant" (Exodus 34:29). One midrash asks: where did these rays originate? Some suggestions are made based on the biblical account, and two relate directly to our exploration of Torah as participatory event:

> Some say that as the Holy One was teaching the Torah to Moses, sparks from the Holy Presence were turned into rays of glory. And Rabbi Samuel bar Nachman said: the tablets were six handbreadths in length and three handbreadths wide. Moses was holding two *tefachim* and the Holy One another two, and there was a gap between them of two more. That is where the rays of glory emanated.[20]

The particular moment of teaching described here is not an example of *hevruta*, wherein two partners in study are united by a common text. Here the author of all is explicating the words. Nonetheless, the midrash is suggesting that an illuminating spark is created whenever two are joined in learning a mediating text. In that moment of pedagogy, the Divine explicates something to the human. It is not only the sense of communion between the three dimensions that generates light. It is also the distinctions between these zones, the cracks where the light gets in. Occasionally in the course of doing Torah, alone or with fellow learners, the three sets of *tefachim* align and something lights up.

Torah as described in this image is not a matter of stacking data or scoring points. Nor is it a question of attaining *unio mystica*, a blurring of all distinctions. It lives in the tension between giving and receiving and between its constituent parts.

This picture of Torah leaves many thorny problems unresolved. According to Maimonides' eighth Principle of Faith, it is not difficult to differentiate the Pentateuch and the rest of the Hebrew Bible from all other literature: the former is of divine provenance, and all the others are human. The *Bhagavad Gita* and *The Brothers Karamazov* are great, but the Torah is different. My position makes such a statement more challenging. It is certainly true that the Torah has been the foundational document of Jewish civilization and others too. It is also true that I love it, and it is my discourse every day. Finding a metaphysical justification for its innate superiority over every other text is neither possible nor necessary. It is different for me.

Alongside Torah as a particular canon, there is Torah as an activity, and that can take place in a dizzying variety of contexts. In recent centuries increasing attention has been paid to the Torah of the world, represented in our midrash by the stone separating hand from hand. Learning about the planet, its diversity and its processes, the natural sciences, and new technologies—this too is Torah and we need to learn it. In my reading, any subject matter, even the most sacred text, can lose its Torah status if the tension is lost. And indeed, any pursuit which encourages curiosity and leaves open the possibility of discovery can be Torah. I may not be able to define it, but I know it when it is happening. Is any process of study, any moment of curiosity, to be deemed Torah in its broadest sense? I would say yes, providing the activity meets the *tefachim* criteria: that I am present, that the world is present, that God is present, and that all three dimensions are palpable.

John Caputo conceives of revelation in this way:

> A "revelation" is not a supernatural invention from another world that interrupts the course of history and nature with a disclosure of which the world itself would not be capable....If we say a revelation is *tout autre*, that does not mean that it breaks in upon us from *another world* but that it comes as *another worlding* of the world, another world disclosure, another way the world itself opens up, is reconfigured, is "revealed" in an unforeseeable and unanticipated way. The unforeseeability is the revealability: we were blind and now we see.[21]

Caputo's theology has Christian roots and is usually described as radical and postmodern. He argues that, by its very nature, revelation is not exclusive; just as there are many cultural forms of life, so are there many revelations. All this makes his approach unpalatable for some traditional Jewish readers. It is as if, when holding up the Torah in synagogue, we were to declare: this is one of a number of cultural revelations and we celebrate them all. To do so seems to belittle the moral import of our Torah and to ignore the historical record, according to which the Hebrew Bible has had a profound impact on cultures around the world. Another objection can be raised to the maximalist interpretation of revelation. If every time I conceive of the world in a new way there has been a revelation, if every sigh is a Sinai, the term is robbed of meaning.

For over 1500 years Jews have been reading the Pentateuch according to a weekly cycle, encouraged to turn it and turn it again, to find links between quotidian realities and the portion currently being read. Turning to Torah and turning it, knowing that it has been turned and turned again by my forebears in vastly different circumstances, I am constantly struck by how new ideas and possibilities come to mind when Torah is read not as an exercise in information-gathering but as a process of meaning-making. God is revealed in Torah regardless of the process by which the text came to be formed. Indeed, thinking about that process is part of my Torah practice. History, referred to elsewhere in this book using the expression *zeman nakat*, is not a challenge to Torah but part of it. This is true so long as I am trying to learn within the model of *tefachim* and not holding up a text or an idea as a specimen to be dissected.

There is an ethical dimension to Torah. Emmanuel Levinas insists that any meaningful revelation must be accompanied by obligation. In a 1977 essay, he argues that becoming aware of an Other shakes me out of my self-enclosed state. Levinas points to a sensibility developed in the West according to which self-possession is the highest virtue. It is based on the assumption that the ideal condition of the self is "repose, calm and conciliation."[22] Encounter with the reality of the Other, however, serves to bring me out of this secure zone and to consider the obligations I have beyond the quest for self-fulfillment.

Levinas sets aside questions relating to a moment at Sinai at some previous point in history and emphasizes instead the notion of revelation itself. Ethical relation, namely, the acknowledgment of the presence of the other, can be understood as "a modality of the relation with God."[23] This awareness carries with it a command I am obliged to obey. It may not be a commandment to observe this or that culinary discipline or to sacrifice this or that animal, but part of the awakening to the presence of the Other is a call demanding a response. Revelation in Levinas' account is not the imparting of a particular body of knowledge. It is the acknowledgment of the demands placed upon me when I see myself as part of a greater whole. Whether or not you call yourself religious has little bearing on whether or not you have experienced a moment of revelation, as unsettling as it is inspiring.

Of course, how you understand God is bound to impact the way in which you think about revelation. Those who hold with God as a personality—*chai* in my terminology—will find it easier to entertain the idea of some communication from the divine to the human realm than those who see God as the ground of existence—*kayyam*. It might be thought that atheists, rejecting outright any God concept and branding it an illusion or a fraud, would have no time for revelation as a concept. Experience teaches otherwise. If you grapple with ideas and feel the pull of the *tefachim* and if, instead of God, you are impelled to act by climate emergency, social hope, or democratic values, you are doing Torah in my terms.

I disagree profoundly with much of what is done in the name of Torah and understand the temptation to let go of the tablets and let the letters float away. My choice is to hold on resolutely and to engage in the practice of Torah with as much integrity as I can muster. There is a political dimension to my reading of the midrash and my understanding of Torah. They are informed by the notion of balance and the separation of powers. Too much of what passes for Torah actually involves an angry person wielding a rock. In order to be Torah, a delicate balance of the three realms is called for. It is also worth noting that in the metaphor, God occupies a third of the surface, not its totality. There is room in my model for a separation of church and state, that is, to allow the world to operate without clerical interference. After all, those regimes which claim that God has written the constitution are dominated by small male elites determined to preserve their monopoly on what constitutes God's will. This is not a Torah of *tefachim*. One of the midrashim records that the tablets fell because the stone by itself was too heavy for any human to bear. It was the writing that made the burden bearable. "After the writing had floated away the tablets were too heavy for Moses."[24] This is what happens when Torah loses its vital tension and becomes a rock with which to bludgeon and suppress.

Rupture and Replacement

Some versions of our midrashic tradition involving the *tefachim* suggest an alternative version of events leading up to the destruction of the first set of tablets. Rather than Moses dashing them to the ground at the sight of Israelite idolatry, the tablets fall as a result of some epic struggle on high:

> Moses' hands were emboldened and he took hold of the tablets and broke them...[25]

> After Israel did "that deed" the Holy One wanted to take the tablets from Moses' hands, so Moses's hand was emboldened and he grabbed them from God...
> The tablets wanted to float up to the sky and Moses attempted to grab them...
> The writing itself floated up.[26]

In all these cases, one of the constituent parts of the dynamic retreats or advances such that the balance is lost, the tension departs, and the tablets fall. Here is a conscious undermining of the well-known biblical story. It is not that Moses expresses his outrage and breaks them; rather, something at the moment of transmission goes awry. Moses overreaches. Like Adam before him, he has been forbidden a certain precinct of existence, and just like Adam, he wants to know what he is missing.

The breaking of the tablets represents dismay and disgrace but also opportunity. In a bold statement, David Weiss Halivni asserts: "If the tablets had not been broken, the Oral Torah would not exist." In contrast to the opinion advanced by Maimonides and others that the Oral Law is the result of pristine revelation of the original divine message, Halivni speaks of "a fractured and reconstituted Torah, assembled from the shards of the tablets, so to speak, fraught with ambiguity and uncertainty and even lacunae and in need of augmentation and human repair."[27]

Perhaps this is the turning and turning again in which we are instructed to engage. For me, Torah is my life and the measure of my days, but it is not static. I hold on tight and then occasionally let go or overreach. As the tablets I was holding are shattered, the possibility of a new set emerges.

The Torah is the basis, the rock from which my wider understanding of doing Torah is hewn. In order to hold our *tefachim*, it is necessary to prepare. Jewish education should encourage the learner to want to grab on to the tablets and to hold on tight. Torah happens when I pull and I feel something pulling back. If all that happens in the Torah process is that my opinions were confirmed and my self-regard massaged, I did not get beyond my own handbreadths. If all that occurs is that my sense of insecurity is deepened and a finger is being wagged, the tension of Torah is lost and something far less salutary takes its place.

Turn the Torah, but do not twist it. Hold on tight, but do not overreach or turn it into a blunt instrument. It may fall, but do not lose hope. We have been putting it back together for thousands of years.

NOTES

1. Deuteronomy 4:44. According to Soferim 14:14 and Shulchan Arukh Orach Chayim 123, Psalm 19:8 is also recited.
2. Soferim 14:14.
3. Mishnah Avot 5:22.
4. For a thorough analysis of the use of the word in the Hebrew Bible, see Beecher, "Torah." For a presentation of seven possible meanings of the term, see Neusner, *Torah*. Solomon, *Torah from Heaven*, offers a clear, systematic, and witty discussion of different understandings of the term. For a fascinating study of attitudes to Torah and revelation in some Hasidic sources, see Mayse, "The Voices of Moses."
5. BT Berakhot 62a.
6. Fishbane, *Sacred Attunement*, 229.
7. This phrase is used with reference to the ark in BT Sotah 35a.
8. This is originally found in Maimonides' commentary on the tenth chapter of Tractate Sanhedrin in the Mishnah.
9. See Mishnah Sanhedrin 10.1.
10. Heschel, *Heavenly Torah*. The first volume of this Hebrew work was originally published in 1962. The English translation cited here is based on the original Soncino edition of that work. In 2021 a new Hebrew edition was published under the editorship of Dror Bondi and has cast exciting new light on the original project, bringing to light chapters which were omitted from the original edition.
11. See Feldmann Kaye, *Jewish Theology*, 99–124. Ross is only one example of what is now a burgeoning group of thinkers, scholars, and practitioners of traditional Orthodox Judaism who reject what might be termed a simple fundamentalist position. See Ross, *Expanding Palace*.
12. See Lebens, "Is There Primordial Torah?," in which he wrestles with the question of whether contemporary Orthodox Jews should hold with the idea of a Torah existing on another realm. Lebens' assumptions are far from my own, but he cites a number of important sources in the course of

his argumentation. Many traditions relating to the meaning and nature of Torah can be found in Heschel, *Heavenly Torah*, particularly 368–386 and 542–544.
13. For a discussion on the writing upon the tablets, see Frankel, "What Did God Write?"
14. BT Baba Batra 14a, BT Nedarim 38a and Numbers Rabbah 4.2 (both of which include the information that they were three handbreadths thick).
15. PT Ta'aniot 4.8, 68c; PT Shekalim 6.1, 49d; Tanhuma Ki Tissa 37; and Tanhuma Buber Ki Tissa 20. The representation of the tablets as curved at the top, well known to anyone who has seen Charlton Heston as Moses in *The Ten Commandments*, is medieval in origin.
16. Exodus Rabbah 28.1.
17. For a variety of rabbinic sources on the rivalry between Moses and the angels, see Ginzberg, *Legends*, vol. 3, 109–114. For analyses of these traditions, see: Halperin, *Faces of the Chariot*, 289–307, which offers a thorough reading of homily 20 of Pesikta Rabbati and related sources; Kasher, "Mythological Figure of Moses"; and Schultz, "Angelic Opposition." In esoteric literature we find the idea that the angels subsequently become reconciled with Moses and imparted mysterious knowledge to him. See Halbertal, *Concealment and Revelation*, 9, and Idel, "Tefisat Hatorah."
18. Exodus Rabbah 28.1. I have omitted the textural reasoning employed in the midrash and the ingenious interpretation of Psalms 68.19: "When you ascended on high, you took many captives; you received gifts from people." In its original context, the verse refers to God. The midrash daringly applies it to Moses.
19. Halivni suggests that according to the Bible itself, the giving and the receiving were separate events. This is part of his theology of what he calls "the maculate Torah." For my purposes in this chapter, I am suggesting that the Torah is given and taken at the same moment. See Halivni, *Revelation Restored*, particularly 84–85.
20. Tanchuma Ki Tissa 37. See also Tanchuma Buber Ki Tissa 20, and Exodus Rabbah 47.6.
21. Caputo, *Insistence of God*, 93.
22. Levinas, *Beyond the Verse*, 149.
23. Ibid.
24. PT Ta'aniot 4.8, 68c.
25. Tanchuma Ekev 11.
26. These three traditions are found in PT Taaniot 4.8, 68c.
27. Halivni, *Breaking the Tablets*, 98–99.

Open Access This chapter is licensed under the terms of the Creative Commons Attribution 4.0 International License (http://creativecommons.org/licenses/by/4.0/), which permits use, sharing, adaptation, distribution and reproduction in any medium or format, as long as you give appropriate credit to the original author(s) and the source, provide a link to the Creative Commons license and indicate if changes were made.

The images or other third party material in this chapter are included in the chapter's Creative Commons license, unless indicated otherwise in a credit line to the material. If material is not included in the chapter's Creative Commons license and your intended use is not permitted by statutory regulation or exceeds the permitted use, you will need to obtain permission directly from the copyright holder.

Yetzer Lev Ha'adam: On Human Nature

The story at the heart of this chapter is gruesome and disturbing. Like many traditions enshrined in folktales, it may not be suitable for children and for those of a particularly sensitive disposition. The rest of us will have to try to face up to its dark implications.

Reform Judaism has tended to espouse an optimistic worldview. In a 1910 essay (the date is significant because it predates the signature horrors with which the twentieth century was to become synonymous), Hermann Cohen affirmed that the moral ideas of Judaism are "closely related and in full accord with the exemplary ethics of the new era ushered in by the French Revolution."[1] He went on to implore his readers:

> Let us be sure … not to lose our Messianic optimism. The evil spirits, in league with pessimism, will vanish once again. Moral soundness, human lucidity and integrity and, along with them, the creative cultural force of our eternally young religion will be universally acknowledged as surely as progress towards the realization of the god is and remains world history's goal.[2]

It is possible to explain the persistence of "evil spirits," atrocities and desecrations with which recent history has been littered, as the vestiges of a vanishing world clinging on with the last of their powers before fading into oblivion. Another response has been to question the validity of the liberal assumption of progress toward human perfectibility. Cohen, in other words, was either not yet right or simply wrong.

This chapter considers human nature and the persistence of evil through the *aspaklaria* of one story—an invitation to ponder the darker side of existence. Cohen was sure the evil spirits will soon vanish. In the meantime, they need to be addressed.

The Dark Side

To some degree the tolerance one displays for unpalatable topics is a matter of personality. Abraham Joshua Heschel's final work was concerned with one of the great misanthropes of Jewish tradition, Rabbi Menachem Mendel of Kotzk. In his introduction to the book, Heschel reflected on the impact of the Baal Shem Tov, the founder of Hasidism, on the one hand, and the Kotzker, on the other. Unlike the churlish pessimism for which the Kotzker was famous, the Baal Shem Tov advanced a Torah of affirmation and celebration. Heschel was influenced by both:

> I was taught about inexhaustible mines of meaning by the Baal Shem; from the Kotzker I learned to detect immense mountains of absurdity standing in the way. The one taught me song—the other silence. The one reminded me that there could be a Heaven on earth, the other shocked me into discovering Hell in the alleged Heavenly places in our world.[3]

Heschel discovered that these two spiritual influences spoke to different aspects of his own personality. In his later years, both ways of looking at the world—an embrace of creativity and possibility alongside a sense of tragedy and irony calling for ruthless honesty—came to expression in his life and work.

Judaism constitutes a rich lexicon, a profound resource through which it is possible to process many of the most troubling aspects of existence. It is as much a language of rupture as of rapture.[4] I want to point to two strategies typically employed to keep the dark side of existence at bay: expulsion and ingestion. The first response is to banish the darkness to some other realm—a motif I explore later in my discussion of *Azazel*. The second, our present exploration, involves "swallowing" that which we abhor, often leading to spiritual indigestion and moral heartburn. We internalize our trauma and then often suffer from reflux.

In recent decades, combining Hermann Cohen's moral optimism with a more recent appetite for welcoming inclusivity, Reform Judaism has garnered a reputation for cheerfulness and positivity. The tunes are upbeat, the sermons are friendly, and the hospitality is audacious and relentless. Yishai Mevorach, an important Israeli thinker who is largely unknown outside a particular circle of postmodern Israeli theologians, expresses his disdain for this kind of mawkish, saccharine, feel-good Judaism:

> In Israeli pre-army educational programs, in research institutes, in evenings devoted to liturgy and poetry, in the pluralistic areas of discourse of progressive Judaism, in *kabbalot shabbat* employing verse and prose, in egalitarian and inclusive prayer gatherings, at times of joint eye-level learning—those who participate believe that they have control over the letter learned or pronounced. They believe that they can keep a safe distance from this letter or, alternatively, they imagine it clean and free of any harmful dimension.[5]

In fact, Mevorach asserts, there is no meaningful religion that sanitizes the underside of existence, no way of grasping religion while avoiding its threatening thorn, no way of ignoring its neuroses and compulsions. For him, the dark side is inescapable. The letter, each molecule of Jewish life, is imbued with guilt and pain, as much as it is marinated in hope. Judaism without tears is not an option.

Mevorach's position should be considered in the context of a much broader debate which has characterized modern Judaism in the West. In a letter written to Salman Schocken in 1937, Gershom Scholem explained that he was drawn to the study of mysticism and mythology as a reaction against Saadia Gaon, Maimonides, and Hermann Cohen, all of whom, he claimed, "saw their primary function in setting up antitheses to myth and pantheism."[6] The turn to pre-modern roots was, in part, a critique of rationalism and modernity, which were considered cerebral and anodyne. The Jewish exposure to modernity has been characterized by a pendulum swinging between rationalism and romanticism, logic and myth, and disenchantment and re-enchantment. Its implications—religious, cultural, political—are playing out at a furious pace. Each side of the debate points to the other's inadequacies and remains largely blind to its own.

This pendulum dynamic is complex, and any attempt to draw the lines too neatly between the camps is bound to be inadequate. Modernity has not played out as a simplistic battle between the children of darkness and the children of light. Mevorach characterizes the pluralistic areas of progressive Jewish discourse without accounting for the thoughts of those like Rachel Adler, Eugene Borowitz, and Emil Fackenheim, each of whom demonstrated a keen awareness of the darker aspects of human existence.

Nonetheless, behind his caricature, there is a kernel of truth. There can be something self-satisfied and platitudinous about much of progressive Judaism with its constant reminders that we are partners in the work of creation and its calls for acts of world mending.

Over recent years, due to environmental threats, pandemic risks, and political polarization, we progressives have become increasingly aware of the threats to stability. In its coming manifestations, Reform Judaism and similar expressions will need to find a way of staying true to Enlightenment values while remaining aware of the perpetual presence of the dark. What characterizes the ancient text at the heart of this chapter is that moral depravity is not identified with a rival camp, such as the Amalekites or the backsliders. Here the source of evil is located within the heart of every one of us.

Samael Pays a Visit

Little is known for sure about the midrash I am about to cite. Its manuscript was published by the scholar Louis Ginzberg in 1913, originally found nestled within the pages of a Yemenite *machzor* (festival liturgy). It shows many signs of Islamic influence, and it is close in many aspects to a number of Muslim texts.[7]

The midrash begins with Genesis 8:21, a verse which includes the expression *yetzer lev ha'adam*, usually translated as "the inclination of the human heart." The activity from which the word *yetzer* is derived is the production of clay vessels. The *yetzer* of the heart may therefore be that which is formed in the workshop of the heart or "every product of the thought of man's mind."[8] Over time and in its other biblical contexts, the word took on "a more developed meaning: human thoughts, plans, imagination, or even dispositions and tendencies."[9]

The entire midrash is only a few paragraphs in length and is presented here in italics interspersed with some commentary and reflections.

> *'For the inclination of the heart of humanity is wicked from their youth' (Gen 8:21). I will now reveal to you the secret of this verse.*
>
> *At the time when the Holy One, blessed be He, created His world, Samael came down (to earth) and with him was what appeared to be a small boy. He went to Eve and said to her: "Can my son stay with you while I make a journey to a distant place?" She said to him: "He may stay." Then Samael went on his way.*

> Now on that day Adam had been walking about in the Garden of Eden. The moment Adam came back to his house, he saw that boy crying. He said to Eve his wife: "Whose son is this?" She said to him: "He is the son of Samael." He said to her: "What has this trouble to do with us?" Now the boy kept weeping ever more loudly and bitterly to the point that he was aggravating Adam. What did Adam do? He arose and slaughtered him, but the boy continued weeping all the more! Adam (again) arose and chopped him up into little pieces, but afterwards each piece was individually screaming! What did Adam do? He (again) arose and cooked him, and he and Eve his wife ate him.

The story opens with the first childminding engagement in human history. Samael, one of the great archdemons, appeals to Eve's good nature and exploits her willingness to look after who she believes to be his son.[10] It is worth mentioning here that some ancient traditions speak of a sexual union, either consensual or coerced, between Samael and Eve,[11] whereby Adam's question to Eve "Whose son is this?" can be read as an expression of jealousy and not simply puzzlement. Adam's Eden state, free to live in the garden with no intergenerational tensions of family responsibilities, is brought to a premature close. He may not have been expelled from the garden, but he has been removed from a state of bliss and introduced to the annoyances and insecurities of quotidian life.

Adam's question to his wife is in fact a quotation from the Mishnah. The question "What has this trouble to do with us?" is put in the mouth of a potential witness in a judicial proceeding when they understand the gravity associated with giving testimony. Such a potentially recalcitrant witness is reminded of the verse from Leviticus clarifying that the person who fails to give testimony is subject to punishment.[12] The use of that phrase here represents an intertextual hint. Adam, who has lived so far free of responsibility, is confronted with the needs of rearing a child, and his question to Eve reflects a well-known human response known ever since Adam: why has this anything to do with us?

What follows is a nightmarish decline from a familiar experience (the inability to calm an agitated baby) to heinous and inhuman acts. Each of the stages in this ghoulish bloodbath is appalling, but before we turn away with a shrug and question the mental health of the ancient or medieval progenitors of this tradition, it should be noted that none of them is unknown in our time. There are too many reports of parents and others killing babies who were making too much noise. Even the act of eating another person remains a resonant theme; indeed, an article in British

Vogue asked whether cannibalism should be seen as the defining cultural trope of 2022.¹³

Adam is portrayed in this dreadful tale as active. The failure of each of his attempts to silence the child provokes another act, even more unthinkable than the last. I read this tale as an insight into the human condition. Coping with the unforeseen outcomes of one act, we make the situation worse. Each of these stages—murder, dismemberment, cooking, consumption—are intended to banish the child but ensure that the guilt is more thoroughly ingested. Adam and Eve swallow the evidence.

> *As soon as Samael realized that they had eaten his son, he came to them and said to them: "Give me back my son, and I'll be on my way." They said to him: "We have not seen (him), nor do we know (where he is)." He said to them: "Are you telling a lie? The Holy One, blessed be He, will eventually give the Torah to Israel, and it is written within it that you should keep your distance from one telling a lie!" While they were talking, the son of Samael began speaking from within Adam and Eve, saying to Samael: "Go on your way. I have now entered into their heart, and I will never depart from their heart, whether they or their descendants or the descendants of their descendants until the end of all generations." At that time Samael went on his way.*

This section of the tale cannot be read without calling to mind the Genesis narrative concerning both Adam and Eve and then Cain and Abel. In this account, it is Samael who plays the role assigned in the original to God. Remarkably, he expresses moral outrage not at the heinous acts which have been committed but because Adam and Eve are lying. Perhaps the most crucial and tragic moment in this entire sorry tale comes when Samael's avatar, who had played the part of the child, banishes Samael. There is no longer a need for monsters and devils—external manifestations of a demonic urge. The monster has now been consumed and internalized, and a kind of irreversible original sin has been committed.¹⁴

It is possible to read this paragraph as an alternative history of modernity. The process of disenchantment does indeed take place. Ghosts and demons are disproved and banished to folklore and nightmares. However, their dismissal is not because humans have outgrown the belief in some demonic drive causing mayhem but, rather, because the virus has been successfully implanted and the ghost is now within the machine. It is as if this obscure text, with roots in the second century BCE or perhaps 1200 years later, is saying: you no longer need to carry around the unwieldy metaphysics of foreign deities and devilish spirits. You can now talk about mental processes and instincts honed in the name of evolutionary aims. You moderns in future centuries will have no need for the paraphernalia associated with external demons. As Hermann Cohen predicted, the evil spirits will vanish.

And, indeed, we find Sigmund Freud employing the imagery of a previous age in the construction of his modern theories in such comments as: "The theory of the drives is so to say our mythology. Drives are mythical entities, magnificent in their indefiniteness."[15] These words were spoken in 1933 as a mythical drive for absolute power swept over Germany and prepared to engulf the world. Decades earlier Freud had observed: "No one who, like me, has conjured up the most evil of those half-tamed demons that inhabit the human breast and seeks to wrestle with them, can expect to come through the struggle unscathed."[16] Sending Samael away, the boy in the human heart remains, leaving us with a version of the human condition, in which "all humans are beings whose destructiveness is as basic as their love."[17]

I grew up in postwar London, the child of a father who had seen Hitler's Ukraine and Stalin's Siberia and a mother who had survived a ghetto and a death camp. We believed that destructiveness was now on the wane and that the son of Samael had been excised from the human heart. These days such confident predictions are more difficult to digest.

Torah as Cure

Thereupon Adam was sad, and he put on sackcloth and ashes. He was afflicting himself with innumerable periods of fasting until the Holy One, blessed be He, revealed Himself unto him and said to him: "My son, do not be afraid of him! I am providing for you a remedy, for he came to you only as my emissary." He said to him: "What is this remedy that you are giving to me?" He said to him: "The Torah.'" He said to him: "Where is the Torah?" At that time he handed over to him the Book of Raziel the Angel, and he was studying it both day and night.

After some time, the ministering angels came to Adam for they were jealous of him. They told him that he was a divinity superior to them and were worshipping him. But Adam said to them: "Do not be worshipping me! Magnify the Lord your God with me, and let us extol His Name together, for I also like you am a created being!" What did the ministering angels do? On account of the great jealousy they felt toward Adam, they took from him the book which the

> *Holy One, blessed be He, had given to him and pitched it in the sea. They then went on their way.*
>
> *Adam searched for the book but could not find it. He was highly distressed, and put on sackcloth and ashes. He afflicted himself with innumerable periods of fasting until the Holy One, blessed be He, revealed Himself unto him from the supernal heavens and said to him: "Do not fear! I will restore the book to you!" At that time the Holy One, blessed be He, summoned the Prince of the Sea and said to him: "Go under My agency to the sea, rescue the book, and give it to Adam!" The Prince of the Sea, whose name is Rahab, went and rescued the book and gave it to Adam. It is the one mentioned in the verse "this is the book of the generations of Adam" (Gen 5:1). May the Lord, blessed be He, deliver us from the evil inclination! Amen, may God's will be done!*

Adam is bereft, jealous, and confused. He is suffering from the earliest and most consequential case of heartburn. It is in this extreme state that Adam is privileged to experience a direct encounter with the Divine, who offers him the Torah as a salve (the Hebrew word employed is *refu'ah*, a cure). Indeed, in rabbinic literature, the Torah is described as an antidote to the ravages of the evil inclination:

> The words of Torah are like an elixir of life. This is comparable to a king who was angry with his son, struck him a violent blow, and placed a bandage on his wound. He told him: My son, as long as this bandage remains on your wound, you may eat whatever you please and drink whatever you please, and bathe in either hot or cold water, and you will come to no harm. But if you remove it, it will immediately fester. Thus the Holy One, blessed be He, said to Israel: my children, I created your evil *yetzer*...Be occupied with words of Torah and it will not reign over you.[18]

This statement, one of many in rabbinic literature in praise of the salutary effects of Torah, is challenging. In recent years, as the social climate has made it possible to overcome some of the layers of obfuscation and denial, several examples of abuse and excess perpetrated by those who are presented as exemplars of Torah rigor and virtue have come to light. Further, the theological picture painted here is one of God perpetuating the need for a drug of which he is the sole supplier. Engagement with Torah is no excuse for abuse and exploitation—such behavior is a desecration. Nor is Torah study a guarantee of moral rectitude. Too many individuals cloaked in piety and erudition have proven to be powerless to the dictates of the son of Samael embedded in their hearts, for it to be plausible to claim that the Torah cure is failsafe.

Rather than dismiss the idea of Torah as a response to the complexity of the human condition, it may be possible to reinterpret it. To be engaged in Torah should be to embrace tension and to explore distinct realms: *tefachim*—the human, the divine, and what lies between them. Studying Torah seriously also affords the opportunity to learn a methodology which helps mold a way of thinking. The exegetical principles, the *middot* by which the Torah is interpreted, encourage its devotees to think in supple and creative ways. Torah at its finest should open the possibility for new ideas and new possibilities, encouraging us to consider a life which is not simply a bad infinity—a repeat of all that has come before.

God gives Adam a book to read, not the Pentateuch but the Book of Raziel the Angel. Noting that the idea of a special book revealed to Adam was known in rabbinic literature, Oded Yisraeli has identified this tradition regarding the origin of the Kabbalah with a universalist trend in medieval esoteric sources.[19] Adam is intrigued by the book, and here again the familiar theme of rivalry with the angels finds its way into the narrative. Perhaps Adam's perusal of the book is akin to Moses' kidnapping of the Torah in the midrash discussed in the earlier discussion of *tefachim*. In both cases, the angels experience unease at the prospect of humans overtaking them in terms of insight and capacity.

The book is thrown into the sea, so God summons the sea deity to pluck it from the waters. In an alternative to the Sinai revelation, the Torah here is birthed from the waters. The Torah is not beyond human reach, not beyond the sea or sunk beneath it for eternity. It is accessible as a way of grappling with the complex dynamics of the human condition. Will Herberg wrote in 1951: "Human existence *is* crisis, *is* insecurity, peril, conflict, urgency, judgment and decision. Not merely human existence today, in this period of war and social convulsion, but human existence as such, the existence of man."[20] This bizarre midrash shares Herberg's insight. It suggests that a life of Torah offers a means not of solving the conundrum or dissolving the complexity but of finding meaning and a possibility of coping.

There are few heroes in this ancient tale. Samael, his avatar son, Eve and Adam, the angels—none of them is simply virtuous. God's own role is ambivalent, offering a cure for a God-ordained sickness. Since coming across the tale some years ago, I have not been able to forget it, and every passing year brings it new resonance and relevance. We behave with moral numbness, and since we have nowhere to bury the evidence of our deeds and omissions, we end up ingesting it. It comes back to haunt us, burning our hearts. In Israel, where I have lived for four decades, this mythic cycle is hard to ignore. The violence which accompanied the birth of the State was, we hoped, nothing to do with us but simply something we were forced to commit as part of the process of attaining independence. We buried the violence, swallowed it, and it comes back to haunt us in the home and on the streets. We did not bestow democratic rights on all who live in the territory we occupy, persuading ourselves that it would be suicidally naïve to do so and promising ourselves that in time we would find an equitable settlement. In the meantime, circumstances have conspired, along with most of the protagonists, to ensure that the temporary has become quasi-permanent, and the deeds we swallowed continue to torment us. We and the Palestinians are held in the grip of a relentless dyspeptic cycle.

Will Torah save us from the son of Samael? Not automatically, of course. Wherever a veil of piety or a wall of authority is employed to cover up unethical behavior, it should be removed. I believe that traditional Torah virtues—deep study, debate, diligence—are virtues worth preserving. Over the generations, conceptions of Torah have changed as the world changes. Now, as technological transformation, social alienation, political polarization, and spiritual angst are all around us, our Torah is in urgent need of renewal. Recovering, reconsidering, and reinterpreting traditions on the edge of our traditional canons may prove to be part of this process.

Perhaps, at the point of the service when we open the ark and hold up its contents to the community, we might add a declaration: this is the Torah, our version of a book given to Adam in his time of despair and confusion, reclaimed from the ocean when the jealous angels cast it beyond human reach. We turn to it with our *yetzer*, the contents and the products of our restless hearts.

Notes

1. Cohen, *Reason and Hope*, 89.
2. Ibid., 89.
3. Heschel, *Passion for Truth*, xiv.
4. I am indebted to Rachel Sabath Bet Halachmi for this formulation.
5. Mevorach, *Aron Ha'edut*, 88,
6. Scholem, *On the Possibility*, 4.
7. Ginzberg, "Beno shel Samael." The Muslim parallels are explicated in Hadromi-Allouche, "The Death and Life."

8. Rosen-Zvi, *Demonic Desires*, 3. See Aitken, Patmore, and Rosen-Zvi, *Evil Inclination*, particularly the essay by Mizrachi, "Reconsidering the Semantics."
9. Rosen-Zvi, *Demonic Desires*, 3.
10. On the character of Samael, see Dan, "Samael, Lilith"; Scholem, *Kabbalah*, 385–389. Fredrick, "Disarticulating Lilith" is particularly interesting in the context of this chapter. She argues that in medieval Jewish folklore Samael and Lilith are conceived as servants of God. Samael appears as a kind of contract killer working on God's behalf rather than some independent entity.
11. See Adelman, *Return of the Repressed*, particularly 98–107.
12. Leviticus 5:1. The phrase is to be found in Mishnah Sanhedrin 4:5.
13. The article "From Yellowjackets to Dahmer" is by Chelsea G. Summers, who has explored the theme in her own fiction. For discussions of the biblical theme, see Anderson, "Parents Eating Their Children" and, particularly, Graybill, "Child Is Being Eaten." For a fascinating and disturbing treatment of this theme from a gendered perspective relating to the early modern period, see Idelson-Shein, "Monstrous *Mame*."
14. For an analysis decades old but still useful, see Cohon, "Original Sin." For a thorough account of medieval Jewish refutations of this doctrine, see Rembaum, "Medieval Jewish Criticism." This theme is discussed from several angles in Mittleman, *Human Nature*.
15. Quoted in Bloom, "Freud," 115.
16. Freud, *Case Histories 1*, 150. For a critique of Freud's scientific mythology, see Bock, *Human Nature Mythology*, 61–79.
17. Goldenberg, "Anger in the Body," 48–49.
18. Sifre to Deuteronomy Piska 45. In his masterful study, *Demonic Desires*, Rosen-Zvi describes this source (from which I have quoted an excerpt) as "the longest and most developed presentation of the evil *yetzer* in the entire tannaitic corpus," 21. In parallel to this source in BT Kiddushin 30b, and also in BT Baba Batra 16a, the Torah is described as *tavlin*, which reads in this context as an antidote or salve.
19. For rabbinic traditions according to which Adam was given a book of some kind, see: BT Baba Metzia 85b-86a; BT Sanhedrin 38b; and Genesis Rabbah 24.2. See Yisraeli, "Jewish Medieval Traditions," particularly 31–40. The medieval work *The Book of Raziel the Angel*, claiming to be the book originally bestowed to Adam, was published in Amsterdam in 1701. A Latin translation of the Hebrew-Aramaic manuscript was produced under Alfonso X of Castile during the thirteenth century. In *Possibility of Jewish Mysticism* Scholem declares: "Kabbalah is, so to speak, the authentic wisdom and knowledge given to Adam by the angel Raziel," 124.
20. Herberg, *Judaism and Modern Man*, 9.

Open Access This chapter is licensed under the terms of the Creative Commons Attribution 4.0 International License (http://creativecommons.org/licenses/by/4.0/), which permits use, sharing, adaptation, distribution and reproduction in any medium or format, as long as you give appropriate credit to the original author(s) and the source, provide a link to the Creative Commons license and indicate if changes were made.

The images or other third party material in this chapter are included in the chapter's Creative Commons license, unless indicated otherwise in a credit line to the material. If material is not included in the chapter's Creative Commons license and your intended use is not permitted by statutory regulation or exceeds the permitted use, you will need to obtain permission directly from the copyright holder.

Kosot Yeshu'ah: Frameworks of Jewish Thought

Teaching Jewish thought presents some methodological challenges. It is tempting to focus on particular thinkers, surfacing the theological and political issues they faced through the *aspaklaria* of each life and body of work. Another approach is to select themes such as chosenness, revelation, redemption, and authority, and to consider the ways in which these beams have been absorbed and refracted through the generations.

It is also possible to address the challenge of conveying complex material in an accessible way by adopting a modal approach. The question animating such a method is not who a thinker was and what they said nor how a set of individuals set their minds to a certain problem. From a modal perspective, what matters more is the basic paradigm at work: what kind of question is being asked and what is the model animating the work of the thinkers under discussion?

Thomas Kuhn developed the notion of paradigms in his portrayal of the history of science, suggesting that scientific revolutions occur as one paradigm gives way to another.[1] Kuhn explained that he was using the term to refer to both "the entire constellation of beliefs, values and techniques…shared by the members of a given community" and "one sort of element in that constellation, the concrete puzzle-solutions which, employed as models or examples, can replace explicit rules."[2]

This chapter searches for paradigms that help explain some of the key preoccupations of modern Jewish thought and frame them in explicitly Jewish terminology.

Paradigms Lost

Richard Rubenstein was one of the most influential and controversial Jewish thinkers of his time. He died in 2021 at the age of 97, but his exit from mainstream institutional Jewish life took place almost fifty years earlier, when he decided that he could no longer pursue the life of a conventional rabbi. In a remarkable memoir published in 1974, Rubenstein recorded the various factors which led up to his change of heart. He made short shrift of American Reform Judaism, which he saw as a classic example of the secularization process. The German Jews who came to the United States after 1848, he wrote

> were a distinctly privileged community. They thought of themselves as almost Protestant.…Confident in themselves, they saw their diluted Judaism as somehow a paradigm of religious rationality. At no point did it stand in their way, especially when the opportunity arose for the most affluent among them to escape the final stigma of Jewishness through marriage.
> They were prepared for everything but the twentieth century.[3]

This last sentence deals a blow to the self-understanding of Reform Judaism. Modernists to a fault, its adherents thought they were adapting Judaism to the new reality, but their reality changed far more profoundly than their reforms could comprehend.

Rubenstein's stinging critique was that of an insider–outsider. He was describing the Reform movement which had educated him and with which he maintained contact. In this sense, he is one of a long line of thinkers who have offered a diagnosis of what ails the movement of which they are a part. A book published some fifty years after Rubenstein's memoir suggested, similarly, that Reform Judaism is not prepared for the twenty-first century.[4] At stake is not this or that article of faith, policy, or practice but rather the wider question: what are we trying to achieve? Does the model in which we are engaged still make sense?

Every movement, ideology, and institution are plagued by structural instabilities, acknowledged or not. The aphorism attributed to Irving (Yitz) Greenberg comes to mind: "I don't care which denomination you belong to, as long as you're embarrassed by it." The two modernist Jewish responses which have been most consequential to me—liberal Judaism and liberal Zionism—are both teetering on the brink of something huge and disruptive. It may be a new chapter. It may be the abyss.

Cups as Paradigms

Seder night is characterized by a number of key symbols, none more central than the four cups of wine which are drunk in the course of the evening. Finding symbolic significance in the details of the meal is an ancient activity, perhaps as old as the Seder itself. A passage in the Talmud of the Land of Israel includes a number of suggestions for their allegorical meaning: most famously, four languages of redemption (we will return to this presently) but also four cups of Pharaoh, four kingdoms, or four cups of doom.[5]

According to the most well-known of the various explanations, the reference here is to four terms used for redemption in certain verses in the sixth chapter of Exodus. Different traditions are associated with these verses, and it is possible that a variant interpretation finding five such terms rather than four was the basis for an opinion that an extra cup of wine be imbibed.[6] This potential fifth symbol is linked in some traditions with a further dimension of redemption to be accomplished at some future time. It may be that Elijah's Cup, primed with wine but not blessed, is a vestige of this old debate about the requisite number of cups of wine to be drunk at the feast.[7]

These cups brim with symbolic meaning in the Jewish religious imagination. Indeed, one Seder cup, a chalice, found its way into the Christian imagination too—it is one of the possible explanations for the origin of what has become known as the Holy Grail.[8] This chapter uses four cups, and then a fifth, to describe different modes or sensibilities that characterize approaches to modern Jewish thought in our times. They represent different versions of redemption.

We might thus consider four kinds of cups—full, overflowing, empty, broken—and the fifth, a cup of presence and absence. Seder night is also characterized by the asking of four questions. As they appear in the Mishnah there were in fact five,[9] and my five cups also represent Big Questions to which modern Jewish thought has sought to provide a response. As an alternative to some of the better-known methods of making such distinctions—traditional and progressive, left and right—my hope is that looking at strategies and philosophies in this way may help clarify them. None of the thinkers referred to here is concerned with one cup to the exclusion of all the others; this is a matter of emphasis not a winner-takes-all battle to the death. Like the Seder itself, without tasting from all of the cups, we are not allowed to leave the feast.

The First Cup: Bourgeois Decency

The immigrant American Jews described in Rubenstein's memoir were in search of a way of asserting themselves as Jews while assuring for themselves lives of economic security and social mobility. While the term "bourgeois" is imprecise—and some are suspicious of it due to its intensive employment by Karl Marx—it helps to evoke the kind of reality this cup represents.[10] Millions of Jews in the nineteenth and twentieth centuries situated themselves in urban settings around the world, and many of them—in Melbourne, Montreal, Johannesburg, and Boca Raton—sought an expression of Judaism that would match their personal and social aspirations. This was to be a Judaism that addressed the vision of a life well lived.

The biblical phrase which best summarizes this first cup is the image of each person sitting beneath their vine and their fig tree, which appears twice in the Hebrew Bible. In the Book of Kings, it is a description (idealized to be sure) of political conditions throughout the land during the reign of King Solomon. For the prophet Micah, living after this golden age, the vision is a prophesy, set in the as yet unattained future and disembodied from his political reality[11] which speaks of a person shrouded in security and free from want, living the successes and disappointments of the life cycle.

In one of his early routines, Woody Allen described the values of his parents as "God and carpeting." The world evoked by this phrase is the world of the Jewish bourgeois, the postwar Jew in the West determinedly building a life of wall-to-wall security and shag-pile certainty. Ignaz Maybaum, a leading theologian of postwar Reform Judaism in Britain, took this idea of the Jewish bourgeois into the domain of theology:

> What makes the Jewish bourgeois a religious figure far beyond ambiguity and neutrality is the Jewish attitude to power, to force, to violence. Jew and bourgeois walk through history like priests. The priest does not wield a sword. No ideology lures the bourgeois into battle. The bourgeois remains a bourgeois as long as he is a private person.[12]

Maybaum, who had come to England from Nazi Germany, took seriously the urge of many, Jews and non-Jews alike, to live a life of purpose and value within the comfort of a secure family structure, presumably amassing the various accoutrements and comforts to be found along the way. He attached dignity to the attempt, common to many of us, to build stable lives imbued with stability and made beautiful with art and culture. Exposure to the perils of extremism confirmed for Maybaum that, in our day, redemption was not to be sought through stirring calls to national redemption but through smaller-scale deeds designed to strengthen family and community. To put it simply and a little unfairly, Maybaum finds God *in* the carpeting.

Much influenced by Franz Rosenzweig, the essence of Judaism was for Maybaum a withdrawal from the sphere of political history. Wedded to eternity rather than the vagaries of current affairs, the Jew's prophetic calling was beyond time and historical circumstance. Christianity and Islam are attempts to serve God within the framework of political power and realpolitik; Judaism, he claimed, was different:

> Rome stands for military virtues, for fortitude in battle, for glory achieved on the battlefield, all noble virtues, but not Jewish virtues, even if the Jews have proved themselves as heroic fighters. Jewish virtues are kindness, charity, justice, humility.... Military man sheds blood mercilessly. Who is a Jew? A man shaped by mercy, his own and that of his forefathers.[13]

In Maybaum's conception of the Jewish Mission, it is in the monogamous family and outside the political sphere that the monotheistic Jew comes to full expression: "Jews are not gentiles, because they are rooted not in history, but in the family."[14]

Our first cup is thus the cup of plenitude, the life of fullness and fulfillment, in which the Jew pulls back from the hurly-burly of history and builds a miniature sanctuary at home.

The Second Cup: Spiritual Overflowing

Psalm 23 includes the immortal phrase "my cup runneth over." The image, as Rashi and others suggested, is one of plenitude: my cup contains all I need. I have enough. The phrase can also be taken to mean not sufficiency but overabundance. This second cup does not strive for a life of plenty and earthly security but yearns for exposure to that which lies beyond. Not the well-regulated flow of life but the overwhelming overflow. Some Jews have turned to pre-modern esoteric traditions in this quest. In the spirit of these traditions, we can note, to return to the psalmist's expression, that the Hebrew word for cup, *kos,* has the same numerical value as *Elohim*, one of God's names, as is taught in the Zohar and elsewhere.[15] Some mystical sources link this phrase with emanations of light from the divine visage.[16] To drink from the second cup is to seek out this divine light: in some versions to be warmed by its illumination and in others to be dazzled by its force.

There is an inherent critique of the first cup in the second. Articulating a decent, conventional Judaism may be good for community and family, but it says little to the individual on a quest for spiritual adventure and fulfillment. The sociological distinction between dwellers and seekers may be relevant here. A Judaism of the full cup is for dwellers, nestled into their suburban lives, aware of how fragile and fleeting those lives can be, keen to find ways to shore them up. In terms of the American Jewish community, it is the established institutional Judaism of the 1940s and 1950s. It is challenged by a new generation of Jewish seekers—the second cup—who want to be exposed to moments of experience and possibilities of encounter. These words of Marcia Prager, taken from a work subtitled *Experiencing the Energy and the Abundance*, help give a sense of the mood of this second cup Judaism:

> We are human beings whose souls are a spark of the living God whose name is I AM. We are also human "doings" whose work is to reflect the divine character of that spark. Where is God? Living with us in holy relationship, flowing through us in holy intention, fulfilled in the covenant binding us to holy action.[17]

The first cup is about security. The second goes beyond the sensible and reaches for the sublime. The explosion of interest in Jewish Spirituality in recent decades illustrates the strength of the urge is to drink from the cup that runneth over.

The Third Cup: Response to Injustice

Just as one of the reactions to a focus on happy families living in a world of plenty was to look for wellsprings of spiritual meaning, another was to emphasize where resources have dried up, where there is hunger and want. This is the sensibility of the third cup. There is a long history of Jewish concern with questions of poverty and privilege, stretching back to the repeated biblical emphasis on the stranger, the widow, and the orphan.[18] In modern times, the prophetic call to clothe the naked and feed the hungry was expressed by some as a core value: for some replacing parochial and religious sentiments (socialism is an example), and for others representing the very heart of Judaism.[19]

In a 1916 essay, Hermann Cohen stated that "the prophets became the *founders of social religion* and thus of social consciousness in general by severing the love of God from mysticism."[20] To use the terminology of this chapter, he articulated in this a theology of the third cup and a rejection of the second. Thinkers as diverse as Cohen in Germany, Levinas in France, and Schweid in Israel placed responsibility for the other at the heart of their reading of Judaism. While the thought of each of them was far more intricate than any simple typology can reflect, they are all exemplars of third cup Jewish thought. In America, viewing social questions through the *aspaklaria* of Judaism and understanding Judaism through the *aspaklaria* of these questions became a central feature of Jewish thought. As the 1885 Pittsburgh platform of the Reform Central Conference of American Rabbis averred:

> In full accordance with the spirit of Mosaic legislation… we deem it our duty to participate in the great task of modern times, to solve, on the basis of justice and righteousness, the problems presented by the contrasts and evils of the present organization of society.[21]

Like the second cup of spiritual uplift, the third cup of social engagement represents a critique of the first. The idea of bourgeois plenitude is seductive: as the world revolves around our ears, we choose to concentrate on our own lives and our children's education. A necessary corollary to this flight away from history is a flight from confronting the economic realities of our contemporary lives. By building "gated communities" in which our families live comfortable lives away from the realities outside, we turn our backs on the suffering of the majority.

The third cup is the empty cup we occasionally glimpse as it is proffered by a street beggar or the empty refrigerator characterizing a rapidly growing number of Israeli households. It is the empty stomach of a child in Gaza or sub-Saharan Africa or the empty gaze of a child forced to flee to a domestic violence shelter. The empty cup serves as an uncomfortable reminder of the flip side to the bourgeois dream. It holds every social issue we would rather not think about or need to construct some elaborate rationalization in order to ignore.

For many liberal Jews, Jewish texts and creeds and practices seem inaccessible, but mobilizing in the name of social amelioration and political improvement is understood as an expression of Judaism's finest legacy.

The Fourth Cup: The Broken Cup

There is an important strain of contemporary Jewish thought which emphasizes the enormous rupture of the contemporary Jewish experience. The tablets have been broken, and something new must come in their place. Adapting the existing model to reflect a changing environment was not considered a strategy equal to the challenges of Auschwitz and Hiroshima.

For proponents of the sensibility represented by the fourth cup, the systematic destruction of six million Jews changed the nature of the theological debate and caused an irreparable rupture of the fabric of Jewish life and the entire Western philosophical tradition. To carry on with the theological discussion as if the Shoah had never happened is an act of breathtaking denial, and thinkers such as Emil Fackenheim were outraged by those in the liberal camp unable or unwilling to shift their worldview in the shadow of the gas chambers.

More recently, the argument that epoch-making, paradigm-busting change has broken the existing mindset has been extended to include rapid and rampant technological change, climate catastrophe, and more. The specter of populism and quasi-fascism rearing its head in regimes previously deemed to be stable liberal democracies has added to the sense that a large rupture has taken place. The cup from which our forebears drank has been shattered.

Advocates of the fourth cup come from left and right, and the responses they propose differ greatly. The theology of the broken cup does not proclaim an end to all hope. Fackenheim makes use of the kabbalistic term *tikkun*, a mending, a repair. While the term *tikkun olam* has been used in relation to each of the other approaches, it is with the fourth cup that the term takes on particularly strong relevance.[22] Fackenheim's *To Mend The World*, perhaps his most significant work, confronts the enormity of the rupture while seeking a way to continue living meaningfully:

> It is true that because a *Tikkun* of *that* rupture is impossible we cannot live, after the Holocaust, as men and women have lived before. However, if the

impossible *Tikkun* were not also necessary, and hence possible, we could not live at all.²³

The fourth cup is invoked not only in relation to the Shoah. It is not exclusive either to right or to left. Its chief characteristic is its radical tone: the call for some fundamental reorientation in the wake of irrevocable epoch-making change.

Four Cups and a Fifth

I have presented here four current approaches or emphases employed by those who try to mediate the challenges of living as a Jew in the modern world. The full-cuppers strive for what Maybaum called "happiness outside the state," a life of fulfillment in the family and outside history. The overflowers seek the kind of spiritual rapture which goes beyond bourgeois comfort and social engagement. The empty-cuppers are driven by a sense of the injustice in the world and strive for greater equality and equilibrium. The broken-cuppers remind us that these other strategies have come down to us from the days when modernity was innocent, when we might still have believed in the infinite perfectibility of the human race. Those days are gone, they tell us.

The fifth cup is neither full nor empty. It takes account of both presence and absence. It shares much with its predecessors but is distinct from each of them. In the first book of an important theological trilogy, Yishay Mevorach proposes a theology of absence. While more familiar theologies present religion as the cure to life's ills, Mevorach sees religion in ironic and paradoxical terms as a kind of illness. Influenced by his teacher Rabbi Shimon Gershon Rosenberg, known as Rav Shagar, as well as three other less direct teachers—Rabbi Nachman of Bratzlav, Franz Rosenzweig, and the French psychoanalyst Jacques Lacan—Mevorach sets out a theological approach infused with postmodern irony. In the terms referred to in this book's introduction, his theology is crunchy and not always immediately accessible, but I predict that it will prove to be of much significance for a wider audience than it currently enjoys.

The quest for spiritual fulfillment is itself a response to a generation in which we were not expected to seek individual gratification but rather to find it in the advancement of the common good. Heschel sought to correct this overemphasis on the needs of the collective, criticizing the tendency to privilege social affiliation over personal conviction:

Our future depends upon our appreciation of the reality of the inner life, of the splendor of thought, of the dignity of wonder and reverence. This is the most important thought: God has a stake in the life of man, of every man.[24]

For me, the image of the half-full cup is also a theology in the most traditional sense of that term. The God I praise and to whom I am committed is a God of presence and of potential. God becomes present in the act of learning when the sense of what is left to learn does not overwhelm but inspires. God becomes present in prayer when the inadequacy of my halting worship is its own liturgy, when "to You silence is praise."[25] God becomes present in society when the awareness of all that must be achieved galvanizes rather than paralyzes. God becomes present in community when the inadequacies and foibles of a congregation are also the sublime sanctity of a *kehillah kedoshah*.

God is also experienced as absence. This theme is to be found within the Jewish esoteric tradition, in Eastern spirituality, and in Western modernity.[26] Gershom Scholem identified this theme in the work of Franz Kafka, which became, for him, a way into Jewish mysticism:

> The void is the abyss, the chasm or the crack which opens up all that exists. This is the experience of modern man, surpassingly well depicted in all its desolation by Kafka, for whom nothing has remained of God but the void— in Kafka's sense, to be sure, the void of God.[27]

The fifth cup is in conversation with all the others. It identifies with the quest for judicious balance typified by the first but challenges its bourgeois certainties. It appreciates spiritual search and social activism but warns against becoming enveloped in either to the exclusion of all else. It acknowledges that everything is broken but warns against an extreme response which can legitimize absolute despair or absolute messianism.

My father, Dow Marmur, once wrote that "one way of defining Judaism would be to say that it is a way of living with ambiguity."[28] The action of pouring the cups at the Seder is described in the Mishnah with a word which actually denotes mixing. It is the same word used in modern Hebrew for the pouring out of a cup, *mizug*, even though the way in which wine is drunk has changed over the centuries. It used to be preserved in concentrated form and then water added at the moment of drinking. Dilution, the term Rubenstein used to describe a watered-down

Judaism incapable of commanding real commitment from its adherents, is preferable to myths of absolute concentrated purity.

We are forever mixing our drinks, working out how watered-down they need to be in order to be potable while retaining their flavor. I do practice a diluted Judaism. The price I pay for this *mizug*, this combination of grape and water, is a heavy one. It is a price I prefer to pay when the alternative is consuming an impossibly thick Judaism, free of all external influences. I believe we should strive to change the internal consistency of the beverage. Its flavor, expressed in our practices, commitments, study, and language, should be stronger. But we should never stop diluting our Judaism. That is how it is meant to be drunk, poured from various cups in diverse permutations. Herein lies the promise evoked each year at our feast of freedom and articulated by the psalmist:

כוס ישועות אשא ובשם ה' אקרא
I shall raise the cup of redemption, and call in the name of God.[29]

Notes

1. See Kuhn, *Structure of Scientific Revolutions*.
2. Ibid., 175.
3. Rubenstein, *Power Struggle*, 50–51.
4. Schiff, *Judaism in a Digital Age*. As an example from the 1930s, see the references to Reform Judaism in Kaplan, *Judaism as a Civilization*, 91–125.
5. PT Pesachim, 10.1, 37 a-b.
6. See: BT Pesachim 118a; Kasher, *Haggadah Shelemah*, 90–95; Leibowitz, *Studies in Shemot*, Vol.1, 114–131; Priel, "Kamah Leshonot Geulah." Priel notes that some sources have suggested six, seven, and eight words of redemption in Exodus 6.6-8. I am drawn to the idea that "you shall know" is one such term: not a promise of divine intervention but of human consciousness. Contemporary Zionist readings have attributed particular significance to the fifth term relating to arrival in the land. Rabbi Shlomo Goren, chief rabbi of Israel, suggested that since the return to the Land and the establishment of the State, five cups be drunk. See Fixler, "Hakos Hachamishit."
7. See Tabory, *Pesach Dorot*, 131–191. Tabory's methodological assumption that the evidence from the Mishnah reflects practices from an earlier period is highly contentious.

8. Recent scholarship is cautious about both the identification of the Last Supper with the feast of the Eve of Passover and the idea that in the time of Jesus there would have been a Seder as the Mishnah presents it. See Bokser, *Origins of the Seder*, particularly 1–28 and, more recently, Kulp, "Origins of the Seder."
9. The Mishnah in question is Pesachim 10:4.
10. For an excellent historical survey of the breeding grounds for what are often known as bourgeois values, see Seigel, *Modernity and Bourgeois Life*.
11. See I Kings 5.5, and Micah 4.4.
12. Maybaum, *Happiness Outside the State*, 45.
13. Ibid., 91.
14. Ibid., 75.
15. See, for example, Zohar III 244b and 273b.
16. See Hellner-Eshed, *Seekers of the Face*.
17. Prager, *The Path of Blessing*, 167.
18. For aspects of poverty, charity, and social justice from the biblical to the rabbinic periods, see: Gray, *Charity in Rabbinic Judaism*; Greenspoon, *Wealth and Poverty*; and Houston, *Contending for Justice*.
19. For examples of contemporary expressions of a concern for social justice framed in explicitly Jewish terms, see Cohen, *Justice in the City* and Rose, Kaiser, and Klein, *Righteous Indignation*.
20. Cohen, *Writings on Neo-Kantianism*, 110.
21. Quoted in Marmur, "Ethical Theories," 212. The rest of that article is also germane to the themes explored in this chapter.
22. A number of fascinating studies have traced the redeployment of the term *tikkun olam* from its Tannatic roots to its modern applications. See: Cooper, "Assimilation of Tikkun Olam"; Krasner, "Place of Tikkun Olam"; and Sherwin, "Tikkun Olam."
23. Fackenheim, *To Mend the World*, 254. In conversation, Fackenheim would disagree with those he called the "go-beyonders"; he found their readiness to "go beyond" the Holocaust reprehensible.
24. Heschel, "Israel and Diaspora," in *The Insecurity of Freedom*, 213–214.
25. Psalms 65.2.
26. Two recent works which offer profound explorations of these themes are Fagenblat, *Negative Theology* and Wolfson, *Heidegger and Kabbalah*.
27. Scholem, *On Jews and Judaism*, 283.
28. Marmur, "The Here and Hereafter."
29. Psalms 116.13.

Open Access This chapter is licensed under the terms of the Creative Commons Attribution 4.0 International License (http://creativecommons.org/licenses/by/4.0/), which permits use, sharing, adaptation, distribution and reproduction in any medium or format, as long as you give appropriate credit to the original author(s) and the source, provide a link to the Creative Commons license and indicate if changes were made.

The images or other third party material in this chapter are included in the chapter's Creative Commons license, unless indicated otherwise in a credit line to the material. If material is not included in the chapter's Creative Commons license and your intended use is not permitted by statutory regulation or exceeds the permitted use, you will need to obtain permission directly from the copyright holder.

Lehaniach: The Assumption of Ritual

One of the students of Rabbi Judah the Prince, so the Babylonian Talmud recounts, came to his master with a question concerning tefillin. Known also as phylacteries, these Jewish ritual objects are worn (by those who choose to wear them) every day except for Shabbat and major festivals, usually at morning prayers. Verses from the Hebrew Bible are inscribed on parchment, encased in two boxes, and bound to the arm and head respectively by means of leather straps.[1] The student asked the following question: on which head does a person with two heads don tefillin?[2]

The image of this two-headed person can serve as an emblem of the ambivalence characterizing modern Jewish attitudes to commandment and ritual.[3] Words of Torah set close to the heart and mind in this ritual practice came to signify the choice to be bound to tradition or to be liberated from it as Jews encountered the modern world.[4] Centuries earlier, tefillin were already the object of intra-Jewish polemics about observance.[5]

I am in two minds about tefillin. One head distances me from their arcane choreography of piety; they appear to be hide-bound in the most literal sense of the term. My other head is attracted to their immediacy, their physicality, and their invitation to bind myself to that which is beyond me. One head tells me this has nothing to do with me. The other tells me it is part of who I am. Every morning these two heads argue it out. Whether or not I bind the straps, I am bound to pay attention to the debate.

Binding Suppositions

The dynamic of binding, releasing, and perhaps binding again is evoked in Dara Horn's novel *In The Image*. An aging Jew close to the end of his life recalls arriving decades earlier in New York Harbor and witnessing Jews "throwing their tefillin overboard. Because tefillin were something for the Old World, and here in the New World they didn't need them anymore."[6] The dying man tasks one of the book's main protagonists to dive down to the bottom of the harbor and retrieve the tefillin previously rejected as detritus.[7] These ritual objects are dumped and then searched for in a dynamic of rejection and retrieval.

Modern Orthodox responses offer a range of strategies all designed to prevent the tefillin from ever being cast aside. While they differ widely, they share a common "right answer" to the tefillin question. If I am a man, it is incumbent upon me to wear them tomorrow morning in the approved manner. If I am a woman, most opinions suggest that I may do so.[8] Samson Raphael Hirsch, a key figure in the establishment of Modern Orthodoxy, justified the ritual act in symbolic and theological terms. In the chapter dedicated to this practice in his 1837 work, *Horeb*, Hirsch set out what it is that the act of wrapping phylacteries represents and the salutary ethical outcomes it may deliver.[9] In keeping with his wider project of explaining all of the established practices of Jewish tradition in symbolic terms designed to appeal to sophisticated and curious Jews of his day and to steer them away from the perilous seductions of Reform, he argued that tefillin stand for the fundamentals of Jewish belief and promote purity and sincerity in our actions: "To dedicate all the powers of our mind, heart and body to the service of the All-One is the lesson of *tefillin*."[10]

Hirsch's assertion that "if truth is to produce results, it must be impressed upon the heart and mind repeatedly and emphatically"[11] highlights the educative aspect of ritual, noting that we are habituated to certain behaviors in the hope that they help inculcate exalted values. For Yeshayahu Leibowitz, that most unorthodox of Orthodox Jewish thinkers, Hirsch's symbolic and romantic interpretation of the practice is to be condemned as a reprehensible exercise in apologetics. In his view, there is only one legitimate and unsullied reason for performing this practice mandated by Halakhah: because it has been mandated by Jewish law. For Leibowitz, any attempt to argue for the efficacy of the *mitzvah* as a prophylactic (it keeps me from harm), a reminder (it keeps me on the right track), or any other benefit is profoundly wrong. When I place these boxes on my arm and between my eyes for the sake of self-actualization or consciousness-raising, it is a false god I worship. Indeed, Leibowitz averred: "a man has no motivation for performing this act and there could be no other motivation than compliance with the will of God."[12] Do not bind yourself up with these straps in the hope that you will be elevated in some way or that values will be impressed upon you by osmosis; bind yourself because you are bound by the Torah of Moses and for no other reason. Anyone suggesting some reward (one can even find examples of health-based justifications[13]) is, in Leibowitz's view, either a fool or a charlatan.

If these Orthodox voices convinced me, I would not be engaged in the daily two-headed debate as to whether I should wrap or desist from wrapping. I am on the search for other theological approaches. Leopold Zunz argued for the inclusion of this ritual in the lexicon of an engaged modern Jew but, unlike Hirsch or Leibowitz, he did not begin from the premise that anything mandated by Jewish law is a commandment to be followed come what may. He was far too aware of historical development to accept such a predicate. Rather, his position, as summarized by his biographer, was that "ritual is a civilizing force ... [and] also a vehicle for preventing the dilution of memory."[14]

Zunz was arguing here not from some a priori conviction that Jewish ritual is the crown of perfection and that regularized piety is mandated by God. He was instead motivated by a concern for the perpetuation of cultural and ethical integrity. In an era in which proponents of radical Reform Judaism were arguing for the dismantling of rituals and external accoutrements, Zunz felt obliged to take a stance against the widespread denigration of Jewish ritual practice. He objected to such an approach both on practical and ethical grounds. Practically, he argued, there is little chance that young people will be inspired by a Judaism denuded of specific practices, ignorant of the Hebrew language, inclined to vapid and self-aggrandizing pronouncements. Ethically, to turn our backs on the heritage of our ancestors and to deride their customs and practices smacks of opportunism, fickleness, and even treachery: "It is always better to bind oneself with *tefillin* than to heretics."[15]

Ironically perhaps, Zunz was himself in favor of a range of reforms considered heretical by some. He sided with the introduction of the organ into the synagogue, the confirmation of girls, the recitation of the *Haftarah* (the weekly reading from the Prophets) in the vernacular, the removal of *Kol Nidrei* and kabbalistic accretions to the liturgy, and more.[16]

There is no indication that he called for every good Jew to don tefillin every day or that he himself did. The heresy to which he objected was the notion that it is possible to eschew all external forms and to settle for a posture of disengaged anthropological curiosity about the outmoded mores of bygone ages. Zunz saw in tefillin a counter to a rapidly evaporating solidarity with the past, present, and future of Jewish creativity.[17]

There is a correspondence between two of the greatest Jewish intellectuals of the nineteenth century relating to these ritual boxes and straps. In opposition to this embrace of tefillin, Abraham Geiger wrote a letter to Zunz in March 1845. Along with protestations of respect, Geiger also expressed surprise and disappointment. His arguments summarize well the other side of the debate about Jewish ritual—the second of my two minds about phylacteries:

> There is no doubt that any ceremony may take on a deeper meaning and that it is never altogether devoid of significance. But should this rite, which is based on a misinterpretation of certain biblical passages, which is linked purely with those excesses associated with charms and amulets, and which is so completely alien to our own thinking and to our own culture and sense of beauty, truly have such beneficial effects? What is dead remains dead; the spirit which was once contained within it still continues to manifest itself, but in other ways and in other forms. To seek to reawaken it now would be a vain endeavor and, even if it were to meet with success, would only have deplorable, soul-killing and demoralizing consequences.[18]

In Geiger's estimation, there should be no place in the Judaism of tomorrow—both tomorrow morning and in the emerging future—for boxes, straps, and amulets. The rabbis who had concocted the ritual were offering an incorrect reading of some biblical passages, which are in fact a call to take the words of Torah to heart and should be read metaphorically. By perpetuating this misreading, the rabbis were allowing customs reflecting the worst of surrounding cultures to infiltrate the higher religion of the Hebrews. The practice belonged to the behavioristic husk rather than the moral kernel of Judaism, and it was to be discarded. To choose to start the day tangled up in obscurantist debris was to misread the demands and possibilities of a new day. Tefillin were to be rejected as mistaken, derivative, and unaesthetic. Geiger and many who succeeded him[19] pronounced tefillin dead on arrival in the modern world. Dead letters cannot be resuscitated, not even by strapping them on to live people.

Zunz and Geiger conduct their argument in my two minds every morning. One strong motivation for retrieving tefillin from the bay into which early Reform tossed them is to perpetuate the discussion, which is more generative than it is paralyzing. Franz Rosenzweig is often reported as having answered the question whether he wraps tefillin with the words "not yet."[20] As I read him, he is saying: for me now to adopt the daily practice of donning phylacteries would be inauthentic, but I do not place that practice outside the realm of possibility or legitimacy. He too was giving an audience to both of his two minds. The phylacteries in all their strangeness—the act of affixing words of scripture encased in boxes to my body—is not an impurity to be purged but rather a possibility yet to be explored, one of many offered by the layers of Jewish existence which have preceded me. Even when he did not lay tefillin, Rosenzweig laid claim to his patrimony in its entirety. A horizon of hope is thus set out before him. Had he but time (which tragically he did not) he would have been able to explore other aspects of Judaism and, by engaging with them, turn them from abstract law into intimate commandment. This approach moves me. Even if the tefillin have been flung overboard, I want to hang onto their straps that they might be brought back to the surface at some future time.

A remarkable halakhic teaching dating back at least as far as the fourteenth century offers another expression of ambivalence, in this case concerning the act of donning tefillin.[21] The word *lehaniach*, the key verb employed in the first of two blessings recited according to most traditions, can be written using two different vocalizations, and some medieval rabbis insisted on precise usage.[22] At the heart of this ruling lies an awareness that the term *lehaniach* can mean more than one thing. It can mean to rest, to settle, to place, to assume, to suppose; it implies setting down with intention and focus. The same word, however, can be employed to mean: to set aside, to leave, to let go.[23] While the normative blessing is intended to be, "Blessed are You, Adonai Sovereign of all, who has commanded us *lehaniach* (to place/don/set/lay) tefillin," it also bears another meaning: "Blessed are You, who has commanded us *lehaniach* (to let go/release/set down tefillin." I adhere to a Judaism which sees this letting go as a blessing. It is, to be sure, a threat and a risk as well. But it is also a blessing.

It is in the exchange between the two heads—or the two voices in our heads—that the remarkable creative energy of Judaism is to be found. In the tension between *lehaniach* and *lehaniach*, new chapters in Jewish life are being written. Modern feminist readings of Jewish ritual, for example, have often expressed the two minds of our Talmudic image. As Susannah

Heschel has commented: "Putting on tefillin is ambiguous: does it empower women or does it reconfirm the perception that Judaism is a male phenomenon and women striving for piety must imitate male acts?"[24] People previously excluded from the normative circle of tefillin wearers are now grappling with tefillin, entangling and disentangling them in search of the new and the true.[25] Creative artists decontextualize and recontextualize the tefillin, sometimes in bold and radical ways.[26]

Moses Mendelssohn described Jewish religious practice as representing a living script: more visceral, more ephemeral, and less susceptible to the risk of idolatry than words written on a page. In Francis Bacon's terminology, ceremonies are gestures, "transitory hieroglyphics."[27] In the act of donning tefillin, letters are created by means of the leather straps and set down on the flesh.[28] More than any other Jewish ritual act, this one exemplifies Mendelssohn's imagery. To don tefillin is to vivify a script, to live a text, to embody words. Theodor Reik, one of Sigmund Freud's original students, offered a detailed analysis of the ritual and proposed an explanation rooted in psychoanalytical theory. Noting that some scholars believed that tefillin originated as stylized forms of bodily mutilations or amulets, Reik was convinced that at a yet more primary stage the ancient Hebrews had wrapped themselves in the skins of animals: "The tephillin are a substitute for those parts of the totemic pelt the ancient Israelites wore in order to identify themselves with their totemic god."[29]

Reik's theory has not fared well in the decades since its publication, and it apparently lacks historical credibility. Nonetheless, his conclusion is striking:

> While at a later period the tephillin may have assumed the indifferent character of religious amulets, everything goes to indicate that they were once the substitutes for the sacred animal pelt, the living garment of the god. Their function, within the framework of an "enlightened" Judaism and a tepid rationalism, may have been merely accessory and purely symbolical. Analytical investigation, however, is able to show that the unbroken, unconscious thought association of the pious with the emotional and intellectual life of their ancestors comes closer to the mystery than the ... seeming objectivity of ... science.[30]

Reik is saying that when Jews decide to don tefillin, they are wearing the skin of their ancestral people yearning for their primal embrace in the

Divine. He doubts that tepid rationalist accounts of the ritual can account for its hold on so many.

That which Geiger pronounced dead still lives, and it holds the possibility of fleeting encounters with an ancestral faith. Classical Reform Judaism wanted to exfoliate, to clean out the pores of obscurantism and superstition. I see no good reason to throw tefillin into the bay and would rather leave open the possibility of binding myself up in my people's pelt. I doubt that a Judaism stripped to the bone offers greater opportunities for creative expression and spiritual depth.

I have one set of tefillin in my study at home and one in the seminary where I teach. Each day I make a choice: *lehaniach*, to lay them against my heart and between my eyes, or *lehaniach*, to set them aside, to leave them be. Were they not part of my Jewish vocabulary, my spiritual lexicon and intellectual palette would be diminished. I cannot, however, bring myself to make their application as regular as the brushing of teeth and the combing of hair. For years I have been embarrassed by this fact, evidence no doubt of inconsistency, inconstancy, and incapacity. Now, however, I realize that it is simply the conversation between two heads jousting to decide who will hold sway today, consoled by the thought that tomorrow the outcome of the head-to-head will likely be different.

The tefillin rejected by the founders of Reform can become the cornerstone of a new approach to Jewish ritual practice. It may not have the proven advantages of Orthodox diligence—consistency, educability, clarity, and mystery. But it keeps tefillin and much besides as part of a vocabulary of spiritual search. It allows for moments in which the close embrace of former generations is experienced at first hand. In such moments the black strap of my wristwatch, keeping me on schedule in the here and now, is replaced by the black straps of my tefillin, offering me access to a longer timeframe. It reminds me that I cannot explain everything I do but that need not stunt my quest for greater understanding. It invites me to thick engagements with worlds of discourse from which I am separated by centuries and ideologies. In our polarized world, it may seem that to don tefillin implies being wrapped up in fundamentalist convolutions. It does not.

There are mornings in which the act of laying tefillin is impossible for me because I am preoccupied or late or because one of my two heads is shouting too loud. There are other mornings in which this act is replete with profundity, intimacy, and reflection. And there are, of course, many mornings in which nothing occurs other than the physical act of tightening and loosening bonds. Years ago, my colleague Mike Comins, who was then serving as a prison guard in the Israeli Army, told me that there were days in which prayer was quite impossible for him. All he could manage in good faith was to don the tefillin and shortly after remove them.

I am not a Jew who affords a priori authority to a halakhic system to define my every waking hour. I have no ambitions to become such a Jew. The notion that the only alternative to this position is nihilism is spurious. I am looking for a way to embody, to enact, and to engender a creative, responsible, and rich Jewish life. As part of this search, I listen to my two minds: one with Geiger and one with Zunz, one throwing the tefillin overboard and one diving to retrieve them.

I do not pray every day with tefillin, but every day I recite a blessing involving *lehaniach*. I thank God for opportunities *lehaniach*, to assume the tradition. And I thank God for the freedom *lehaniach*, to let go.

Notes

1. The origin of tefillin is, like so much else in Jewish history, the focus of controversy. Some facts are known beyond contention. Findings in the Judean desert demonstrate that in the first century various Jewish groups made use of tefillin bearing a strong resemblance to those currently in use. One of the most fascinating questions concerning the development of tefillin as a central feature of Jewish worship is the extent to which the biblical verses typically understood to represent the basis for the practice are in fact their origin or the extent to which they reflect the local adoption of an amulet ritual imported from other cultures. For a thorough discussion of these and related questions, see Cohn, *Tangled up in Text*.
2. BT Menachot 37a. For a striking reading of the Tosafot commentary offering a way of judging whether a two-headed person should be considered one person or two, see Soloveitchik, *Kol Dodi Dofek*, 57. The context of this Talmudic discussion, both literary and medical (relating to conjoined twins), lies beyond the scope of this chapter.
3. For an important discussion of approaches to Jewish ritual observance in modern Jewish thought, see Eisen, *Rethinking Modern Judaism*.
4. Moses Hess recounted the story of an assimilating Jew who boasted to Mendelssohn that his son no longer wore tefillin. For this anecdote and Hess' reading of it, see Koltun-Fromm, *Moses Hess*, 115.
5. See Kanarfogel, "Rabbinic Attitudes Toward Nonobservance," particularly 7–14, and Wolfson, "Mystical Rationalization," particularly 249. The statement in Zohar I 130b in the name of Rabbi Elazar is relevant in this

context: "Happy is the person who dons tefillin and knows the reason for doing so." Earlier still, Ulla's comment in BT Berakhot 14b implies that there were those who prayed without tefillin (and were subject to his opprobrium).
6. Horn, *In The Image*, 50.
7. See Lewin, "Diving into the Wreck," particularly 56–59.
8. For a survey of the halakhic literature, see Golinkin, *Status of Women*, 51–75.
9. Hirsch, *Horeb*, 175–180. For a twentieth-century reprise of Orthodox theological engagement with tefillin, see Lookstein, "Tefillin and God's Kingship."
10. Hirsch, *Nineteen Letters on Judaism*, 84.
11. Ibid., 83.
12. Leibowitz, *Judaism, Human Values*, 20.
13. For one example see Schram, "Tefillin."
14. Schorsch, *Leopold Zunz*, 116. The relevance of this exchange in the 1840s is discussed in Schorsch, "Ideology and History." For a discussion of Zunz's 1822 sermon on tefillin, see Gottlieb, *Jewish Reformation*, 168.
15. Schorsch, *Leopold Zunz*, 119.
16. Ibid., 129.
17. See Levy, *Vision of Holiness*, 129–132. This account of how tefillin can bind Reform Jews is remarkable to the extent that it mirrors some of the symbolic explanations employed by Hirsch and Zunz. Levy describes the performance of the *mitzvah* in highly lyrical terms: for example, "It is as though the press of leather into our skin was God's redeeming arm, strengthening our own and acting through us" (130). Another theological reading of the act of donning tefillin is offered by Heschel in *Man's Quest for God*: "God wants me to be close to Him, even to bind every morning His word as a sign on my hand, and between my eyes," 99.
18. Wiener, *Abraham Geiger*, 113.
19. See, for example, Kohler, *Jewish Theology*, 455, where he emphasizes that the Jew is now forging a different kind of relationship with his non-Jewish neighbor. Here is another expression of rejection from a later Reform theologian, Ignaz Maybaum: "The phylacteries make Jewish prayer the worship of a primitive religion. The medieval Jew was not aware of their primitivity. After all, he was a medieval Jew. But for the post-medieval Jew phylacteries cannot but appear as a medieval device for the attainment of religious aims" (*Ignaz Maybaum: A Reader*, 63–64). Maybaum was a student of Rosenzweig but parted ways with him on this matter. There is no "not yet" to be found in this statement but rather "no longer." Our medieval precursors need make no excuses for their engagement with this ritual, but for us this has become impossible.

20. This statement has been widely quoted. It appears in a letter from Rosenzweig to Rudolf Hallo dated March 27, 1922, and it refers to an earlier conversation between the two. The "not yet" is a significant part of Rosenzweig's thought, independent of his comment, first made (according to a later letter) in a conversation with Hallo around 1920. For more on the "not yet" in Rosenzweig's thought, see Kavka, *Jewish Messianism*, 135–157, where he presents Rosenzweig's position regarding messianism and the future and compares it (quite unfavorably) with the views of Emmanuel Levinas. For other perspectives on the wider question of the "not yet" in Rosenzweig, see Hollander, "Significance of Franz Rosenzweig," particularly 156–160, and Wiener Dow, *Uvlechtecha Baderech*, particularly 83–84, 151–156. When Rosenzweig told Hallo (apparently in response to a question highlighting the examples of both tefillin and fasting) "not yet," it was not a casual throwaway line but part of a larger system of thought and reflection.
21. See, for example, *Sheelot Uteshuvot Maharil Hahadashot* (Jerusalem, 1977) Orach Chayim 2, 4. Rabbi Yaakov ben Moshe Levi Moelin explains the difference in meaning between the two pronunciations of the blessing.
22. For detailed discussions of the development of these blessings see Amit, "Curious Case of Tefillin" and Rosenthal, "Al Birkot Hatefillin." Both of these articles note that there were significant discrepancies between the Babylonian custom and the custom practiced in the Talmudic period in the Land of Israel.
23. See, for example, the commentary by Shneur Zalman of Liadi, *Shulchan Aruch Harav*, Orach Chayim 25, which links the second version of *lehaniach* with abandonment.
24. Heschel, "Jewish and Muslim Theologies," 30.
25. For example, see: Hauptman, "Women and Conservative Synagogue"; Tucker, "Gender and Tefillin"; and Weisberg, "On Wearing Talit."
26. For a fascinating and multilayered discussion of Yona Wallach's provocative poem "Tefillin," see Frumkin, "New Insights." See also Tsoffar, "Staging Sexuality" and Zisquit, "Innovation and Tradition." The poem appeared in an Israeli literary magazine in 1982 accompanied by photographs of Wallach with a man wearing nothing but tefillin. In the area of dance, in 2019, Moriah Ella Mason premiered a work entitled "Queer, Jewish," in which the straps of tefillin are employed in iconoclastic ways. In both of these examples, sexual dimensions of the tefillin ritual are explored. In his 1927 poem "Toil," Avraham Shlonsky used tefillin imagery to describe what he saw as the redemptive power of the construction of a new society: "My land wraps in light like a prayer shawl/Houses stand like phylacteries/And like bands of phylacteries glide hand-laid asphalt roads" (Mintz, *Modern Hebrew Poetry*, 184).

27. The phrase appears in Book 2, Chapter 16 of a classic work by Bacon first published in 1605. See Bacon, *Advancement of Learning*, 131. Quoted in Freudenthal, "Moses Mendelssohn: Iconoclast," 359.
28. In his responsum *Tashbetz* I.118, Shimon ben Tzemach Duran noted that forming the letters *shin*, *dalet* and *yod* from the straps was not known to the Sages of the Talmud or their successors, the Geonim, but was an innovation of the Jews of Spain as an expression of their love of the *mitzvot*.
29. Reik, *Pagan Rites*, 145. In my mind this analysis is linked with BT Bekhorot 57b, where a tradition is preserved according to which a newborn animal is clothed in the flayed skin of its mother for protection.
30. Ibid., 145–146.

Open Access This chapter is licensed under the terms of the Creative Commons Attribution 4.0 International License (http://creativecommons.org/licenses/by/4.0/), which permits use, sharing, adaptation, distribution and reproduction in any medium or format, as long as you give appropriate credit to the original author(s) and the source, provide a link to the Creative Commons license and indicate if changes were made.

The images or other third party material in this chapter are included in the chapter's Creative Commons license, unless indicated otherwise in a credit line to the material. If material is not included in the chapter's Creative Commons license and your intended use is not permitted by statutory regulation or exceeds the permitted use, you will need to obtain permission directly from the copyright holder.

Masoret: Tradition!

Judith Plaskow has suggested that theology can be understood as "sustained and coherent reflection on the experiences and categories of a particular religious tradition, and as reflection on the world in the light of that tradition."[1] It comprises training an *aspaklaria* on tradition and allowing that tradition to serve as an *aspaklaria* through which the world is perceived.

Theology as a self-conscious discipline is not a popular activity. Only small groups engage in it. Tradition, in contrast, is ubiquitous. None can escape its pull since "avant-gardes endlessly replace themselves in a 'tradition of the new' ... Closely examined, all culture is recycled."[2] To see (even without eyes) is to see through the prisms provided consciously or otherwise by traditions. But what is tradition? According to our tradition, more than one answer to this question can be found.

Tradition!

Jaroslav Pelikan, a leading historian of Christian theology, opens his important work on the meaning of tradition by referring to *Fiddler on the Roof*, a show which first opened in 1964 and has ever since been, like tradition itself, constantly revived. In Tevye the Milkman's opening soliloquy, he suggests that tradition provides a way for each person to keep their balance in precarious circumstances. It assigns clear roles and practices to the community as a whole and to particular ages and genders. Its origins may be unclear but its power is undeniable:

> You may ask, how did this tradition start?
> I'll tell you—I don't know. But it's a tradition ...
> Because of our traditions,
> Everyone knows who he is and what God expects him to do.[3]

Pelikan notes that this speech and "Tradition!"—the rousing song it introduces—were not part of the original score. Rather, they came into being when the writers and producers asked themselves what the plot, based on a series of stories by the great Yiddish writer known as Sholem Aleichem, was really about. They came to the conclusion that, at its heart, the show concerned "the disintegration of a whole way of life."[4] It was therefore necessary to conjure up that tradition which was then to be challenged and undermined as the story unfolds.

"Tradition!" was thus composed in order to evoke something at risk of being lost. Zygmunt Bauman has suggested that tradition "only lives posthumously, in the experience of detraditionalization."[5] One of modernity's key characteristics has been a questioning of traditional attitudes; such is the irony of history that modernity itself has become an endangered tradition. Anything, including anti-tradition, can become a tradition. And every tradition is threatened by the specter of obsolescence.

Pelikan distinguishes between tradition and traditionalism. The former is a constant, dynamic feature of human endeavor, while the latter can become a way of neutralizing debate and stunting growth:

> Tradition is the living faith of the dead, traditionalism is the dead faith of the living. And ... it is traditionalism that gives tradition such a bad name. The reformers of every age, whether political or religious or literary, have protested against the tyranny of the dead, and in doing so have called for innovation and insight in place of tradition.[6]

To read Pelikan as a radical iconoclast would be an error: his own journey took him from the Lutheran to the Orthodox Church. He offers a pungent critique of the Enlightenment confidence that universal values, embodied imperfectly within traditions, can be retained while those traditions are cast aside:

That view of traditions seems to assume ... that the tradition will not be replaced by something far worse, and that universal truths and values, once attained, no longer need the tradition to sustain them—an assumption for which the past two centuries does not provide any great measure of reassurance.[7]

Accordingly, both the elevation of traditions to the status of a cult[8] and the illusion that tradition can be escaped are to be avoided.

But what do we mean by tradition? The sociologist John B. Thompson distinguishes between four aspects of this contested term. He suggests that it refers, first, to "an interpretative scheme, a framework for understanding the world,"[9] then to "a normative guide for actions and beliefs in the present," and to "a source of support for the exercise of power and authority."[10] Along with these dimensions—hermeneutic, normative, and legitimizing—Thompson sees tradition as a key marker of identity: "As sets of assumptions, beliefs and patterns of behavior handed down from the past, traditions provide some of the symbolic materials for the formation of identity both at the individual and at the collective level."[11]

Thompson's framework aims at universal validity. It suggests that from the farthest east to the uttermost west, in urban sprawl or rural seclusion, human beings employ networks of tradition to interpret texts, events, and emotions, establish modes of behavior, legitimize the exercise of authority, and provide core components of identity.

It is not surprising that a story about Jews should have yielded the anthem with which Pelikan opens his reflection on tradition. Jews around the world have been maintaining, transforming, undermining, and forgetting traditions for as long as anyone. The Jewish experience of modernity is one in which internal processes and external pressures have made questions of tradition central: are tradition and modernity on a collision course or can they be reconciled? Are traditions to be jettisoned or preserved?

Jewish Conceptions of Tradition

The thirteenth-century work *Sefer Hachinuch* articulates a position on tradition that has characterized much of Jewish life across centuries and continents. It lists the prohibition against straying from the teachings of our ancestors as one of the commandments of Judaism:

We were prevented from disagreeing with the masters of the tradition, peace be upon them, and from changing their words and to not remove ourselves from the commandments in all matters of the Torah. And about this it is stated (Deuteronomy 17:11), "you shall not stray from the matter that they tell you right or left."[12]

Unsurprisingly, there is an innately conservative dimension to a civilization which has perpetuated itself for 3000 years. It is striking, however, that Jewish tradition is riddled with challenges to this ideal of unerring adherence to previous practice. Take, for example, Jewish garb. From biblical times, the addition of fringes to the corners of a garment has been a feature of traditional Jewish menswear. No other item of clothing can claim biblical authority. A number of later sources quote a midrash which states that the refusal to change one's clothing was one of the four things that assured Jewish survival during the years of slavery in Egypt.[13] In fact, a number of midrashim had already listed reasons why the Israelites merited redemption from Egypt, among them refusing to change their names and their language, eschewing slander and sexual impropriety,[14] offering the blood of the paschal sacrifice and the blood of the circumcision ceremony,[15] and declining to reveal the secret mysteries of the religion.[16] The citation by later sources of the ancient precedent for keeping one's clothing distinct from the surrounding world is, however, an innovation. Not only is the text absent from ancient sources, so too is the practice: "Medieval European Jews did, in fact, dress distinctively (often not by choice). In antiquity, by contrast, Jews did not dress distinctly."[17]

My purpose in bringing this example is not to catch Jewish tradition in an inaccuracy. To engage in such a hunt would be to mistake tradition for history—a mistake common to many fundamentalists and anti-traditionalists alike. Rather, I want to suggest that Jews have developed robust and flexible strategies to ensure continuity and creativity.

While a number of terms are used in Hebrew sources to relate to tradition,[18] one above all others plays this role in modern Hebrew. Intriguingly, this term, *masoret*, appears on only one occasion in the Hebrew Bible—a fact which makes understanding even its basic etymology a considerable challenge. *Masoret* is a word whose core meaning has been contested within the Jewish interpretive tradition. There is, therefore, good reason to be suspicious of anyone claiming to know what Jewish tradition definitively is and what is demanded of those aiming to be true to it. Our tradition does not speak with one voice when seeking to understand itself.

Three Roots, Many Branches

Masoret appears only once in the Hebrew Bible. Ezekiel 20:37 reads, something like: I will cause you to pass under the rod, and I will bring you in the *masoret* of the *brit*. Most English translations, following the King James Version, render this phrase as "the bond of the covenant."

Scholarly proposals for the root meaning of *masoret* have covered a broad range of possibilities.[19] I want to consider the *masoret* of the *masoret*[20] by offering some thoughts about the nature of Jewish tradition through a consideration of this one word. Almost all Hebrew words have three-letter roots, each of which opens up a broad semantic field. Most modern Hebrew speakers would assume that the root of *masoret* is *m-s-r*. Moses is portrayed at the start of Tractate Avot in the Mishnah as receiving the Torah and passing it on, and the word used to denote this act of transmission is *m-s-r*. This root is employed in diverse settings: a message is a *meser* and dedication is *mesirut*.[21] Based on his examination of local languages and other sources, Ben-Hayyim suggested that the root *m-s-r* originally also had the sense of counting (it is striking that in the ancient Greek translation of the Ezekiel verse, *masoret* is translated as "number"). The different meanings all speak to aspects of tradition: it is that which is passed on, that to which I am dedicated, that which carries a freight of meaning. It counts.

The expression *masoret hi beyadenu*—we have a *masoret* in our hands, we possess a *masoret*—is used in a number of rabbinic sources which tell of a family of Temple craftsmen who refused to share their wisdom with anyone beyond their kin. When challenged to explain this behavior, they replied: according to the tradition we hold, the Temple will eventually be destroyed, and we do not wish to divulge our secrets in case they are abused.[22] The tradition is transmitted only within the family, and the prohibition against revealing the secret is explained in terms of an attitude or prediction passed on through the generations. This early rabbinic usage of *masoret* highlights the intimate family dimension which so often connects to tradition. The thing that a revered relative would always say, the way in which a certain act is carried out in our household, or, in this case, a prediction about the future carried from generation to generation—all these are at the heart of tradition. It is worth adding that another important part of the dynamic of tradition is figuring out which family traditions should be discontinued and which secrets brought to light.

Another potential root for this unique word is *y-s-r*, from which the word for suffering is derived as well as *musar*, ethical or moral conduct. One midrash uses this etymology to support the idea that suffering is an innate part of the covenant and that tribulations have a salutary effect.[23] For many adherents of classical Reform Judaism, this reading of tradition, according to which "the rigor of tradition was the protecting shell that preserved intact the delicate kernel of essential ideas," was most compelling.[24]

The usage of the word *masoret* has changed over time and, in the form *masorah*, it came to refer to the text of the Hebrew Bible tended to with precision by the Masoretes.[25] As I mentioned in the introduction to this book, the Masoretes came to play the crucial role of fixing the vocalization of the text. Here, too, the fate of this one word teaches something about Jewish understandings of tradition. There is a fixed aspect: the text is presented to each generation of readers as a given. The question, though, of how the latent unvocalized text is to be pronounced, namely, the form of expression it is to take, turns each generation into heirs of the Masoretes.

"Masoret!" is the Hebrew version of the musical's opening number. It is the word used today to denote tradition. In modern Israel, the term *masorti* has taken on further layers of significance. As well as its adoption by the Israeli movement for Conservative Judaism, it has also come to be associated with a major marker of identity. Analyzed in a number of studies by Yaacov Yadgar and others, the phenomenon of Jewish Israelis choosing to describe themselves as *masortim* should be noted here. This appellation deliberately rejects the notion that the spectrum of Jewish ideological and religious commitments offers a binary choice between religious and secular. In recent years the term has become increasingly prevalent particularly among Jews from non-European, mostly Muslim countries.[26]

Appearing only once in the Hebrew Bible, *masoret* defies definitive interpretation. It can mean a bond, a number, an account, a transmission, a fence,[27] a condition, a commitment, a chastisement, an imperative, and much more. Like tradition itself, *masoret* changes over time and context. This is our *masoret*. Those who say our tradition should never be altered are not only ignoring the dynamic of historical development; they are also perpetrating an unintended irony since there is no more traditional Jewish response than change.

BOUNDED INDETERMINACY

T.S. Eliot's statement that "tradition … cannot be inherited, and if you want it you must attain it by great labor"[28] rings true in a Jewish context. For Jews born into active Jewish families, it may be that an invitation to the tradition is offered and access skills provided without conscious effort. But, like it or not, every person who considers themselves a Jew is obliged to consider what the *masoret haberit* calls them to learn and experience.

My approach is wary of essentialist notions of The Jewish Tradition.[29] Nonetheless, I am convinced that any Judaism which does not see itself in light of the Judaisms which have preceded it is unlikely to thrive. This sentiment was given powerful expression by Abraham Joshua Heschel, who asserted that a Jew is a person "in whose life Abraham would feel at home, a person for whom Rabbi Akiba would feel affinity, a person of whom the Jewish martyrs of all ages would not be ashamed."[30] He also averred that "our way of life must remain to some degree intelligible to Isaiah and Rabbi Johanan ben Zakkai, to Maimonides, and to the Ba'al Shem."[31]

The debate between progressive and conservative approaches to tradition hinges on our understanding of the three words "to some degree." The degree to which Isaiah would have understand anything about the life of the Ba'al Shem is itself limited: the creed they professed, the rituals they enacted, the world of assumptions they inhabited were vastly different. Nonetheless, they—and every Jew implicated in the tradition—are linked to some degree. Unintelligible often to ourselves and our contemporaries, we remain intelligible to some degree to our forebears and, such is the hope of tradition, to our descendants.

Michael Rosenak, a great philosopher of Jewish education, made extensive use of a distinction between "language" and "literature" first proposed in different contexts in the work of Michael Oakeshott and R.S. Peters. Rosenak suggested that these two terms can be used "to suggest the distinction between source and commentary respectively; between sacred tradition and interpretation, and between the foundations of the good life and the ways it may actually be lived."[32] Rosenak not only acknowledged but celebrated the fact that inevitably there are "differing opinions about the point at which sources end and interpretations begin."[33] His use of the distinction is helpful in bringing to the fore some key questions about Jewish education, and for thirty years it has been a staple of discourse in this field.

Rosenak's insight is instructive as a description of how we tend to think about tradition. There is a core, a beating heart, an essence, and beyond it the rest is commentary. In his work on intermarriage, Avinoam Rosenak summarizes his late father's work and provides concrete examples of what constitutes language. He asserts that language represents the permanent cultural canon, aspects of Judaism which may never be retired. The examples he then gives are instructive: the Hebrew Bible, laws of levirate marriage and *chalitzah*,[34] circumcision, and the ban on intermarriage.[35]

This is when essentialist discourse about tradition becomes tricky. Imagining Judaism without the Bible is, I would agree, an impossible task. But levirate marriage, according to which a surviving brother has the responsibility to wed his widowed sister-in-law? Or chlalitzah, the ceremony by involving spitting and the untying of laces by which the surviving brother can escape this requirement? These are unshakeable foundations of Jewish experience? It is not clear on what basis to draw the line separating sacred tradition from its interpretation.[36] He (it is usually a he or group thereof) who decides what may not be changed becomes a self-appointed bouncer for God, deciding who may enter and who has failed the entrance requirements. In my understanding, each movement, congregation, family, and individual is called to act as their own gatekeeper, to find a way of expressing the covenantal imperative to pass on something that was passed on to them. None of us should shy away from expressing our understanding of *masoret haberit*, what tradition asks of us. This includes those who fight with the traditions they have inherited; that, after all, is a Jewish tradition too.[37]

I do not accept the notion that there is sacred tradition on one hand and its interpretation on the other. Interpretation *is* sacred tradition. Tradition is well described by the expression "bounded indeterminacy."[38] Its bounds, perhaps like the bonds often identified in the verse from Ezekiel, are crucial. Each person lives within a bounded context, and one of the secrets of the endurance and creativity of the Jewish story has surely been the inculcation of traditional norms, assumptions, responses, and behaviors. Either through a determined act of will or through negligence and apathy, many Jews situate themselves outside any Jewish bounds. They are unbounded. This alarms me, but the response required should not, in my opinion, be conservative or reactionary. At its heart, our tradition calls for itself to be re-imagined. Isaiah, who according to Heschel might visit any one of us and attempt to recognize us, called out: "Behold, I am making a new thing, now it will sprout, now you shall know it."[39]

In my reading, tradition—characterized as it is by indeterminacy—inevitably involves commitment. In this sense, it is both bounded and binding. But clucking and tutting and telling people they ought to live within the covenant will not work. We have to find ways for iterations of *masoret* unimaginable to us to come into existence. Jaroslav Pelikan dedicated his book on the rediscovery of tradition to the memory of his parents and to his children, appending a verse from Goethe's *Faust*, translated as:

> What you have as heritage,
> Take now as task;
> For thus you will make it your own![40]

Notes

1. Plaskow, "Jewish Theology," 64.
2. Noyes, "Tradition," 245.
3. The lyrics are by Sheldon Harnick.
4. This quotation from a book by Richard Altman about the making of the musical is found in Pelikan, *Vindication of Tradition*, 3.
5. Bauman, "Morality in the Age" 49. In the same essay, Bauman offers the insight that "the insecurity of speakers is the true subject matter of the discourse whose ostensible topic is the security of tradition" (50).
6. Pelikan, *Vindication of Tradition*, 65.
7. Ibid., 56.
8. Traditionalism in an extreme form can yield toxic political results. Umberto Eco placed "the cult of tradition" at the top of a list of fourteen characteristics of nascent fascism ("Ur-Fascism," 78–79).
9. Thompson, "Tradition and Self," 91.
10. Both of these phrases are taken from Ibid., 92.
11. Ibid., 93. For another approach to tradition, focusing on three metaphors—tradition as language, narrative, and horizon respectively—see Yadgar, "Tradition."
12. *Sefer Hachinuch*, 496.
13. Two examples of nineteenth-century rabbis deeply engaged in the struggle against modernizing influences who cited this source should suffice here. Rabbi Moses Schreiber, known as the Chatam Sofer, quoted the midrash, including the ban on changing one's form of clothing, in his *Torat Moshe* (Pressburg 1929-1943), vol.3. 31b; and Rabbi Zvi Elimelech Shapira of Dinov, a great figure of Polish Hasidism, mentioned this tradition in his *Igra Dekala* (New York, 2003), vol.1, Shemot, 177a.
14. Leviticus Rabbah 32.5.

15. See Mekhilta deRabbi Yishmael, Bo, 5 (Horovitz-Rabin, 14); Pesikta Rabati 17; Pesikta deRab Kahana, 7.4.
16. Numbers Rabbah, 20.22; Tanchuma (Buber), Balak, 25.
17. Fine, "How Do You Know," 20.
18. In "Jewish Tradition" (325) Himmelfarb notes *kabbalah* and *yerushat avot* along with the word which is at the heart of the present chapter.
19. Ben-Hayim, "Mesorah Umasoret" is an excellent 1957 Hebrew article, which makes illuminating use of parallel usages in Arabic and, particularly, Samaritan Aramaic. Greenberg, *Ezekiel 1-20* (372–373) covers many of the main theories concerning the meaning of the term.
20. *Masoret Hamasoret* (Venice, 1538) is the title of a grammatical work by Elijah Bachur.
21. For an ingenious suggestion that *musar* (ethics) is related to *mesirat nefesh* (dedication and willingness to stake one's life), see Aharon of Zhitomir, *Toldot Aharon*, (Berditchevm 1817), Vayera, 12a.
22. See PT Yoma 3.9 4a: BT Yoma 38a; PT Shekalim 5.2 48d and 49a. See also Yalkut Shimoni to Genesis 130, 161.
23. Midrash Tehillim (Buber), Psalm 94. While the suggestion that the word *masoret* is derived from the root *y-s-r* is rarer than the other proposals, it can also be found in the Syriac translation of the Hebrew Bible dated to the second century CE and also in medieval exegesis. See Eliezer of Beaugency's twelfth-century commentary to Ezekiel (Warsaw, 1910), 32.
24. Lazarus, *Ethics of Judaism*, 218.
25. In "Mesorah Umasoret" Ben-Hayim proposes that the word first came to be applied to the wording of the text through the meaning of *m-s-r* as counting. These textual experts counted the letters and words of the entire Bible and engaged in various calculations. Greenberg, *Ezekiel 1-20* (373) shows how linguists such as Judah ben David Hayyuj (Morocco, tenth to eleventh century) suggested that the primary meaning of the root concerns counting.
26. There is a burgeoning literature on *masorti* expressions of Judaism in Israel. For an analysis of this phenomenon in English, see Yadgar, *Secularism and Religion*.
27. Avot 3:17.
28. Eliot, "Tradition and Individual Talent," 38.
29. Two reflections on Jewish tradition which, though very different from each other, have impacted my thinking are Braiterman, *(God) After Auschwitz* and Himmelfarb, "Jewish Tradition."
30. Heschel, *Moral Grandeur*, 47.
31. Heschel, Man's *Quest for God*, 112. See also Heschel, *Moral Grandeur*, 9. See Marmur, *Abraham Joshua Heschel*, 14–17.
32. Rosenak, *Roads To The Palace*, xiv.

33. Ibid., 21.
34. The former requires a brother to take his dead brother's wife as his own if there was no issue from the marriage (see Genesis 38:8, Deuteronomy 25:5-6); the latter provides an alternative for the brother not able or willing to perform his duty. See Deuteronomy 25:7-10, and also Ruth 4. Tractate Yebamot is dedicated to levirate marriage.
35. Rosenak, *Zehuyot Mitnagshot*, vol.1, 98.
36. For a thorough discussion, see Levisohn, "What Work."
37. Biale, *Not in the Heavens*, surveys this anti-traditional tradition, quoting Isaac Deutscher's declaration that "the Jewish heretic who transcends Jewry belongs to a Jewish tradition" (1).
38. I learnt this expression from Simão, "Bounded Indeterminacy of Tradition" and, through her work, learnt something of the ideas of Jaan Valsiner, who started using this term in the 1970s.
39. Isaiah 43:19.
40. Pelikan, *Vindication of Tradition*, on the dedication page. Another translation of the verse (from the first part of *Faust*) reads: "What from your fathers' heritage is lent/ Earn it anew, to really possess it!" Pelikan quoted this verse often: for example, when receiving a major prize toward the end of his life.

Open Access This chapter is licensed under the terms of the Creative Commons Attribution 4.0 International License (http://creativecommons.org/licenses/by/4.0/), which permits use, sharing, adaptation, distribution and reproduction in any medium or format, as long as you give appropriate credit to the original author(s) and the source, provide a link to the Creative Commons license and indicate if changes were made.

The images or other third party material in this chapter are included in the chapter's Creative Commons license, unless indicated otherwise in a credit line to the material. If material is not included in the chapter's Creative Commons license and your intended use is not permitted by statutory regulation or exceeds the permitted use, you will need to obtain permission directly from the copyright holder.

Neder: Vows and Commitments

In Berlin, in 1938, a twenty-two-year-old student in a Reform rabbinical seminary wrote a short essay on Halakhah. He opened with the question of perspective. People today, argued the student, tend to judge Halakhah in terms of standards external to it. "Whether the standard is rationalist or irrationalist, whether the appeal is to society or to the individual, in common is the fact that religion is measured by the one who does the judging."[1] The student's name was Emil Fackenheim, and he continued to ask searching questions throughout his long career as a Jewish philosopher. In the essay and later, it was not his conclusion that every detail of Jewish law was to be observed scrupulously. He did call, however, for an attempt to perceive Halakhah from within its own *aspaklaria* and not simply observed from a polite distance. Halakhah, he asserted, "confronts us as *Commandment*."[2]

How is a modern Jew, blessed with multiple perspectives, to relate to a commanding call and to translate that call to a way of living? The young Fackenheim declared himself unable to believe either that the detailed prescriptions of the halakhic system were the Commandment in full or that nothing other than full observance was required:

> It will hardly be possible for us to possess Halakhah as a fixed order of our lives. To be sure, Halakhah is to be practiced in the whole of life, but it cannot be for us an unquestionable reality, which at bottom it never quite ought to be.[3]

This chapter explores the relationship of a modern liberal Jew to Halakhah.

Children of the *Chatzufah*

Neder, the vow, might be reclaimed by non-Orthodox Jews in search of what Eugene Borowitz termed "a compelling sense of Jewish duty."[4] To help explain why such a search should be underway, it may prove helpful to decontextualize and repurpose *chatzufah*, a Talmudic image taken from Tractate Nedarim (Vows) in the Babylonian Talmud. Having introduced the *chatzufah* and explained her relevance, it will be possible to move on to *neder* itself.

In BT Nedarim 20b, it is suggested that if a fetus is conceived in morally compromised circumstances, the effects will be palpable after birth. A list of such cases includes children conceived when the mother has been terrified or raped, when she is despised or banned by her husband, and when he had relations with her while inebriated, confused, or with someone else in mind. The last examples of children whose lives are impacted by the circumstances of their conception are *b'nei chatzufah*, children conceived by a "brazen woman."[5] This descriptor is a version of the word *chutzpah*, which made its way into English thanks to its Yiddish usage. The *chutzpah* of the *chatzufah*, the bold daring of this woman, is that she initiates sexual intimacy rather than waiting demurely for her husband to make the first move.

The rabbis of the Talmud were conflicted about the *chatzufah*. Her case is quite distinct from the other examples provided on the list, which relate to the husband's moral failings, and they were not sure that sexual assertiveness on the part of the wife is to be decried as a negative attribute. An alternative opinion asserted that any man whose wife who behaves thus "will have children the likes of whom did not exist even in the generation of Moses our teacher."[6] The men of the Talmud, uncertain what to make of something beyond their ken, were torn between blanket condemnation and extravagant admiration.

Any image taken from the area of intimate relations can backfire, and I am not employing it here in order to be unnecessarily provocative. I am conjuring up the *chatzufah* because in my reading she best symbolizes the approach adopted by modernizing Jews. Rather than wait coyly for modernity to arrive, such Jews initiated contact and went out to meet modernity with alacrity.

To exemplify this enthusiastic adoption of what some parts of Europe were offering to Jews in the wake of the French Revolution, I have chosen a text published in 1793, before the founding of institutional Reform

Judaism, by Lazarus Bendavid, a Berlin-born philosopher and mathematician. A fervent adherent of Immanuel Kant, Bendavid wrote a pamphlet designed to persuade his fellow Jews to throw off the shackles of primitive Jewish observance. The tract, a "deist manifesto, addressed to that group of Jews who hesitated to abandon the commandments for fear they would lose the very anchor of morality,"[7] includes this clarion call:

> Open a new page! Now, without doubt, everything has changed: the state treats you well, it wants your good, and to merit this you must abolish all the pointless commandments and tell your children what you know well to be true: that they were introduced only as a fence around the garden, which protected the inner core in previous centuries when the spirit of enslavement prevailed, and is no longer suitable nor is it effective. And [tell them] that you want to relinquish the fence so long as the inner core is not damaged, and you admit that the pure Mosaic code, the doctrine of natural religion, is the basis for your faith.[8]

In the name of ethics and progress, Bendavid aimed for a dissolution of distinct Jewish expression. In the decades which followed, Reform Jews acted in the name of these same principles but with a view to perpetuating and developing Judaism in the spirit of the new age. In a 1931 work, David Philipson contrasted Reform with rabbinical Judaism:

> It lays as great a stress upon the *principle* of tradition as does rabbinical Judaism, but it discriminates between separate traditions as these have become actualized in forms, ceremonies, customs, and beliefs, accepting or rejecting them in accordance with the modern religious need and outlook, while rabbinical Judaism makes no such discrimination.[9]

Reform Jews ever since have taken modernity as their yardstick. To live in the modern world is to be impacted profoundly by modernity. There seems to be no way of avoiding it, despite the attempts of many. Some Jews, among them most in the Reform camp, embrace modernity with enthusiasm, welcoming the blessings of rationality, scientific discovery, technological advance, tolerance, and humanism which it promises.

While the encounter of some Jews with modernity has been forced or distracted, Reform Jews have tended to seek it out intentionally. Reform Judaism is not the result of an unwitting or half-hearted union with the modern world but rather an enthusiastic coupling. There were other outcomes of this meeting. Many sought ways to divest themselves completely of a Jewish identity which seemed at odds with the new world opening up to them. Those born into the traditions of liberal Judaism and those choosing to identify with it are children of the *chatzufah* who opted to stay Jewish and to build a Judaism for tomorrow on the basis of this identity.

Halakhah and Reform Judaism

Some Reform Jews continue to emphasize the values and even the aesthetic of the originators of Reform Judaism, while others have become warier of both modernity's honey and its sting. Halakhah, inadequately translated as Jewish law and better understood as "the normative structure undergirding Jewish life in both its private and public dimensions"[10] until the onset of modernity, has been at the heart of this internal Reform debate about the best way to ensure the perpetuation and flourishing of Judaism in a new and rapidly changing reality.

In 1885, the first platform of American Reform averred that ritual laws "fail to impress the modern Jew with a spirit of priestly holiness; their observance in our days is apt rather to obstruct than to further modern spiritual elevation."[11] The platforms adopted by the movement in subsequent years demonstrated a marked change in their tenor and content, much to the chagrin of those still loyal to the spirit of the *chatzufah*.

Speaking of Torah, the 1937 Columbus Platform stated that "it preserves the historical precedents, sanctions and norms of Jewish life, and seeks to mould it to the patterns of goodness and holiness."[12] Torah certainly reflected the transient circumstances of its composition, and as a consequence

> certain of its laws have lost their binding force. … But as a depository of permanent spiritual ideals, the Torah remains the dynamic source of the life of Israel. Each age has the obligation to adapt the teaching of the Torah to its basic needs in consonance with the genius of Judaism.[13]

In the 1976 Centenary Perspective, the emphasis had moved still farther from the spirit of 1885. Like the two earlier documents, personal autonomy was cherished, but now it was to be put to the service of informed choice:

Within each area of Jewish observance Reform Jews are called upon to confront the claims of Jewish tradition, however differently perceived, and to exercise their individual autonomy, choosing and creating on the basis of commitment and knowledge.[14]

The 1999 Statement of Principles overturned the original Pittsburgh's certainty about the irrelevance of ritual and other laws, and the language of informed choice had also been transformed. Now, a commitment to lifelong study of Torah was to provide the possibility of hearing the call of the commandments, described as

> the means by which we make our lives holy. We are committed to the ongoing study of the whole array of מצות (*mitzvot*), and to the fulfillment of those that address us as individuals and as a community. Some of these *mitzvot*, sacred obligations, have long been observed by Reform Jews; others, both ancient and modern, demand renewed attention as the result of the unique context of our own times.[15]

These Reform declarations spanning a century all express aspects of a restless search to forge an appropriate relationship with Halakhah. For the young Emil Fackenheim and for many others who trace their ancestry back to the *chatzufah*, outright rejection of the halakhic canon, the halakhic process, and halakhic norms impoverishes the fabric of Jewish life and does an injustice to the balance between Halakhah and Aggadah which has characterized Judaism for millennia.[16] A priori acceptance of Halakhah as it is expressed, say, in the Shulchan Arukh, is however impossible to square with core values. Some mediating mechanism is called for.

Informed Choice Reconsidered

Different terms have been used in non-Orthodox Jewish circles to articulate the desired balance between autonomy and commitment. One of the most persistent Reform slogans has been "informed choice," implying that the right of each individual to decide how they behave demands a high level of education and maturity. Thoughtful Reform Jews have not been shy to express their discomfort with the implications of these beliefs while not suggesting that hard-earned freedoms be abandoned. The British Reform theologian Tony Bayfield interrogated the non-Orthodox approach with five uncomfortable questions:

If Judaism is to move, as for many Jews it has already done, into a post-*halakhic*, post-legal mode, what is to happen to the *halakhic* tradition? And, perhaps, more urgently still, what is to stop mere anarchy being loosened upon the Jewish world? How can Judaism survive the whims of the autonomous individual? Moreover, is not the elevation of autonomy the ultimate arrogance and dethronement of God? Does this not represent the triumph of modern, western, secular thinking over religion?[17]

These questions are difficult to confront but impossible to ignore. Eric Yoffie, a former head of the Reform Movement in North America, observed:

A revelation that is more ongoing than fixed is liberating both for the individual and the community, but it is also unsettling. It makes the Reform revolution a permanent one, and imposes the onerous burden of informed choice on every Reform Jew, in every era.[18]

Informed choice is, therefore, an inevitable burden and an inalienable right of Reform Jews. The idea of "choosing and creating on the basis of commitment and knowledge," in the language of the 1976 Centenary Perspective quoted above, offered a means of privileging the principle of personal autonomy while seeking to avoid some of the risks alluded to in Bayfield's five hard questions.

There are good reasons to be skeptical about informed choice as an abstraction. What is the basis of learning upon which choices are to be made? Who is to be entrusted with these choices?[19] Too often, the way in which our practices are established mistake thin pretext for deep learning and preference for choice. All of us make choices, but they may not be the choices we imagine them to be, activated as we are by our drives, our social standing, and cultural assumptions. Our choices are influenced not only by our rational judgments but by a host of factors, some more explicit than others.

Determinism has been making a comeback. Increasingly, in recent years, it has been suggested that free will is a hoax and that we are all in the grip of our genes, our instincts, neurological processes, market forces, or the Powers That Be. To my mind, it is sufficient for us to construct our lives on the assumption that we do in fact possess a degree of agency. Acting on the assumption that "if free will did not exist, it would be necessary to invent it"[20] is more productive than simply turning one's face to the wall and waiting for that which has been preordained to play out.

While the conclusion that free will and choice are all illusions is too paralyzing an insight to be useful, it does behoove us to acknowledge the enormous degree to which our choices and preferences are programmed or massaged. New technologies have rendered this situation all the more acute. The image of autonomous rational individuals making informed choices as if they were disembodied judges does no justice to the complicated ways in which our decisions are made.[21] Even without the efforts of marketers and power brokers, choices are informed by much more than data gleaned for the purposes of making decisions. They are informed by the words we speak, the habits of our heart, and the patterns of behavior to which we are exposed and which we perpetuate within families and communities. Our choices are informed by experiences, upheavals, and rituals—as much perhaps by quotidian activities as by peak emotional states.

"Informed choice" by itself is inadequate. In its stead, I want to offer an example of a term taken from halakhic vocabulary which respects individual choice and encourages the shouldering of personal responsibility. This term calls for the involvement of the community and highlights the role of language and speech. It mandates perpetual learning for every person at a level which makes sense for them. It invites those who choose to engage with it to a constant process of development. My suggestion is to articulate a compelling sense of Jewish duty by repurposing an ancient instrument of choice and commitment: the *neder*.

Vows and Oaths

Before offering a brief description of some Jewish understandings of vows and oaths, a word of warning is warranted. This is a complicated field, and it is challenging to give enough information to make the topic comprehensible without becoming swathed in obscurity. Both the *neder* and the *shevu'ah* appear in the Hebrew Bible and then have tractates dedicated to them in the Mishnah and beyond. Typically, they are translated by the words vow and oath, respectively, and while the rabbis often emphasized the difference between the two terms by relating to the formula employed and the subject and intention of the formula recited, the distinction has not always been maintained.[22] For many Jews today, the term *neder* may be familiar from the formula beginning with the words *Kol Nidrei* at the start of the evening service for Yom Kippur. Some may know it from the practice of adding the waiver *bli neder* (without making a vow) whenever a statement is made that could be construed as a binding commitment. Beyond these popular usages lies a rich and complex Jewish literature concerning vows and oaths.[23]

The roots *n-d-r* and *sh-v-ʿa* are the main biblical terms concerning verbal undertakings and appear in in most books of the Hebrew Bible. Perhaps the most famous vow in the Hebrew Bible is uttered by Jacob at Bethel:

> Jacob then made a vow saying, "If God remains with me, if God protects me on this journey that I am making, and gives me bread to eat and clothing to wear, and if I return safe to my father's house—Adonai will be my God. And this stone, which I have set up as a pillar, shall be God's abode; and of all that You give me, I will set aside a tithe for You."[24]

Relating specifically to the *neder*, Jacques Berlinerblau highlights four aspects of the Israelite vow, each of which is relevant for our quest for a currency of Jewish duty. In the Bible, a *neder* is typically a declaration of something to the Temple or to God. He notes, firstly, that a vow is usually initiated by an individual. The classic cases of vowing as recorded in the Hebrew Bible involve particular characters: Jephthah (Judges 11), Hannah (1 Samuel 1), and Absalom (2 Samuel 15).[25]

Berlinerblau's second category is privacy. He argues:

> The making of a vow is an individual (as opposed to interactive) practice, that does not require the presence, assistance, or scrutiny of any other human being, even if the petition is made in a public setting (such as the temple).[26]

However, as his third insight clarifies, the vow is not wholly internal. It is a spoken invocation. The tragic words of Jephthah in the gruesome episode from Judges 11 come to mind here, after it transpires that the first creature to come into view was his beloved daughter and thus, according to the terms of the vow, she must be sacrificed. He exclaims, "For I opened my mouth to Adonai and I cannot retract," and his daughter concurs: "Father, you opened your mouth to Adonai, do to me as you said" (Judges 11:35–36).[27] The fourth key characteristic proposed by Berlinerblau is autonomous regulation. In his reading, "the votary [the person making the vow] had the freedom to decide exactly what item would be offered and requested from the deity."[28]

To these four characteristics—individual initiation, privacy, spoken invocation, and autonomous regulation—another factor of the biblical vow is particularly resonant in our contemporary context. Numbers 30, the primary Pentateuchal treatment of the *neder*, differentiates between a vow uttered by a man, on the one hand, and a woman under the thrall of either her husband or her father, on the other. While the vow of the man is sacrosanct, there is an override clause allowing the husband/father the possibility of suspending the validity of the vow in certain circumstances. The discourse here is about gender and power, and it raises the question of when the freedom of the votary is limited or compromised by considerations of gender, identity, and status:[29] "Vowing is ... a powerful medium, but one with ambiguous limits and ambivalent implications for gender roles and relations."[30]

In rabbinic literature, the term *neder* typically applies as a promise to ban the use of a specific property by either the votary or another person. In the latter case, the term *konam*, probably a substitute for *korban* (sacrifice), or some similar term is frequently used to suggest that a certain item is prohibited to the person making the vow—just as a sacrifice is prohibited to someone once it has been offered up to the Temple.[31] By making the vow, something otherwise permissible is rendered off limits by employing a formula of words. It is uncoerced, but once the words have been pronounced, I am bound by them.

A frequent theme in rabbinic and later sources is the need to be cautious before uttering a *neder*: "The Rabbis insisted that it is preferable entirely to abstain from swearing."[32] The cautionary tale of Jephthah served as an extreme example of the danger inherent in taking a vow. Alongside this stern warning, postbiblical Judaism developed a mechanism by which a person could be released from their vow under certain circumstances, known as *yadot*, handles. The process of seeking ways to free a person of a verbal commitment brought the ancient sages of Judaism into a world of discourse about language and intention.[33] It is quite possible that the pre-history of *Kol Nidrei* is related to the wish to guard people from uttering a rash vow whose implications might prove to be grave. BT Nedarim 23b tells of a High Holyday declaration made, however, at Rosh Hashanah, the New Year, and not ten days later on Yom Kippur.

> He who desires that none of his vows made during the year shall be valid, let him stand at Rosh Hashanah and declare: "Every vow which may make in the future shall be cancelled," provided that he remembers this stipulation at the time of the vow.[34]

Perhaps a predecessor of what was to be become *Kol Nidrei*, this is a remarkable suggestion. It is discretionary, vocal, and self-regulated but perhaps hints at a communal dimension which was certainly to be developed in subsequent centuries.

Unsurprisingly, the halakhic system has been keen to emphasize that oaths and vows are not intended to cancel the fundamental commitment to Halakhah. Hence, for example, an oath which involves the contravention of a biblical prohibition is rendered invalid.[35] Nonetheless, the Talmudic position is that a *neder* can indeed override *mitzvot*, at least in certain circumstances.[36] Nachmanides states that "vows take precedence over the Torah, and therefore they apply to commandments just as to optional matters."[37]

I am proposing a renewed interest in the *neder* from a post-halakhic perspective. I am convinced that for contemporary Jews (or that segment of contemporary Jews who have embraced core aspects of modernity) recovering a sense of Jewish duty will not come as the result of simply accepting the whole system a priori. The neder, specific and personal in nature, may provide an alternative. To be bound to *mitzvah* is to bind oneself through one's intention by one's spoken word.

Neder as Praxis

The Scottish philosopher David Hume was intrigued by the mysterious act of promising. He observed:

> Since every new promise imposes a new obligation of morality on the person who promises, and since this new obligation arises from his will; it is one of the most mysterious and incomprehensible operations that can possibly be imagined, and even be compared to *transubstantiation* of *holy orders*, where a certain form of words, along with a certain intention, changes entirely the nature of an external object, and even of a human creature.[38]

Four years after Hume's death, Rabbi Nachman of Bratzlav was born. He too saw the act of vowing as miraculous. Rabbi Nachman marveled at the power afforded a Jewish person to forbid what the Torah has permitted and attributed this to the divine element within each individual.[39] Both Hume and Rabbi Nachman saw some great mystery and power in the utterance of words with intention.

I suggest that we reexamine this instrument of commitment present in Jewish tradition from earliest times. It will no doubt undergo significant transformation—that, as I understand it, is the essential dynamic of *masoret*. What does a praxis of Jewish duty centered around the *neder* look like? For some this might be experienced as a purely individual pursuit, either because their circumstances do not allow them the opportunity to be with like-minded people or because they are not prepared to give up any of their autonomy.

Engaging in a Judaism of the *neder* as a lone wolf is not the preferred option. I see the community aspect of this educational and religious process as crucial. I envisage communities of studying Jews who come together, select an aspect of Jewish life, research it, research it some more and, after a meaningful process, encourage each member of the *chavurah*, the learning unit, to make a self-regulated verbal commitment. It may be that of the fifteen of us who choose to dive into kashrut, some choose to become or already are vegan, some vegetarian, some observe a separation between milk and meat, and some are unbound by any version of traditional Jewish food discipline but adopt some other values-informed position. It may be that as a result of a process of study and rumination I decide to give ten percent of my expendable income to *tzedakah*, or recite Grace After Meals, or volunteer in a shelter, or study the Talmud every morning. There may be *nedarim* of environmental responsibility or of ritual piety. I am suggesting that we beef up the informed part of informed choice and consider turning our choices into something other than declarative preferences.

There will be no *neder* patrol to enforce whether you keep your word. The purpose of the communal dimension is not to police or to judge but to inspire and support. The Hebrew calendar offers ample opportunities to consider one's commitments. *Kol Nidrei*, uttered on the eve of Yom Kippur, could play this role, as could Shavuot, which can be read to mean not only the Festival of Weeks but the Festival of Oaths. This version of the *neder* should give new meaning to the liturgy of *Kol Nidrei*, wherein each of us is invited to consider which areas of life warrant renewed commitment and where we have failed to live up to our *nedarim*—choices translated into spoken commitments. The hope is to give new meaning to community, education, and individual responsibility.

The legacy of the *chatzufah* calls for an embrace of modern values. The mechanism of the *neder* offers a way of staying true to this embrace while providing the possibility of creating a version of *Torah Sheba'al Peh*, a Torah spoken with intention. This may be too loose for some and too binding for others. As a way for liberally minded Jews to be involved in a constant process of inquiry and growth, it offers an intriguing possibility. It calls for translating our thoughts into words, and our words into binding commitments. It is a way of living the letters.

Notes

1. Fackenheim, *Jewish Thought*, 21.
2. Ibid., 22.
3. Ibid., 24–25.
4. Borowitz, *Renewing the Covenant*, 254.
5. BT Nedarim 20b. The list purports to give nine examples but actually lists ten. In some versions children of rape are not listed. The *chatzufah* is unique among the cases since all others relate to an act or a state of mind concerning the man. For brief mention of this text, see Boyarin, *Carnal Israel*, particularly 109–113 and 129–131; and Lawrence, "Rape Culture," particularly 143.
6. BT Nedarim 20b. Prooftexts for this assertion are provided from Genesis 30:14–18 and 1 Chronicles 12:33. Read in conjunction, they imply that Leah was assertive in claiming her right to sleep with Jacob in return for her provision of mandrakes and that the issue of Leah's intercourse with Jacob on that occasion, Issachar, was endowed with remarkable powers of perception.
7. Feiner, *Origins of Jewish Secularization*, 232. The pamphlet is discussed in conjunction with a work by Fichte from the same year in Rose, "Lazarus Bendavid's."
8. Cited in Feiner, *Origins of Jewish Secularization*, 232.
9. Philipson, *Reform Movement*, 4–5.
10. Blidstein, "*Halakhah*," 37.
11. Levy, *Vision of Holiness*, 260.
12. Ibid., 264.
13. Ibid.
14. Ibid., 272.
15. Ibid., xvii. For rationalist rebuttals of the fourth platform, see Seltzer and Sussman, "What Are Basic Principles" and Aaron, "The First Loose Plank." The platforms are compared in Zola, "The Common Places."

16. Two remarkable reflections on the interplay between Halakha and Aggadah have been offered by Hayim Nahman Bialik and Abraham Joshua Heschel. See Bialik, *Revealment and Concealment*, 45–87, and Heschel, *Heavenly Torah*, particularly 1–29.
17. Bayfield, *Sinai, Law and Responsible Autonomy*, 15.
18. Yoffie, Foreword to Kaplan, *The New Reform Judaism*, ix.
19. Ellenson, "Borowitz and Dorff" presents a debate about informed choice between leading theoreticians of the Reform and Conservative movement.
20. Pockett, "If Free Will."
21. See Schmookler, *The Illusion of Choice*.
22. For the distinction between *neder* and *shevu'ah*, see Lieberman, *Greek in Jewish Palestine* (115–143) who notes that in the early centuries of the Common Era, "in practice the people seem not to have discriminated between these two terms" (117).
23. For oaths and vows in the biblical period and the Ancient Near East, see: Cartledge, *Vows in Hebrew Bible*; Kawashima, "Oaths, Vows, and Trust." For Second Temple and rabbinic aspects of the theme, see particularly Benovitz, *Kol Nidre* and Lieberman, *Greek in Jewish Palestine* (115–143). Mann, "Oaths and Vows" is over a century old but remains enlightening. See also Lichtenstein, "Philosophy of the Laws" and Gershon, *Kol Nidrei*, which looks at the origin and development of the declaration across history. For more insights on Kol Nidre, see Hoffman, *All These Vows*. For medieval dimensions, I found Yisraeli, "Taking Precedence" to be of interest regarding the thirteenth century and Morell, "Samson Nazirite Vow" concerning the later medieval and early modern context to be of particular significance. See also Rosenblatt, "Relations Between Jewish and Muslim Laws." The modern philosophical literature on promising is large and lies beyond my scope and capacities. Nevertheless, I would highlight: Agamben, *Opus Dei*, particularly 89–125, and Liberman, "On the Rationality of Vow-Making."
24. Genesis 28:20–22.
25. An apparent exception to this rule can be found in Numbers 21:2, where it appears that the Israelites as a whole take a vow, but even there the terminology emphasizes the individual. Milgrom, *Numbers*, 172, suggested that each individual uttered the vow. See Berlinerblau, *The Vow*, 48–53.
26. Ibid., 82.
27. BT Nedarim 28a, Kiddushin 49b and elsewhere include the statement that "words uttered in the heart are not words." They have to be spoken out loud in order to become something. Friedland Ben Arza, *Yehi*, is a remarkable discussion of speech act theory from a Jewish perspective. See 77–81 for her discussion of the *neder*. See also Faur, "Maba Bitzui." Weinroth, "Tafkid Hamilim," particularly 229–240, discusses the role of words in vows in rabbinic and later halakhic literature. Weinroth suggests that while

the Talmud of the Land of Israel focuses on the intention of the votary, the Babylonian Talmud considers the words to have an independent formal function, and therefore the precise formula employed is of crucial significance (238).
28. Berlinerblau, *The Vow*, 101. Malachi 1:14 provides an example of the self-regulated nature of the biblical vow: the cheater is condemned, but it appears that he can get away with it.
29. See Dolansky, "Why Can Women's Vows" and Niditch, *The Responsive Self*, 72–89. For a discussion of Hannah and Elkanah in this context, see Fidler, "A Wife's Vow." For a reading of a section of BT Nedarim in the light of Lévi-Strauss and Bourdieu, see Stein, "Linguistic Liaisons."
30. Niditch, "*The Responsive Self*," 89.
31. See Benovitz, *Kol Nidre*, 13–16.
32. Lieberman, "Oaths and Vows," 115.
33. For a remarkable Hebrew essay on some conceptual implications of this mechanism, see Rosenberg, "Yadot Nedarim." BT Nedarim 25a includes a remarkable midrash, according to which Moses makes clear to the Israelites that the Torah is not given as a *shevu'ah* according to their interpretation of the words but rather according to the interpretation of Moses and of the *Makom*, the Omnipresent.
34. See Gershon, *Kol Nidrei*, 19–26.
35. Shulchan Arukh Yore Deah 239:20.
36. BT Nedarim 16b, 18a.
37. Nachmanides to Numbers 30:3. This is brilliantly discussed in Yisraeli, "Vows and Oaths."
38. Hume, *Treatise of Human Nature*, 524 (Book 3, Part 2, Section 5).
39. *Likkutei Halakhot* Yore Deah, Nedarim 3.1.

Open Access This chapter is licensed under the terms of the Creative Commons Attribution 4.0 International License (http://creativecommons.org/licenses/by/4.0/), which permits use, sharing, adaptation, distribution and reproduction in any medium or format, as long as you give appropriate credit to the original author(s) and the source, provide a link to the Creative Commons license and indicate if changes were made.

The images or other third party material in this chapter are included in the chapter's Creative Commons license, unless indicated otherwise in a credit line to the material. If material is not included in the chapter's Creative Commons license and your intended use is not permitted by statutory regulation or exceeds the permitted use, you will need to obtain permission directly from the copyright holder.

Safek: The Benefit of Doubt

When setting Ira Gershwin's lyrics for "It Ain't Necessarily So," a song in which the literal veracity of the Bible stories is treated with skepticism, George Gershwin turned to Ashkenazi liturgical music for inspiration. The attentive listener will hear the strains of the traditional Blessings of the Torah as the character known as Sportin' Life tells us that "the things that you're liable to read in the Bible" may not quite have occurred in the way they are described.[1]

Doubt is sometimes seen as an adversary to be overcome; indeed, the postbiblical Hebrew word for doubt, *safek*, has the same numerical value as Amalek, the Israelites' nemesis in the wilderness. This fact is cited in various sources to suggest that doubt is just as implacable an enemy. Already in the Garden of Eden we are introduced to one of doubt's great mythological expressions. "Just don't eat from the fruit of that tree," says God to Adam and Eve. "Is that really what God said?" asks the cunning serpent, who offers Eve an alternative interpretation of the divine prohibition.[2] Doubt slithers in the undergrowth, undermining certainties. It is a foe on our tail, a snake in the grass.

Utilizing the cadences of Jewish piety in the service of a sublime expression of doubt challenges the picture of religion as a certainty designed to eradicate doubt. At least in the case of Judaism through the ages, it ain't necessarily so.

Self-doubt and Other Varieties

The Proto-Indian-European root of the English word doubt is *dwo*, two. Doubt is what happens when the allure and certainty of the uniformity is undermined by the possibility—seductive, unsettling, exciting—of an alternative. Doubt is a mental state, but it is also a philosophical and scientific method. It can paralyze, but it can also galvanize. Doubt is more than one thing. It presents as an implacable foe, a pathology,[3] a lack of information,[4] or an instrument of thought. The scientific revolution is built upon it, but modernity is threatened by it. One key distinction between varieties of doubt is whether the doubt is open-ended or bounded by some other certainty. If I doubt a belief or a claim because it contradicts a belief or claim I believe to have precedence, my doubt is in service of another certainty. If, on the other hand, my doubt is radical and universal, the doubt threatens to undermine not the possibility of this or that belief but the possibility of belief itself.[5]

Another variety of doubt is turned in on oneself. Instructed by God to tell Pharaoh to release the Israelites, Moses offers a classic portrayal of self-doubt: the Israelites would not listen to me so how then should Pharaoh heed me, a man of impeded speech?[6] Moses' question is reasonable. Based on his record in speaking to his own people, the chances that he will enjoy success with Pharaoh seem slim. Self-doubt lives in the gulf between what is expected of me and what I believe I can achieve. It is also a reminder to behave with humility. Hillel's advice not to believe in yourself until your dying day is not to be interpreted as an instruction to lack confidence in one's own abilities.[7] Rather, it is intended to prevent a person from believing that a fault observed in another could never be found in oneself.

Self-doubt can be debilitating and tragic. Nonetheless, it is an inevitable and indispensable part of being human: "The experience of self-doubt is unknown only to the thoughtless 'enlighteners' and positivists, to those who live in the obtuse self-certainty of conventions, whether ecclesiastic or non-ecclesiastic."[8] The rest of us are bound to live with doubts, enraged and enfeebled but also enriched by them.

It may be that self-doubt is the original doubt, or perhaps it is that moment of rupture and release when the word of one's parents and other figures of authority is brought into question. In any case, the term doubt covers a range of emotional states and intellectual postures. It relates to claims of truth, authority, value, prediction, and motivation. Truth claims concern historical veracity and contemporary facts: what happened and what is. Authority claims, in contrast, do not relate to a particular fact but to the basis upon which a claim is made. A claim of value asserts that a particular action or disposition is good or bad or, indeed, that it has significance of any kind. Predictions deal with what is yet to be, while statements concerning motivation speak to the intention of an act's perpetrator and not the details of what happened. Each of these assertions can be met with a response of doubt. Sportin' Life's undermining of the literal truth of Bible stories in the Gershwins' musical combines doubt about whether things really happened the way they are described with doubt about the authority upon which religion founds the notion that this *necessarily* happened thus. Like most examples of doubt, it represents a blend of different strains.

Shakespeare's Hamlet experiences doubt as an existential challenge. He is an exemplar not only of personal anguish but of national, social, and global insecurity: to be sustainable or not to be sustainable, to be moral or not to be moral, to be proportionate or not to be proportionate, to cope with trauma and loss or to crumble, to be or not to be. This chapter has been written in winter 2023/2024 during a time of war when insoluble questions are unavoidable. How to balance the need for security with the imperative of humanity? How to restore deterrence and return the displaced and the kidnapped? What does the future hold for Israelis and Palestinians? While certainty is promoted as a means of coping with tragedy, collective existential doubt simmers beneath the headlines. How to be who we are meant to be? That is the question.

Yes and No

According to a midrash, there are certain human qualities and behaviors through which a person will be accepted as God's very own. These include solidarity, reverence, amity, truth, peacefulness, deference, humility, diligence at study, and lack of excessive concern for worldly business. The tradition further asserts that this prized status can be attained through attending to the needs of scholars, engaging in discussion with disciples, displaying gladness of heart, and right conduct. This catalog of ethical rectitude and decency ends with two words, each repeated: *lav lav* and *hen hen*. In Aramaic they read literally as: no no and yes yes. One translation suggests "the No that is really No, and the Yes that is really Yes."[9]

An ideal is expressed in this phrase. In one rabbinic source the Children of Israel answer "yes" to every "thou shalt" in the Ten Commandments and "no" to every "thou shalt not,"[10] proposing a model of absolute obedience according to which our "yes" is in complete accord with the divine "yes." However, "no no, yes yes" indicates more than disciplined compliance; it is an expression of integrity and clarity:

> Rabbi Yose, son of Rabbi Judah, says: what does the verse mean when it states "A just *ephah*, and a just *hin*, shall you have" (Leviticus 19:36)? But wasn't the measurement *hin* included in the measurement *ephah*? Rather, this serves to teach that your yes [*hen*] should be just and your no should be just. Abaye says: that means that one should not say one matter with his mouth and think another matter in his heart.[11]

The rabbis play with the word *hin* in Biblical Hebrew, used to denoted a measurement, based on its similarity to the Aramaic word for "yes." Probity is achieved when ambivalence and duplicity are removed, when the mouth affirms what the heart perceives. There is, however, a phrase to be found in a few rabbinic sources which offers an alternative to this ideal of the irrefutable yes and the unequivocal no. One example of this alternative approach appears in Tractate Shabbat of the Babylonian Talmud. The principle exists that sacred scriptures should be saved from fire even at the risk of contravening Sabbath work prohibitions. Rabbi Abahu was asked whether sacred texts which were situated in the house of Abidan, where apparently they were used by sectarians for purposes of debate, should be saved on the Sabbath. On the one hand, their sanctity should demand it; on the other, any act seeming to legitimize the activities of that institution should be discouraged. The Talmud records that Rabbi Abahu said yes and he said no, and the matter was uncertain to him. Literally, the expression reads: "Yes and no, and the matter was light in his hands."

In a famous essay on Halakhah and Aggadah, Hayim Bialik used this expression to characterize Aggadah: "[Halakhah] commands and knows no half-way house. Her yea is yea, and her nay is nay. ... The other advises, and takes account of human limitations: she admits something between yea and nay."[12] Bialik's characterization of Jewish law represents an ideal, a striving for clear distinction between the yes and the no. However, one of the key characteristics of Jewish law is the inclusion of doubt in its methodology.

Why were yes and no loose in the hands of Rabbi Abahu when offering an opinion about the scriptures kept in the House of Avidan? Not because of chronic indecision, but because he felt the pull of competing goods.

That moment of holding yes and no in one's hands is as far from indifference as it is possible to be. It is not affected hesitancy or cultured ennui. Rather, it is a great expression of humanity. God, the Talmud assures us, does not doubt.[13] But human beings do, not only when we eschew the possibility of truth and meaning but also when we hold yes and no lightly in our hands.

The Birth of *Safek*

There is no word for doubt in the Hebrew Bible, but even without a vocabulary, doubt is to be found within it. Jeremiah admits to crises of faith, moments in which God seems to him "like a deceptive brook, like a spring that fails."[14] Perhaps more than anywhere else, in Job and Ecclesiastes doubt finds a voice.[15]

It is in rabbinic literature that a word to express doubt becomes prevalent. The origin of the Hebrew word *safek* is not, like the English, the number two, but it is more likely connected to the act of bringing together. It is also connected to a word meaning "to clap" and "to slap." One commentary suggests a link between the word *safek* and the process of grafting or linking vines.[16] The root *s-p-k* is also shared by the word denoting supplying and satisfying. *Safek* is born when two contrasted or contradictory possibilities come into contact with each other or are grafted on to each other or simply collide. Contrary to Bialik's typology, according to which Halakhah is all about the clarity of yes and no, Jewish Law is the birthing ground of *safek*.

In a brilliant study, Moshe Halbertal examined the use of the term *safek* in early rabbinic literature. He demonstrated how this literature deals with cases of doubt relating to questions such as the status of forbidden foods, purity, lineage, monetary uncertainty, and circumstances of inherent vagueness like discerning when the afternoon becomes the evening. Halbertal posited a distinction between the rabbinic method and sectarian thinking:

> One of the social definitions of sectarian existence is the construction of a demarcated and all-encompassing social reality that reduces friction with the environment and, consequently, conflict with the reality of uncertainty. Such a sweeping prohibition removes, with a wave of the hand, all primary interest in the sorts of uncertainty of which the Mishnah speaks.[17]

Rabbinic literature does not close down the possibility of *safek* but develops mechanisms for coping with it. Part of the genius of the system is its approach to doubt. While sectarians waged a war on doubt, the rabbinic system found a way of integrating it into its worldview, thus allowing a more fruitful interface with the world out there. The Sages of the Mishnah and the Talmud created procedures through which doubts could be measured and managed.

Here is one example. The Babylonian Talmud offers a thought experiment. Nine stores in a city sell only kosher meat, and a tenth sells meat which has not been slaughtered in this manner. A person is in possession of meat but does not know where the meat was purchased. In this case, the Talmud states, the meat is to be regarded as unfit for consumption despite the probability that the meat is indeed kosher. So far so predictable: one must act with an abundance of caution and assume that a prohibition applies. The Talmud goes on to state, however, that if the meat was found somewhere in the streets of that city but not in one of the stores, a different calculation is employed. Since the majority of butchers' shops in that city offer only kosher meat, a presumption of probability can be employed, and the meat is kosher.[18] For those imagining non-kosher status as a kind of infection which either has invaded the meet or has not, such a ruling makes no sense. For the systems developed by rabbinic Judaism, this conceptualization of doubt has a paradoxical double effect: it imagines an abstracted parallel reality in which flights of fancy can be indulged and theoretical possibilities explored, and it allows for engagement with society as a whole. The rabbis developed frameworks of doubt to allow for the complexity of big city living.

Halbertal noted that over many centuries, the study of uncertainty in its various manifestations has become a major preoccupation of yeshiva learning and provides an arena within which scholars can demonstrate mental agility and analytical rigor. At the same time:

> The ramified development of states of uncertainty and rules governing them within the Tannaitic literature stems from the rejection of the basic premises of sectarianism, so when a person loyal to halakhah finds himself in spaces that are always susceptible to uncertainty, the Mishnah and Tosefta provide him with rulings that allow him to chart his course through an uncertainty-laced world.[19]

For 2000 years, Judaism has not only provided salves and alternatives to doubt but also integrated doubt into its system. The term *aspaklaria* was given an inaccurate but informative etymology by Maimonides and other medieval commentators. They suggested that it should be read to say *safek reiya*, doubtful vision.[20] I suggest that *safek* is part of the *aspaklaria* through which Jews have looked at the world. Doubt is not simply an obstruction. It is also a prism.

It might be imagined that a faithful Jew is expected to accept the divine source of commandments as an article of faith. This is not, however, the case according to biblical scholars such as Tikva Frymer-Kensky, who asserted that "a careful examination of several texts in the Pentateuch ... leads to the inescapable conclusion that in fact there were distinct voices in Israel that did not automatically accept the God-given nature of statements declared to be from God."[21]

The Judaism I profess does not battle *safek* as if it were Amalek. My Judaism is unimaginable without healthy doses of doubt, present in every act of interpretation, every consideration of a consequential idea, and every attempt to articulate belief. *Safek* is built in to my *aspaklaria*.

Sefek Sefeka

One of the most intriguing constructs of the rabbinic science of *safek* is a concept known as *sefek sefeka*, a doubt within a doubt or a compound uncertainty. Actuaries and risk assessors employ comparable criteria when calculating probability. Moshe Koppel expressed the essence of this principle thus: "If a particular prohibition holds only if both conditions A and B hold, and in fact both A and B are in doubt, then we can assume that the prohibition does not hold."[22]

The intricacies of this methodology and the disputes between classical halakhic commentators concerning its application are beyond the purview of this chapter. I suggest interpreting the expression *sefek sefeka* to represent "the doubt of doubt." Different social systems can be judged according to the space they allow for doubt: "If the danger of relativism to a stable society is an excess of doubt, the danger of fundamentalism is a deficit of doubt."[23] My own preference is for an abundance of doubt over a surfeit of certainties. Nonetheless, I am alarmed at the prospect of an approach so riddled with doubt that it leaves no room for action.

Peter Berger and Anton Zejderveld argue convincingly that a healthy dose of doubt is crucial for tolerance, science, and democracy, and they recommend that each religious tradition find ways of not only accommodating but also celebrating doubt. They list "the core of the highly non-dogmatic and skeptical rabbinical method" as one of the religious options for steering a middle position between faith and doubt.[24] The question, impossible to answer definitively but equally impossible to avoid, is when doubt should give way to conviction. For some, Halakhah provides a mechanism by which this measure is calibrated. My ideas may not be kosher, they say, but my lunch is. For me, doubt extends to that system too. While halakhic conformity does not establish the boundaries of my doubt, Jewish fidelity and human solidarity do.

Wherever the lines are set, there are in fact limits to our doubt: "The suspicion of scepticism may redound to the honor of a man searching for truth."[25] At certain moments, the necessity to act or to resist strikes us with pellucid clarity—not unlike the way Descartes described the experience of certainty which surpasses even his method of universal doubt. Shaul Magid offered an ingenious suggestion for grappling with the dilemma of doubt and certainty from a Jewish perspective. Melding some insights of Luther and Montaigne with the writings of Nachman of Bratzlav and Yosef Yuzel Hurvitz of Novordok, Magid is in search of

> a rubric whereby one's inner life can function with a posture of certainty, enabling focus and depth to one's devotional life without resulting in fundamentalism ....
>
> I am certain at every moment. What makes me unable to universalize that certainty and thus force it on others is that I know, potentially, in another moment, I may be certain of something else. This is not a question of ambivalence as much as an understanding that every moment requires a decision, an act of separation ... yet that which one chooses, and about which one then becomes certain, is never predetermined.[26]

Like Elijah on Mount Carmel, it is necessary to stop vacillating and take a stand. The challenge is how to do so without aiming to uproot doubt completely and without succumbing to the lure of the absolute.

In my lexicon, *safek* has an honored place. Its root is not in the abstraction of duality but in the encounter between differences and the provision of possibilities. It should not be fetishized, but nor should one fantasize about its final destruction. Constant vacillation is no virtue, but doubt should not be abolished. "It Ain't Necessarily So" is part of Torah.

This poem by Yehuda Amichai gives doubt its true place: a vital role in the cycle between dense certainty and looser potential for growth:

> From the place where we are right
> Flowers will never grow
> In the spring.
>
> The place where we are right
> Is hard and trampled
> Like a yard.
>
> But doubts and loves
> Dig up the world
> Like a mole, a plow.
> And a whisper will be heard in the place
> Where the ruined
> House once stood.[27]

Notes

1. See Gottlieb, *Funny, It Doesn't Sound Jewish*, 218.
2. The sixteenth-century commentator Rabbi Ovadiah of Sforno offered an interpretation of Genesis 3:1 according to which the snake represents the imaginative capacity which places doubt in the weak intellect of the woman.
3. In a 1918 letter to Lou Andreas-Salomé, Sigmund Freud wrote: "I have the feeling ... that your derivation of the phenomenon of doubt is too intellectual, too rational. The tendency to doubt arises not from any occasion to doubt, but is the continuation of the powerful ambivalent tendencies in the pre-genital phase, which from then on become attached to every pair of opposites that present themselves" (Freud and Andreas-Salomé, *Letters*, 77).
4. Heschel, "Quest for Certainty" presents Saadia Gaon's understanding of doubt as being the absence of knowledge, thus distinct from error which is false knowledge (292–293).
5. Descartes, often cited as a proponent of this second kind of doubt, did in fact hold with certainties—not only the fact of his thinking but also truths that struck him in a profound way. His proposal to doubt everything is a method of ascertaining certainty.
6. Exodus 6:12.
7. Mishnah Avot 2:4. Joseph ben Hayim Jabez interpreted this teaching as a warning directed against those faithful Jews who allowed themselves to study external wisdom in the belief that they would not be negatively impacted by the heretical content to which they were exposed. Maimonides

took a somewhat different approach, citing the example of Yochanan the High Priest, described in BT Berakhot 29a, who became a Sadducee at the age of eighty. This position is made yet more explicit by the Renaissance scholar Abraham Farissol, who read the Mishnaic teaching as a reminder not to look disdainfully upon the shortcomings of others. See Farissol's Mishnah commentary (Jerusalem, 1969), 20–21.

8. Jaspers, *Philosophical Faith and Revelation*, 361.
9. This expression is employed on p. 205 of *Mishkan T'filah*, the 2007 American Reform Siddur, in a reading adapted from Seder Eliyahu Rabba 23. Braude and Kapstein, *Tanna debe Eliyyahu*, suggest "through his Nay being Nay, and through his Yea being Yea" (317).
10. Mekhilta de Rabbi Ishmael Yitro, Bachodesh 4, Horovitz-Rabin 218. It is interesting to note that the model lauded by Rabbi Ishmael has the people saying yes to yes and no to no, while for Rabbi Akiva they say yes to everything. In the parallel to this tradition in Mekhilta de Rabbi Shimon bar Yochai Yitro 20, Epstein-Melamed 146, it is God who tells the people when no is no and when yes is yes. See also Midrash Tehillim, 8; Otzar Hamidrashim, Midrash Aseret Hadibrot, 450.
11. BT Baba Metzia 49a.
12. Bialik, *Revealment and Concealment*, 45.
13. BT Gittin 6b.
14. Jeremiah 15:18.
15. See Hecht, *Doubt*, 45–85 and Pardes, *Countertraditions in the Bible*, 145–151. Sneed, *Politics of Pessimism*, 6, sees Ecclesiastes as the apogee of doubt in the Hebrew Bible. For important discussions of skepticism in Ecclesiastes and in Second Temple Jewish literature, see Kiperwasser and Herman, *Sceptical Topoi*.
16. See Rabbi Yisrael of Kozhnitz, *Avodat Yisrael* to Avot 1:16, referring to Mishnah Orlah 1:5.
17. Halbertal, *Birth of Doubt*, 14.
18. BT Ketubot 15a, discussed at length, including comparisons with the Tosefta in Halbertal, *Birth of Doubt*, 34–39.
19. Ibid., 210.
20. See Maimonides Commentary to the Mishnah, Kelim 30:2.
21. Frymer-Kensky, "Revelation Revealed," 287.
22. Koppel, "Resolving Uncertainty," 42.
23. Berger and Zejderveld, *In Praise of Doubt*, 87.
24. Ibid., 115.
25. Heschel, "Quest for Certainty," 266.
26. Ibid., 225.
27. Amichai, "The Place Where We Are Right" in Vecchione, *Faith and Doubt*, 71.

Open Access This chapter is licensed under the terms of the Creative Commons Attribution 4.0 International License (http://creativecommons.org/licenses/by/4.0/), which permits use, sharing, adaptation, distribution and reproduction in any medium or format, as long as you give appropriate credit to the original author(s) and the source, provide a link to the Creative Commons license and indicate if changes were made.

The images or other third party material in this chapter are included in the chapter's Creative Commons license, unless indicated otherwise in a credit line to the material. If material is not included in the chapter's Creative Commons license and your intended use is not permitted by statutory regulation or exceeds the permitted use, you will need to obtain permission directly from the copyright holder.

Azazel: Gaza and Expulsion

Theology drawn from today's headlines is soon outdated. At its best, theology set apart from those headlines can prove timeless; more often it is toothless.

Zeman nakat: history happens, and it makes a difference. Jewish thought since the Enlightenment has related to deep processes but also to specific events. Two above all, the Shoah and the creation of the State of Israel, have had an impact so profound that a Jewish thought written in our day without taking them into account is beside the point.

Many of the big questions apply regardless of specific events. Suffering, authority, redemption, joy, justice—these perennial issues and others still occupy us. It is possible to read Philo, Saadia Gaon, and Bahya ibn Paquda and to resonate with their concerns but not in the same way they did. The anxieties and hopes of different generations have common themes, perhaps, but distinct iterations.

Long before the war broke out in October 2023, I had decided to devote a chapter to Gaza, believing that it represents an existential challenge to the future of Israel and to the nature of Judaism. At the time of writing these words, the grim circumstances of the atrocity with which the war begun and the immense suffering which ensued is unabated and unresolved. I cannot make this chapter timeless since it has been formed on time's bleeding edge. By the time you read these words, the specific events may be felt less acutely. I predict that the fundamental issues they address will remain for years to come.

Expulsion and Expiation

Regarding *Yetzer Lev Ha'Adam*, a shocking tale was recounted according to which Adam, unable to quell the cries of a mysterious and threatening baby he has murdered, ends up burying the evidence by ingesting it. This brutal story constitutes a mythological account of a psychological and political phenomenon still prevalent. Confronted with guilt and shame, we often swallow them. We think our trauma has been buried, when in fact it has been planted deep within us and resurfaces periodically.

Ingestion and internalization is one model for dealing with our greatest challenges. Expulsion and expiation is another. Leviticus 16 tells of a ritual involving two goats to be performed by Aaron, the High Priest. While one is to be designated "for Adonai" and set aside to be sacrificed as a purification offering, the other is to be marked "for Azazel" and is left to wander into the wilderness.

The meaning of Azazel remains shrouded in uncertainty. Aron Pinker categorized the various attempts to understand it into four main categories: the name of a supernatural entity, the name or description of a place, an abstract noun, and a description of the dispatched goat. Alongside these four interpretive approaches, various additional suggestions have been made.[1] Countless theories have been loaded up on this poor goat as it is set out into the wilderness. One offered by Ida Zatelli is particularly resonant. She argues that "this fascinating ancestral rite is not a sacrifice; it represents a struggle against chaos, against transgressions and disorder, which threaten the harmony and safety of man, and it expels them to the desolation which they pertain."[2] It is not only in biology that ingestion and expulsion are twinned mechanisms; they are fundamental human responses to complexity and pain. The banished goat epitomizes the expulsion instinct.

One of the interpretations of Azazel is geographical: it is understood to be the destination to which the goat is headed, described in the Talmud as a tough and desolate place.[3] In the social psychology of contemporary Israel, the role of Azazel as a physical destination to which our sins are banished is played by *Aza*, known in English as Gaza. The Gaza Strip is an Azazel for Israelis: a wasteland on the edge of our consciousness, the place to which we banish our doubts and fears. The creeping annexation of the West Bank is Samael, while the disengagement from Gaza and the belief that it no longer concerns us is Azazel. Indeed, in colloquial Hebrew, telling someone they can "go to Azazel" is to invite them to go to hell. Gaza has become Azazel.

Hawks and doves, Zionists and non- or anti-Zionists, we all make use of these ingestion and expulsion mechanisms. Those who believe that the State of Israel is a perversion of the finest Jewish values, who share with Daniel Boyarin the fear that his Judaism may be dying as a result of Israeli occupation of Palestinian lands,[4] may (however much we may want to banish the thought) prove to be right—seventy-five years into the story of Jewish statehood, the long-term prospects for decency and stability are still in the balance. Like the rest of us, these critics also internalize assumptions and banish unthinkable thoughts. Those convinced that Israel is a beacon of moral probity must also work hard to swallow and exile inconvenient truths. We all digest and expel in one way or another.

The strategy which has informed Israeli government policy ever since the assassination of Yitzhak Rabin has related to the Palestinian people with a combination of ingestion and expulsion: we suck it up and we throw it out. The plan seems to be to wear down Palestinian political aspirations on the West Bank, and to leave them in the wilderness beyond our attention and responsibility in Gaza. If Israel can prove its geopolitical worth as an economic powerhouse and regional superpower in a changing Middle East, so the argument goes, the plight of the Palestinians will disappear from our consciousness. Some on Israel's right have not given up on a more literal and odious version of the expulsion myth: not only to remove Palestinians from our frame of reference, but from the land in general. In this appalling scenario, the people of Gaza can go straight to Azazel.

The disengagement from Gaza in 2005, an act met with genuine anguish by many, was in my reading a version of the scapegoat episode. Any sins imputed to the Israeli side and any responsibility for this crowded and benighted stretch of land were now removed. What more do you want of us?—we said to our critics. We have left. It is no longer our business. In fact, frequent attacks and military operations have persisted since the disengagement, and Israel continues to exercise a high degree of control on what and who comes in and out of Gaza.[5] Sending our responsibility out into the wilderness, we find that the goat keeps wandering back. In October 2023, the murderous rage we thought could be held at bay stepped across what proved to be a flimsy border, wreaking catastrophe. If we thought that we had left Gaza, and Gaza had left us, we were terribly wrong.

Doubt and Certainty in a Time of War

On October 7, 2023, thousands of Hamas terrorists attacked Israeli settlements close to the border with Gaza, a border they managed to cross with scandalous ease. The massacre which ensued not only evoked a deep-seated dread lurking in the recesses of the Israeli psyche, it exceeded it. The attack and the war which followed it has claimed tens of thousands of lives and left hundreds of thousands displaced. There are other, less obvious, potential victims of this and every war—among them doubt, nuance, and hope. Expressing understanding of Israel's security needs and strategic dilemma is considered by some to betray the cause of justice; for others, acknowledging the immense suffering of innocent Palestinians or interrogating the attainable goals of the war is tantamount to treason.

Alain Finkielkraut summed up the complexity and uncertainty that attend extreme situations:

> God sees clearly, but in the beautiful phrase of Milan Kundera, "man proceeds in the fog." Fog is his fate, even when he thinks he is living under the sun of reason or the honest light of feeling. … Joining the humanitarian side and supporting the victims does not mean, despite appearances, that we have made the right choice. No matter what we do, it is risky and uncertain.[6]

The subject of this chapter is not the 2023 war. The fog is too dense. Rather, our topic is evoked in a statement made by my father, Dow Marmur, in a book published in 1991: "By being in control over territory and over the Arab minority, Jews have had to test the teachings of their tradition in a new way."[7] Palestinian citizens of Israel, Palestinian residents of Jerusalem, Palestinians in the West Bank, and Palestinians in Gaza are all in some measure under the sovereign control of the State of Israel—a state that is at pains to assert its fundamentally Jewish nature. This fact sets the contemporary Jewish experience in Israel apart from Diaspora communities in the present and from almost every Jew in the preceding two millennia.

Non-Orthodox Jewish thinkers have been slow to grapple with the implications of this profound change. Among the exceptions to this general observation, Judah L. Magnes certainly deserves particular mention. Magnes argued that if the Jews in Palestine were not to live perpetually on their bayonets, a radically new approach to the "Arab question" was called for. Most Zionists tended to regard Magnes and the other intellectuals in his set as fatally naïve. In his own mind, he was holding a flame first lit long before by the great prophets of Israel.[8]

Magnes died in the year of Israel's establishment. His position, deeply rooted in his progressive religious views and out of step with the mainstream of Zionist thought, was regarded for decades as a curiosity, little more than a footnote. The small groups, such as *Berit Shalom*, Covenant of Peace, in which he was involved, did not set the tone for what was to ensue in Israel's first decades. The beliefs of Martin Buber, Ernst Simon, Magnes, and others were not compatible with the challenge of state-building. However, in order for the State of Israel to survive its first century and embrace a better future, the legacy of these and others may need to be resuscitated and made fit for purpose in a radically new context.

Originally a pacifist, the Second World War persuaded Magnes to shift his position, asserting that "war is not for something good, but against the greater evil – to help put down the devil."[9] He remained convinced, however, that "there is no other way of peace and progress in Palestine, except through Jewish-Arab cooperation."[10] The alternative offered by Magnes and others like him did not offer a practical program to win the struggle for Israel's existence. The struggle for Israel's soul may yet have recourse to their ideas, appropriately modified and translated.

The Legacy of Vivian Silver

Vivian Silver was born in Winnipeg in 1949. Already involved in progressive Jewish causes before moving to Israel in 1974, she was to become one of the most effective activists at the heart of a dizzying array of initiatives, most relating to gender equality and peacebuilding, right up until the day of her murder in Kibbutz Be'eri on October 7, 2023.

In an interview with *Forbes* magazine conducted two years before her death, Silver is quoted as saying: "I hope that both sides realize that nothing will come out of war, other than continued destruction. And that if our leaders care about their people, then they're going to have to change the paradigm."[11] She added that she was putting her life on the line for the possibility of peace between Israelis and Palestinians, referring not only to her wholehearted commitment to the cause but also to the fact that she chose to live a short distance from the border with the Gaza Strip.

In another interview, Silver described herself as a "conditional Zionist," believing firmly in the right of the Jewish people to self-determination so long as the same right was afforded to the Palestinian people. She fostered close relations with partners in the Gaza Strip and among Israel's Palestinian population, never losing faith in the possibility of a changed paradigm. Her commitments were strong and her perspective sharp.

Vivian Silver's views on Jews and Palestinians fell outside the Israeli consensus. She insisted on discussing what has come to pass since Israel's military victory in 1967. Hundreds of thousands of Jews live in the West Bank, and the infrastructure created makes the prospect of any future dismantling extremely difficult. Some of these settlers and some of those who provide them with political and material support aim to annex the West Bank and remove any distinction between post-1948 and post-1967 territories. Any distinction but one: no provision will be made to afford rudimentary democratic rights to some three million Palestinians living there. The fact that many are advancing this project in the name of Judaism demands a Jewish response from those who oppose it.

It is not surprising that no fairytale ending to the conflict has been achieved. This disappointing outcome might have resulted even if Israel had worked tirelessly for a negotiated peace. Many of Israel's policies seem to be designed to ensure that no settlement could ever come about. Jerusalem, it appears, is becoming Sparta, resigned to a permanent state of conflict.

What should Israel do regarding the Palestinian people's quest for sovereignty? It would be possible to understand a strategy of postponement: since the conditions for a negotiated arrangement between Jews and Palestinians do not currently exist, we will act in such a way that when the wind finally changes direction, the basis of such an agreement can be resurrected. This would mean freezing settlement expansion and investing in constructive relationships as much as possible. I could also understand a strategy arguing that there will never be a perfect time to negotiate and we should grab the bull by its horns now, allowing for the establishment of a Palestinian political entity alongside a sovereign state of Israel or an ingenious version of this comprising a confederative or some other model with security safeguards built in as a precondition.

Rather than either of these approaches, the plan seems to be to hold out the possibility of a degree of economic development for the Palestinians of the West Bank and to deny them the hope of any national political expression. As for Gaza, so goes this argument, we have disengaged and left them to their own devices (unless those devices are explosives aimed at Israel). If the perpetual cycle of aggression convinced Silver that a new paradigm had to be found, it has convinced many on the settler right that any saplings of change should be swiftly eradicated. We persevere, make business deals with whoever we can in the region, and hang on until the Palestinians give up on their dreams. This is not only the plan of a few ideologues. It has become the dominant policy of the State, enthusiastically supported by some and tacitly accepted by most. Recent developments and pronouncements have even encouraged some Israelis to believe that the Palestinians may leave the stage altogether, a belief to be resisted as venal and derided as fanciful.

Is there a way to change the paradigm? And is this a Jewish question?

A Jewish Question?

Even when clothed in secular garb, major themes of Western modernity, like progress, salvation, redeeming knowledge, and confrontation between good and evil, are versions of much older religious ideas. Rather than overthrow religion or ignore it, the path of the liberal religionist calls for a reimagining of the religious message to face up to the challenges of the day.[12] Critics of liberal religion claim that this engagement with contemporary problems is, in fact, a rehearsal of commonly held progressive opinions lightly decorated with religious terminology. This critique is often justified, but that should not render invalid the search for a genuinely religious voice offering an alternative to intransigence and chauvinism. Steven Schwarzchild framed the quest for social amelioration in Jewish terms:

> Judaism always advocates, in the name of the God absolutely concerned with the world, the greatest possible human, religious attention to the welfare and progress of this world—and if this be called "secularism", then so be it—but it teaches convincingly that this can be done only under the aegis of a Law put forth by the transcendent God.[13]

We humans are tasked with the complicated job of discerning what God commands us to do here and now, not as *bittul Torah*, a waste of valuable Torah time, but as the heart of our Torah.

Many Israeli Jews are strongly motivated by a belief system which regards territorial compromise with the Palestinians as heresy, error, betrayal, or sin.[14] Whatever the destructive potential inherent in such intransigence may be—and I fear that it may yet prove to be the ruin of Israel as a democratic state—there is no doubting the powerful influence it exerts on many and the degree of commitment it engenders.

Some voices (outnumbered and shouted down though they are) are being raised in Israel in favor of compromise as a Jewish imperative.[15] I believe that such a response is crucial and should be part of my proposed Jewish lexicon. Either we go in the direction of peace and compromise with all the risks and pitfalls attached, or we go to *Azazel*. The price to be paid by shifting our paradigm is heavy, outweighed only by the price we continue to pay for refusing to do so.

In my reading, Vivian Silver's voice belongs in a chain of prophetic tradition, pointing to a future she was not privileged to see. While apparently farther away than ever, her legacy—a profoundly Jewish one—has never been more relevant. While some have ridiculed her memory as if she deserved her grim fate,[16] for me and others her courage and her activism is a great inspiration. She called for a change in the paradigms which have informed the relationship between Jews and Palestinians for a century, and as such she spoke a profound Jewish truth.

SAMSON: POWER, VENGEANCE, BLINDNESS

Political Zionism, the modern political movement dedicated to the establishment of a Jewish homeland, offered a diagnosis of the Jewish condition, arguing that only by taking on the yoke of political power would it be possible to provide a sustainable response to the plight of Jews scattered around the world. For those who disagree with the diagnosis or find the cure more harmful than the condition it claims to treat, the impact of exercising control over millions of Palestinians seems little more than the logical outcome of a Eurocentric colonialist adventure. For those on the other side of this polemic, deeply impressed by the palpable achievements of Israel, Zionism's reading of the Jewish condition, its response to the legacy of anti-Semitism, and its engagement with political power and sovereignty all seem to have been a signal success.

Then there are the rest of us, not willing to condemn out of hand the Jewish Return into History nor able to ignore the momentous moral challenges it brings. If Zionism speaks of power, response to oppression, nation-building, and vision, the model of Samson in Gaza can be read as a warning of the negative aspects inherent in all these: misdirected force, vengeance, destruction, and blindness.

Gaza features prominently in the story of Samson recounted in Chapters 13–16 of the Book of Judges. Samson, a remarkable figure among the major protagonists of the Book of Judges, was famed as a symbol of strength. In the Babylonian Talmud he is described as a kind of archetype of outlandish power who, ultimately, is laid low by it.[17] Since biblical times, Jewish images of power have typically lauded intellectual prowess and moral excellence, eschewing physical strength.[18] The last century has seen the most extreme examples of Jewish power and of Jewish powerlessness in all of our long history, and it is not surprising that perceptions of power have been altered as a result.[19]

The image of Samson as an epitome of raw strength has played a role in Israeli political culture. Levi Eshkol, Prime Minister of Israel in the 1960s, was involved in the development of the Samson Doctrine, according to which a mortal threat to Israel's security would engender a nuclear response threatening to bring down Israel's enemies along with it. Eshkol, again, turned to the figure of Samson when describing Israel as "Samson the Weakling," while, earlier, a commando unit in Israel's fledgling army was known as "Samson's foxes."[20]

A verse from the Samson tale has become a popular song in extreme nationalist circles in Israel. It reads: "Please, God, strengthen me just once more, and let me with one blow get revenge on the Philistines for my two eyes."[21] Here the link between vengeance and blindness is made explicit: rather than a measured use of power in the name of defensible military goals, the story descends into vendetta.

While the temptation to be sucked into the vortex of revenge can be overwhelming, there are also remarkable examples of a stubborn refusal to fall. One such example was heard at the funeral of Evyatar Kipnis, a man slain at Kibbutz Be'eri. In his eulogy, Evyatar's son Yotam declared that rather than read the Hebrew word *nakam* as vengeance, he chooses to pronounce it *nakum*, meaning: we will rise.

One of the features of occupation is an epidemic of blindness. Most Jewish residents of pre-1967 Israel have little idea what is happening in the Occupied Territories and only a scant grasp of the rapid construction of a huge infrastructure designed to make Jewish presence an irreversible fact. Jews and Palestinians in Israel may occasionally find themselves in the same place, but they rarely see each other. When Israel is flattening parts of Gaza, it is very hard for most Israelis to think about the Palestinians being flattened. It is much more comfortable to believe that anti-Israel interests are misreporting and exaggerating (which they sometimes do) and to focus on our own pain and on security concerns (which are real). By making the other invisible, we help assure that basic empathy—a necessary component of any workable compromise—is kept permanently at bay.

Samson, eyeless in Gaza, epitomizes not a grudging and sober exercise of physical power for the sake of survival but rather an indiscriminate and desperate use of power. His example should serve as a warning. His is the tragic end of a man whose raw power cannot save him from the inexorable logic of self-destruction. How can we prevent Gaza being our perpetual Azazel? How might the fate of Samson be avoided?

Psalm 85

Mercy and truth have met together;
Righteousness and peace have kissed each other [*nashaku*].[22]

While this translation of the verse from Psalm 85 presents an ostensibly harmonious picture, the words can be interpreted quite differently. The root *n-sh-k* carries the meaning of both a kiss and a weapon. One rabbinic tradition understands it as a debate between abstract principles at the dawn of creation debating the advisability of creating humanity.[23] The tension between these abstract values has been employed to great effect by John Paul Lederach in his work on peacebuilding. He notes that while it is possible to pit these principles in a kind of boxing match, the chance for reconciliation exists when "the four different energies are embraced."[24]

Even though the prospects for reconciliation seem distant, to continue to believe in them is a commandment. The time will come when Jews and Palestinians will seek to hold mercy and truth and righteousness and peace in their hands. In order for this to happen, it will be necessary for much to change, including an honest reckoning with the process by which sovereignty was attained. The pro-Palestinian activist Sylvain Cypel has predicted that "as long as Israel does not own up to the constitutive facts of its own existence and those of its Palestinian partner … no real reconciliation will occur."[25] While many of his formulations and assumptions enrage me, I believe that in this he is correct. The day will yet come when not only the stirring aspects of the Jewish Return into History but also the compromises and tradeoffs that accompanied Israel's founding will need to be confronted. Ingesting and expelling will not be enough. We will have to confront. In my understanding of Zionism, this is as important an act of taking responsibility as heroism in battle and pioneering acts of social construction.

What Next?

In his *Star of Redemption,* Franz Rosenzweig adopted the image of the six-pointed star and suggested that on a foundational triad of God-World-Humanity, a further triangle could be superimposed, comprising Creation-Revelation-Redemption.[26] Dow Marmur argued that so enormous is the upheaval in Jewish life since the days of Rosenzweig (who died in 1929) that a star should be added to stand alongside his Star of Redemption. Marmur said that, together with the star of redemption, we need to think about a new one created in the white heat of the twentieth century: Faith-People-Land together with Hope-Righteousness-Power.[27] This second triangle represents a particular challenge: to find hope, to deploy power, and to act with righteousness and fundamental decency.

Every year Jews are encouraged to recall the drama of the Azazel expulsion as part of the cycle of Torah reading. For most of the last 2000 years, it has been understood metaphysically or metaphorically, relating to that which each of us has committed and omitted. In recent decades, the drama of Azazel has expanded to include the national and political domains. This new situation calls for a recalibration of the ingestion-expulsion dynamic.

If a Judaism of moderation sidesteps the question of Jewish sovereignty and responsibility—either by settling for hollow patriotic slogans or by removing itself from the messiness of engaging with Israel—it will fail to rise to the demands of this hour, leaving the field for fundamentalists to dominate unchallenged. As mercy and truth and justice and peace are caught in an impossible embrace, we have to work out a possible future, making common cause with others, religious and secular, motivated by a similar imperative. In a hail of bullets, under a pile of rubble, a paradigm is waiting to be developed. Through the fog, a star.

Notes

1. See Pinker, "Goat to Go." The literature concerning the Azazel conundrum is extensive. See Milgrom, *Anchor Bible,* 1059–1084, for an extensive commentary on the ritual and particularly 1071–1079, where he provides a survey of elimination rites in the Ancient Near East. This approach is impressively expanded on by one of Milgrom's students in Wright, *Disposal of Impurity.* Tawi, "Azazel the Prince," reviews a range of opinions, noting, for example, Saadia Gaon's rejection of the notion that Azazel was a deity and preferring to interpret it as a mountain. Tawil him-

self prefers to identify Azazel with the Canaanite deity Môt. Blair, *De-Demonising the Old Testament*, particularly 17–26 and 59–67, takes issue with the identification of Azazel with a demon. For the notion that the ritual owes less to cognate Near Eastern practices than it does to a reading of the story of Joseph and his brothers, see Carmichael, "Origin of Scapegoat Ritual." Orlov, *Atoning Dyad*, particularly 22–31, shows how Jacob and Esau are symbolically represented in some traditions. Orlov has done much important work on the Azazel tradition, particularly through the prism of Second Temple literature. De Roo, "Was the Goat," suggests that the word refers not to a foreign deity but to the wrath of God.
2. Zatelli, "Origin of Biblical Scapegoat Ritual," 263.
3. See BT Yoma 67b. See also Pseudo-Jonathan to Leviticus 16:10. Haketav Vehakabbalah to Leviticus 16.8 discusses this idea, noting the lack of any reference to a mountain.
4. See Boyarin, *Border Lines*, xiv.
5. For a survey of the situation in Gaza in June 2023, see Gisha, "Gaza Up Close."
6. Finkielkraut, *In the Name of Humanity*, 93. Kundera's expression is found in his 1995 work, *Testaments Betrayed*, 240. The riskier and more uncertain the situation becomes, the more ferociously the war on *safek* is waged. It is easier to brand an idea defeatist or treasonous than to grapple with its implications. Stone's *Perilous Times* is a fascinating survey of the question of free speech in wartime throughout American history. He writes: "A critical function of free speech in wartime is to help the nation make wise decisions about how to conduct the war, whether its leaders are leading well, whether to end the war, and so on" (531).
7. Marmur, *Star of Return*, 36.
8. On the life and thought of Magnes, see Magnes, *Dissenter in Zion*, and Barak-Gorodetsky, *Prophetic Politics*.
9. Magnes, *Dissenter in Zion*, 363.
10. Ibid., 449.
11. Norlian, "Israeli and Palestinian Women."
12. Girard, *Things Hidden*, makes the ingenious suggestion that in many modernist circles, religion itself is turned into a scapegoat sent to Azazel: "Religion always scandalizes in periods of decomposition because the violence that had entered into its composition is revealed as such and loses its reconciliatory power. Human beings are soon moved to make religion itself into a new scapegoat failing to realize once more that the violence is theirs," 32.
13. Schwarzchild, *Pursuit of the Ideal*, 75. This sentence is taken from his 1966 article "The Lure of Immanence – The Crisis in Contemporary Religious Thought," first published in *Tradition*.

14. For compelling presentations of aspects of these theological trends, see Inbari, *Messianic Religious Zionism* and Inbari, "Psychology in Religion and Politics." For an analysis of state acquiescence, see Mendelsohn, "State Authority in Balance." For a critique and a proposal for a religious alternative, see Manekin, *End of Days*. Manekin's efforts to form a religious camp opposed to the settler ideology may prove to be highly significant, although at the time of writing it is unclear how the Gaza War will impact this initiative. For an important study comparing the messianism of Kook with what he terms the Promethean messianism of Ben Gurion, see Ohana, "Politics of Political Despair."
15. In the course of 2023, for example, a group calling itself *The Believing Left* has sought to carve out for itself an explicitly religious place in Israel's peace camp.
16. On the day when her death was confirmed, a month or so after the October 7 attack, Minister of National Security Itamar Ben Gvir, an arch disruptor and disciple of Meir Kahane, posted on social media that Nazi Hamas (Holocaust imagery is never far from his lips) had deliberately killed Silver, who in his perverse opinion had been in their service throughout her life.
17. See BT Sotah 10a, where Samson is portrayed as being glorified in his strength and ultimately compromised as a result of that strength.
18. In *Unheroic Conduct* Boyarin writes: "My point is not to deny that there was ever a Jewish martial tradition, nor to assert that being violent is un-Jewish, which would be at best a nonstrategic essentialism. As it developed historically, however, Diaspora Jewish culture had little interest in Samson, and its Moses was a scholar," 273.
19. For important explorations of this theme, see the broad historical sweep of Biale, *Power and Powerlessness*, the in-depth reading of Zionism in Luz, *Wrestling with an Angel*, and the anti-liberal polemic of Wisse, *Jews and Power*.
20. For a reading of the Samson traditions in a contemporary Israeli context, see Abulof, "Samson, Unchained."
21. Judges 16.28. For a thorough analysis of this theme of vengeance and its links with the law of talion, see Paynter, "Revenge for Two Eyes."
22. Psalm 85.11
23. Genesis Rabbah 8:5.
24. Lederach, *Journey Toward Reconciliation*, 61. See the entire essay "The Meeting Place," 51–61. Sarah Bernstein introduced me to this interpretation and continues to use it in her peacebuilding work.
25. Cypel, *Walled*, 485.
26. See Rosenzweig, *Star of Redemption*. For an ingenious discussion of Rosenzweig's triangles and other aspects of his thought from the perspective of systems theory, see Zwick, "Words and Diagrams."
27. Marmur, *Star of Return*, particularly 33–39.

Open Access This chapter is licensed under the terms of the Creative Commons Attribution 4.0 International License (http://creativecommons.org/licenses/by/4.0/), which permits use, sharing, adaptation, distribution and reproduction in any medium or format, as long as you give appropriate credit to the original author(s) and the source, provide a link to the Creative Commons license and indicate if changes were made.

The images or other third party material in this chapter are included in the chapter's Creative Commons license, unless indicated otherwise in a credit line to the material. If material is not included in the chapter's Creative Commons license and your intended use is not permitted by statutory regulation or exceeds the permitted use, you will need to obtain permission directly from the copyright holder.

Pi Yagid: Prayer and Language

Prayer and language are usually bound up together in Judaism. Usually but not invariably. Quoting verses from the psalms, Maimonides argued in his *Guide* that given the limitations of language, the ideal for prayer should comprise "silence and limiting oneself to the apprehensions of the intellect."[1]

Many important world traditions have privileged the non-verbal—the silence that comes after language has been used—as the locus of ultimate truths. Jewish thinkers have, on the whole, kept their distance from such views: it may be that the eternal truths are beyond our capacity for expression, but they still exist in language. Sam Fleischacker offered a grounded Jewish critique of theologies of wordlessness, making a philosophical case for "an understanding of language as bearing God's presence in its mystery, as a meeting place for God and humanity rather than a purely human product."[2]

This chapter explores Jewish prayer in its overwhelmingly verbal context. The verse appended to the Amidah prayer calls upon God to open my lips that my mouth declare (*pi yagid*) God's glory.[3] Verses from the psalms, words sanctified by generations of pious repetition, are employed to ask for more words, just as they are deployed to illustrate that words are ultimately insufficient.

In the main, Jews have not sought redemption from words but through them. Language is not to be understood as a clumsy semaphore for the sublime but as a way to encounter God. There is, of course, a time for deep silence and a need to escape the ubiquity of language. This chapter is about all the other times.

Jewish Theologies of Prayer

In the introduction to this book I suggested that the biblical question "What does this ritual mean to you?" is a fundamental theological challenge. The question is often posed in relation to the act of prayer. What in heaven and what on earth do I think I am doing when I pray? Before relating to language and prayer, the focus of this chapter, it is worth dwelling on wider aspects of the question. I often ask my students to complete the sentence "when I pray I…" and their responses vary widely. Here are a few: When I pray I express gratitude for all the good that is; I mark time; I give voice to my identity as a Jew; I make space for the inarticulate speech of the heart; I express yearning for a better future, acknowledging the gulf between what is and what might yet be. When I pray I conform, rebel, confront, avoid; I am certain, uncertain, alienated, connected. When I pray I pray that I may be able to pray. For many people, the act of praying in a religious framework is as elemental as primary biological and social functioning. For many others, vestiges of prayer activity persist when no theological basis is allowed. Ritual, community, tradition, meditation, and commitment to something beyond the self are on display at sporting events, in temples of culture, on meditation retreats, in political rallies, and many other venues besides. Even when prayer is rejected out of hand, it is not readily dislodged from the heart.

Distinct from history, phenomenology, and textual interpretation, the theology of prayer asks a question addressed with different tools by the psychologist and the anthropologist: what is the meaning of prayer? A variety of theological accounts of prayer has emerged in the course of history.[4] In the Hebrew Bible, according to Moshe Greenberg, "there was a constant refinement of the idea of worship" away from a notion prevalent in the ancient world that the gods are to be propitiated by flattery to intercede in times of crisis, to "the acknowledgment of dependence upon God. Prayer became a vehicle of humility, an expression of un-self-sufficiency."[5]

There is little evidence of a regularized system of prayer in the biblical period.[6] Rabbinic literature, however, offers a range of implicit rationales for prayer, deploying rich imagery to suggest, for example, that God yearns for the prayers of the righteous, that an angel turns all the prayers into a crown worn by God,[7] and even that God prays.[8] It was rabbinic Judaism that developed a rigorous system of fixed regular prayers to be carried out both when the worshipper is inspired and focused, and also when the words are being recited out of duty or inertia. Alongside this structured framework, the Sages emphasized in parallel the importance of *kavanah*, often translated as intention. This term came to include both the intentional performance of the prayer and a directing of the mind to God, the ultimate addressee.[9] The rabbis made prayer an obligation while also insisting that it be more than an obligation. Had either of these aspects been missing, it is unlikely that the great edifice of Jewish prayer could have been constructed or, subsequently, maintained.

By privileging duty and performance over explicit explanation, the system generated intense loyalty and prayer literacy while also leaving much space for further exploration of the essence of prayer itself. The great medieval thinker Bahya ibn Paquda describes a practice combining the recitation of traditional formulas and meditation upon their profound intention: "For know that words are uttered with the tongue and are like a shell, while meditation on the words is in the heart, and is the kernel."[10] For Bahya, devotion in prayer is "nothing but the soul's longing for God, humbling itself in His presence, exalting its Creator, offering praises and thanksgiving to His name, casting all its burdens upon Him."[11] Each human being carries bears a soul of divine provenance, and prayer provides moments at which the soul can commune with its source. To pray, suggests Bahya, is to facilitate the reunion of the soul with its home. It is to be judged not primarily by the veracity of its assertions or the proof of its efficacy; its essence is the communion of the soul with its source.

Jewish esoteric literature of the Middle Ages developed a number of theologies of prayer, often in direct polemical contrast to the rationalists and the philosophers.[12] The praying individual is involved in a cosmic drama charged with erotic passion, and the words uttered with conviction have the power to break through from the earthly realm and influence the higher reaches. When the circumstances conspire and the intention is pure, the Shekhinah, the Divine Presence, "is present in his prayer and is raised to the Holy One."[13]

Building on this foundation, Hasidic conceptions of prayer were developed with a particular emphasis on the overcoming of the dictates of the self, leading Louis Jacobs to conclude that "in Hasidism prayer is essentially an exercise in world-forsaking and abandonment of self."[14] There is, however, a strong strand of Hasidic thought which sees prayer as a sublime expression of engagement with the world. In his *Yetev Lev*, for example, Rabbi Yekusiel Yehuda Teitelbaum stated that to pray is to do more than to fulfill a personal religious responsibility. It is "for the sake of the entire people Israel and in order to benefit one's fellow person."[15]

Thus, even before the dawn of modernity, there was already a wide array of theologies of prayer. The person at prayer propitiates the divine for a good outcome, helps create a crown for God, gives the soul a chance to call home, strives for intellectual perfection, participates in a metaphysical creative drama effecting change in the higher reaches, engenders practical results in this world, battles against the restrictions of the self, and reaches out to one's fellow persons, to name but a few.[16]

An eighteenth-century anecdote recounted in Solomon Maimon's autobiography may help to introduce the particular challenges of modernity to the praying Jew. He tells of his conversations with his teenage friend Moshe Lapidoth about the latest science, poetry, and philosophy with which they were preoccupied. They noticed that this appetite for discourse and inquiry was eating into the time appointed for prayer. Lapidoth said to Maimon: "Friend, what is going to become of us? We do not pray now at all."[17] The challenge of Western modernity, carrying with it the possibility of leaving prayer behind, encouraged the questioning of old theologies, and, for some, the creation of new ones. It was no longer a matter of finding an explanation for a normative act. Now the norm itself was in question. Lapidoth's question still echoes not only for those who have abandoned prayer but also for those who continue to strive with it.

Some modern theologies of Jewish prayer constituted a modern twist on pre-modern theories. Yeshayahu Leibowitz promoted a view, couched in Kantian terms, according to which the purpose of prayer was the fulfillment of the halakhic obligation itself. Any attempt to explain its therapeutic qualities or life-saving potential should roundly be rejected as idolatry.[18] If Leibowitz's views can be read as a modernized version of Lithuanian Orthodoxy, Abraham Joshua Heschel's many writings on the theme of prayer can certainly be seen in the context of the Hasidic milieu in which they were promulgated: "The purpose of prayer is to be brought to His attention, to be listened to, to be understood by Him; not to know Him, but to *be known* by Him."[19] While historians of Jewish prayer note that it served as a substitute for the sacrificial system, Heschel insisted that in its fullest expression, the act of praying is not a symbolic replacement but a moment during which one places oneself on the altar.[20] To use imagery taken from his ancestor the Apter Rav, at prayer the heart, punctuated by holes generated by concern for the woes of the community, is ripped out of the chest and held up for God to behold.[21] Even for the person less likely to tear their heart out at every moment of prayer, Heschel suggested that it can act as "a perspective from which to behold, from which to respond to, the challenges we face."[22] Prayer by this account is more than a formal obligation: it is a shattering experience and an *aspaklaria* through which we strive to see and to be seen.

Other modern theories are explicitly modernist. To cite two examples, Mordecai Kaplan offered a functionalist reading of prayer, deeply influenced by pragmatic philosophy. In his formulation, "prayer aims at deriving, from the Process that constitutes God, the power that would strengthen the forces and relationships by which we fulfill ourselves as persons."[23] Marcia Falk called for a feminist Jewish reconstruction of prayer, condemning the maleness and anthropocentrism of God language, which she termed "liturgical idolatry."[24]

In the spirit of this venerable tradition of interpreting prayer, I want to sketch the contours of a theology of prayer focusing on language—not the specific terminology of Jewish liturgy but language as a meeting place of the human and the divine.

GOD OF LANGUAGE[25]

This theology of prayer is focused on language: a particular language (it is almost impossible to enter the world of Jewish prayer without Hebrew) but also a language of gestures and silences, movements, and moods. Beyond the language of Hebrew and the body language of *tefillah*, prayer points to God who lives and exists, *chai vekayam*, within all language.

The connection between Jews and the study of language is well attested. In George Steiner's formulation, "Jewish thought has played a pronounced role in linguistic mystique, scholarship and philosophy."[26] He regards it as no accident that, in his formulation, with the exception of Saussure "the master-players in the critique of language, in philosophic and formal linguistics have been Jews or of Jewish origins."[27]

Jews, who have played the role of insider/outsider in many societies over several eras, have been deeply engaged with questions of language ever since Babel. The obvious reason for this is the proliferation of languages they encountered as they moved around and the necessity, both cultural and economic, of operating within more than one language system. There may also be something about the nature of language itself which mirrors the insider/outsider status of the Jew. Language lives within (almost) every person but depends on conventions which cannot be wholly self-referential in order to work. Language dwells both "in here" and "out there."

Philo of Alexandria, described by Maren Niehoff as "the first Jewish thinker to have developed a theory of language,"[28] conceived of it as a divine emanation, constituting the basic structure of the universe. This link between language and the Divine is developed throughout the Jewish esoteric tradition. Joseph Dan noted that in the kabbalistic concept of God's Holy Name, "language stops being a means and becomes an independent divine essence, in which language and divinity are united. The holy name of God is not an expression of the divine: it is the essence of divinity itself."[29] The thought that in some way God is in language or parallel to language may offer an escape from the banal distinction between "exists" and "does not exist." Elliot Wolfson suggested that the authors of the Zohar imagined language as evolving, driven by the impulse to overflow its own boundaries. Language, like God, unfolds.[30]

This more expansive and more theological approach to language continues into modernity. In an essay entitled "Language and Proximity," Emmanuel Levinas saw language as "fraternity, and thus a responsibility for the other, and hence a responsibility for what I have not committed, for the pain and the fault of others."[31] The essence of Levinas' ethical turn to the other is mirrored in or constituted by language.

Sara Friedland Ben Arza has written an important work in which she argues that there is something important to be gained from thinking about God in relation to the work of philosophers of language such as Austin and Searle.[32] She suggests that from as early as the account of creation in Genesis, language is presented as fulfilling two distinct roles: one is generative, creative, essential, ontological—language creates; the other is indicative, suggestive, referential—language represents. This dual function of language mirrors a distinction to be found in the way "God" is perceived. Like language, God creates and God represents.

The great questions about God—essence, uniqueness, incorporeality, communicability, mystery, commandment—have parallels in discourse about language.[33] Is it we who create God or God who creates us? We speak language, but also, in Heidegger's formulation, language speaks.[34] This blurring of the boundary between acting and being acted upon is echoed thrice daily in traditional Jewish prayer. The third-century Palestinian sage Rabbi Yochanan asserted that the Amidah prayer, the central liturgy of every prayer service, should begin with the verse "Adonai, open my lips, and my mouth will declare your praise"[35] and end with "May the words of my mouth and the meditation of my heart be pleasing to you, Adonai, my rock and my redeemer."[36] The first of these verses is a remarkable statement of Divine–human interaction in speech in general and prayer in particular. God's prerogative causes my lips to open, and my mouth will reciprocate with words of praise. I initiate the request, beseeching God to take the initiative to allow me to speak.[37]

In a 1916 essay, Walter Benjamin rejected both what he called a "bourgeois" theory of the word (a word is just an arbitrary signifier) and what he called a "mystical" theory (a word is the essence of that which is signified). In contrast to each of these approaches, Benjamin offered a remarkable reading of the early chapters of the Book of Genesis. He suggested that in the second account of the creation, humanity is not created from the word but rather invested with language as a gift and thus elevated above nature. In his reading, the bestowal of language to Adam and Eve sets it free from the divine act of creation: "God rested when he had left his creative power to itself in man. This creativity, relieved of its divine actuality, became knowledge. Man is the knower in the same language in which God is creator."[38] The language is the same, but this does not make humanity divine because we are limited in comparison to "the absolutely unlimited and creative infinity of the divine word."[39] In Benjamin's exciting theory, all of nature, including the inanimate parts of it, is involved in language, seeking to communicate their meaning. It is language, released from the sole domain of God, which gives creativity to human beings, who are then charged with the task of interpreting the vestigial language of the Divine inherent in all things and, in some way, speaking that language back to God.

Although he may not have been a conventional worshipper, Walter Benjamin's theory provides the basis for a theology of prayer. Language is freed from divine servitude and freed up for divine service. God is immanent and transcendent, absent and present, parallel and incommensurable. God exists as surely as these words exist. God is not to be accepted or rejected but recited.

Prayer is what happens when intention meets language.[40] Like all language, it is generated by individuals in specific communal and cultural contexts. Prayer, in Hermann Cohen's formulation, is "the language of the congregation, the language of the religious community"[41]: when I speak the language of prayer, even alone in my room, I am not alone.

"The process of prayer," writes Michael Fishbane, "keeps one alert to the fragility of speech and its necessities in all areas of life; but it can also simultaneously help one remember the role of language as signs between our eyes of the sacred mysteries of existence."[42]

When I pray, I place myself within the evolving prayer traditions of my people, allowing me an opportunity to fulfill the primal role of Adam and Eve: to speak God's reality back to God. This is a language of praise and joy but also of anguish and confusion. When the statements made in this prayer language are untenable, I have to either reinterpret them or replace them, and both of these responses are part of this *masoret*.

LANGUAGE ACQUISITION AND LANGUAGE FLUENCY

Some people are tone deaf to prayer. It leaves them cold, and the act of mumbling imprecations seems ridiculous to them. Another objection to prayer has less to do with personal predisposition than with a theological objection. The question here is not why should I bother praying but rather: how can anyone pray in the wake of all the horrors to which we are exposed?

My response to these questions is not to seek some platitudinous explanation to make this *safek* evaporate. Such an approach is as patronizing as it is ineffective. Instead, I would encourage such a person, any person, to find for themselves a vocabulary and a practice which allows them to speak their rejections and affirmations, to give voice to the inarticulate speech of the heart. To find it impossible to utter words of faith and praise in light of catastrophe is neither heretical nor new: a Talmudic tradition attributes similar responses to Jeremiah and to Daniel, each of whom has a book named for them in the Hebrew Bible.[43] For both prophets, it was a particular word of the traditional prayer which had become unsayable; in modern times, it is the enterprise of prayer itself that has come into question. There is no reason to see such an honest (and understandable) response as an adversary to be defeated. At the risk of over-psychologizing, I would suggest that those who find such a rejection of prayer so objectionable are grappling with a *safek* within themselves.

Illiteracy and indifference offer a much graver threat to the future of Jewish creativity than do the rejection of this or that religious premise. Knowing Hebrew is, by itself, no guarantee of mastering the language of Jewish prayer, but it helps. The words of Jews implacably opposed to religious axioms but able to converse in the language of prayer represent some of the most penetrating Jewish prayers of all.[44]

To speak in favor of prayer fluency may sound like an ultra-conservative position, but it follows directly from the language-based theology of prayer I am presenting here. To have prayer flowing in one's mouth, in the words of the Mishnah,[45] is an educational aim of great cultural significance. The great obstacle to this aim is faced by teachers of language everywhere: it is very hard to learn a language one has no intention of using. The educational challenge is to find a way of teaching and learning the language of Jewish prayer, with its fixed texts and a great sea of additions, embellishments, melodies, and choreographies, in such a way that contemporary Jews can speak their own values and vacillations in this language. God is invited to open our lips, but it is our own mouths that will do the talking.

The second paragraph of the Shema, from the eleventh chapter of Deuteronomy, instructs parents to teach God's words to their children so that the coming generation will speak them. When I pray, I take the words taught to me. Often the words are just repeated, husks with no kernel. Sometimes the words speak to me, and I marvel at the privilege of being part of an old and wise tradition. Often I refuse to even say the words. And occasionally I get close to the intention of Deuteronomy, adopting and adapting the words I have been taught and really speaking them. Occasionally in living the letters, the letters live.

I end this chapter with two excerpts from my own language of prayer, gleaned in the course of prayer digressions, distractions, and explorations. The first is taken from a reflection found at the start of the Morning Prayer in the Yemenite rite (not a version of the prayer with which I was accustomed as a British Reform Jew). It starts thus: "May it be Your will, my God and God of my ancestors, to clarify my ways of thinking, and to establish my capacity for verbal response." The second comes from a Hebrew poem by Michal Govrin. It uses as its structure a penitential poem from the liturgy of the High Holydays which contrasts the people Israel and God: "We are Your people and You are our God, we are Your children and You are our Father, we are Your servants and You are our Master."[46] Govrin adopts this structure, but the addressee, presumably God however perceived, is conceived of in terms of language:

> You are the voice and we are your speech
> You are the voice and we are your letters
> You are the voice and we are the tongue you cut
> And we are the lips that pronounced
> And we are the teeth that enunciated your words

The final verse of this poem, which is redolent with imagery from the Jewish esoteric tradition as well as layers of contemporary thought about language, reads thus:

> See your speech rise in us from the world
> See your voice calling from our lives
> See us writing you day and night
> May these words be on your tongue
> Thou shalt not forget.[47]

Notes

1. Maimonides, *Guide*, 1.59. The verses he cites are Psalms 65:2 and 4:5. See also *Guide* 3.32. For a presentation of the complexity of Maimonides' position on prayer, see Fox, "Prayer in the Thought." For other examples of prayer beyond or without language in Jewish tradition, see Ehrlich, *Nonverbal Language of Prayer*.
2. Fleischacker, "Words of Living God."
3. See Psalms 51:17.
4. For a highly informative survey, see Rosenberg, "Prayer and Jewish Thought," which proposes six approaches to prayer: "simple," theurgic, mystical, didactic, existential, and institutional. For a tripartite distinction made not by a contemporary scholar but by the MaHaRaL of Prague in the sixteenth century, see *Netivot 'Olam*, Avodah, 9. He suggests that prayer can be understood in terms of its impact on God, on the human–Divine connection, and on the individual. The term "theology of prayer" is employed by Gotlib, "Theologies of Prayer," in his brief discussion of two contemporary exemplars of the field: Arthur Green and Dov Singer. Green has made a significant contribution to the study of Hasidic attitudes to prayer, to commentary on the traditional prayer book, and to the promulgation of a contemporary theology of prayer which might be called Hasidic naturalism. For a personal reflection on his approach to prayer, see Green, *Judaism for the World*, 36–51. Many of the ideas discussed in this chapter were developed in conversation with Michal Muszkat-Barkan.
5. Greenberg, "On Refinement," 90. There is something overly positivistic in Greenberg's assumption of an arc of "refinement."
6. In the sixth chapter of the Book of Daniel we read of his practice of thrice daily prayer. This is not attested to in earlier biblical works.
7. Both of these images are found in Exodus Rabbah 80.21. For a discussion of Jewish prayer in the Second Temple period, see Falk and Harkins, "Early Jewish Prayer" and Reif, "Place of Prayer."

8. See BT Berakhot 7a. Hayim of Czernowitz (*Be'er Mayim Hayim*, Noach, 6) learns from God's prayer to God's self that the essence of prayer is to sweeten or mitigate harsh judgments from on high.
9. See Heschel, *Heavenly Torah*, 204–205.
10. Bahya ibn Paquda, *Duties of the Heart*, Heshbon Hanefesh, 207.
11. Ibid., 211. In the twentieth century this idea was expressed by Rabbi Abraham Isaac Hakohen Kook, who describes (*Olat Haraya*, Inyanei Tefillah, 3) a kind of spiritual cholesterol that gathers around the heart and that can be cleaned out by the use of prayer, thus ingeniously combining the metaphysical with the therapeutic.
12. Swartz, *Mystical Prayer*, relates to theories about early mystical prayer literature. He argues that while "prayers in *Hekhalot Rabbati* may indeed have been composed for the purposes of engendering a mystical trance," the primary purpose of the prayers at the heart of *Ma'aseh Merkavah* was "evocative rather than instrumental" (7). For a selection of Zoharic sources on prayer, see Tishby, *Wisdom of the Zohar*, 940–1075, specifically the mention of Moses de Leon's polemic against rationalist views of prayer (952). For a discussion of early Kabbalah, see Dan, "Divine Will Clothed in Human Will: The Intention of Prayer in Early Kabalah" in *Heart and Fountain*, 115–120.
13. *Tikkunei ha-Zohar*, Tikkun 21, quoted in Tishby, *Wisdom of the Zohar*, 1053. For a later expression of the belief that the act of praying effects a change in the higher orders, see, for example, Yaakov Zvi Yulis, *Kehillat Ya'akov* (Lemberg, 1870) 24b.
14. Jacobs, *Hasidic Prayer*, 21.
15. *Yetev Lev*, Hayyei Sarah, on the Baraita in BT Shabbat 127a.
16. Some Jewish theologies of prayer are explicitly educational. They claim that a key purpose of prayer is to train the soul and the intellect to achieve a higher level of consciousness or moral excellence. See, for example, *Or RaShaZ*, Vayikra, 473; *Ye'arot D'vash*, 2.3.
17. Maimon, *Autobiography of Solomon Maimon*, 143.
18. Leibowitz, *Judaism, Human Values*, 30–36.
19. Heschel, *Man's Quest for God*, 10.
20. Ibid., 70–72.
21. Heschel, *Moral Grandeur*, 38. It would be equally plausible to bring Rav Soloveitchik as a representative of the Lithuanian *mitnagged* tradition and Arthur Green as an exemplar of a neo-Hasidic approach. See Lichtenstein, "Prayer in Teachings." For a recent example of Green's reflections on the prayer book and on prayer itself, see Green, *Well of Living Insight*.
22. Heschel, *Moral Grandeur*, 259.
23. Kaplan, *Questions Jews Ask*, 103.
24. Falk, "Notes on Composing," 45.

25. Many of the ideas in this section are adapted from Marmur, "God of Language." In that article these ideas are discussed more fully, and the reader is directed to further reading.
26. Steiner, *After Babel*, 60.
27. Steiner, *Grammars of Creation*, 281. Gross, *Berit Halashon*, charts the preoccupation of Jewish thought with issues of language and speech from the earliest times—in Genesis 1, Psalms 33 and 119, for example, the creation of the cosmos is described as a speech act—to the present day.
28. Niehoff, "What Is in a Name?" 220.
29. Dan, "The Name of God, The Name of the Rose, and the Concept of Language in Jewish Mysticism", in *Jewish Mysticism*, 132. See also Scholem, *Origins of the Kabbalah*, 332. Dan's analysis is in response to Scholem, "Name of God," which is a fascinating exploration of the notion that the name of God serves as the foundation point of all language.
30. See Wolfson, *Language, Eros, Being*, particularly 284.
31. Levinas, "Language and Proximity," 123.
32. Friedland Ben Arza, *Yehi*.
33. For Christian theological parallels, see Ebeling, *Theological Theory of Language*, and Küng, *Does God Exist?* particularly 502–508.
34. Heidegger, *Poetry, Language, Thought*, 188.
35. BT Berakhot 17a. The verse is Psalm 51.17. See also Psalm 145.21.
36. Psalm 19.15.
37. See Rabbi David Kimhi to Psalms 19:15. See also Sarna, *Songs of the Heart*, 94–96.
38. Benjamin, "On Language as Such," 323.
39. Ibid. Benjamin's article was written with his friend Gershom Scholem in mind, and, in turn, Benjamin's essay had a crucial impact on Scholem's much later essay, "Name of God." See particularly 178 for a reference to prayer. For more on Benjamin and prayer, see: Buck-Morss, *Dialectics of Seeing*, particularly 14; Jacobson, *Metaphysics of the Profane*, particularly a comment on 171, note 312; and Wolosky, "Gershom Scholem's Linguistic Theory."
40. For a discussion of one central part of Jewish liturgy from the perspective of language theory, see Marmur, "Kaddish as Speech Act."
41. Cohen, *Religion of Reason*, 391.
42. Fishbane, *Sacred Attunement*, 142. Fishbane suggests that beyond this layer of language lies a great silence.
43. PT Berakhot 7.4, 11c; BT Yoma 69b.
44. For a remarkable collection of such poetic expressions and an analysis of their content, see Sagi, *Prayer After the Death of God*.
45. Mishnah Berakhot 4.3 and 5.5. The etymology of this phrase and its implications are discussed in Naeh, "Boreh Niv Sfatayim."

46. The authorship of this highly popular liturgical poem, a staple of the Ashkenazi rite from early times, is unknown. See Song of Songs Rabbah 2.45 for a parallel or basis to the prayer.
47. Guvrin's poem appears in Derrida and Guvrin, *Guf Tefillah*, 150.

Open Access This chapter is licensed under the terms of the Creative Commons Attribution 4.0 International License (http://creativecommons.org/licenses/by/4.0/), which permits use, sharing, adaptation, distribution and reproduction in any medium or format, as long as you give appropriate credit to the original author(s) and the source, provide a link to the Creative Commons license and indicate if changes were made.

The images or other third party material in this chapter are included in the chapter's Creative Commons license, unless indicated otherwise in a credit line to the material. If material is not included in the chapter's Creative Commons license and your intended use is not permitted by statutory regulation or exceeds the permitted use, you will need to obtain permission directly from the copyright holder.

Tzechok: Judaism and Humor

This chapter is about the centrality of humor in Jewish life. It involves neither reviews of the greatest Jewish comedians nor analyses of the best Jewish jokes. It makes no claim to the superiority or exclusivity of Jewish humor over any other variety. There are no tips here on how to be funny, nor any guidelines on how to avoid insulting or boring people in the process. Instead, the claim here is that laughter, comedy, and humor have always been a part of Jewish life and a claim that a Jewish life without laughter, comedy, and humor is not a life one should seek to lead.

I regard humor as something more than a distraction from the serious business of being a Jew. I do not assert that everything is a cheap gag. The tendency to turn everything into one typically stems from an instinct to deny or deflect what is actually taking place—an instinct that sometimes needs to be overcome. Indeed, boundless ridicule is not a compelling life strategy. Radical humor, in contrast, is.

But is it Jewish? Just as there is no word in Biblical Hebrew for doubt, there is no Hebrew word at all for humor. Modern Hebrew has simply adopted the word known in English and cognate languages, a term originating in Greek theories according to which the human temperament was governed by the balance of fluids. As far as the Hebrew language and Jewish culture is concerned, "humor" is an imported liquid.

Jews and Humor

Judaism, it might be argued, is no joke. Merriment and frivolity should be avoided as the business of fulfilling God's commandments demands *koved rosh*, seriousness of mind, and diligent obedience.[1] The Jews' tragic history has justifiably inspired dirges and lamentations; just securing a viable future for the Jewish people is a serious and often grim undertaking. Every morning, so one classic work of Jewish law decrees, a Jew is to gird their loins in strength, determined to perform the commandments despite potential mockery.[2] It might be assumed from this that laughter not only was seen as inappropriate to the seriousness of existence but also represented a threat to be resisted.

John Morreall argued that throughout Western thought, humor has been regarded with suspicion, denigration, or downright rejection. He listed three objections based on hostility, irrationality, and irresponsibility, respectively. Humor is characterized (or caricatured) in many of these Western traditions as being an assertion of arrogance (deriding the shortcomings of the other), absurdity (celebrating incongruity to the point of incoherence), or escapism (deflecting one's attention from the demands of life in the real world). Morreall noted that some non-Western approaches, such as Zen Buddhism, find a more congenial place for humor in their worldviews and speculated that "the comic view of the world may well be the most cosmic view of all."[3]

Sociologists remind us that for many contemporary Jews in North America, it is the legacy of Jewish humor that persists long after creedal and behavioral dimensions of Jewish life have receded.[4] A continent away from Hollywood and the Catskills, Sigmund Freud offered an outstanding example of humor as a constituent of modern secularized Jewishness: his Jewish identity was closely tied to his connection to Jewish humor.[5] Often, the more alienated Jews are from the traditional moorings of Jewishness, the more central the role of Jewish humor seems to be.

But humor is not simply a measure of distance from Jewish tradition. It has been a core characteristic of the Jewish experience since earliest times.[6] Laughter, *tzechok*,[7] was there from the beginning. It is, so the Book of Genesis suggests, the origin of Isaac's name, Yitzchak. The birth of laughter in the biblical account is itself a prime example of the sense of nuance, irony, and absurdity to be found in the key sources of Jewish tradition. Abraham is described as laughing at the prediction that a centenarian father would successfully impregnate a nonagenarian mother.[8] However, it is Sarah's incredulous laughter which attracts divine attention. Situated at the entrance to the tent, she overhears three guests predicting her imminent fertility, although her inner laughter is described as being subtly different to that of her husband. While Abraham thought the chances of either spouse being able to play their required biological role were slim, it is her husband's capacity that seems doubtful to Sarah.

The biblical narrator offers a master class in the absurdities, frailties, and misunderstandings inherent in family relations and in the human–Divine encounter.[9] In an echo of the Eden story, Sarah attempts to deny the accusation that she laughed, only to be upbraided either by God or by her husband (ambivalence and uncertainty have always been engines of humor), with the words: "*lo ki tzachakt,* no, you *did* laugh."

Laughter is not necessarily cheap or derisive. The twelfth-century commentator Rabbi Samuel ben Meir describes Sarah's laughter in Genesis 21 after she has given birth as "the joy of wonder"[10]; laughter born in the encounter with new possibility. The greatest expressions of humor in Jewish culture, as in all others, cannot be reduced to the level of adolescent sniggering or nihilist mockery. There is divine comedy, rooted in the most profound human experiences, wrought from joy as from pain, alert to new connections, and opening up new pathways.

A distinction between two modes of laughter, represented by Homer and the Bible, respectively, is proposed by Agnes Heller. Homeric laughter is that of the gods, ridiculing the shortcomings of other deities or mortals. Biblical laughter, exemplified by its first occurrence when Abraham and Sarah find the prospect of imminent childbirth preposterous, is of a different nature: in other words, "Homeric laughter humiliates the inferior; biblical laughter indicates a lack of faith in the superior's promise. The first is a merry laughter, the second a laughter of doubt and despair."[11] This suggestion appropriately highlights the role of power in the dynamics of humor. Conquerors and conquered often laugh at different things.

Humor is a complex mechanism, deeply embedded in the human psyche.[12] One of the most compelling accounts of humor from within Hebrew sources can be found in a work authored by Solomon Pappenheim. His *Yeriot Shlomo* delves into the meaning of Hebrew words, and in his discussion of a number of biblical roots denoting laughter and amusement,[13] he describes laughter as an attempt to attain perfection through an awareness of contrast. Humor dwells in the opposition between what is predicted and what is found. Pappenheim argues that what he terms the perfection of essence and the perfection of function are tangible perfections: something can be fully itself or perfectly effective. The perfection of contrast is fundamentally different. It demands a feat of the imagination, by which the gulf separating the "is" from the "ought" is somehow bridged.

The prospect of Abraham and Sarah bringing forth a child at their age runs counter to all we know about human reproduction, and the gulf between what we know and what God predicts is bridged by laughter. The ingenuity and creativity of humor is often sparked either by the surprise of discrepancy or by the wonder induced when two comparable things appear in incongruous contexts. Whether humor is being employed to mock or deflate an adversary or to poke fun at oneself, whether it is blunt and explicit or subtle and concealed, it is often the gap between expectation and reality which provides grist for its mill.

Humor is about perspective. It "sets up specific conflicts ... between its intentional perspectives."[14] It is the interplay between these perspectives wherein humor is to be found, and also humanity and a sense of proportion. Humor is an *aspaklaria*, and when it is lost, our vision is often corrupted or impaired. Comic entertainment may be designed to distract. Profound humor is a way of seeing.

Playful Rabbis

There is immense playfulness to be found in much of Jewish literature and folklore. In the Babylonian Talmud (Nedarim 25a), for example, in the midst of a highly technical discussion of the *neder*, a story is told about a man accused of lying about having repaid a loan who is brought to court to take a vow. He places the coins that he had indeed not returned in a hollowed-out walking stick and appears in the court leaning on this stick. When the time comes to make the oath, he needs both hands to hold the Torah scroll so he asks the creditor to hold his cane. The borrower then swears (truthfully!) that the money he owes is in the possession of the creditor. The plan goes awry, however, because the creditor is so enraged that he dashes the stick to the ground, and the ruse, like the money owed, is revealed. Nevertheless, notes the Talmud, the wily borrower spoke the truth when uttering the *neder*.

The tale is redolent with irony and suffused with an appreciation of human frailties and consequent absurdities. Handing the hollowed-out staff to the creditor is an ingenious way of avoiding making a false vow, something which is assumed by all the dramatis personae to be an unacceptable outcome. The borrower overreaches, however, since the creditor's anger leads to the scam being exposed. The fact that the Torah is involved in the machinations makes the episode all the more dramatic. Slapstick, intrigue, courtroom drama—these and other ingredients all combine here. The humor lives in the gulf between the moral indignation of the creditor and the devious tactics of the debtor, between the intended deception and the literal accuracy.

The humor of the rabbis was often connected to language, comprising interplay between different languages, words sounding similar to other words, insights yielded through punning, and other techniques. A discussion in the fifth chapter of Tractate Eruvin in the Babylonian Talmud dwells on the ambiguity in understanding some words when they are pronounced in different ways. A distinction is suggested between Judeans and Galileans concerning both their accents and the precision they employ in speech. An anecdote is recounted concerning a Galilean who went along his way proclaiming, "Amar Leman, Amar Leman!" Those who heard him (presumably Judeans) said to him: "Foolish Galilean! Do you mean a donkey (*chamor*) to ride, or wine (*chamar*) to drink, wool (*amar*) to wear, or a lamb (*eimar*) to slaughter?"[15]

This derogatory comment to the Galilean can also be read as a celebration of the multivalence of language. The ambiguity of words, written or spoken, is the basis not only for misunderstanding and error but also for ingenious insights. The Talmudic account goes on to include examples both of what is perceived as Galilean clumsiness and what as Judean acuity. Having explored the differences between residents of one region and those of another, the discussion turns to gender and lists a number of cases in which a dignified sage receives his comeuppance from a brilliant woman. The incongruity here is supplied by the cultural assumption that a woman would be uneducated and therefore incapable of holding her own in the cut and thrust of halakhic discourse. One of the examples concerns Rabbi Jose the Galilean and Beruriah. He meets her on the road and asks her: "On which path shall we walk toward Lod?" She says: "Foolish Galilean! Did not the Sages say: 'Do not talk much with women?' You should have phrased your question more succinctly: 'Which way to Lod?'"[16]

A rabbi is upbraided by a woman for talking too much to a woman (in this case, her), and then taught how he can avoid wasting so many words in the future. Not everyone who reads this ironic tale is struck by its humor. For example, in the great seventeenth-century work *Shnei Luchot Haberit* Beruria's words are quoted to support the rabbinic notion that excessive chatter with women is indeed dangerously seductive and is therefore to be avoided.[17] But there is a comic and ironic dimension to this and many other rabbinic sources, whether latent or explicit.[18]

The question of whether a text was originally composed with humorous intent is always open to debate.[19] As I hear Beruriah's words today, noting the fact that the redactors of the Talmud chose to enshrine them, they make me laugh, and they make me think. Perhaps this is one of the advantages of choosing to identify with a very old tradition: it may take centuries or longer for a joke to become clear, but sooner or later, its moment arrives. The fact that generations of men have failed to get the joke only makes it more poignant.

The rabbis of the Talmud praised humor as a pedagogical tool[20] and a therapeutic salve, noting, for example, that the provision of amusement and relief to those in distress is a deed likely to guarantee those who perform it a place in the world to come.[21] Humor is more than a benign force. It is a theological category.

Humor and Theology

The episode involving Rabbi Jose and Beruriah exposes the absurdity of the notion that men should grapple with the excesses of their libidos by limiting the number of words they address to women. In a discussion in the Talmud of the Land of Israel,[22] the startling assertion is made that God made a point of not speaking to women in the Hebrew Bible and only spoke directly to Sarah when accusing her of laughing. One rarely quoted sage, Rabbi Biri, rejects this thinking out of hand and instead declares that God goes above and beyond in order to hear the discourse of righteous women. Employing the same logic as Beruriah, he notes that God uses more words than were strictly necessary in conversation with Sarah. In my reading, Rabbi Biri is not only protecting the fundamental dignity of Sarah; he is also taking a stand against gross anthropomorphism and anachronism.

To portray God as a man concerned with limiting communication to the bare minimum so as to avoid temptation is to perpetuate an idolatrous reading of the Bible story. Rabbi Biri rejects this line of thinking and sees God engaging Sarah in conversation. Rabbi Biri, who makes almost no other appearances in rabbinic literature, deserves our gratitude for saving his contemporaries from yet again turning God into a self-conscious male. The God he imagines yearns for the sound of women in conversation. Here humor is in the service of theology.

Reinhold Niebuhr took humor seriously but saw it as appropriate primarily for dealing with the obvious absurdities of life: "It must move toward faith or sink into despair when the ultimate issues are raised."[23] It is fine to laugh in the playground, so this argument goes, but we must be focused and intense in the classroom when the lesson begins. I disagree. Our humor should come with us all the way to the Holy of Holies.

Humor should be an essential part of a believer's toolkit, helping expose our own cant and pomposity as well as everyone else's, for "there is no better solvent for truth than laughter, and nothing is more laughable than a truth that claims to be absolute."[24] A God who is truly absolute has nothing to fear from humor and much to fear from exploiters and manipulators who act in God's name without anyone to question them or to poke fun at them. *Tzechok*, laughter, deserves its place in this theological lexicon. Desecration of God's name is more likely to be perpetrated through a dearth of humor than through a surfeit.

The Future of Jewish Humor

Berger's *Redeeming Laughter* suggests that modernity represents a profound change in the role to be played by humor and the comic:

> Modernity *pluralizes* the world. It throws together people with different values and worldviews; it undermines taken-for-granted traditions; it accelerates all processes of change. This brings about a multiplicity of incongruencies – and it is the perception of incongruence that is at the core of the comic experience.[25]

The self-deprecating,[26] absurdist, language-based, survival-oriented kind of Jewish humor is the result of the encounter of traditional Jewish modes of life with modernity. One of the most consequential encounters of that same encounter, namely, Zionism and Israel, have often been portrayed as deficient in that kind of "Jewish humor." In his work on Jewish humor, Joseph Telushkin played into this characterization and offered an explanation:

> There is not a great deal of humor being created in Israel, and most of what exists is not very funny, at least not to non-Israelis. Because people in power are able to deal with their problems directly, they have no need to settle for the personal gratification of a sharp put-down or witticism.[27]

There is much humor to be found in Israel, packaged for media consumption and doled out more spontaneously on the street. It is different from its counterparts in North America for a host of reasons: some no doubt connected to issues of power, some to the hardships of state-building, and some to the influence of non-European cultural influences.[28] Whether it is better or worse than other forms of humor is not my concern here. As an Israeli, I am convinced that we cannot afford to lose the traditions of irony, subversion, and incongruity. We need to foster a healthy culture of humor in Israel directed in particular at all sources of power: religious, social, and political. In 2025, at the time of this book's completion, news emerged of a swoop organized by the Jerusalem police on the Educational Bookshop in Eastern Jerusalem. The shop carries books in English and Arabic, but the officers sent to inspect the titles spoke neither, and used applications on their phones to translate the book titles. There is nothing amusing about gagging free speech, restricting the flow of ideas, or accusing peace activists of terrorism; and yet the absurdity of the situation calls for laughter as well as protest. The laughter, indeed, is a form of protest.

Human beings everywhere are striving and struggling, growing and loving, losing and grieving. The alphabet of Jewish elements offers ways to process all of these universal human experiences. Some of these ways involve community, ritual, and politics. Some offer solace. Some of them activate the intellect, others the digestive system. Humor is part of this alphabet. The laughter of Sarah is not to be read as a sin or a weakness but as a profound way of processing complexity, absurdity, and challenge. It is an approach to life.

The story of the Jews is said to begin when Abram heeded a divine call. Perhaps it really began a little later, when a woman in her late eighties, standing by the entrance to a tent preparing a meal, burst out laughing.

Notes

1. See Mishnah Avot 3.13.
2. This instruction is to be found in the very first section of Jacob Ben Asher's fourteenth-century work *Arba'ah Haturim*.
3. Morreall, "Rejection of Humor," 263.
4. In the 2013 *Portrait of Jewish Americans* by the Pew Center, an affinity with Jewish humor is listed as one of the highest indicators of Jewish identity.

5. See Oring, *Jokes of Sigmund Freud*. One of Freud's first students published a classic work on Jewish humor in 1962: see Reik, *Jewish Wit*. In *Philosophy of Laughter*, Morreall brings fifteen thinkers' approaches to laughter and humor to represent traditional theories; Freud is the only Jew among them. Wisse, *No Joke*, 33–34, suggests that in his 1905 book *Jokes and Their Relation to the Unconscious*, Freud was not interested in what jokes have to say about the Jewish condition but rather what universal conclusions can be adduced from Jewish jokes.
6. For a survey, see Greenspoon, *Jews and Humor*, including an excellent essay by Eliezer Diamond (33–54). Wisse, *No Joke*, provides an excellent survey of modern Jewish humor in Europe, America, and Israel. See also Cohen, *Jewish Wry*. In his important work, *Redeeming Laughter*, Berger surveys many great religious traditions and judges that "Judaism, Christianity and Islam ... are comparatively underprivileged in the department of mirth," 197.
7. Apart from the name Isaac, the root *tz-ch-k* is found in the Hebrew Bible some fifteen times, mostly in the Book of Genesis. A variant reading with a *sin* rather than a *tzadi* is more prevalent, appearing over fifty times, mainly in Wisdom literature. Rabbenu Bahya ben Asher to Genesis 28.13 proposes a difference of meaning between *tz-ch-k* and *s-ch-k*. For an analysis of the historical development of this change, see Moreshet, "Tzachak-Sachak."
8. Genesis 17:17.
9. Kaminsky, "Humor and the Theology of Hope," offers a comprehensive survey of discussions of humor in the Hebrew Bible in general and a close reading of the figure of Isaac in particular.
10. RaShbaM to Genesis 21:6.
11. Heller, *Immortal Comedy*, 30. The mocking laughter of God described in Psalms 2:4, 37:13, and 59:9 seems to conform to the Homeric rather than the biblical model, as does the tone of Psalms 115:4–8 regarding idols and the taunting of Elijah on Mount Carmel in 1 Kings 18.27. Another attempt to distinguish between kinds of laughter can be found in *Tiferet Shimshon* by Rabbi Shimshon Dovid Pincus. Unlike most traditional interpretations which see Sarah's laughter as an expression of derision, he ingeniously suggests that while her initial laughter implied lack of faith, the laughter of Genesis 21:6, in which she celebrates the fact that all will laugh with her, represents a purer form of humor—a celebration of creation.
12. Goldstein and McGhee, *Psychology of Humor*, offers an excellent introduction to some of these complexities, especially Patricia Keith-Spiegel's account of early theories of humor (4–39).
13. *Yeri'ot Shlomo* Part 2 (Roedelheim, 1831), 31b-35a. The Hebrew roots are *tz-ch-k, s-ch-k, l-tz-tz, l-'a-g,* and *k-l-s*.

14. Vandaele, "Narrative Humor," 735. Vandaele's work relies heavily on Wright, *Narrative, Perception, Language and Faith*.
15. BT Eruvin 53b.
16. Ibid. The rabbinic tradition quoted by Beruriah is attributed to Yose ben Yochanan in Mishnah Avot 1.5.
17. Isaiah Halevi Horowitz, *Shnei Luchot Haberit* (Jerusalem: Sha'arei Ziv, 1990), vol.1, She'ar Otiot, 'Emek Haberakha, Hilkhot Bi'ah, 5, 436a. He quotes Beruriah's words and then launches into a warning against the temptations of sexual depravity.
18. Boyarin, *Socrates and Fat Rabbis*, particularly 133–192, explores this comic dimension as one of two competing or contrasting voices to be found within Talmudic discourse.
19. For an example of a debate between eminent Bible scholars over the degree to which a text (in that case a chapter from the Book of Joshua) is to be read through a humorous prism, see Zakovitch, "Humor and Theology" and Cross, "Response to Zakovitch." In BT Menachot 29b a famous tale is told according to which Moses is afforded a glimpse into Rabbi Akiva's house of study. The midrash records that Moses did not understand what was being discussed, and most contemporary readers would assume that this was due to changes in language and assumptions that had occurred in the 1500 years separating them and also due to Rabbi Akiva's penchant for squeezing laws out of the flimsiest textual basis. Rashi, however, has a more prosaic and far less humorous explanation: it was simply that in the midrash, Moses had not yet been given the Torah when the time travel took place. The assumption is that had Moses been given the Torah he would have understood every aspect of what was being taught by Rabbi Akiva. This is another example of killing the irony in order to neutralize the perceived theological threat.
20. See the example of Rabba in BT Shabbat 30b, although there it is made clear that he would start his teaching with a joke and then engage in the core of study with great seriousness.
21. BT Ta'anit 22a.
22. PT Sotah 7.1 21b. See also Genesis Rabbah 20.6 and 48.20.
23. Niebuhr, *Discerning the Signs*, 130–131. Berger, *Redeeming Laughter*, note 9, 203–204, identifies Niebuhr's position with that of Kierkegaard and expresses his disagreement with both of them.
24. Sands, "Ifs, Ands, and Buts" 507.
25. Berger, *Redeeming Laughter*, 202. Wisse, *No Joke*, notes that it is only in modernity that humor becomes the aim of entertainment "as opposed to a delightful by-product of otherwise-earnest interpretation" (24). So it is not just that modernity opens up the possibilities of humor but also that in modernity, humor is commodified.

26. Ben-Amos, *Myth of Jewish Humor*, takes issue with the idea that Jewish humor is characterized by self-mocking.
27. Telushkin, *Jewish Humor*, 173. Wisse, *No Joke*, particularly 182–220, disagrees with Telushkin's statement.
28. Regarding non-Ashkenazi expressions of Jewish humor, it is instructive to consider France, where the work of such figures as Michel Boujenah, Yvan Attal, and Gad Elmaleh has been highly influential.

Open Access This chapter is licensed under the terms of the Creative Commons Attribution 4.0 International License (http://creativecommons.org/licenses/by/4.0/), which permits use, sharing, adaptation, distribution and reproduction in any medium or format, as long as you give appropriate credit to the original author(s) and the source, provide a link to the Creative Commons license and indicate if changes were made.

The images or other third party material in this chapter are included in the chapter's Creative Commons license, unless indicated otherwise in a credit line to the material. If material is not included in the chapter's Creative Commons license and your intended use is not permitted by statutory regulation or exceeds the permitted use, you will need to obtain permission directly from the copyright holder.

Kehillah: Community

In retrospect, the excommunication of Baruch Spinoza by the community of Portuguese Jews in Amsterdam in 1656 was a watershed moment. Life before modernity was largely defined in terms of communal affiliation. Spinoza's philosophy looked to a time in which individuals would chart their own ethical course. Symbolically, then, the act of excommunication reads like the closing of one era and the dawn of a new one. The ban was enacted "by decree of the angels and by the command of the holy men … with the consent of God, Blessed be He, and with the consent of the entire holy congregation."[1] Spinoza is said to have received news of the community's decision with equanimity:

> All the better; they do not force me to do anything that I would not have done of my own accord if I did not dread scandal. But, since they want it that way, I enter gladly on the path this opened to me, with the consolation that my departure will be more innocent than was the exodus of the early Hebrews from Egypt.[2]

At the age of twenty-four, Spinoza had already come to the conclusion that his own intellectual journey placed him in conflict with his home congregation and that it was necessary for him to part ways with them in order to follow his own path to freedom and truth. The arc of Moses' growth as described in the Book of Exodus saw him transition from a child of Pharaoh's court with no awareness of Hebrew affiliation to the leader of a people bound for the Promised Land. Spinoza's exodus, symbolic of so many moderns who were to follow in his footsteps, saw him tread the opposite path: from "thick" affiliation to hard-fought independence.

The contrast between Moses' and Spinoza's journeys, between self-fulfillment within the confines of the community and beyond them, has been a central feature of the modern Jewish experience ever since. In the summer of 1781, for example, a dispute erupted between Netanel Posner, a businessman from Altona-Hamburg, and the rabbi of the community, Raphael Kohen. When some men from the community came to wake him to join the *selichot* services of penitential prayers leading up to the High Holydays, Posner remarked with derision: "Yesterday I went to a comedy and then to a ball, and today you are waking me from my sleep for such nonsense."[3] In response to a number of public comments by Posner that revealed his freethinking views and his rejection of communal authority, the rabbi attempted to employ traditional sanctions in order to coerce the recalcitrant into conformity. Kohen sent a letter to the Danish authorities then ruling Altona in which he declared that "I see it as my main function to guide the community under my care in the ways of worshipping and loving God, and to thwart any freethinking and irreligion."[4] Posner, for his part, remained stubbornly resistant to the attempt of the community to force him to bow to their dictates.

For many of us today, the remarkable and unfamiliar aspect of this episode is not Posner's refusal to be bound by certain rituals and beliefs. Rather, it is the expectation that the community has the right to enforce conformity of practice and thought. In 1781, that expectation, a feature of medieval Jewish life, was on the wane. Today, it has largely disappeared outside ultra-Orthodoxy. Even there, continued adherence is increasingly predicated on personal choice. Western modernity has involved a redrawing of the relationship between the individual and the community, and few have been unaffected by this change.

Both Spinoza and Posner, each in their own way, threatened the old order since each epitomized the individual in search of philosophical truth, untrammeled by conventions and dogmas, unwilling to bow to the dictates of the *kehillah*, the community. *Kehillah* has been under threat from various quarters, not only from recalcitrant rebels. The concept of the modern nation state often undermined its centrality, and more recently radical transformations in economics and technology have cast doubt over the very notion of community.[5] Individualism, globalization, nationalism (including Zionism),[6] secularization, digitization, and alienation—all these and other factors have put the pre-modern Jewish community in retreat in modern times.

Reports of the death of community are, however, premature. In the face of all these challenges, new ways of imagining and realizing *kehillah* continue to emerge.

COMMUNITY AND THE SOCIAL IMAGINARY

Discourse about "community" tends to be imprecise. Elizabeth Bounds listed a number of distinct meanings attributed to the term, describing them as desires rather than descriptive states. When we speak today of community, she suggests, we may mean a desire for "immediate relations," an arena of meaningful love, solidarity, and perhaps spirituality in contrast to more mechanical roles prescribed by society; a desire for collective connection in reaction to a conflicted society; or "a desire for the experience of a unified transcendence … so that life is lived in relation to something *greater* than the self."[7] She notes that the term may also be employed to evoke a desire to reaffirm lost traditions and practices; a desire to establish new practices in response to societal pressures; and, lastly, "a desire for effective political participation, seeing oneself as a citizen among fellow citizens with relations and responsibilities."[8]

The *kehillah* may be hard to define, and it may be undergoing profound change, but it is not dead. It continues to be part of our "social imaginary," a term employed by Charles Taylor to describe "the ways people imagine their social existence, how they fit with others, how things go on between them and their fellows, the expectations that are normally met, and the deeper normative notions and images that underlie these expectations."[9] Notions of community feature prominently in most social imaginaries, be they of conservatives or progressives. The gulf in the ways in which community is imagined is often great. To take an obvious example, if you are a practicing Orthodox Jew, you will not move to an area unless you know that certain needs will be met: if there is not a synagogue you can pray in within walking distance, you will not be changing your address by choice.

Non-Orthodox Jews may yearn for community and may love it, but their connection to it is imagined in a different way. In the main, our relationship with community is more negotiable and more malleable. Our ideal communities (mine at least) notice when we are not there but refrain from judging or policing us. We want a *kehillah* "thick" enough to be significant but not enough to stifle. As is the case in most of our significant relationships, our expectations of community are complex and sometimes self-contradictory. We want affiliation without asphyxiation, connection but not at the price of independence, to be supported but not to be overwhelmed.

Community has often been imagined in contrast to some other model of social organization. Ferdinand Tönnies' distinction between community (*Gemeinschaft*) and society (*Gesellschaft*), first proposed in the 1880s, is still compelling.[10] As part of his analysis of the impact of modernity on forms of social organization, Tönnies posited two ideal types: the former associated with traditional expressions of communal existence, and the latter more characteristic of modernity. According to this distinction, "community" is where individuals are bound together by common norms and intimate interactions, while "society" is more contractual in nature, where individuals navigate their way through a web of institutions guided by market forces and self-interest. Community is where our web of emotional responses is woven, where rules are implicit, and where our conscience is nurtured. Society is where our capacity for reason and distance is honed, where rules are explicit, and where our personal private consciousness comes into its own.

For a Jewish expression of this distinction, the name of Martin Buber, who was consciously influenced by Tönnies' seminal work, can be invoked. One of the most significant Jewish thinkers of the twentieth century, Buber is perhaps best known for his proposed distinction between two modes of relation which he termed "I-It" and "I-Thou." The former describes a relationship which is fundamentally instrumental and transactional. When the inspector checks my bus pass they can likely only spare two seconds of thought for me because there are many people on the bus and many more buses to be inspected. They are an It to me (indeed they have been replaced by machines in many places), and I am an It to them. This does not mean that we dislike each other. Were they to strive for a relationship of I-Thou with every passenger, few tickets would be checked. There are indeed all kinds of connection between subjects which are necessarily functional: "without *It* man cannot live. But he who lives with *It* alone is not a man."[11]

The second kind of relationship, "I-Thou," is immediate and profound. At that I-Thou moment, my affinity with the other person is not exclusively or primarily about what we are providing each other: endorphins, reassurance, monetary compensation, whatever. It is about seeing the other person in their humanity and being truly in their presence. It is about real connection. The other is not an It to me, but someone I encounter in a more authentic way.

Buber extended this notion beyond the bond formed between two subjects, reaching out into the social realm. Here the distinction he posited is between collective and community: the former describes the bundling together of humans for some instrumental purpose and it is based on "an organized atrophy of personal existence"[12]; the latter stands for the increase and conformation of personal existence "in life lived toward one another."[13] Influenced by the social thought of Tönnies and others, particularly Gustav Landauer,[14] Buber advanced the ideal of community as a crucial element in the construction of lives of meaning.[15] Tönnies contrasts community with society and Buber contrasts it with collective. In each case, "community" stands for a profound non-instrumental connection with other persons, while the alternative term relates to the essential yet alienating structures of modern life.

Mordecai Kaplan described the prevalent model of synagogues offering almost exclusively religious service to privileged members as congregations, which in his view ought to be replaced by communities, thus responding to a much wider range of communal needs for all the Jews living in a particular area. Kaplan emphasized that the new Jewish community would need to reflect new conceptions of democracy rather than outmoded hierarchical models. In Kaplan's view, a community was needed which would counteract a process of fragmentation according to which the various functions offered within the community appeared to have nothing to do with each other:

> The only way to overcome that fragmentation of Jewish life is to have Jews form themselves into organic communities that would function as the instruments of Jewish life as a whole, and that would meet all its needs, in order of their urgency and importance.[16]

While Tönnies and Buber imagined community as something smaller and more intimate than society or collective, Kaplan's conception of *kehillah* was rooted in a critique of congregations offering too limited a range of services (mainly prayer services). He imagined organic communities and set out pragmatic steps designed to bring them to life.

In 1990 Judith Plaskow devoted an entire section of her foundational work of feminist Jewish theology to a reimagination of community, folding into this analysis considerations of difference, chosenness, and the State of Israel. She argued convincingly that a feminist reading of Judaism necessitates a re-reading of the concept and practice of communal life. She described a "struggle to bring the manifold riches of a complex human heritage to the careful nurturing of communal and individual life."[17]

The tension between particularism and universalism, so central to the modern Jewish experience, plays out in communal life. Some are so engaged in the microcosmic drama of their own community that nothing else seems to matter. When the world "out there" seems hostile and controversial, it is all the more tempting to stay within the comfort zone of one's own community and keep wider political and social questions at bay. *Kehillah*, a community of search and support, is a place where people can be nurtured and experience growth, a place of refuge and retreat. It can also be a springboard—a way of acting in the wider world.

In *Sacred Attunements*, Michael Fishbane identifies three spaces which "separately and together … cultivate the values of community and its continuity."[18] They are home, synagogue, and homeland. Each of these sites de-emphasize the centrality of the individual, which has preoccupied the discourse of modernity. He describes home as "the primary ground of self-transcendence" and "first community."[19] Then comes the synagogue, which he portrays as a foundational "second community, transcending the family unit."[20] An enthusiastic adherent of communal life, Fishbane warns against the risk of insularity:

> Members of a synagogue must bear in mind that their spiritual enclave both includes and excludes, not solely by virtue of language and memory, but by dint of its traditions of membership and acceptance. A house of gathering for Jews must therefore always be preparatory for and proleptic of a more inclusive congregation.[21]

The *kehillah* described here is a springboard. It is local and specific, informed by particular tastes and tunes and idiosyncrasies. It also looks beyond itself to other communities within and beyond the Jewish people. As communities imagine themselves, they would do well to employ Fishbane's terminology in asking themselves: are we a spiritual enclave nurturing those within, or are we also active—not just as individuals, but as a *kehillah*—in the society beyond our community? Each community strikes its own balance between the inward looking and the outward facing.

For those who imagine their community as a place of nurture and retreat, the springboard image is unappealing. For those of us who want our communities to be conduits through which we express our values in tangible ways in the wider society, the metaphor is more alluring but still problematic. I cannot assume that everyone in my community shares my certainties and doubts. I know that there is more than one *aspaklaria* through which the world is perceived. On the other hand, communal life necessarily involves value-laden decisions, even for the most consensus-minded and conflict-averse. Will families not conforming to the heterosexual norm be welcomed, banished, or tolerated? Is the pulpit a place in which the great moral issues of the day can be discussed, or do we insist on platitudinous homilies whatever the situation?

It is impossible to avoid the challenge of a community's political and ideological stance and equally impossible to get the balance right, which is why from time to time there are splits and reconfigurations (these can also occur as a result of non-ideological factors like personality clashes). New communities are imagined, often in contrast to the old ones. Often, they end up looking remarkably similar to the *kehillah* left behind.

The Chorus and Pool

Here are two more images of *kehillah* which may find their place in an emerging social imaginary. A *kehillah* offers its members the opportunity to play a variety of roles. To borrow terminology from a choir (the Hebrew word for which, *makhelah*, is closely related to *kehillah*), life in a community ideally allows all of its members to experience being a soloist, participating in small ensembles, and singing in the chorus.

Modernity has put the emphasis on individuals, and the market economy has discovered that new technologies are perfectly suited to the task of separating us from our discretionary income. As a result, each of us is bombarded with the message that we are special, we are worth it, and we should be all that we can be. This is attractive but it is also exhausting. Framing every encounter as one in which I must attain complete fulfillment sets unrealistic and undesirable expectations. A community is a place in which I am not expected to be a soloist all the time.

A small digression about clergy is called for at this juncture. Particularly in modern Western communities with an emphasis on frontal, performative ritual, clergy members are cast as perpetual soloists, always "on" and usually the center of attention. This is unhealthy, and in the broad sweep of Jewish history, untraditional too. My advice to students training for positions of communal leadership is to spend time in the chorus. To cite another image, community life provides an opportunity to be part of a repertory company of actors, in which I may be playing Hamlet one week and third tree from the right the following week. The star system, according to which I will only participate when I can get top billing, often ends badly. When a clergy member leaves communal life upon retirement, they sometimes express an unwillingness to sing in the chorus if they are not offered the lead.

Kehillah is a chorus in which I am occasionally the soloist. The Kaddish prayer offers a good example of this dynamic.[22] While in many Reform circles it has become customary for the entire community to recite all parts of this prayer, the Kaddish originates as antiphonal liturgy in which one individual leads and the community as a whole (a quorum of ten is required) respond. The formula of response, which has parallels in other liturgies such as the communal call to prayer and the Grace After Meals, is accorded religious significance.[23] Rabbinic Judaism created a network of interactions between members of a close-knit community which necessitate role-switching: we need each other to be present sometimes as chorus, other times as soloist. The Kaddish is in fact a reflection on need. From its earliest roots as a doxology, a declaration of praise and messianic hope at the end of a study session, in the Middle Ages under the influence of Christian society it became associated with death and mourning, ascribing an active role to those who have survived.

The Kaddish thus expresses the idea of "the living helping the dead" by means of releasing them from an unresolved state and allowing them to attain eternal rest.[24] Whether or not the living can help the dead, the congregation can certainly help the mourner fulfill their need: no congregation, no Kaddish. The reality of congregational life expresses a truth likely to outlive the metaphysical assumptions of a bygone era. It is a matter of faith whether reciting the Kaddish releases my loved one from purgatory—that was not the faith of those who first formulated the Kaddish nor is it mine. But it is a matter of fact that showing up for my fellow congregant and being the chorus for their solo meets their need. The Kaddish helps release its reciter from a purgatory of solitude.

The last image of community in this chapter was first suggested to me by my father, Dow Marmur. He described community as a kind of *mitzvah* pool. The concept that there are 613 commandments to be fulfilled by each individual is a stirring call to individual responsibility, but it is also an unattainable ideal. Community acts as a kind of reservoir of *mitzvot*. He was not implying that if my neighbor makes a point of avoiding armed robbery, I am therefore free to engage in it. Each of us is indeed bound by certain fundamental ethical commitments, and membership of a community will not help absolve us if we are derelict in their fulfillment. Beyond these fundamental commitments, however, there is a great ocean of *mitzvot*. Rather than simply eschewing them, on the one hand, or perpetuating the fantasy that each of us can fulfill all of them, on the other, I can conceive of my community as a kind of *mitzvah* offset scheme. Your passions and skills lead you to be active in learning, or volunteering in a soup kitchen, or raising money for a new building, or interreligious dialogue, or Torah reading, or a host of other activities. A community provides a framework in which the various interests and capacities of its members can be pooled.

This idea of a *mitzvah* pool sounds unacceptable from the perspective of Orthodox Judaism, according to which each Jew is bound to each commandment large or small. Nonetheless, parallels to my father's image can be found in works of impeccable Orthodox lineage. Rabbi Avraham Shmuel Binyamin Sofer was one of the leading rabbis of Hungarian Jewry of his day and a strong opponent of liberal religious trends. In his commentary to the Pentateuch he asserted that "it is impossible for any one person to fulfill the entire Torah," adding:

> It can only be achieved together. And this is why Rabbi Akiva taught that "you should love your fellow as yourself is a cardinal rule, for when everyone is united together, then each individual has the possibility of fulfilling the Torah .... Only in *Kehillah* may we live Torah in its entirety.[25]

Similarly, Rabbi David Leifer of Nadvorna averred:

> Fulfilling the Torah can only take place along with one's fellows, because no individual is capable of fulfilling all the Torah. Rather, one person carries out a certain mitzvah, and the next person fulfills another mitzvah, and together the whole Torah is fulfilled. When there is unity within the people Israel, the mitzvot of each individual are counted with the collective.[26]

My father, the Reform rabbi, perhaps conceived of the *mitzvah* pool in a different way from his Orthodox predecessors, but the fundamental notion holds: to live in community is to take on the yoke of religious obligation together so that we are less concerned with judging our neighbors' shortcomings than we are in celebrating their achievements.

Bound together by blood, place, mind, practice, neighborhood, or friendship, we humans cluster together in a variety of human associations. Our lives are lived out within a variety of social structures. Frameworks such as ethnic identity, cultural affinity, shared history, class interest, gender, creed, local pride, interest groups, the state, and others inform every person's existence to some degree. In my understanding, to live a Jewish life means to live in *kehillah*, in community. It is more than an organizing principle or an institutional configuration.

I cannot tell how *kehillah* will be understood in the face of immense cultural change. The State of Israel both challenges and enriches models of Jewish community, as do new technologies and lifestyles. To live without some form of meaningful *kehillah* is, however, a grim fate and a profoundly un-Jewish condition. To be deprived of community is to be left high and dry with neither springboard, chorus, nor pool. Surrogates offering influence, resonance, and solidarity may be offered by, perhaps, private companies or state agencies. I predict that none will replace the *kehillah*. Thousands of years after Moses and hundreds of years after Spinoza, the *kehillah* lives on.

Notes

1. Quoted in Nadler, "Why Spinoza Was Excommunicated."
2. Quoted in ibid.
3. Quoted in Feiner, *Origins of Jewish Secularization*, 167.
4. Quoted in ibid., 168.
5. See Schiff, *Judaism in A Digital Age*.
6. Friedmann, *End of the Jewish People?*, which was published in 1968 and is therefore dated but offers a strong expression of the concern that what is taking shape in Israel is fundamentally different from previous modes of Jewish life.
7. Bounds, *Coming Together*, 2.
8. Ibid.
9. Taylor, *Modern Social Imaginaries*, 23.
10. Tönnies, *Community and Society*.
11. Buber, *I and Thou*, 34.
12. Buber, *Between Man and Man*, 31.
13. Ibid.
14. This connection is discussed in Engel, "From the Neue Gemeinschaft."

15. For Buber's consideration of community from the perspective of cultural creativity and a selection of Buber's writings on community in a range of contexts, see Buber, *On Intersubjectivity*, including the introduction by Eisenstadt (1–22), and Buber, *Paths in Utopia*. In "Secular Religiosity," Mendes-Flohr wrote: "Bereft of sociological sacrality, Buber's Judaism could only speak to select Jews, or perhaps rather to select aspects within the soul and spiritual imagination of many modern Jews. It could not, however, provide the basis of a communal identity. This is indeed ironic for one such as Buber who was so passionately devoted to the renewal of Jewish community" (15).
16. Kaplan, *Greater Judaism*, 456. As might be expected from a pragmatist such as Kaplan, he offered a range of reasons why such a community would better serve the real needs of contemporary Jews.
17. Plaskow, *Standing Again at Sinai*, 120.
18. Fishbane, *Sacred Attunement*, 176.
19. Ibid., 178.
20. Ibid., 178.
21. Ibid., 180.
22. For a collection of essays relating to different aspects of the Kaddish, see Birnbaum and Cohen, *Kaddish*. For a remarkable extended musing on aspects of the Kaddish and an important contribution to American Jewish literature, see Wieseltier, *Kaddish*.
23. See, for example, BT Shabbat 119b, and BT Berakhot 57a.
24. Freehof, "Ceremonial Creativity," 214.
25. Sofer, *Ketav Sofer* (Tel Aviv: Sinai, 1980), 275.
26. Leifer, *Ohev Hesed* (Netanya, 2001), 224a.

Open Access This chapter is licensed under the terms of the Creative Commons Attribution 4.0 International License (http://creativecommons.org/licenses/by/4.0/), which permits use, sharing, adaptation, distribution and reproduction in any medium or format, as long as you give appropriate credit to the original author(s) and the source, provide a link to the Creative Commons license and indicate if changes were made.

The images or other third party material in this chapter are included in the chapter's Creative Commons license, unless indicated otherwise in a credit line to the material. If material is not included in the chapter's Creative Commons license and your intended use is not permitted by statutory regulation or exceeds the permitted use, you will need to obtain permission directly from the copyright holder.

Reshit: The Flowering of Our Redemption?

In 1949, the two chief rabbis of the nascent State of Israel were charged with the task of composing a prayer to give liturgical expression to this new moment in Jewish history. In keeping with the rabbinic injunction to pray for the welfare of the government,[1] they formulated a blessing, with some help from the distinguished author S.Y. Agnon, which is still recited on Shabbat and festivals in congregations identifying with some version of Religious Zionism. The most memorable phrase in this blessing describes the State as *reshit tzemichat geulatenu*, the first flowering of our redemption.[2]

This phrase, while novel at the time, is resonant.[3] It echoes one of the blessings in the thrice-daily Amidah prayer, where the root *tz-m-ch*, implying organic growth, is used in relation to the Davidic dynasty, the original messianic line. It is a phrase redolent with messianic expectation and reminiscent of the thought of Rabbi Abraham Isaac Kook, the pre-State chief rabbi whose thought (or versions thereof) has animated Religious Zionism for decades. These three words express what might be termed cautious messianism:[4] the State is not described as the fulfillment of all messianic expectation, the apogee of a great metaphysical transformation, but rather as a stirring by dawn's early light, an intimation of some redemptive process still in its infancy. A parallel sentiment led Isaac Mayer Wise to choose as a slogan for the Hebrew Union College a phrase from Genesis 44:3, "With the first light of morning," hinting at the process of modernity and enlightenment.[5]

The maverick thinker Yeshayahu Leibowitz condemned the expression *reshit tzemichat geulatenu* as a Sabbatean heresy, referring to the failed seventeenth-century messianic movement. For Leibowitz, a state was nothing more than a political instrumentality, and its elevation to some theological status could only be construed as idolatry. The ultra-Orthodox do not tend to employ the expression. Some in the moderate wing of the Religious Zionist camp preferred to insert a small adaptation of the blessing which prays that the State "may become" the first flowering of our redemption as opposed to the assertion that it already is. In some quarters it has been argued that the expression is not applicable because Israel today is not sufficiently messianic. When the Israeli government voted to withdraw from Gaza in 2005, a polemical suggestion was made in settler circles that the phrase be changed by one letter: from the first flowering (*tzemichat*) of our redemption to the first abandonment or decline (*tzenichat*) of our redemption. For those in this camp, the state is holding back the upsurge of fervor which will eventually enable the delicate flower of messianic promise to meet its full potential. For me, it is that fervor and the kind of blunt ethno-nationalism with which it is often twinned that undermine the vision of Israel as a greenhouse for redemption.

The first hues of dawn in the aftermath of 1948 signified a release from the darkness in which Jews in Europe had been enveloped through the 1930s and 1940s. My father, Dow Marmur, credited his Zionist commitment to a stop on a long train journey from Uzbekistan to Poland in 1946 at the age of eleven. In a relentlessly grim and uncertain reality, he encountered members of a Zionist youth group who met the train with singing and dancing. They were preparing to move to Eretz Yisrael and represented for him a metaphor for hope, a glimmer of redemptive possibility, a hint of tomorrow.[6]

When Israel was all tomorrow for Jews of many ideological stripes, it did represent a first flowering. Now Israel is a concrete reality, more populous and developed than most could have predicted in those early years. So much has changed in the intervening decades. Does the formula from Israel's founding years still hold? For a person espousing values of justice and decency, how might the State of Israel be seen in theological terms? Does the flower of redemption yet bloom?

Getting Across the River

Political systems, like religions and nations, rely on founding myths. Years ago, Israeli embassies around the world used to distribute a pamphlet entitled *Myths and Facts*. It set out all a young Israel activist needed to know in two columns, somewhat like the blessings and curses ranged against each other on two mountains described in the Book of Deuteronomy.[7] On one side of the page were the "myths"—the libelous calumnies perpetrated and disseminated by Israel's enemies; on the other side were the "facts" of the case. The booklet allowed no space for ambivalence or complexity. Rather, the power of facts was prescribed as an antidote to the poison of myth.

A myth, however, is not a lie. It is a story, an *aspaklaria*, a way of marshaling experiences and memories and attitudes. Myths are not the opposite of facts but rather the way in which we prioritize and deploy them in order to serve a communal or personal need, explain a mystery, or bridge a conceptual gulf. It would be nice to believe that people who believe what I believe walk in the clear light of the truth, while those who believe something different are condemned to stumble around in the gloom. But such a banal binary does not capture the complexity of our reality.

There are certainly lies, perpetrated through either ignorance, laziness, or malice, and it is important to call them out wherever possible. Often, however, the more relevant question is which truths are being mustered and which ignored. There is too much truth for us to bear. There are also dizzying facts: institutions built, advances made, injustices perpetuated, lives shattered. At their best, myths sort facts into truth. At their worst, they rely on quasi-facts to keep the truth at bay.

Israel—people, land, state—is both a myth and a fact. When Israel is regarded either as all fact or as all myth, distortion typically ensues.[8] The following tale from the Babylonian Talmud can serve perhaps as a productive myth through which Israel's priorities and horizons may be understood:

> Rabbi Pinhas ben Yair was once traveling in order to ransom captives, and he encountered the River Ginai. He said to the river: "Ginai, split your waters for me so that I can cross through you." The river replied: "You are on your way to fulfill the will of your Maker, and I am on my way to fulfill the will of my Maker. You may or may not accomplish your task: I am certain to accomplish mine." Rabbi Pinhas said to the river: "If you do not split, I decree upon you that water shall never again flow through you!" The river split for him.

> There was a certain man carrying wheat for Passover. Rabbi Pinhas said to the river: "Open up for this person too, for he is engaged in the performance of a mitzvah." The river opened up for him too.
>
> There was also an Arab merchant who had accompanied them on the way. Pinhas ben Yair said to the river: "Open up for this person too, so it should not be said 'Is this how they deal with traveling companions?'" The river opened up for him too.[9]

The sage is on a mission to perform the mitzvah of *pidyon shevuyim*, the redemption of captives held hostage by bandits. He encounters an argumentative river who mounts a persuasive argument: why is your effort to save the life of a kinsperson more pressing than mine, which is to perform the will of my maker and to flow without interruption? Pinhas has no time for philosophical debates with bodies of water and coerces the rivers to open up without further ado. But the story does not end there. There is another person charged with bringing wheat for the preparation of matzah in celebration of the Passover festival. Here, too, there is a time constraint, and there is no time to search for a bridge or construct a raft. A suspension of the natural order is called for, and the rabbi presses the river into service once again. Lastly, regarding an Arab merchant who is also keen to get across the river, Pinhas invokes a traditional Jewish argument to explain why this third pedestrian should also benefit from the miracle: it will not look good for the Jews if it becomes known that we only look after our own. While the narrative falls short of conjuring up an abstract universalism, it does insist that in order for the Jewish story to be fulfilled, we must recognize the other's story.

Redeeming those in distress—and, more broadly, ensuring the physical and economic wellbeing of a people that has experienced the degradations of powerlessness—is indeed one of the core aims of the State of Israel. It is not, however, the only one. The wheat bearer in this tale symbolizes another agenda item: cultural creativity. In the midrashic imagination, uncultivated wheat is likened to the Written Torah, namely, raw material from which something new might be created.[10] Along with security and creativity, the third traveler calls us to justice, empathy, and solidarity.

There is a fourth character in this mythic tale: the river, who challenges the rabbi's innate conviction that his quest justifies the suspension of natural laws and processes. In my allegorical reading, the river questions the arrogance underlying the confidence of political Zionism that it can change the course of history by sheer force of will.

I hear the troubling, insistent voice of the river every time I repeat the slogan that Israel can be both a Jewish and democratic state. This ambition, like much in Israel's Declaration of Independence, offers a vision of what Israel strives to be. Those who formulated it were motivated by the deep conviction that, at this stage in our history, the alternative route eschewing sovereignty and dreaming of our harmonious acceptance in host societies was practically unavailable and even morally unacceptable. I share the hope that Israel can find a way to be both Jewish and democratic, but I hear the relentless voice of River Ginai with its uncomfortable question: what makes you think this outcome is achievable?

The Talmud's coda to the tale undermines the notion that the story recounts three separate miracles. Rather, in order for this Talmudic parallel to the crossing of the Red Sea to be fulfilled, all the protagonists have to get across the river. These are therefore not three discreet crossings but one tripartite miracle:

> Rav Yosef said: how great is this person! Greater than Moses and the six hundred thousand! In that earlier case, the water split only once, here it split three times. But perhaps here it also split only once? Let's say he was as great as Moses and the six hundred thousand.[11]

The Talmudic tale was not told with the modern State of Israel in mind. It cannot help solve the numerous difficult questions to be faced as the daunting challenges of sovereignty only increase. It does not reveal the particular form of political organization that the State of Israel should adopt in the coming decades: will we be Sparta, a lone warrior state repelling all attackers, or Canada, a new binational story forged out of conflict and difference? Like all political regimes, this paradigm is bound to shift with every turn in the river as circumstances and geopolitical realities change.

I believe that while the contours of a future Israel remain unrevealed, whatever develops will need to grapple with the four characters in this foundational story: a Jew striving to secure the wellbeing of their fellow Jews, the bearer of a sack full of cultural possibilities waiting to be explored and developed, another people sharing the land, and a call to keep our dreams within reasonable parameters. So great are the challenges that it is tempting to focus on one or other of these "miracles" to the exclusion of the others. That is why conversations about Israel are often hopelessly mismatched, with each of the interlocutors speaking past each other. But perhaps here too these processes have to unfold simultaneously. A siloed reading cannot do justice to our intertwined reality in which security, culture and morality are all in play.

A Conditional Zionism

Some argue that the time has come to jettison Zionism, an ideology mired in nineteenth-century attitudes devoted to a cause which has already been achieved. Recent years have seen an efflorescence of new terminologies: post-, anti-, and counter-Zionisms abound, some of which distinguish between Zionism and Israel.[12] Within mainstream Israel, however, the word Zionism is increasingly used to describe every good and noble sentiment.

Little is to be gained by becoming embroiled in confusions of terminology. I am a Zionist in the sense that I am moved by the emphasis on agency, responsibility, and creativity that it promises. Other strategies of Jewish response to modernity, such as the attempt to bolster a robust Jewish life in the Diaspora, are honorable and laudable, and I wish them only success. My severe doubts about the health of the Zionist project are matched by doubts that these alternatives can offer sufficiently compelling frameworks to bolster a Judaism strong enough to prevail, survive, and flourish.

My love for the land, the language, and peoples of Israel is immense. My gratitude to those who act heroically in defense of the three linked miracles—security, creativity, and justice—is unreserved. My Zionism is, nonetheless, conditional. It requires every part of the Talmudic allegory to be fulfilled or at least attempted: when one or other component is ignored, no good outcome can be expected. There are leading political figures and opinion makers in Israel who retell the story such that only two figures cross the river. They promote a picture of Israel armed to the hilt, in which Palestinians have either been cowed into submissiveness or even herded onto trucks and sent away. Some of them regard the trappings of democracy and the rule of law as unwanted debris left over from the assimilatory West to be jettisoned along with all doubt and nuance.

This picture of Israel's future is, tragically, growing in popularity. One reason for this is the progressive camp's inability to offer a competing vision which meets the bar of credulity. A new Middle East in which all coexist in dignity and security is beyond reason and hope for most Israelis as these words are written. The task at hand is to find a workable version of this inclusive mythic framework, one encompassing security, creativity, a commitment to decency, dignity and justice, and an acknowledgment of the bounds of the possible. My Zionism is proudly conditional insofar as it calls for all these conditions to be addressed.

The German expression *Alt-neu* is usually understood as "old-new": a famous synagogue in Prague was named the Altneuschul in the sixteenth century; Herzl used it to describe the "Old New Land" in his eponymous 1902 novel. One explanation of the name of the synagogue suggested that it was in fact a corruption of the Hebrew expression *al tnai*, meaning conditional, based on a Talmudic teaching that all synagogues outside the Land of Israel have only a provisional presence.[13] Accordingly, Herzl's imagined land was both old and new—a modern expression of an ancient longing—and also subject to conditions. However, it is not only Diaspora institutions which were afforded a conditional status in our tradition. An ancient midrash applying traditional rabbinic argumentation based on the interpretation of biblical verses declares startlingly that the Land of Israel, the Temple, and the Kingdom of the House of David were all given *al tnai*, conditionally.[14]

Zionism, too, is *al tnai*, conditional in nature, and it is not easy to fulfill its various conditions. Take, for example, the challenge of balancing security considerations with ethical principles—a dilemma from which the Jews as a people have been largely spared for two millennia. Princeton's Jeffrey Stout made a theoretical argument that reads painfully against the backdrop of Israeli realities:

> I, for one, aspire to belong to a society that would treat the commission of horrible acts like the intentional bombing of civilian populations as literally inexcusable, even in situations where such a tactic is thought on plausible evidence to be necessary in fending off terrorist destruction. I fear that anything less than an absolutely overriding prohibition of such acts will tempt our leaders to commit moral horrors in situations that only seem, at the time, to be emergencies .... I am also prepared to bite the bullet in the event of an actual emergency. A society resolutely committed to avoiding the infliction of moral horrors would rather go down in flames, while treating this commitment as a matter of integrity, than survive by instructing its leaders in advance to perform such acts on its behalf if an emergency arises.[15]

Stout claims that he would rather have his society disintegrate than license morally repugnant acts committed in the name of national security.

Faced with emergencies and perceived existential threats, concerned lest our squeamishness be interpreted as weakness by our neighbors, Israelis do not adopt Stout's position. However, when exceptional circumstances are allowed to become the norm and extreme acts are given the imprimatur of Jewish tradition, I believe that Israel's future comes under threat.

I marvel at the achievements of Israel in a few short decades, but this sense of wonder is accompanied by grave and abiding concerns. I share the alarm expressed by Menachem Fisch in light of "the Pandora's box of traditional Jewish eschatological yearning for Zion that it [political Zionism] inadvertently opened."[16] Writing from within Israeli society and with a pain and concern which match the incisiveness of his analysis, Fisch states:

> Political Zionism's vision of establishing a Western democracy committed to nation-building and statecraft motivated by values of equality and fairness has given way to a self-conception of Israel as a well-armed and fortified ghetto, whose sole aim is to protect its Jewish population from a dangerous and inherently anti-Semitic world.[17]

Immanuel Jakobovits underlined the importance of emphasizing the conditional nature of Zionism:

> Each of the three assumptions, which I considered mistaken – the belief in the establishment of Israel as *definitely* the beginning of the Redemption, the belief in miracles as Israeli realism, and the disbelief in the conditional character of our title to the Land – could lead to unwarranted and reckless decision, based on the premise that the events we witnessed were irreversible.[18]

Articulating views such as these has become anathematized and demonized, as if by giving them voice one is lending succor to Israel's enemies. However, circling the wagons and thinking wholesome patriotic thoughts is not, to my mind, an effective strategy. I see an honest acknowledgment of our challenges as a more compelling Zionist response in keeping with our tradition of vigorous and passionate debate. If we are to hang on to Israel, described some eighteen centuries ago as being a conditional gift, we must foster a more robust culture of self-criticism. This conditional Zionism may prove to be a condition of our survival.

Two Reform Rabbis

Two Reform rabbis of earlier generations accompany me as I think about Israel: one nestled on my left shoulder, the other stridently positioned on my right.

From his arrival in Palestine in 1922, Judah Leib Magnes, president and chancellor of the Hebrew University, was involved in political activity deemed beyond the pale by most in the mainstream Zionist camp. He argued that Jewish immigration, settlement on the land, and the promotion of Hebrew life and culture were more important than the achievement of statehood. He was convinced that these aims could be achieved without incurring Palestinian antagonism. In a 1929 letter to Chaim Weizmann, he set out in stark terms the moral and political boundaries of the question to be determined in the coming decades:

> Do we want to conquer Palestine now as Joshua did in his day – with fire and sword? Or do we want to take cognizance of Jewish religious development since Joshua – our Prophets, Psalmists and Rabbis, and repeat the words: "Not by might, and not by violence, but by my Spirit, saith the Lord." The question is: can any country be entered, colonized and built up pacifistically, and can we Jews do that in the Holy Land? If we can not (and I for one do not say that we can rise to these heights) I for my part have lost half my interest in the enterprise. If we cannot even attempt this, I should much rather see this eternal people without such a "National Home", with the wanderer's staff in hand and forming new ghettos among peoples of the world.[19]

Here and elsewhere Magnes is saying: if the price of statehood is endless conflict, I am not sure I want any part of it. He lived long enough to express dismay at some of the events surrounding the 1948 War, but we have no way of telling how he would have responded to the successes, failures, compromises, and challenges of the State—no longer the subject of theoretical musing but an undeniable fact.[20] He might have taken Stout's position and argued that he no longer has any truck with the experiment in Jewish sovereignty.

In the course of the ensuing decades, Magnes' position was rejected and often reviled. He claimed that fidelity to the core principles of Judaism as he understood them set limits on the means to be employed in pursuit of the goal of political independence. While many Reform thinkers of his age saw Zionism as a diversion from or even a perversion of the loftiest

Jewish values, Magnes saw the prospect of Jewish society cultivated on the land as fulfillment of those values and a new chapter in the development of Jewish values in the world. In order for this result to be achieved, the urge for conquest would have to be replaced by the capacity for compromise; indeed, he yearned for a country built up not by might or power but by spirit.

Graced with hindsight, we can say that Magnes was tragically credulous, overestimating progress and reason while underestimating the disasters set to befall the Jews within only a few short years. Arguing that diasporic wandering was preferable to the price to be paid for political sovereignty seems incongruous: a nineteenth-century sensibility of optimism unable to adapt to the cruel realities of the twentieth century. With the activities of Magnes, Martin Buber, and others in mind, Emil Fackenheim, the Reform rabbi (better known as an eminent Jewish philosopher) perched on my right shoulder, was later to comment that "whereas in some circumstances powerlessness may indeed be a moral virtue, in others it is indulgence in a moral luxury."[21] German-born Fackenheim described the events leading to the establishment of the State as the "Jewish Return into History." He had no time for Magnes' argument regarding moral decline and statehood. Indeed, such a position seemed petulant in the face of the Shoah.

In a sense, Magnes and Fackenheim, two Reform rabbis from different backgrounds and generations, embody two sides of the perennial question: is it better to perpetrate injustice upon another or to have injustice perpetrated against oneself? Fackenheim believed that the obscenity of Jewish powerlessness had made it abundantly clear that the risks of power were to be preferred to the ignominy of destruction. Making a virtue of weakness was not only a foolish policy but also a kind of moral cowardice.

In recent decades, Fackenheim's caution has been much closer to the Israeli zeitgeist than Magnes' idealism. I predict that in the difficult decades to come, some of the Zionist roads not taken[22] may be re-explored in search of ways by which all three individuals from the Talmudic tale can cross the river in the context of one concerted episode. While Magnes has been largely forgotten,[23] discourse about the shape of Israel and Palestine in the future may, in time, reconsider his legacy.

This may sound little more than wishful thinking since every war and every atrocity render us less keen to question our founding myths and less receptive to Palestinian voices. Nevertheless, I am convinced that, sooner or later, both Jews and Arabs will come to recognize that we are fated to cross this river together or not at all. In the process, Judaism will change, perhaps to an uncomfortable degree. In a playful and compelling retelling of the story of the spies from the Book of Numbers mentioned in the introduction to this book, Emmanuel Levinas suggests that one reason why ten of the twelve spies gave a negative report of the prospects for entering the Land is that the gift of prophecy was bestowed upon them and they saw, with dismay, the generation of Sabras, native Israeli Jews, that would one day spring up in the land with whom they would have nothing in common.[24] Tomorrow's Israeli Judaism will look different, but this is the kind of radical transformation which has long been part of Jewish tradition. I predict that when this phase of Israel's history transitions to a new one, the vision of Magnes and his like may find its way back into the discourse.

Geulatenu

The State of Israel faces dramatic challenges, and there is no telling what may yet befall it. Palestinians also have some fateful decisions ahead of them. The redemption that Israel symbolizes is not a banal happy-ending to history. In the Hebrew Bible the root *g-a-l*, from which *geulah*, redemption, is derived, relates not only to the act of release but also to the prosecution of justice. More surprisingly, the root relates also to staining and defilement. There is mess in messianism and the ever-present fear that low instincts will be indulged in the name of high ideals.[25] Israel's occupation of the West Bank represents for some the guarantee of its redemptive potential. In my eyes, if no horizon of possibility is presented for compromise, if no possibility of a future characterized by decency, dignity, and security is held out to the Palestinian people, the occupation is a desecration. To "redeem" the entire land promises not the early dawn of redemption but a long night of suffering.

Perhaps the most disturbing question concerning Israel is whether the State in its current form must be rejected *on Jewish grounds*. I believe that, on Jewish grounds, the struggle for the soul of Israel must continue. Each question epitomized by each of the travelers crossing the River Ginai is exhausting in its scope. How do we guarantee security, inspire a diverse and plural outpouring of Jewish creativity, and foster a consciousness of shared society and common humanity with the Palestinians?

Religion has not, on the whole, played a salutary role in the quest to cross the river with security, creativity, justice, and proportion. The

Pandora's Box of romantic or messianic fervor has had a disproportionate influence on the debate. Somewhere, on the other side of a long night is a religious sensibility allowing for a new way of imagining the future for Jews and Palestinians. It is largely dormant, nestled under the soil of a beautiful and bloodstained land. Listen closely and you may be able to hear its first stirring.

Notes

1. Mishnah Avot 3:2.
2. Tabory, "Piety of Politics," 233–238, surveys both the differing opinions concerning the provenance of the expression (whether it originated with Rabbis Herzog and Uziel or with Agnon) and its messianic overtones. See also: Golinkin, "Prayers for the Government"; Marx, "Prayer for the State"; and Rappel, *Hatefillah*. It is possible that Rabbi Frank, Ashkenazi chief rabbi of Jerusalem, coined the expression, although the hunt for its originator matters less in this context than the debate about its meaning.
3. For a medieval foreshadowing, see Rashi to Psalm 143:8, where morning is interpreted as the flowering of redemption.
4. See Penslar, *Zionism*, 59.
5. For a fifteenth-century example of citing the Genesis verse in the context of redemption, see Abraham Saba, *Eshkol Hakofer* to Ruth (Bartfeld, 1907), 3a.
6. See Marmur, *Six Lives*, 22.
7. Deuteronomy 11:29.
8. In my reading, Heschel's *Israel*, penned in the immediate aftermath of the 1967 War as a theological riposte to ambivalence about Israel's actions in some Christian circles, operates almost exclusively on the level of myth. The question of Heschel's approach to Israel is an interesting one. After the publication of *Sabbath* in 1951 Heschel was criticized by Trude Weiss-Rosmarin for being so lax in his presentation of the dimension of space only a few years after a Jewish state had been declared in the Jews' ancient land. He was sufficiently stung by this barb to issue a clarification of his position. Notwithstanding this appendix to his work, Heschel was keen to redress what he considered an imbalance which had skewed in favor of the dimension of space and to refocus the debate around time and eternity. Heschel the social critic was, however, also aware of problems to be addressed. On a visit to Israel in 1958, for example, he commented that while soldiers were being encouraged by army rabbis to ensure that their

food was kosher, they had no such guidance from religious leaders about whether their military actions were kosher. This comment, lacking in the 1967 work, shows a blending of the mythical and the factual. See Heschel, *Insecurity of Freedom*, 216.
9. BT Hullin 7a.
10. See Seder Eliyahu Zuta, 2.
11. BT Hullin 7a.
12. A number of important recent works have challenged the political Zionist narrative, adopting a range of positions. For most in the conventional Zionist or pro-Israel camp, these works are anathema. In my view, they need to be read and engaged with by anyone who cares deeply about the prospects for Israel's future. In alphabetical order, I would mention in this context: Beinart, *Crisis of Zionism*; Boyarin, *No-State Solution*; Butler, *Parting Ways*; Magid, *Necessity of Exile*; and Penslar, *Zionism*. Palestinian narratives must also be read, among them Khalidi, *Hundred Years' War*.
13. BT Megillah 28b.
14. Mekhilta de Rabbi Ishmael, Jethro 2. Three things were given conditionally: Eretz Yisrael, the Temple, and the Kingdom of the House of David, but the Torah scroll and the covenant of Aaron were given unconditionally. In a parallel text, the Midrash of Three and Four (*Batei Midrashot* 2, 22), the proximity of Israel to God is also listed as an unconditional feature.
15. Stout, *Democracy and Tradition*, 200.
16. Fisch, "Tragic Paradox," 29.
17. Ibid., 33.
18. Jakobovits, *If Only My People*, 142. See also Jachter, "The Great Reishit."
19. Magnes, *Dissenter in Zion*, 277.
20. Martin Buber, with whom Magnes cooperated in these political efforts, did live to see the State come into existence. He declared in 1958 that he had come to accept the State of Israel in the form in which it had come into being. See Buber, *Israel and the World*, 257.
21. Fackenheim, *Political Philosophy*, 8. See also Wisse, *Jews and Power*.
22. See Pianko, *Zionism and the Roads*, where some alternatives to political Zionism, today largely forgotten, are presented and analyzed.
23. For some explorations of Magnes' life and thought, see Barak-Gorodetzky, *Judah Magnes* and Kotzin, *Judah L. Magnes*.
24. See Levinas, *Nine Talmudic Readings*, 61. For a reading of this Talmudic dialogue and an examination of Levinas's changing views on Israel, see Eisenstadt, "Rhetorical Subterfuge."
25. See, for example, Menahem ben Saruq, *Machberet Menachem* (London, 1854), 50a.

Open Access This chapter is licensed under the terms of the Creative Commons Attribution 4.0 International License (http://creativecommons.org/licenses/by/4.0/), which permits use, sharing, adaptation, distribution and reproduction in any medium or format, as long as you give appropriate credit to the original author(s) and the source, provide a link to the Creative Commons license and indicate if changes were made.

The images or other third party material in this chapter are included in the chapter's Creative Commons license, unless indicated otherwise in a credit line to the material. If material is not included in the chapter's Creative Commons license and your intended use is not permitted by statutory regulation or exceeds the permitted use, you will need to obtain permission directly from the copyright holder.

Sha'at Hamefazrim: Judaism Thick and Thin

> The division of bodies into gaseous, liquid, and solid, and the distinction established for the same substance between the three states, retain a great importance for the applications and usages of daily life, but have long since lost their absolute value from the scientific point of view.[1]

If these words were true when they were published in the first decade of the twentieth century, they are all the more valid today. Other states of matter have since been identified, and the distinctions between the three original states reconsidered. However, the old tripartite distinction continues to be significant for applications and usages of Jewish life.

Throughout history, Jews have been attracted to organizing principles by which a complex totality can be summarized. The world, we are taught, stands on Torah, worship and acts of loving-kindness,[2] and, later in the same chapter of the Mishnah, on justice, truth, and peace.[3] In his Hebrew translation of Harald Othmar Lenz's 1861 work on science, S.Y. Abramovitz, known as Mendele Mocher Seforim, adapted the Mishnaic teaching and asserted that the tripod upon which the world stands are the categories of animal, vegetable, and mineral.

Medieval Judaism was influenced by Aristotle's theory of matter as well as by other theories, such as the idea of the *pneuma*, an all-encompassing air at the foundation of Stoic physics.[4] *Sefer Yetzirah*, an immensely important work of the Jewish esoteric tradition, connected these Greek understandings of the physical elements with its own distinctive theory of language. It also introduced the triad of *olam*, *shanah*, and *nefesh*, representing the cosmos, time, and the soul respectively.[5]

Employing the classic division into three states of matter may prove helpful in thinking about the various ways in which Jews affiliate, articulate, and educate. In this chapter we will consider this distinction through the *aspaklaria* of a Talmudic distinction between a time of density and a time of dissemination, *sha'at hamefazrim*.

Denominations for and Against

If Judaism is the language by which I speak as a human, Reform is the dialect and the accent in which I speak Jewish. Like any accent, Reform has changed over time, and there is significant variation within the dialect: indeed, not every Reform Jew speaks Judaism in the same way, as archrationalists rub shoulders with New Age spiritual seekers and ironic postmodernists. Having grown up in Britain and lived for some four decades in Israel, I speak a version of the dialect which is hard for some of my fellow Reform Jews to follow. Some are sure it is not Reform at all. In view of all this and in light of the prevalent trend away from denominationalism, why not drop the accent?

Contemporary Jews in the West have often employed denominational or ideological distinctions to explain differences of belief and practice. We may assume that a student in the Mir Yeshiva in the Lithuanian ultra-Orthodox tradition entertains a different belief regarding an all-powerful God guiding destiny and exercising judgment than does their avowedly secular counterpart (although our beliefs do not always match our uniforms). A Reconstructionist will tend to reject both a notion of the Jews as a Chosen People espoused in Orthodox circles and the concept of the Jewish Mission which had currency among Classical Reform Jews. A Bundist[6] would likely feel differently about the prospect of being seen in public eating a cheeseburger than would a Gerer Hasid.

Denominational categories provide some with a satisfying way of answering the question: what kind of Jew are you? However, these categories have their limitations. Many reject them altogether, noting that Jewish expression in modern times is more complex and paradoxical than any typology can contain. There are whole sections of the Jewish community which have been largely ignored by most of the labels. In recent years in Israel there has been an important discussion concerning Jews from non-European backgrounds who have been subject to this kind of exclusion.

Yaakov Yadgar pointed out that when the categories of affiliation do not know what to do with the reality of, for example, a modern Israeli Jew loyal to their Moroccan family's traditions, they suggest that such an identity is somehow inauthentic. Yadgar argues that the problem lies not with the person in question but with the inadequacy of the conceptual model.[7]

David Ellenson, an expert in denominational distinctions within Judaism from the nineteenth century in Europe through to contemporary North America, stated that while there are substantive differences between the various movements,

> the charge that confronts all of them is how to make Judaism relevant, compelling, joyous, meaningful, welcoming, comforting and challenging to American Jews who have infinite options open before them, yet still ask that the human needs of meaning and community be fulfilled.[8]

Ellenson's insight applies beyond continental boundaries. Movements and ideologies, with all their differences, share similar challenges.

The adjective Reform has not outlived its relevance for me, and it tells you something about me. Something, but not everything. It is the house I grew up in and the instrument with which I want to continue building. Reports of the demise of denominations are premature, but declarations of their significance are exaggerated. Hence the search for additional *aspaklariot*—prisms through which the currency and intensity of Jewish commitments can be understood.

Solid, Liquid, Gas

"Solid" iterations of Jewish life are easy to identify. Halakhah is replete with tangible expressions of a thick Jewish identity. The words that come out of my mouth and the food that goes into it, the straps I place on my arm and the sukkah I build in the fall—all these and much more articulate a solid Jewish mode of being. Zionism, too, even in its non-religious manifestations, has offered a specific and solid remedy to the ills of contemporary Jewish existence. Real estate is more real than abstract notions of home, and in order to create the conditions in which the Jewish people can survive and thrive, it is necessary to reemphasize the physical element after centuries of rarefied abstractions. Rabbi Leon Ashkenazi is said to have quipped that Herzl was right when he said: if you will it, it is not an *aggadah*, a dream or a tale. It is not an *aggadah*, he said, to be engaged in the building up of Israel; it is Halakhah—it involves countless detailed acts, both concrete and tangible.⁹

All intense commitments, be they Buddhist or Baptist, might be described as "solid" or "heavy." There is, perhaps, something about Judaism that makes it particularly suited to the image of solidity. Our God might be intangible, but the life of the Jew is punctuated with tasks to be performed and stuff to be obtained. The candles and the wine, the lulav to be waved and the sukkah to be erected on Sukkot, the frenzy of cleaning and eating around Pesach. Will Herberg expressed this notion in an important 1951 work:

> Hebraic religion strikes an unmistakably *this*-worldly note: this world, the world in which we pass our lives, the world in which history is enacted, the world of time and change and confusion, is the world in which the divine Will is operative and in which, however strange it may seem, man encounters God. Depreciation of this world in favor of some timeless world of pure being or essence is utterly out of line with the realistic temper of Hebraism.[10]

Liberal streams of Judaism have tended to replace one kind of solidity—halakhic conformity—with surrogates; social action, battling poverty and prejudice, became a quasi-Halakhah for some opposed to Halakhah. But *tikkun olam*, repairing the world, has its own demands. Those unconvinced that one ought to wake up early in the morning to fulfill God's commandments in ritual conformity and legal precision were nonetheless prepared to do so to participate in a protest or to staff a soup kitchen.

Our lives inevitably have a solid dimension, but collectively we are living in what the great sociologist Zygmunt Bauman described as liquid times. Bauman found this image to be particularly helpful in explaining the changes of modern times. Prophets of modernity, like Karl Marx, were interested in dissolving the solid doctrines of older times in order to replace them with new certainties, new solidities. Now, in late modernity, the liquidizing tendency is yet more profound:

> "Dissolving everything that is solid" has been the innate and defining characteristic of the modern form of life from the outset; but today, unlike yesterday, the dissolved forms are not to be replaced … by other solid forms – deemed "improved" in the sense of being even more solid and "permanent" than those that came before them, and so even more resistant to melting.[11]

Modernity in its various manifestations engaged in loosening up some of the certainties: namely, the metaphysical structures upon which the medieval world had been based. In our century, fluidity is everywhere. National identity, gender, the relationship between time and space, sexual orientation, and other dimensions of existence are understood in liquid terms. Many modern (and post-modern) Jews have tended toward Judaism in its liquid form, emphasizing change and adaptability. Bauman and other theoreticians of modernity noted that in recent decades rapid technological and cultural changes have impacted the traditional ways in which space and time were experienced.

What I want to call gaseous or ephemeral Jewish expression has little use for "solid" expressions of Jewish community and continuity and suspects that the liquid camp presents nothing more interesting than a watered-down version of the old absolute certainties. Before discussing an example of this concept of Judaism as gas, I want to connect this solid–liquid–gas model to a rabbinic adage.

A Talmudic teaching attributed to Hillel the Elder reads: "At the time of gathering, disseminate. At the time of dissemination, gather."[12] To judge from the context, this maxim refers to Torah and suggests that one should run counter to the prevalent trend. When Torah learning is being stored in houses of study by an intellectual elite, that is the time to bring Torah to the masses. And when opportunities for study are widely available, that is the time to engage in a more rarefied kind of Torah study which will have little impact on the general public.[13]

I read this teaching in light of the distinction between states of matter. When Judaism is being presented as "too too solid,"[14] it is time to emphasize its more fluid aspects. And at a time of dissemination, *sha'at hamefazrim*, when it seems as though the trace of Jewish substance may disappear on the wind, it needs to be solidified.

What does it mean for Judaism to be conceived of as an ephemeral whiff?

Michael Chabon and the Ghetto of Two

In May 2018, the author Michael Chabon was invited to give an address at a graduation ceremony held by the Hebrew Union College's Los Angeles campus. While wishing success to the graduates, Chabon took the opportunity to attack one of the fundamental priorities of the Jewish community since the days of Ezra and Nehemiah: endogamy. In parallel, he excoriated Israeli government policies as indefensible and immoral. The occupation and intermarriage were intriguingly intertwined in his speech, which unsurprisingly garnered controversy.

Chabon did not pull his punches. "An endogamous marriage is a ghetto of two," he asserted.[15] It is an enclave, comparable to that perpetuated by the Jewish extremists in Hebron. Judaism is designed to make every adherent a "boundary maven," charged with "wall-building and boundary-patrolling." The only tribe into which Chabon wants his children to marry is "the tribe that prizes learning, inquiry, skepticism, openness to new ideas ... that enshrines equality before the law, and freedom of conscience, and human rights ... that sees nations and antiquated canards and ethnicity as a construct prone ... to endless reconfiguration." It may happen that you marry a Jew, but this should be only a by-product or coincidence.

Chabon ended his address with an appeal to the Jewish leaders of tomorrow to tap into the proven capacity of Judaism to reinvent itself and to agitate against injustices perpetrated in the names of the Jewish people:

> This is my charge to you, class of 2018, Jewish leaders of the future: Knock down the walls. Abolish the checkpoints. Find room in the Jewish community for all those who want to share in our traditions ... Seize every opportunity to strengthen and enrich our cultural genome by embracing the inevitable variation and change that result from increased diversity.

The author said two contradictory things to the graduating class: first, a distinct, thick, stolid Jewish existence is unethical and therefore undesirable; second, go out and help craft a Jewish existence worthy of prevailing and flourishing into the future. He told our students to tear down all the walls that today confine and define Jewish life and to make that tearing down of walls the definition of a new Judaism. If you insist on this Jewish thing, I heard him say, bound it with a lack of boundaries. Remove not only the physical barriers and checkpoints but the conceptual ones too. Make of it a gas. You may store it, but the higher aim is to release it.

Chabon's Judaism has no need for weight or extension. Its preferred fate is to be dissipated into the greater atmosphere, the hybrid bricolage, the pastiche and creole of human existence. He doubts that Judaism will indeed disappear or dissipate in this way, but he makes a case, both aesthetic and moral, for privileging this approach to Jewish existence. He stated that the 1994 massacre of Muslim worshippers in Hebron by Baruch Goldstein was the turning point for him. It was then or around then that he realized that a friendly liberal version of Judaism, which I refer to here as liquid in nature, is too unstable to last. Boundaries of any kind will eventually lead, he implies, to barricades of the worst kind. Liquid Judaism will eventually congeal.

There is a certain grandeur to Chabon's way of thinking about Judaism. Often articulated in response to a Jewish establishment which seems preoccupied with the dictates of physical continuity and communal strength, this voice—an echo of the prophetic voice—calls for a constant emphasis on the ethical essence of the Jewish project.

A Judaism of pure spirit, however, is no Judaism. It rests on a distinction which is foreign to Judaism's own categories of thought as they have developed in all their variety over millennia. It is naïve to believe that any concern for security is a self-serving lie, and it is odd to suggest that two members of a group who choose to perpetuate their identity by creating a household together are guilty of creating a ghetto. The rage with which Chabon's comments were met in some circles is unwarranted, but the criticism that his analysis lacks a grounding in the rich complexity of Jewish culture has merit. The risk of a gaseous Judaism is that while striving to be abstract and universal, it may be insubstantial. This is the weakness of a Jewish physics comprising only one fundamental substance. If ephemeral Judaism risks being vapid, the liquid variety is plagued by the possibility that it will become tepid and the solid version by the dangers of extremism—it may become frigid or torrid or both.

Chabon's speech is discussed in an important 2023 work in Hebrew by Avinoam Rosenak.[16] Rosenak considers the phenomenon of intermarriage from the perspectives of philosophy, theology, and educational thought. His pessimistic thesis, developed over 850 pages of close argumentation, is that attempts to fuse Western and Jewish thought have proven incapable of providing a convincing rationale to persuade westernizing Jews to marry a fellow Jew and to perpetuate the Jewish collective. His analysis includes the liberal wing of Orthodoxy, and his critique is not leveled at this or that thinker but at the liberal project itself.

It is to be sure a project under significant pressure, but in my reading its foundational insights have not lost their validity. In a refutation of Chabon in the *Jewish Review of Books*, Elli Fischer cites a Mishnah from Tractate Baba Batra in which the necessity of maintaining distinctions is upheld: farmers must keep bees away from mustard plants. Fischer omits to mention that the same Mishnah cites a minority opinion which actually allows this very same mixture.[17] There is more fluidity in the tradition than some are prepared to admit.

The Dangers of a One-State Solution

I disagree with at least half of what Michael Chabon said to the graduating class of 2018, but I am grateful for him and for others whose views I do not share. I want to live in a world safe for difference and strongly held opinions, preferably expressed with love and care. Chabon's assertion that there is something reprehensible or unjustifiable about a Jew marrying another Jew is best read as a provocation and a *cri de coeur*. As a call to Jews to participate actively in their own dismemberment or their transformation from a thing of substance to a fleeting shadow, I reject it. The thought that in order to be fully human I must renege on my identity as a Jew is insulting and unconvincing. I do not, however, reject or reprove Michael Chabon. I want him to be part of this ecosystem comprising gaseous, liquid, and solid components.

There have always been Jews who have wanted to stop being Jews, and in the millennia of our history there has never been an easier time in which this ambition can be filled. For the rest of us, the question is how to maintain the optimum mixture of states of matter. If Chabon is taking his leave of any vestige of Jewish connection, we should wish him well and bid him farewell. If, as I suspect, he is actually imploring us, the fashioners of so many reinventions, to recast the internal balance of our Jewish raw materials so that being Jewish can be an adventure for him and others like him, we should invite him to join us in thinking through what Judaism needs to look like in this age of extremes.

The more fundamentalist a worldview, the more "solid" it tends to be. Solidity has clear advantages: it is educable and tends to engender high levels of loyalty. Acts of heroism and self-sacrifice are often motivated by solid commitments. The risks that go along with it are no less apparent. When slogans and certainties take the place of complexity and nuance, the results can be dire.

Those (like me) who emphasize the dynamic liquidity of Judaism run the risk that their contributions to the Jewish conversation will be insufficiently passionate and rigorous to make much of an impact. Fleeting and abstracted calls for the furtherance of disembodied Jewish values are likely to dissipate in the atmosphere. It is hard to educate for a faint soupçon of Jewish values. In order to be transmitted, those values have to be embodied; they need to bulk up. Chabon suggests that he has given up on the possibility or desirability of a liberal Judaism. Unlike him, I have little doubt about its desirability. Its feasibility, however, is in the balance, doubted by detractors and sometimes by adherents too.

Calls to privilege one or other of the fundamental states are naïve and unhelpful. They are also frightening. Some voices in Israel and around the Jewish world are becoming increasingly intransigent, increasingly extreme and increasingly dismissive of any approach less "solid" than their own. Anyone who offers an alternative view, anyone more liquid, anyone who solves the equation using moral boundaries and physical barriers differently than the current party line, anyone speaking out against ignorance or intransigence is branded a self-hater, a denier, a traitor. Rather than looking for a balance between fundamental states, more and more seem to be opting—in a sense quite different from the usual parlance—for a one-state solution. Within the corridors of established Jewish life, one is expected to be a solid citizen. In other corridors, meanwhile, questioning every orthodoxy has become a new orthodoxy.

Conservative critics of Jewish progressives tend to adopt one or both of the following strategies, each of which is unnerving to an alert liberal. The first predicts that these wishy-washy liquid and gaseous Jews will soon dissolve into the ether. Demographers and demagogues predict our imminent shrinkage and eventual oblivion. Chabon, they argue, will soon get his way for everyone except the solidly committed, who will remain immune to the silent but deadly gas of self-diffusion.

The second critique suggests that the liquid and gaseous reaches of the Jewish world are in fact caught in the grip of an orthodoxy no less solid and intractable than the ideologies they condemn. The liberal certainties—that self-fulfillment is an ultimate virtue and that thick boundaries of faith and identity should be attenuated or removed—amount to their own dense solidity and leave no room for difference and challenge.

I come to the solid, the liquid, and the yet more intangible dimensions of Jewish life with love for and concern about all of them. It behooves us to strive for a balance between our strong beliefs and convictions, on the one hand, and our openness to accept difference, on the other. I am a modern Jew, and I refuse to give up on being Jewish because I wish to be modern. I want to keep looking for a successful combination of these fundamental states because I believe that walking away from this coming chapter of Jewish history would impoverish me and impoverish Judaism too. I continue to look to my Jewish identity as a key to my identity as a person in the world. I came to Israel forty years ago because I was drawn to the prospect of adding to the spirit of Judaism by drawing a liquid Torah out of the solid ground of a nascent society. I am still in search of a multi-state model.

Here are three states of matter: the solid and tangible; the liquid and changeable; and the gaseous and ephemeral. They resonate with the old formula of *olam-shanah-nefesh*, highlighting "thinginess," impermanence, and disembodied spirit, respectively. Given the fact that contemporary physics has moved beyond the three-state theory, future metaphors developed by scientifically minded individuals may ponder what plasma Judaism might look like or, for that matter, a Bose-Einstein condensate Judaism.

There is a great deal to ponder with the three classic states alone. Take, for example, the feminist critique of images and notions relating to fluidity and the way they have been associated with the feminine.[18] Elizabeth Stephens, has interrogated the manner in which "the 'fixed' is invariably aligned with the conservative and the normative, while the 'fluid' is associated with the positive, progressive, and resistant."[19] Or, from another perspective, consider the elaborate sacrificial system described in the Hebrew Bible and in later literature, according to which the solid is transformed by fire into a pleasing odor to God, a sacred aroma.

A century before Michael Chabon, Hayim Nachman Bialik hoped that the time would come when conditions would allow the word of the Jews to go out into the world. In a 1922 speech entitled "On Duality in Israel," Bialik identified two great leitmotifs that have run through Jewish culture from its inception: "the tendency to abstraction and expansion and the urge for enclosure and uniqueness," namely, the universalist and the particular, respectively.

Bialik regarded the story of the Jews as a particular iteration of a universal truth, and this innate tension as an instance of

> the ways of humanity from the concrete to the abstract. This is the meaning of progress ... and the Israelite nation walked and continues to walk on two paths. When we were connected to our land, we based our lives on the concrete ... during the period of exile the second fundamental quality grew stronger, the quality of abstraction.

Writing in Germany in the 1920s, the poet laureate of the Hebrew national revival was in search of a workable balance between the concrete and the abstract. His speech ends with words which still have the capacity to stir, looking forward to *sha'at hamefazrim*, the time of dissemination: "And who knows? Perhaps after hundreds of years we will be emboldened to make another exodus which will lead to the spreading of our spirit over the world, and to the unending quest for eternity?"[20]

Notes

1. Poincaré, *The New Physics*, 105.
2. Avot 1:2.
3. Avot 1:18.
4. Gad Freudenthal's many books and articles have explained aspects of this deep influence: for an example of the Aristotelian theory on Maimonides, see, "Maimonides' Philosophy of Science" and for the impact of Stoic physics on medieval Jewish thought, see "Stoic Physics." For a general overview of the impact of theories of matter on Jewish thought, see Langermann, *Jews and the Sciences*.
5. See Sefer Yetzirah 6:1, where the cosmos, time, and the soul appear alongside water, air, and fire, and other triads.
6. The General Jewish Labor Bund was a secular Jewish socialist Yiddishist organization active from the 1890s in Eastern Europe.
7. See Yadgar, "Transcending Secularization."
8. Ellenson, "American Jewish Denominationalism," 15.
9. The anecdote is mentioned in Sharvit, "Harav Yehuda," 282.
10. Herberg, *Judaism and Modern Man*, 49. In his footnote to this comment, Herberg quotes B.H. Streeter's assertion that to the Hebrew, the world of phenomena is not an illusion but "the field of values."
11. Bauman, *Culture in Liquid Modern World*, 11–12.
12. BT Berakhot 63a.
13. It is interesting to note that Yosef Haym of Baghdad (*Ben Yehoyada*, Jerusalem 1898, 56c) reads the proverb beyond the context of Torah learning and suggests that the expression relates originally to the world of philanthropy. When charitable donations are scarce, that is the time to give generously. When contributions are plentiful, that is the time to save, presumably so that there will be money to make up for shortfalls in the future.
14. For the origin of this phrase, see Hamlet, Act I Scene 2.
15. All quotations from the speech are taken from Chabon, "Those People, Over There."
16. Rosenak, *Zehuyot Mitnagshot*, volume 1, especially 359–361.
17. Fischer, "Michael Chabon's Sacred and Profane." The reference is to Mishnah Baba Batra 2:10.
18. For a provocative discussion of the association between the fluid and the feminine, see Irigaray, "The 'Mechanics' of Fluids" in *This Sex*, 106–118. The implications of Irigaray's theories are examined in Stephens, "Feminism and New Materialism."
19. Ibid., 186.
20. Bialik, *Revealment and Concealment*, 44.

Open Access This chapter is licensed under the terms of the Creative Commons Attribution 4.0 International License (http://creativecommons.org/licenses/by/4.0/), which permits use, sharing, adaptation, distribution and reproduction in any medium or format, as long as you give appropriate credit to the original author(s) and the source, provide a link to the Creative Commons license and indicate if changes were made.

The images or other third party material in this chapter are included in the chapter's Creative Commons license, unless indicated otherwise in a credit line to the material. If material is not included in the chapter's Creative Commons license and your intended use is not permitted by statutory regulation or exceeds the permitted use, you will need to obtain permission directly from the copyright holder.

Taluy: Dependence and Independence

If you are an ultra-Orthodox Jew and you are reading these words, one of three things has happened. It may be that an error has occurred, and you find yourself in front of this book by accident. You might be scouting out the opposition. Or the third possibility is that you are gripped by a curiosity that is likely to take you outside the confines of your current lifestyle before long. In any case, you are welcome, but this work is not addressed to the ultra-Orthodox segment of the Jewish world. Nor is it aimed at those who have decided that 3500 years of distinct Jewish life can come to an end in this generation without any great loss to humanity. If that is your position, this book is also not for you.

My *aspaklaria* is different, and it spawns a question posed to Jews in neither of these camps: what does the future of Judaism depend on? Before hazarding some responses, a word about the Hebrew term for depending is called for.

HANGING IN DOUBT

The root *t-l-h* relates to the act of hanging, draping, or suspending. In the Hebrew Bible it is typically applied to an inanimate object or more frequently a body, such as Haman in the Book of Esther, hoisted by his own petard.[1] Within two verses in the Book of Deuteronomy the word is employed twice to refer to the general category of capital punishment:

> If a man is guilty of a capital offense and is put to death, and you hang him (*talita*) on a tree [or a stake], you must not let his corpse remain on the stake overnight, but must bury him the same day. For a hung body (*taluy*) is an affront to God: you shall not defile the land that the Lord your God is giving you to possess.[2]

The carcass of a hung offender is itself an offense, and the sanctity of the Land demands that it be buried without delay. While the root is used in most cases to describe something being thus hung or draped, there are some exceptions in which a more idiomatic and metaphorical meaning is intended. Deuteronomy 28:66 is part of the catalog of grim circumstances to be faced by those who fail to live up to the terms of the covenant. The verse includes the expression translated as "the life you face shall be precarious" or "your life shall hang before you," which employs the word *taluy*, hung uncertainly in the balance.[3] Rashi explains: "This is because of *safek*. Any *safek* may be termed *taluy*, hanging. You will always be saying: 'perhaps I will die today through the sword that is coming upon us.'"[4]

Safek (doubt or uncertainty) is likened to the state of hanging by a thread, unsure of whether one's fate will go one way or another. Failure to act in accordance with the divine plan will be punished by perpetual insecurity. To this day, there are many for whom anything uncertain, *taluy*, is regarded as offensive to God—as a carcass left to rot to be removed with all speed.

In the transition from biblical to rabbinical literature,[5] the Hebrew term *taluy* and its Aramaic equivalent *talya* are deployed less in the literal sense of suspension and more in a metaphorical sense, used to denote dependence or proportionate linkage. To cite one example, two sages are engaged in a disagreement on a matter of inheritance law in BT Baba Batra 142b. Rabbi Yirmiya expresses the opinion that the matter should be decided as normative practice in line with his view, since those agreeing with his opinion have the advantage of seniority over the camp of Rabbi Abahu. His interlocutor retorts: Does the matter depend (*talya*) on age or, as he asserts, on the strength of the reason behind the ruling?

Both in English and in these Hebrew sources, depending is a paradoxical business: "it depends" denotes uncertainty, and contingency, while "you can depend on it" suggests fixity and reliability.

The World Hangs by a Thread

It was widely held by the ancient Hebrews that the world stood on pillars whose foundations perhaps lay deep in the oceans.[6] One verse in the Book of Job reflected "a poetic cosmology which deviated from the major Israelite tradition."[7] In a resonant turn of expression, Job describes the power of God, who "spreads out the northern skies over empty space, suspends the earth over nothing."[8]

The last words of this verse, *toleh 'al blimah* are not easy to translate. Assuming that *blimah* is comprised of two shorter words, *bli mah*, it can be rendered as "without anything" or "dependent on no thing." In other words, Planet Earth appears to hang in the firmament unsupported.[9] Rashi suggests that the northern skies and the Earth "stand in the air sustained by the strength of the arms of the Holy One."[10] Whether God is imagined playing the role of Atlas, holding up this planet through constant exertion of strength, or as the designer of a complex system in which Earth is motionless at its heart, the teaching is fundamentally similar: the world depends on no external support but solely on the Creator. The world is independent, held in place by—nothing.

Hebrew, a language highly susceptible to multiple meanings, offers another possible interpretation of *blimah*, carrying such meanings as to close one's mouth, to repel, and to soak up. In modern Hebrew, the root is used when applying the brakes in a car or referring to a defender in a soccer game.[11] This semantic field is explored in a Talmudic reading of the Job verse where it is employed to further an ethical teaching about the virtue of self-restraint: "Rabbi Ilea says: the world endures due to the merit of one who restrains themselves during a quarrel, as it is stated: He hangs the earth upon *blimah*."[12] This second reading transfers the meaning of the verse from the astronomical to the social. The suggestion, moralizing in tone rather than an assertion of scientific truth, is that a person who manages to avoid losing control in the heat of disagreement is performing an act of cosmic preservation. The world depends on it.

These two interpretations explore different dimensions of dependence. The former asks a physical question and proposes a metaphysical response: our planet is propped up by nothing, thanks to the power of a creating and world-sustaining God. The latter ascribes ultimate significance to the manner in which individuals contrive strategies of coexistence. The two strands are connected by a sense of wonder and an awareness of precariousness. The world does not rest on unshakable foundations; rather, it depends on goodwill, both human and divine. It hangs by a thread.

What does our future depend on? Exploring this question involves reflecting on both dependence and independence.

INDEPENDENCE

Just as Job's image conjures up the image of a world suspended in the ether, the Mishnah relates to a love so pure that it depends on nothing:

> All love that depends on a particular thing (*teluya bedavar*) ceases when that thing ceases. All love that is dependent on nothing, will never cease. What is an example of love that depended on something? Such was the love of Amnon for Tamar. And what is an example of love that did not depend on anything? Such was the love of David and Jonathan.[13]

Like a skeptic at a séance, modernity offers prosaic physical explanations designed to demystify both the Bible's cosmology and the Mishnah's ideal of love free of all interest. Physics, psychology, evolutionary science, and the other instruments of disenchantment undermine the notion that the physical or emotional spheres can ever be wholly pure or independent. It is magnetic force that keeps the Earth hanging, and even a love experienced as pure can be approached through a range of psychological, social, chemical, and other prisms.

Ironically perhaps, while modern science was debunking pre-modern notions of independence (such as Job's cosmology and the Mishnah's description of pure love), modern politics and social theory were advancing notions of self-determination, self-governance, and self-authorization.[14] Western modernity privileges a view of the individual free from conceptual and political shackles, celebrating "a fuller independence from time-honored beliefs and pieties."[15] Movements of national independence have paralleled, and often inspired, struggles for personal self-realization.

Rejecting the notion of the "self-made man," Frederick Douglass wrote: "No possible native force of character, and no depth of wealth and originality, can lift a man into an absolute independence of his fellowmen, and no generation of men can be independent of the preceding generation."[16] Douglass, whose own life was testament to the difference an individual can make, nevertheless questioned the ideal, much encouraged by

Romanticism and capitalism, according to which a person can float freely, untethered to context or tradition. His words serve as a reminder that absolute independence is an illusion.

Independence, radical self-reliance, complete autonomy—these goals were not considered either attainable or even desirable in traditional Judaism:

> Autonomy, which figures as the central organizing principle of liberal consent theories and their attendant ethical systems, is neither a presupposition nor a goal of Judaism....By no traditional accounts is a person "entitled" to act in complete freedom; he or she is required to act in community, in covenant with God, and in accordance with halakhah.[17]

Among Jewish responses to modernity, Reform and Zionism emphasized distinct aspects of independence. The founders of Reform were inspired by a worldview epitomized by Immanuel Kant's statement: "Freedom (independence from being constrained by another's choice), insofar as it can coexist with the freedom of every other in accordance with a universal law, is the only original right belonging to every man by virtue of his humanity."[18]

Later iterations of Reform Judaism, in some cases less enthusiastic about the Kantian formulation, retained this enthusiasm for the notion of independence. For example, Eugene Borowitz, one of the most influential Reform thinkers of the twentieth century, spoke of believers who "sense the reality of a God who grounds our values yet makes room for human independence and calls human beings into an active partnership."[19]

Zionist notions of independence tended to focus less on individual self-fulfillment than on national self-determination. The dream was to break out of the pattern, 2000 years in formation, of reliance on the goodwill of host societies and to strive for a new era: "To be a free nation in our land," say the words of *Hatikvah*, Israel's national anthem. In a 1952 speech, David Ben-Gurion set out his vision of political and cultural independence:

> With the establishment of the State there has been a fundamental change in the way we see ourselves, the way we see the world and the world sees us, and thus our image, both inward facing and outward looking, is being reconstituted. We are getting ever closer to the origin and historical root of our people in its early formation and independence, and to the spiritual

legacy from biblical times. At the same time, we are increasingly becoming free citizens of the wide world, integrating into the universal human legacy of every generation and every people.[20]

This is a statement of a classic Zionist view of independence, according to which the creation of a Jewish polity can bring dignity and normality to the attempt of Jews to play their role in world civilization.

There are traditional and contemporary reasons to harbor a deep suspicion of ideologies of untrammeled independence. No man or woman is an island, and no religion or state or multinational conglomerate either.[21] One way of mediating between the promise of greater independence and the dangers inherent in such an absolute ideal has been suggested by the philosopher Marilyn Friedman. Rejecting the possibility of an absolute or abstract independence, she speaks instead of "a relatively low but still humanly possible form of dependence."[22] From within the contours of what is described as "relational autonomy," she proposes an approach which rejects, as did Douglass, a doctrinaire libertarian stance which asserts that any person can achieve any goal if they only try hard enough. Conscious of the deep structural inequalities that characterize our world, Friedman still leaves space for a version of the ideal of independence as a potent aspiration.

A corollary to the growing prominence of notions of personal and national independence is a concern with responsibility. I earlier cited the remarkable Talmudic tale of Rabbi Elazar ben Dordaya, who does all in his power to reverse a prediction that his repentance would never be accepted.[23] With his final breath and at the end of his tether, he says: "the matter depends (*taluy*) on nothing other than myself."[24] The Sage is a tragic and ambivalent figure, but his final words, uttered as he places his head between his knees and weeps, have become a slogan of Jewish and other movements of liberation: we cannot rely on the intervention of others; we have to take responsibility and face the consequences. It is on us.

In our day, the idea that each of us is free to make our choices has been commodified and exploited by market forces and governments. Choice is manipulated and self-realization is hawked by quacks. Nonetheless, those who condemn the ideal of greater independence as a mere illusion are, I believe, profoundly misguided. It is surely better to live in a society which strives for diversity and self-expression than to be forced to submit to someone else's idea of truth. My own religious ideal is one in which individuals blessed with a considerable degree of independence can choose how to express their profound dependencies.

Independence of thought, independence of spirit, a deep engagement with the sources of our people in their own terms (and ideally in their original languages), a willingness to take responsibility for the current chapter in the longest story in the human history—on all this, I believe, the Jewish future depends. There is, however, more.

Dependence

Land-based commandments, *mitzvot hateluyot ba'aretz*, are religious obligations incumbent on Jews only when they are situated in the Land of Israel.[25] Included in this category are a range of laws connected to the sabbatical year, tithing, and many other agricultural practices. Typically, it is these particular kinds of observance to which the phrase is thought to refer, but there is a more radical and surprising reading of the term, according to which the entire system of commandments, including those which have no apparent connection to the Land of Israel, are all dependent (*teluyot*) upon it. By this account, as explained by Marc Saperstein,

> The commandments performed in exile have little intrinsic importance; they have an instrumental value, preserving Jewish distinctiveness, and keeping Jews in practice, for the time when they would return to the Land and perform them as they were truly intended to be performed.[26]

This understanding of Land-based commandments goes against the grain of its literal sense and suggests that the network of Jewish commitments which have molded Jewish life for millennia is dependent and conditional upon the Land. This applies even for those Jews who never set foot in the Land. It is as though the legitimacy of the whole enterprise is designed for and guaranteed by the Land of Israel.[27] Observance of the *mitzvot*, practiced with rigor for many centuries, is like rehearsing your lines for opening night: it is important as preparation, but it is no more than a dress rehearsal.

Dependence in this sense implies priority. There is a strand of Jewish thought that makes even bolder metaphysical claims, asserting that the world itself exists for the sake of Israel.[28] The hierarchical thinking at work here is parallel to pre-Copernican cosmology, in which some fixed object—the land, the people—is situated in the heart of a great cosmic mechanism.

The universe is dependent on Israel[29] or, in some versions, the Torah,[30] the commandments on the Land, and others. Israel plays the role here of a lodestone.

How are we to understand teachings such as the classic declaration that "the Land of Israel is holier than all other lands"?[31] My approach to Judaism is fundamentally historical: *zeman nakat*. It is not hard to understand why Jews have been tempted to elevate their belief to a metaphysical status and to claim that the Torah and the Land and the People are the very purpose of creation.[32] The question to be asked is whether this kind of approach can be maintained today. It could be argued, for example, that the risk of cultural assimilation is so enormous that anything differentiating the Jewish expression and offering Jews a reason for pride should be celebrated. What is wrong with thinking that the world is dependent on Israel?

It is wrong because it is neither defensible nor necessary. It is a pre-Copernican doctrine in a post-Copernican world. It is wrong, too, because as a result of the Jewish Return into History, Israel is now a regional superpower with nuclear capability, and one implication of this change in the power balance is that hyperbolic statements of primacy ought to be replaced by more sober and modest ambitions. It is wrong because in Israel today, a growing minority—some of them elected officials—believe the metaphorical rhetoric to be literally true. Believing that my life has meaning is essential. Believing that the world exists for my sake is dangerous.

The world should be enriched by Israel. Israel should have a place in the world. But the world is not dependent on Israel. Israel is, in fact, dependent on the world. The Talmudic category of *mitzvot hateluyot ba'aretz*, commandments whose fulfillment is contingent on the *eretz*, should now be understood not as *eretz* in the sense of Land but as *eretz* in the sense of World.

Much like the English word "earth," *eretz* bears a multitude of meanings in the Hebrew Bible. It refers to the whole Earth, to earth in contrast to heaven, and to all the inhabitants of the earth. It also means a country, a territory, a piece of ground, and more. One of Israel's well-known newspapers is called *Ha'aretz*. The title is deliberately ambiguous, since it may refer to the Land of Israel, known to this day in Hebrew simply as *eretz*, or to the entire planet.[33] To use a parallel from German newspapers, it is *Neues Deutschland* (New Germany) and *Die Welt* (The World) rolled into one.

Tomorrow's Judaism needs to articulate *mitzvot hateluyot bekadur ha'aretz*, commandments dependent on Planet Earth. These will be based on an awareness that the planet is undergoing a crisis of unprecedented proportions and that acts of world maintenance are fundamentally Jewish acts. Like the Pharisaic paradigm in its day, this will have to translate into practical expressions, including what we eat and how we travel. Much work has been done over recent years to explore the relationship between Judaism and ecological awareness.[34] Hava Tirosh-Samuelson stated that while

> the Jewish religious tradition includes principles that can be very useful in contemporary attempts to think about ecology from a religious perspective...if Jewish environmentalism is to grow, Jews will have to engage the large body of ecological philosophy in greater depth.[35]

This engagement will not only yield heartwarming insights; it will force us to confront the culture of consumption of which we are a part.

The future is uncertain, depending on unknowable variables. In order to prepare for it, all we can do is clarify our fundamental dependencies. Climate crisis should spawn the category of Earth-dependent commandments, incumbent on the pious and the anarchic alike.

INTERDEPENDENCE

Dependence is a scandal of mortality. We depend on the nutrition we can find, the circumstances we are in, the time we have. Substance dependency—drugs, alcohol, and the like—is an extreme and destructive form of a universal dependency on sustenance, love, hope, and more. We are all dependent, striving in different ways for independence. More than ever before, we are learning the degree to which our prospects are bound up with the hopes and dreams of others: other peoples and cultures, other beliefs and ideologies, other species and life forms.

Tomorrow's Judaism will be wrought in the encounter between dependence and independence. The Mishnah's insistence that "every single person must say: the world was created for my sake"[36] relies on every single person being included in the equation. The moment I believe that the universe exists for me but not for you, the path to perdition is set.

Being a Jew, like being any other kind of person, needs no justification. Yearning to sustain and advance the Jewish project beyond one's own generation should not require an apology. The challenge is to pursue this rich and multifaceted channel while never forgetting our fundamental interdependence. We need to find a way of articulating a reason to stay Jewish and to do Jewish which is not predicated on some proof that God intended everyone and everything to be dependent on us. We are not the reason the world exists. However, knowing this should not lead to the conclusion that it is of no consequence whether Judaism continues to be in the world. A sense of interdependence should provide a license for humility and perspective, on the one hand, and for an embrace of identity and specificity, on the other.

The Aramaic expression *ha beha talya* literally means: this is dependent on that. It is a simple thought with significant implications. As an educational principle, it calls for the encouragement of curiosity across disciplinary definitions. As a guide to politics, it reminds us that the wellbeing of one party to a conflict will only be safeguarded when the other party's grievances and needs are addressed. Theologically, it conjures up the bold teaching, well attested in rabbinic tradition, that even God is dependent, while simultaneously being the ultimate independence. God has been imagined as being in need of our involvement. In David Hartman's memorable turn of phrase, "divine perfection is a relational category involving interdependence."[37] This idea is explored in the theology of Mara Benjamin, who has demonstrated that opening the lexicon of divine metaphors to include mothers' experiences deepens our understanding of how God, the radically independent other, can also be dependent on humanity. The dependence/independence dichotomy is too crude to capture this complexity.[38]

Ha beha talya. One thing depends on the other: the human on the divine, vulnerability on agency. I cannot predict what the Jewish future is likely to bring, but I imagine it will involve mediating between a thirst for independence, an acknowledgment of dependence, and a growing awareness of interdependence. We have to work hard to get the balance right. Everything hangs on it.

Notes

1. Some thirty instances of *t-l-h* are listed in the concordance, almost a third of which appear in Esther. In Ezekiel (16:3, 27:10, and 27:11) the subjects to which the verb is applied are non-human.
2. Deuteronomy 21:23. See also 2 Samuel 18:10; Song of Songs 4:4; and Hosea 10:26.
3. For another metaphorical usage of *taluy*, see Hosea 11:7.

4. Rashi to Deuteronomy 28:66.
5. See Ben Sira 7:18 for an example of a Second Temple usage of *taluy*.
6. See 1 Samuel 2:8; Psalms 24:2' 75:4' 104:5` Job 26:11, 38:6. See also Stadelmann, *Hebrew Conception of the World*.
7. Habel, *Book of Job*, 371.
8. Job 26:7.
9. See Rabbenu Bahye ben Asher to Deuteronomy 32:27. The verse is cited, for example, in a twentieth-century anti-Copernican tract by Pinhas David Weberman, appended to his edition of Rabbi Chayim Vital's *Sefer Hatekhunah* (Jerusalem, 1967), 125–126. Over 800 years earlier the point had been made by Abraham ibn Ezra in his commentary to Job 26:7. The verse is taken to support a pre-Copernican view of the universe, according to which the earth is motionless at the center of the cosmos while the other heavenly bodies rotate according to unvarying motions.
10. Rashi to Job 26:7.
11. See Psalm 32:9. See also the commentary of Rabbi Ishmael ben Chakmon to BT Baba Batra 58a.
12. BT Hullin 89a.
13. Mishnah Avot 5.16.
14. This triad, listed as three axes or dimensions of the concept of autonomy, is taken from Mackenzie, "Three Dimensions of Autonomy."
15. Taylor, *Sources of the Self*, 323.
16. Quoted in Friedman, "Relational Autonomy and Independence," 52. First delivered as a lecture in 1859, "Self-Made Men" was published in 1872.
17. Zoloth, *Health Care*, 158.
18. Kant, *Metaphysics of Morals*, 30 [6:237].
19. Borowitz, *Judaism After Modernity*, 160.
20. Ben-Gurion, "Atzmaut Tarbutit."
21. "No man is an island" is from John Donne, and "no religion is an island" is from Abraham Joshua Heschel.
22. Friedman, "Relational Autonomy and Independence," 56.
23. See the chapter entitled *Bi*.
24. BT Avodah Zarah 17a.
25. See PT Shvi'it 6.1, 36b; and PT Kiddushin 19, 61c.
26. Saperstein, "The Land of Israel," 201. This short article offers a good treatment of the debate concerning the commandments and the Land. For an even more thorough discussion, see Ravitzky, "Hatzivi Lakh Tziyunim."
27. See Sarason, "Significance of Land of Israel."
28. See, for example, Midrash Alpha Beta, in Wertheimer, *Batei Midrashot* vol.2 (Jerusalem, 1989), 450, where the verse from Job in which God hangs the world on *blimah* is understood to refer to the people Israel, whose willingness to go without anything places it at the heart of the cosmos.

29. See, for example, Shem Mishmuel to Bamidbar, 1913, according to which God hangs all of the worlds on the perfection of Israel, like a secondary hung on to the primary.
30. See, for example, Kli Yakar to Deuteronomy 32:1: "The existence of the heavens and the earth is dependent (*taluy*) on the Torah, since the higher and the lower realms are two opposites and they need a center to connect them. This is the person, composed of matter and form and the combination of the two is effected by the Torah, for without it a person would be just like a beast, without a dimension from the higher reaches." In this teaching, Shlomo Ephraim ben Aaron Luntschitz uses the metaphor of balance in a precise way: the Torah is that instrument by which the disparate forces of creation are held together.
31. Mishnah Kelim 1.6.
32. See, for example, Rashi to Genesis 1.1 and Gerim 1:5.
33. Idel, "Land of Israel," 172, suggests that the terminologically specific *Ha'aretz* implies the Land of Israel as opposed to *eretz*, the earth in general. On p.179, Idel also notes a pun by Rabbi Isaac of Acre on multiple meanings of the word, relating to both land and earth.
34. See: Waskow, *Torah of the Earth*; Watts Belser, "The Bible and Ecotheology"; Yaffe, *Judaism and Environmental Ethics*; and Yoreh, *Waste Not*.
35. Tirosh-Samuelson, *Judaism and Ecology*, 56.
36. Mishnah Sanhedrin 4.5.
37. Hartman, "Relationship, Memory."
38. See Benjamin, *Obligated Self*, particularly 50. Most relevant in this context is the work of Jessica Benjamin from a feminist psychoanalytical perspective. See Benjamin, *Bonds of Love*, particularly 113–114 and 158–162.

Open Access This chapter is licensed under the terms of the Creative Commons Attribution 4.0 International License (http://creativecommons.org/licenses/by/4.0/), which permits use, sharing, adaptation, distribution and reproduction in any medium or format, as long as you give appropriate credit to the original author(s) and the source, provide a link to the Creative Commons license and indicate if changes were made.

The images or other third party material in this chapter are included in the chapter's Creative Commons license, unless indicated otherwise in a credit line to the material. If material is not included in the chapter's Creative Commons license and your intended use is not permitted by statutory regulation or exceeds the permitted use, you will need to obtain permission directly from the copyright holder.

The Twenty-Third Letter

To Megiddo and Back

As mentioned in the introduction, I decided to write this book in 1990 in Megiddo Jail where I was stationed. I was in my late twenties, studying for the Reform rabbinate at the Hebrew Union College in Jerusalem. The closing words to this book are written some thirty-five years later at a time of great uncertainty in Israel, in Gaza, and in the entire Middle East. Armageddon (the name by which Megiddo is known in the Greek of the New Testament) seems closer now than it did when I was encamped there. The fundamental anxieties which fueled the writing of this book, whether modern Judaism is a viable project and whether Israel can survive and thrive, have only deepened with time.

This book includes elements of old-fashioned theology in that parts of it are explicitly about God. All of it, including the most overtly political sections, constitutes an attempt to articulate a response to Micah's question: What does God require of you?[1] Judging from its frequent mention of Israel, the book should be situated on the Zionist spectrum where some may decry it as an anti-Zionist screed while others condemn it as hyper-Zionist diatribe. It is, I hope, neither.

Taking the notion of *aspaklaria* seriously means celebrating different approaches even when objecting to them. In his 2024 work, *The No-State Solution*, Daniel Boyarin offers a manifesto for the Jewish future which affirms the Jews as a nation but rejects categorically the option of the Jews expressing their nationhood through the vehicle of the State of Israel, which he regards as inevitably mired in racism and injustice.[2] He eschews the notion that Jewish life can be understood simply in confessional religious terms as well as the idea that Jews should settle for a homogenized cosmopolitan identity. I find it more difficult than Boyarin to write off all that Israel may yet be and the millions of my fellow Jews who are committed to building a society here, but I share many of his critiques and concerns. For the sake of symmetry, it should perhaps be also noted that I read and take seriously a raft of Jewish thinkers to the right of me politically and religiously, some of whom dismiss my self-understanding as a religious Jew as self-delusion or fraud. The diagnosis offered in works with which I profoundly disagree is often more compelling than the proposed cure.

We are unlikely to forge a path back from Armageddon unless we are prepared to entertain unsettling and unpopular views and avoid the temptations of insult and outrage. The controversial liberation theologian Marc Ellis proposed a checklist of six challenges which (at approximately the time when I was on guard duty in Megiddo) he predicted would need to be taken up by future Jewish theology. He asserted that such a theology "must be distinctly Jewish in category and speech yet generous toward other religious and humanist communities."[3] Second, it should not settle for disembodied statements of eternal truths but "seek to be present in history." Third, it should be inclusive and critical of all that demands criticism within Jewish life. Fourth, it should not settle for parochial Jewish interests but must balance the imperative of Jewish survival with "a deepening of the witness its values offer to the world." Fifth, it demands an emphasis on the witness against idolatry as that which binds Jews to each other and "as the fundamental link to religious and humanist communities of good will around the globe."[4]

Ellis ends his catalog of criteria for a new Jewish theology thus:

> Jewish theology must in its essence be a call to *teshuvah*: commitment and solidarity in all their pain and possibility, as well as a critical understanding of the history we are creating and the courage it takes to change the course of that history.[5]

It is for readers to judge whether my attempt to delineate a "crunchy" Jewish theology includes at least some of these elements.

A Proposed Lexicon

The theology described here aims to be crunchy yet coherent. It is predicated on a certain reading of *yetzer lev ha'adam*, the human condition. It notes our capacity for ingesting our misdeeds and shortcomings as an attempt to bury the evidence and our parallel urge to expel them. It sees the Torah, stretched out between its *tefachim*, spanning the realms of God, humanity, and the world. Reveling in Jewish particularity, it is alarmed at the destructive potential of chauvinism and affirms the fundamental bond of human solidarity that overrides distinctions of creed and tribe (*vegoralenu*).

This book includes theology in the classic sense, striving for a closer understanding of God from the perspective of existence and of vitality (*chai vekayam*). God is approached in spirituality and responsibility (*bi*) and in language and prayer (*pi yagid*). God is perceived through more than one *aspaklaria*.

The theology touches upon some perennial aspects of Jewish obligation and practice (*lehaniach, neder*) and offers a new understanding of some of its underlying assumptions: a reading of limitations, binaries and boundaries (*gader*), and an interpretation of tradition (*masoret*). It considers the importance of community, *kehillah*, to Jewish life.

My theology suggests that humor (*tzechok*) and doubt (*safek*) are central to Judaism, as are a historical consciousness (*zeman nakat*) and both a thick reading and an intense deployment of Jewish sources (*dovev*). It suggests paradigms through which contemporary Jewish thought (*kosot yeshua*) and various states of Jewish intensity (*sha'at hamefazrim*) can be considered.

In light of the Jews' return to the political arena, this theology is overtly political in nature. Indeed, modernity and sovereignty demand that traditional approaches to peoplehood and chosenness be revised and the fundamental humanity of all people be underlined. The book asks what the State of Israel might and can be (*reshit*) and applies the criterion of decency to the behavior of its politicians and of society in general (*hogenet*). It warns against the risk of moral collapse if we do not face up to all that has been expelled to *Azazel*. This theology asserts that unless and until these notions of solidarity and justice are given priority, Israel's future remains in the balance. Along with such crises as the environment, these are issues upon which our futures depend (*taluy*).

Living the Letters represents one way of combining some of the key themes of modern Jewish life and presenting them in the form of an alphabetical lexicon. Its aim is to spark interest, to provoke response, and to exemplify serious and engaged liberal Jewish thought. Its patchwork comprises elements of a possible Judaism for tomorrow.

Alphabets Change

Alphabets imply completeness, but they themselves change: letters are introduced and others fade away. Geoffrey Chaucer's fourteenth-century alphabetical poem lacks verses beginning with J, U, or W, because these letters were not features of the English alphabet in his day.[6] In chemistry the periodic table, that alphabet of elements listing the building blocks of the natural world, has grown considerably in number since its introduction in 1869. Alphabets change.

This book has followed an ancient Jewish example and employed an alphabetical structure. According to *Magen David*, a kabbalistic work by the sixteenth-century scholar David ibn Zimra, the Hebrew alphabet is also due to change in the future with an as yet unrevealed letter of the alphabet. Ibn Zimra's theories were in the tradition of what has been termed the doctrine of the Sabbatical cycles, which claims that history moves through epochs.[7] The day will come when humanity lives on a higher level of moral perfection, and it is then that a new letter of the alphabet, a new building block of existence, will come to be known. Just as the Rabbis taught that reality now perceived through a speckled *aspaklaria* will come to be seen with pellucid clarity, the teaching here looks to a future time in which we will be able to articulate something fundamentally new.

The twenty-third letter represents the ineffable, the unspeakable, and the unknown. The term ineffable, used frequently by Abraham Joshua Heschel, refers to that which cannot be expressed, often used in reference to both the extremely abstract and the extremely concrete. Neither the overwhelming presence of the sublime nor the intense immediacy of a leaf or a moment lend themselves to being expressed in words.[8]

Something unspeakable is so horrific, so terrifying, that words cannot be found to describe it. Throughout history, and markedly since the 1930s, the world has borne witness to much that is unspeakable—a corollary and obverse to great technological and cultural advances. A new letter is called for to articulate the unspeakable alongside the sublime and the inspiring.

The unknown is different in nature from the ineffable and the unspeakable. It comes into being when something radically new is encountered, be it an anxiety or a hope, a revelation or a threat. When Moses says to Pharaoh, "we shall not know with what we are to worship Adonai until we arrive there,"[9] he is pointing to such an unknown. He cannot yet express what it will be, but he can at least express this not knowing. As I write these words, it is clear that the war which began in October 2023 will have a profound impact on the Middle East and on Israel's standing in the world, but it is impossible to know what that impact will be. To cite another example of the unknown, unrelated to this dreadful war, there can be little doubt that the artificial intelligence revolution will transform our lives and many aspects of Jewish life. Pretending to know the nature of these transformations is to pronounce a letter not yet revealed.[10]

This is the point at which *Living the Letters: An Alphabet of Emerging Jewish Thought* arrives at its conclusion. The idea of a letter still concealed, one which will be used to form words yet unimagined, is an appropriate image for this closure. It denotes the ineffable, the unspeakable, and the unknown. I am unconvinced by the idea that everything ineffable will ultimately be expressed and that all apparent mysteries will eventually be disenchanted. Science continues to shed light on many phenomena previously thought miraculous, but wonder will continue to outstrip understanding. There will always be something beyond our capacity to explain, even when all the current conundrums have been resolved. This axiomatic belief is not based on a scrupulous examination of all the evidence but rather on a sensitivity to the perils of hubris. There is more in heaven and earth than any of our philosophies can contain.

The Jewish experience in the twentieth century has brought us face to face with the unspeakable. The awareness that a catastrophic abandonment of basic humanity is an ever-present risk has informed this book throughout. During the time spent writing this book, great reservoirs of suffering have been filled up and the perverse demons of brutality set free to roam in Israel, Palestine, and many other locations too.

There is almost no mention of antisemitism or indeed of the Holocaust in this book. This is a statement, not an oversight. While there is no denying their significance, I refuse to grant either of them a generative value. The degree to which identity is founded and political positions established on the basis of a sense of victimhood is alarming; the more grim the situation becomes, the stronger the tendency to fall back on this mainstay.[11]

My stubborn resistance to dwell on antisemitism and the Holocaust is not the result of nonchalance. I do not dismiss or downplay these facts but strive for a Judaism that points beyond survival.[12] Judaism after Auschwitz cannot be the same as it was before. The Shoah may indeed be a kind of ground zero, the scorched earth upon which something new is built; however, it must never become a holy of holies. It should be afforded no sanctity of its own even as it galvanizes us to seek sanctity.

Within the intimate vocabulary of my own family, the most articulate expression of striving for the ineffable in the wake of the unspeakable involves no words at all. My mother was nine years old when she was taken from the Lodz Ghetto to Ravensbrück concentration camp. Decades later, when asked whether she would make a *tallit* for her daughter-in-law, she shared a rare memory from that hellish childhood. The guards, she recalled, had forbidden the women inmates of the camp to wear any undergarments. They were prepared to allow one exception: the women could wear re-purposed prayer shawls taken from murdered Jews. Decades after this gross desecration, my mother proceeded to make beautiful and unique prayer shawls for each of her grandchildren and other family members. This is a more cogent response to perversity and inhumanity than any of her more verbose relatives could ever muster. From a place of perversity, an expression of decency and dignity. From rupture, a stitching together. Perhaps the threads of each *tallit* were constituted by the twenty-third letter of the alphabet: a place where the ineffable and the unspeakable meet.

The Unknown

Earlier in this book I introduced the notion of bear-hunt stoicism, suggesting that we cannot evade the greatest challenges of our day. Despite the temptation to evade them, we have to go through them. Writing in the most ominous days the Jews have ever known, Martin Buber gave powerful expression to this imperative, writing in 1940: "The only way to salvation is by the steep and stony path over the recognition of reality."[13] Four years earlier, Buber adopted Kierkegaard's notion of the Single One, re-purposing and democratizing it to refer to the contemporary citizen striving to make sense of a world in turmoil. Such a person, each of us in potential

... must put his arms around the vexatious world ... only then do his fingers reach the realm of lightning and of grace.

... He must face the hour which approaches him, the biographical and historial hour, just as it is, in its whole world content and apparently senseless contradiction, without weakening the impact of otherness in it.[14]

We must face the hour which approaches us, knowing that we do not know what it brings, but employing our moral intuition and intellectual capacities as best we can. Facing the future, it is not only the stoicism of the bear hunt which is called for, but a version of prophecy. I do not mean by this the accouterments and mannerisms of the prophet, for which healthy skepticism is usually appropriate. Our current moment calls for a prophetic reaction from each of us, striving to understand what is demanded of us today so that tomorrow may yet be redeemed.

I believe that if Israel is to survive and thrive, Israeli society will need to change in a way few citizens of the country can imagine, let alone countenance. We will need to take steps to give the Palestinian people a horizon of hope and a prospect of decency, both because it is the pragmatic thing to do and because it is the right thing to do. It will not be easy. We will need to reconsider the lines we have drawn between "us" and "them," between friend and foe.[15] Each time an atrocity is perpetrated, the paradigm is confirmed. A new letter is needed to help us articulate a version of the future in which we are not trapped in an eternal vendetta or sucked ever deeper into a vortex of blood.

I predict that despite the palpable reluctance to offer Palestinians a horizon of hope, failure to do so may spell our end. Since "our hope has not been lost," I prefer to imagine a profound transformation of attitudes and behaviors. The Jews and Palestinians who live in Israel/Palestine in the coming generations will need to be educated together, to learn more deeply about each other's dreams and aspirations, to speak each other's languages, and to respect each other's lexicons.

In response to the unspeakable, we Jews established a state and took on the enormous burden of power. Critics of Zionism see this as untenable and are convinced that we are destined to become exemplars of the brutality whose victims we have until recently been. I understand this critique and find it difficult to dismiss. However, while this drama is still unfolding, I would rather struggle for Israel's future than prepare its obituary.

What of Jewish life around the world? The prospects for the continued thriving of ultra-Orthodox enclaves seem good, but the liberal camp is in decline. In order to flourish, it will need to make a case for continuity which goes beyond survivalism and victimhood. It will also most probably need to function in areas delineated, at best, by blurred boundaries. More people will be Jew-ish in an ephemeral way rather than Jewish in an overwhelmingly solid manner. Neither tutting and scolding nor pretending that a happy ending is guaranteed is an appropriate response. Rather, Judaism will have to develop a thick language of engagement and possibility. If Reform Judaism (along with other non-Orthodox expressions) is going to make it, it will need to recalibrate the relationship between its constituent parts: solid, liquid, and ephemeral. It will need to be more than a case one can make or a flag one can fly. It must be a life one chooses to live and a lexicon one chooses to employ.

My proposed twenty-third letter is one to help engender a new way in which the Jew faces the other, be they in Israel or anywhere else. We have to find new ways of articulating our commitments, passionately Jewish and compassionately human. It is worth noting that once this imagined extra letter has been introduced, it will still be only one among twenty-three. Most of what we are likely to encounter—the sublime, the horrendous, and the unknown—has been experienced by those who came before us. To think otherwise is arrogant and ignorant. To live within a *masoret*, as the prophet Ezekiel knew, is to be part of a *berit*, a covenant that preceded us and that, one way or another, will continue after us.

Describing what she called an engendered Judaism, Rachel Adler set out its core characteristics:

> It must rigorously interrogate the theological languages of the past while illuminating vocabularies of metaphor and devotion through which God and the people Israel can continue to reveal themselves to one another ... we will have to make the theological project as complicated as the world from which we launch it. This requires not a method but an entire repertory of methods for thinking, for reading, for describing, and for imagining how diversely situated and gendered people have lived, do live, and could live Jewish lives.[16]

I invite you, the reader of this attempt to illuminate vocabularies of metaphor and devotion, to think of your own lexicon. What concepts, beliefs, concerns, anxieties, and hopes would be included in your alphabet? What would you seek to impart to a coming generation?

"An alphabet, like a life, is a finite set of shapes. With it, one can produce almost anything."[17] Kaveh Akbar's insight suits the purpose of this book. At their best, our lives offer an opportunity to deploy our limited resources and aim for something unbounded. Your alphabet, whoever you are, will be different from mine. For that matter, were I to write my own lexicon in a year or two, it would be different from this. Held up to the changing lights of events and emotions, the *aspaklaria* constantly throws up new possibilities and fresh insights. This has been true ever since Abram heard the divine instruction: "Raise your eyes and look from where you are."[18]

In my vocabulary, this turning to questions of ultimacy is a turning to God, "to whom our life can be the spelling of an answer."[19] Using the letters by which the world itself was created, as Israel the people and as each Jacob, each Rachel, and each Leah, our lives are spelling out a response.

Notes

1. Micah 6:8.
2. Boyarin, *The No-State Solution*.
3. All of the following quotations are from Ellis, *Toward Jewish Theology*, 111–112.
4. For my own reading of idolatry as a category of contemporary Jewish thought, see Marmur, "On Petrification."
5. Ellis, *Toward Jewish Theology*, 112.
6. See Chaucer, *Complete Works*, 79–83.
7. For a description of the development of this doctrine in the work of Nachmanides and *Sefer Hatemunah* and its parallels with earlier Islamic thought, see Krinis, "Cyclical Time." This teaching is mentioned in Lipiner, *Chazon Haotiot*, 81 and 245.
8. See Zijlstra, *Language, Image and Silence*, particularly 1–31. Heschel made extensive use of the term "ineffable" in his writing. In *God in Search* he distinguishes between the ineffable and the unknown: "thing unknown today may be known a thousand years from now," whereas the ineffable means "that aspect of reality which by its very nature lies beyond our comprehension," 104.
9. Exodus 10:26.
10. For an analysis of some of these trends in the context of Judaism, see Schiff, *Judaism in a Digital Age*.
11. See Rosenstein, "Brief History of Jewish Victimhood."
12. See Marmur, *Beyond Survival*.

13. Buber, *Israel and the World*, 116. For a reading of the 1940 essay "False Prophets" from which this is taken, see Harvey, "Buber on False Prophets." Buber was decried as a fantasist and an optimist by many in the Zionist mainstream, but that did not deter him.
14. Buber, *Between Man and Man*, 65.
15. The influence of Buber is also palpable in these remarks. In his 1936 "Question to the Single One" (*Between Man and* Man, especially 73–76) Buber took issue with Carl Schmitt's rooting of the political in the friend/enemy distinction. For more on that distinction, see Slomp, "The Theory of the Partisan."
16. Adler, *Engendering Judaism*, xxiii.
17. Akbar, *Martyr!*, 426.
18. Genesis 13:14.
19. Heschel, *Man Is Not Alone*, 78.

Open Access This chapter is licensed under the terms of the Creative Commons Attribution 4.0 International License (http://creativecommons.org/licenses/by/4.0/), which permits use, sharing, adaptation, distribution and reproduction in any medium or format, as long as you give appropriate credit to the original author(s) and the source, provide a link to the Creative Commons license and indicate if changes were made.

The images or other third party material in this chapter are included in the chapter's Creative Commons license, unless indicated otherwise in a credit line to the material. If material is not included in the chapter's Creative Commons license and your intended use is not permitted by statutory regulation or exceeds the permitted use, you will need to obtain permission directly from the copyright holder.

Works Mentioned

Aaron, David H. "The First Loose Plank: On the Rejection of Reason in the Pittsburgh Platforms of 1999", *CCAR Journal* 191 (2001): 87–116.

Abulof, Uriel. 2022. "Samson, unchained: Biblical undercurrents in the political sentiments of Israeli Jews". *Israel Studies* 27(2): 1257–144.

Acevedo, Juan. *Alphanumeric Cosmology From Greek Into Arabic: The Idea of Stoicheia Through the Medieval Mediterranean* (Tübingen: Mohr Siebeck, 2020).

Adelman, Rachel. *The Return of the Repressed: Pirqe de-Rabbi Eliezer and the Pseudepigrapha* (Leiden & Boston: Brill, 2009).

Adler, Rachel. *Engendering Judaism: An Inclusive Theology and Ethics* (Philadelphia: Jewish Publication Society, 1999).

Adler, Rachel, and Robin Podolsky. "Sexuality, Autonomy and Community in the Writings of Eugene Borowitz", *Journal of Jewish Ethics* 1.1 (2015): 114–136.

Afterman, Gedaliah. *Understanding the Theology of Israel's Extreme Religious Right: 'The Chosen People' and 'The Land of Israel' from the Bible to the Expulsion from Gush Katif* (PhD Thesis, University of Melbourne, 2007).

Agamben, Giorgio. *Opus Dei: An Archaeology of Duty* (Stanford: Stanford University Press, 2013).

Ahad Ha'am. "Transvaluation of Values" (1898), in *Words of Fire: Selected Essays of Ahad Ha'am* (London: Notting Hill Editions, 2015), 100–124.

Aitken, James K., Hector M. Patmore, and Ishay Rosen-Zvi (eds.). *The Evil Inclination in Early Judaism and Christianity* (Cambridge: Cambridge University Press, 2021).

Akbar, Kaveh. *Martyr!* (New York: Alfred A. Knopf, 2024, Kindle edition).

Albo, Joseph. *Sefer Ha-ʿikkarim, Book of Principles* (Isaac Husik, transl.) (Philadelphia: Jewish Publication Society of America, 1929–30).

Allison, Dorothy. *Skin: Talking About Sex, Class & Literature* (Ithaca: Firebrand Books, 1994).
Almog, Yael. *Secularism and Hermeneutics* (Philadelphia: University of Pennsylvania Press, 2019).
Altmann, Alexander. *Moses Mendelssohn: A Biographical Study* (London: Routledge & Kegan Paul, 1973).
Altmann, Alexander. "Do We Need a Jewish Theology?", *Proceedings of the Institute for Distinguished Community Leaders* (Waltham: Brandeis University, 1986): 1–3.
Altmann, Alexander. "Franz Rosenzweig on History", in: Paul Mendes-Flohr (ed.), *The Philosophy of Franz Rosenzweig* (Hanover: University Press of New England, 1988), 124–137.
Altmann, Alexander. "The Encounter of Faith and Reason in the Western Tradition and Its Significance Today", *Journal of Religion* 101.3 (2021): 326–350.
Amir, Merav. "On The Border of Indeterminacy: The Separation Wall in East Jerusalem", *Geopolitics* 16.4 (2011): 768–792.
Amir, Yehoshua. "Gishot Laraayon Bechirat Yisrael Baet Hachadasha", in: Shmuel Almog & Michael Hed (eds.), *Ra'ayon Habechira* (Jerusalem: Zalman Shazar, 1991).
Amit, Aaron. "The Curious Case of Tefillin: A Study In Ritual Blessings", *Jewish Studies Quarterly* 15 (2008): 269–288.
Anderson, Wendy Love. "Parents Eating Their Children – The Torah's Curse and Its Undertones in Medieval Interpretation." *TheTorah.com*, 2018. https://www.thetorah.com/article/parents-eating-their-children-the-torahs-curse-and-its-undertones-in-medieval-interpretation.
Ardam, Jacquelyn. "The ABCs of Conceptual Writing", *Comparative Literature Studies* 51.1 (2014): 132–158.
Arendt, Hannah. *The Origins of Totalitarianism* (New York: Meridian, 1958).
Arendt, Hannah. "Walter Benjamin: 1892-1940", in: Walter Benjamin, *Illuminations* [Hannah Arendt, ed.], (New York: Schocken, 1969), 1–58.
Armstrong, A. H. *Plotinian and Christian Studies* (London: Variorum Reprints, 1979).
Assis, Elie. "The Alphabetic Acrostic in the Book of Lamentations", *Catholic Biblical Quarterly* 69.4 (2007): 710–724.
Assmann, Jan. "A Dialogue Between Self and Soul – Papyrus Berlin 3014", in: Albert I. Baumgarten, Jan Assmannand and Guy Stroumsa (eds.), *Self, Soul and Body in Religious Experience* (Leiden: Brill, 1998), 384–403.
Athas, George. "Setting the Record Straight: What Are We Making of the Tel Dan Inscription?", *Journal of Semitic Studies*, 51.2 (2006): 241–256.
Atlan, Henri. "Chosen People", in: Arthur A. Cohen and Paul Mendes-Flohr (eds.), *Contemporary Jewish Religious Thought* (New York: Charles Scribner's Sons, 2009), 55–59.

Avis, Paul. *God and the Creative Imagination: Metaphor, Symbol, and Myth in Religion and Theology* (London: Routledge, 1999).
Avishai Margalit, *The Decent Society* (Naomi Goldblum, transl,) (Cambridge: Harvard University Press, 1998).
Baeck, Leo. *The Essence of Judaism* (New York: Schocken, 1961).
Baeck, Leo. *This People Israel: The Meaning of Jewish Existence* (Philadelphia: Jewish Publication Society, 1965).
Baeck, Leo. *The Pharisees, and Other Essays* (New York: Schocken, 1966).
Barak-Gorodetsky, David. *Judah Magnes: The Prophetic Politics of a Religious Binationalist* (Merav Datan, transl.) (Lincoln: University of Nebraska Press, 2021).
Bar-Ilan, Meir. "Hazman Lesugav BeBreshit Aleph", *Mo'ed* 14 (2004): 1–18.
Bar-On, Shraga and Yakir Paz. "Adon Hakol Veyotser Breshit: Aleinu Leshabeach Ketfilla Anti-Binitarit", *World Union of Jewish Studies* 52 (2017): 19–46.
Baroni, Antonio. "Alphabetic vs. Non-Alphabetic Writing: Linguistic Fit and Natural Tendencies", *Rivista di Linguistica* 23.2 (2011): 127–159.
Barrett, Anthony A. *Caligula: The Corruption of Power* (London & New York: Batsford, 1989).
Batnitzky, Leora. "The Philosophical Import of Carnal Israel: Hermeneutics and the Structure of Rosenzweig's *Star*", *Journal of Jewish Thought and Philosophy* 9 (1999): 127–153.
Batnitzky, Leora. *Idolatry and Representation: The Philosophy of Franz Rosenzweig Reconsidered* (Princeton: Princeton University Press, 2000).
Batnitzky, Leora. *How Judaism Became a Religion: An Introduction to Modern Jewish Thought* (Princeton: Princeton University Press, 2011).
Bauman, Zygmunt. "Morality in the Age of Contingency", in: Paul Heelas, Scott Lash, and Paul M. Morris [eds.], *Detraditionalization: Critical Reflection on Authority and Identity* (Cambridge: Blackwell, 1996), 49–58.
Bauman, Zygmunt. *Liquid Times: Living in an Age of Uncertainty* (Cambridge: Polity Press, 2007).
Bauman, Zygmunt. *Culture In a Liquid Modern World* (Cambridge: Polity, 2011).
Baumgarten, Albert I. "Rabbi Judah I and His Opponents", *Journal for the Study of Judaism* 12.2 (1981): 135–172.
Bayfield, Tony. *Sinai, Law and Responsible Autonomy: Reform Judaism and the Halakhic Tradition* (London: Reform Synagogues of Great Britain, 1993).
Bayfield, Tony. *Being Jewish Today: Confronting the Real Issues* (London: Bloomsbury, 2019).
Beecher, Willis J. "Torah: A Word-Study in the Old Testament", *Journal of Biblical Literature* 24.1 (1905): 1–16.
Be'er, Haim. *El Hamakom Sheharuach Holekh* (Tel Aviv: Am Oved, 2010).
Beinart, Peter. *The Crisis of Zionism* (New York: Times Books & Henry Holt, 2012).
Beiser, Frederick C. *Hermann Cohen: An Intellectual Biography* (Oxford: Oxford University Press, 2018).

Ben-Amos, Dan. "The 'Myth' of Jewish Humor", *Western Folklore* 32.2 (1973): 112–131.
Ben-Dov, Jonathan. "Apocalyptic Temporality. The Force of the Here and Now", *Hebrew Bible and Ancient Israel* 3.5 (2016): 289–303.
Ben-Dov, Jonathan. "Time and Natural Law in Jewish-Hellenistic Writings", in: Jonathan Ben-Dov and Lutz Doering (eds.), *The Construction of Time in Antiquity* (Cambridge: Cambridge University Press, 2017), 9–30.
Ben-Gurion, David. "Atzmaut Tarbutit", 1953. *The Ben-Yehuda Project.* https://benyehuda.org/read/37369.
Ben-Hayim, Zeev. "Masorah Umasoret," *Leshonenu* 21.3–4 (1957):283–292.
Benjamin, Jessica. *The Bonds of Love: Psychoanalysis, Feminism, and the Problem of Domination* (New York: Pantheon, 1988).
Benjamin, Mara H. *The Obligated Self: Maternal Subjectivity and Jewish Thought* (Bloomington: Indiana University Press, 2018).
Benjamin, Walter. "On Language as Such and the Language of Man", in: Peter Demetz (ed.) *Reflections* (New York: Schocken, 1970), 314–322.
Benovitz, Moshe. *Kol Nidre: Studies in the Development of Rabbinic Votive Institutions* (Atlanta: Scholars Press, 1998).
Ben-Sasson, Haim Hillel. "'The Name of God and the Linguistic Theory of the Kabbalah' Revisited", *Journal of Religion* 98.1 (2018): 1–28.
Benun, Ronald. "Evil and the Disruption of Order: A Structural Analysis of the Acrostics in the First Book of Psalms", *Journal of Hebrew Scriptures* 6 (2006): 1–30.
Berger, John. *Ways of Seeing* (London: British Broadcasting Corporation and Penguin Books, 1972).
Berger, Peter. *Redeeming Laughter: The Comic Dimension of Human Experience* (New York: Walter de Gruyter, 1997).
Berger, Peter and Anton Zijderveld. *In Praise of Doubt: How to Have Convictions Without Becoming a Fanatic* (New York: HarperOne/HarperCollins, 2009).
Bergman, Ronen. *Rise and Kill First: The Secret History of Israel's Targeted Assassinations* (New York: Random House, 2018).
Berlin, Adele. "The Rhetoric of Psalm 145", in: Ann Kort and Scott Morschauser (eds.), *Biblical and Related Studies Presented to Samuel Iwry* (Winona Lake: Eisenbrauns, 1985), 17–22.
Berlinerblau, Jacques. *The Vow and the "Popular Religious Groups" of Ancient Israel: A Philological and Sociological Inquiry* (Sheffield: Sheffield Academic Press, 1996).
Biale, David. *Power and Powerlessness in Jewish History* (New York: Schocken, 1986).
Biale, David. *Not In The Heavens: The Tradition of Jewish Secular Thought* (Princeton: Princeton University Press, 2011).
Bialik, Hayim Nachman. *Revealment and Concealment: Five Essays* (Jerusalem: Ibis, 2000).

Bielik-Robson, Agata. "The God of Myth Is Not Dead – Modernity and Its Cryptotheologies, A Jewish Perspective", in: Willem Styfhals and Stéphane Symons (eds.), *Genealogies of the Secular: The Making of Modern German Thought* (Albany: State University of New York Press, 2019), 51–80.

Bigman, David. "Katav Leshem Malchut She'eina Hogenet", *Ma'agalim* 6 (2010): 19–35.

Birnbaum, David and Martin S. Cohen (eds.). *Kaddish* (New York: New Paradigm Matrix, 2016).

Birnbaum, David and Martin S. Cohen (eds.). *Modeh Ani: The Prayer of Gratitude* (New York: New Paradigm Matrix, 2017).

Blacker, David J. *Democratic Education Stretched Thin – How Complexity Challenges a Liberal Ideal* (Albany: State University of New York Press, 2007).

Blair, Judit M. *De-Demonising the Old Testament*. PhD Thesis, University of Edinburgh, 2008.

Bleich, J. David. *With Perfect Faith: The Foundations of Jewish Belief* (New York: Ktav, 1983).

Blidstein, Gerald J. "*Halakhah* - The Governing Norm", *Jewish Political Studies Review* 8. 1/ 2 (1996): 37–80.

Bloch, Yigal. "Iyun Mechudash Bemashmaut Hamunach Segulah", *Shnaton LeCheker Hamikra Vehamizrach Hakadum* 21 (2012): 111–140.

Bloom, Harold. *The Anxiety of Influence: A Theory of Poetry* (New York: Oxford University Press, 1973).

Bloom, Harold. "Freud: Frontier Concepts, Jewishness, and Interpretation", *American Imago* 48.1 (1991): 135–152.

Blumenthal, David R. *Facing the Abusing God: A Theology of Protest* (Louisville: Westminster/John Know Press, 1993).

Bock, Kenneth E. *Human Nature Mythology* (Urbana: University of Illinois Press, 1994).

Bokser, Baruch M. *The Origins of the Seder: The Passover Rite and Early Rabbinic Judaism* (Berkeley: University of California Press, 1984).

Borowitz, Eugene B. *How Can a Jew Speak of Faith Today?* (Philadelphia: Westminster Press, 1969).

Borowitz, Eugene B. "Hope Jewish and Hope Secular, A Response to Jürgen Moltmann", in: Eugene B. Borowitz, *Exploring Jewish Ethics: Papers on Covenantal Responsibility* (Detroit: Wayne State University Press, 1990), pp.145–160.

Borowitz, Eugene B. *Renewing the Covenant: A Theology for the Postmodern Jew* (Philadelphia: Jewish Publication Society, 1991).

Borowitz, Eugene. *Judaism After Modernity: Papers from a Decade of Fruition* (Lanham: University Press of America, 1999).

Borowitz, Eugene B. *Studies in the Meaning of Judaism* (Philadelphia: Jewish Publication Society, 2002).

Botha, Phil J. "Psalm 34 and the Ethics of the Editors of the Psalter", in: Dirk J. Human (ed.), *Psalmody and Poetry in Old Testament Ethics* (New York: T & T Clark, 2012), 56–75.

Bounds, Elizabeth M. *Coming Together/Coming Apart: Religion, Community, and Modernity* (New York: Routledge, 1997).

Bourougiannis, Giorgos. "The transmission of the alphabet to the Aegean", in: Łukasz Niesiołowski-Spanò and Marek Węcowski (eds.), *Change, Continuity and Connectivity: North-Eastern Mediterranean At The Turn of the Bronze Age and in the Early Iron Age* (Wiesbaden: Harrassowitz, 2018): 235–257.

Bowring, John. *A Memorial Volume of Sacred Poetry* (London: Longmans, Green, Reader & Dyer, 1873).

Boyes, Philip J. and Philippa M. Steele (eds.). *Understanding Relations Between Scripts II* (Oxford & Philadelphia: Oxbow Books, 2020).

Boyarin, Daniel. "The Eye in the Torah: Ocular Desire in Midrashic Hermeneutic", *Critical Inquiry* 16.3 (1990): 532–550.

Boyarin, Daniel. *Carnal Israel: Reading Sex in Talmudic Culture* (Berkeley: University of California Press, 1993).

Boyarin, Daniel. *A Radical Jew: Paul and the Politics of Identity* (Berkeley: University of California Press, 1994).

Boyarin, Daniel. *Unheroic Conduct: The Rose of Heterosexuality and the Invention of the Jewish Man* (Berkeley: University of California Press, 1997).

Boyarin, Daniel. *Border Lines – The Partition of Judaeo-Christianity* (Philadelphia: University of Pennsylvania Press, 2004).

Boyarin, Daniel. *Socrates and the Fat Rabbis* (Chicago & London: University of Chicago Press, 2009).

Boyarin, Daniel. *The No-State Solution: A Jewish Manifesto* (New Haven: Yale University Press, 2023).

Braiterman, Zachary. *(God) After Auschwitz: Tradition and Change in Post-Holocaust Jewish Thought* (Princeton: Princeton University Press, 1998).

Braiterman, Zachary. "The Emergence of a Modern Religion: Moses Mendelssohn, Neoclassicism, and Ceremonial Aesthetics", in: Christian Wiese and Martina Urban (eds.), *German-Jewish Thought Between Religion and Politics* (Berlin: de Gruyter, 2012), 11–29.

Brand, Joshua. "Aspaklaria (Perek Misefer Al Klei Zechuchit)", in: *Sefer Zikaron De Vries*, (Jerusalem: University of Tel Aviv Press, 1969), 110–118.

Braude, William G. and Israel J. Kapstein (transl.). *Tanna debe Eliyyahu: The Lore of the School of Elijah* (Philadelphia: Jewish Publication Society, 1981).

Brettler, Marc Zvi. *God Is King: Understanding an Israelite Metaphor* (Sheffield: JSOT Press, 1989).

Brettler, Marc Zvi. *How To Read The Jewish Bible* (Oxford & New York: Oxford University Press, 2007).

Breuer, Edward. "Rabbinic Law and Spirituality in Mendelssohn's 'Jerusalem'", *Jewish Quarterly Review* 86.3/4 (1996): 299–321.
Brin, Gershon. *The Concept of Time in the Bible and the Dead Sea Scrolls* (Leiden: Brill, 2001).
Brody, Samuel Hayim. *Martin Buber's Theopolitics* (Bloomington: Indiana University Press, 2018).
Brown, John Pairman. "Proverb-Book, Gold-Economy, Alphabet", *Journal of Biblical Literature* 100.2 (1981): 169–191.
Buber, Martin. "Love of God and the Idea of Deity", in: *Eclipse of God: Studies in the Relation Between Religion and Philosophy* (New York: Harper, 1957), 47–62.
Buber, Martin. *Paths in Utopia* (R.F.C. Hull, transl.) (Boston: Beacon Press, 1950).
Buber, Martin. *I and Thou* (Ronald Gregor Smith, transl.) (New York: Scribner, 1958).
Buber, Martin. *Israel and the World: Essays in a Time of Crisis* (New York: Schocken, 1963).
Buber, Martin. *Between Man and Man* (New York: Macmillan, 1965).
Buber, Martin. "The Election of Israel: A Biblical Inquiry", in: Nahum N. Glatzer (ed.), *On The Bible* (New York: Schocken, 1982), 80–92.
Buber, Martin. *On Intersubjectivity and Cultural Creativity* (S.N. Eisenstadt, ed.) (Chicago & London: Chicago University Press, 1992).
Buck-Morss, Susan. *The Dialectics of Seeing: Walter Benjamin and the Arcades Project* (Cambridge: MIT Press, 1989).
Butler, Judith. *Undoing Gender* (New York: Routledge, 2004).
Butler, Judith. *Giving an Account of Oneself* (New York: Fordham University Press, 2005).
Butler, Judith. *Parting Ways: Jewishness and the Critique of Zionism* (New York: Columbia Press, 2012).
Calderon, Ruth. *Alfa Beta Talmudi: Osef Prati* (Tel-Aviv: Miskal – Yedioth Ahronoth, 2014).
Caputo, John D. *The Insistence of God: A Theology of Perhaps* (Bloomington: Indiana University Press, 2013).
Caputo, John D. *Cross and Cosmos: A Theology of Difficult Glory* (Bloomington: Indiana University Press, 2019).
Carmichael, Calum. "The Origin of the Scapegoat Ritual", *Vetus Testamentum* 50.2 (2000): 167–182.
Carriero, John. "Descartes (and Spinoza) on Intellectual Experience and Skepticism", *Roczniki Filozoficzne* 68.2 (2020): 21–42.
Cartledge, Tony W. *Vows in the Hebrew Bible and the Ancient Near East* (Sheffield: JSOT Press, 1992).
Ceresko, Anthony R. "The ABCs of Wisdom in Psalm XXXIV", *Vetus Testamentum* 35.1 (1985): 99–104.

Ceresko, Anthony R. "Endings and beginnings: Alphabetic thinking and the Shaping of Psalms 106 and 150", *Catholic Biblical Quarterly,* 68.1 (2006): 32–46.
Chabon, Michael. "Those People, Over There." *Tablet,* May 30, 2018. https://www.tabletmag.com/sections/arts-letters/articles/michael-chabon-commencement.
Chaucer, Geoffrey. *Complete Works* (Oxford: Clarendon Press, 1912).
Chernick, Michael. *A Great Voice That Did Not Cease: The Growth of the Rabbinic Canon and Its Interpretation* (Cincinnati: Hebrew Union College Press, 2009).
Cherry, Shai. *Coherent Judaism: Constructive Theology, Creation & Halakhah* (Boston: Academic Studies Press, 2020).
Cirelli, Anthony. "Facing the Abyss: Hans Urs von Balthasar's Reading of Anxiety", *New Blackfriars* 92.1042 (2011): 705–723.
Cohen, Arthur A. *An Arthur A. Cohen Reader* (David Stern and Paul Mendes-Flohr, eds.) (New York: Charles Scribner's Sons, 1986).
Cohen, Aryeh. *Justice in the City* (Brighton: Academic Studies Press, 2012).
Cohen, Hermann. *Reason and Hope: Selections from the Jewish Writings of Hermann Cohen* (Eva Jospe, transl.) (New York: W.W. Norton, 1971).
Cohen, Hermann. *Religion of Reason Out of the Sources of Judaism* (Atlanta: Scholars Press, 1995).
Cohen, Hermann. *Spinoza on State and Religion, Judaism and Christianity* (Jerusalem: Shalem, 2014).
Cohen, Hermann. *Writings on Neo-Kantianism and Jewish Philosophy* (Samuel Moyn and Robert S. Schine, eds.) (Waltham: Brandeis University Press, 2021).
Cohen, Marc A. "The Movement from Ethics to Social Relationships for Levinas, and Why Decency Obscures Obligation", *International Journal for Philosophy of Religion* 76 (2016): 89–100.
Cohen, Mordecai D. (ed.). *Shevarim Neesafim Leshirah* (Israel: Yoav Itamar, 2017).
Cohen, Sarah Blacher (ed.). *Jewish Wry: Essays on Jewish Humor* (Bloomington: Indiana University Press, 1987).
Cohn, Yehudah B. *Tangled up in Text: Tefillin and the Ancient World*, Brown Judaic Studies 351 (Providence: Society of Biblical Literature, 2008).
Cohon, Samuel S. "Original Sin", *Hebrew Union College Annual* 21 (1948): 275–330.
Coogan, Michael David. "Alphabets and Elements", *Bulletin of the American School of Oriental Research* 216 (1974): 61–63.
Cooper, Levi. "The Assimilation of Tikkun Olam", *Jewish Political Studies Review* 25. 3/4 (2013): 10–42.
Copenhaver, Brian and Daniel Stein Kokin. "Egidio da Viterbo's *Book on Hebrew Letters*: Christian Kabbalah in Papal Rome", *Renaissance Quarterly* 67 (2014): 1–42.

Coward, Harold and Toby Foshay (eds.). *Derrida and Negative Theology* (Albany: State University of New York Press, 1992).
Crary, Jonathan. *Techniques of the Observer: On Vision and Modernity in the Nineteenth Century* (Cambridge: MIT Press, 1992).
Cross, Frank Moore. "A Response to Zakovitch", in: Susan Niditch (ed.), *Text and Tradition: The Hebrew Bible and Folklore* (Atlanta: Scholars Press, 1990), 99–104.
Cuddihy, John Murray. *The Ordeal of Civility: Freud, Marx, Levi-Strauss and the Jewish Struggle With Modernity* (New York: Basic Books, 1974).
Cypel, Sylvain. *Walled: Israeli Society at an Impasse* (New York: Other Press, 2006).
Dan, Joseph. "Samael, Lilith, and the Concept of Evil in Early Kabbalah", *AJS Review* 5 (1980): 17–40.
Dan, Joseph. "The Language of Creation and Its Grammar", in: Christoph Elsas (ed.), *Tradition und Translation: zum Problem der interkulturellen Übersetzbarkeit religiöser Phänomene* (Berlin & New York: de Gruyter, 1994), 42–63.
Dan, Joseph. "The Language of the Mystics in Medieval Germany", in: Karl Erich Grozinger and Joseph Dan (eds.), *Mysticism, Magic and Kabbalah in Ancient Judaism* (Berlin & New York: Walter de Gruyter, 1995), 6–27.
Dan, Joseph. *Jewish Mysticism, Volume III: The Modern Period* (Northvale: Jason Aaronson, 1999).
Dan, Joseph (ed.). *The Heart and the Fountain: An Anthology of Jewish Mystical Experiences* (Oxford: Oxford University Press, 2002).
Dan, Joseph. "Otiot Derabbi Akiva Vetfisat Halashon Hachadashah", *Daat* 55 (2005): 5–30.
Daniels, Peter T. and William Bright (eds.), *The World's Writing Systems* (New York & Oxford: Oxford University Press, 1996).
De Kerckhove, Derrick and Charles J. Lumsden (eds.). *The Alphabet and the Brain: The Lateralization of Writing* (Berlin & Heidelberg: Springer, 1988).
Deleniv, Sofia. "The 'Me' Illusion: How Your Brain Conjures Up Your Sense of Self", *New Scientist* (5 September 2018): https://www.newscientist.com/article/mg23931940-100-the-me-illusion-how-your-brain-conjures-up-your-sense-of-self/.
De Looze, Laurence. *The Letter and the Cosmos: How The Alphabet Has Shaped the Western View of the World* (Toronto: University of Toronto Press, 2016).
Demsky, Aaron. "The Interface of Oral and Written Traditions in Ancient Israel: The Case of Abecedaries", in: Christophe Rico and Claudia Attucci (eds.), *Origins of the Alphabet: Proceedings of the First Polis Institute Interdisciplinary Conference* (Newcastle upon Tyne: Cambridge Scholars Press, 2015) 23–31.
Denis, Mathieu and Ulrich Ufer, "Of Modernity's Boundaries, Border-Runners and Toll-Keepers", *Eurostudia* 7.1–2 (2011): 199–211.

De Roo, Jacqueline C.R. "Was the Goat for Azazel Destined for the Wrath of God?", *Biblica* 81.2 (2000): 233–242.
Derrida, Jacques. *Limited Inc.* (Evanston IL: Northwestern University Press, 1988).
Derrida, Jacques and Michal Guvrin. *Guf Tefillah* (Tel Aviv: Hakibbutz Hameuchad, 2012).
De Simone, Pia. "Plato's Use of the Term *Stoicheion*. Origin and Implications", *Archai* 30 (2020): 1–18.
Deutsch, Gotthard. *Philosophy of Jewish History* (Cincinnati: Bloch, 1897).
Diamond, James A. "The Post-Secular: A Jewish Perspective", *Cross Currents* 53.4 (2004): 580–606.
Diamond, James A. *Jewish Theology Unbound* (Oxford: Oxford University Press, 2018).
Dickinson, Colby. "Citing 'Whatever' Authority: The Ethics of Quotation in the Work of Giorgio Agamben", retrieved from *Loyola eCommons, Theology Faculty Publications and Other Works*.
Dinur, Avner. "Secular Theology as a Challenge for Jewish Atheists", *Melilah: Manchester Journal of Jewish Studies* 12 (2015): 131–144.
Diringer, David. *Writing* (London: Thames & Hudson, 1962).
Diringer, David. *The Alphabet: A Key to the History of Mankind*, third edition (London: Hutchinson, 1968).
Dolansky, Shawna. *Why Can Women's Vows Be Vetoed?*, TheTorah.com, 2016. https://www.thetorah.com/article/why-can-womens-vows-be-vetoed.
Dorrien, Gary. "The Crisis and Necessity of Liberal Theology", *American Journal of Theology and Philosophy*, 30.1 (2009), 3–22.
Drucker, Johanna. *The Alphabetic Labyrinth: The Letters in History and Imagination* (London: Thames & Hudson, 1995).
Eagleton, Terry. *Reason, Faith, and Revolution: Reflections on the God Debate* (New Haven: Yale University Press, 2009).
Ebeling, Gerhard. *Introduction to a Theological Theory of Language* (London: Collins, 1973).
Eco, Umberto. "Ur-Fascism", in: *Five Moral Pieces* (London: Secker and Warburg, 2001), 65–88.
Editors of Commentary Magazine. *The Condition of Jewish Belief* (New York: Macmillan, 1966).
Edwardes, Martin P.J. *The Origins of Self: An Anthropological Perspective* (London: UCL Press, 2019).
Ehrlich, Uri. *The Nonverbal Language of Prayer: A New Approach to Jewish Liturgy* (Tübingen: Mohr Siebeck, 2004).
Eisen, Arnold M. *The Chosen People in America: A Study in Jewish Religious Ideology* (Bloomington: Indiana University Press, 1983).
Eisen, Arnold M. "Divine Legislation As 'Ceremonial Script': Mendelssohn on the Commandments", *AJS Review* 15.2 (1990): 239–267.

Eisen, Arnold M. *Rethinking Modern Judaism – Ritual, Commandment, Community* (Chicago: University of Chicago Press, 1998).

Eisen, Robert. *Gersonides on Provenance, Covenant and the Chosen People: A Study in Medieval Jewish Philosophy and Biblical Commentary* (Albany: State University of New York, 1995).

Eisenstadt, Oona. "Rhetorical Subterfuge: A Reading of Levinas's 'Promised Land of Permitted Land'", *Levinas Studies* 13 (2019): 27–42.

Eliot, Thomas Stearns. "Tradition and the Individual Talent", in: *Selected Prose of T.S. Eliot* (Frank Kermode, ed.) (New York: Harcourt Brace Jovanovich, 1975), 37–44.

Elizur, Shulamit. "Limkoram Shel Piyutei Selichot", *Tarbiz* 84.4 (2016): 503–542.

Ellenson, David. "History, Memory and Relationship", in: Michael Signer (ed.), *Memory and History in Christianity and Judaism* (Notre Dame: University of Notre Dame Press, 2000), 170–181.

Ellenson, David. "American Jewish Denominationalism: Yesterday, Today, and Tomorrow", *The Reconstructionist* 71.2 (2007a): 5–15.

Ellenson, David. "The Talmudic Principle, 'If One Comes Forth to Slay You, Forestall by Slaying Him,' in Israeli Public Policy: A Responsum by Rabbi Hayyim David Halevi", *Jewish Law Association Studies* 17 (2007b): 73–79.

Ellenson, David. "Eternity and Time", in: Arthur A. Cohen and Paul Mendes-Flohr (eds.), *Contemporary Jewish Religious Thought* (New York: Charles Scribner's Sons, 2009), 189–193.

Ellenson, David. "Antinomianism and Its Responses in the Nineteenth Century", in: Christine Hayes (ed.), *The Cambridge Companion to Judaism and Law* (Cambridge: Cambridge University Press, 2016), 260–286.

Ellenson, David H. "Jewish Legal Interpretation and Moral Values: Two Responsa by Rabbi Hayyim David Halevi on the Obligations of the Israeli Government Towards Its Minority Populations", *CCAR Journal* 48.3 (2001): 5–20.

Ellis, Marc H. *Toward a Jewish Theology of Jewish Liberation* (Maryknoll: Orbis, 1987).

Emerson, Ralph Waldo. "Quotation and Originality", in: *Letters and Social Aims* vol.8 (Boston: J.R. Osgood, 1876), 175–204.

Engel, Amir. "From the *Neue Gemeinschaft* to Bar Kochba: The Jewish *Communitas* or the Idea of Jewish Politics as Messianism", *Religions* 13:1143 (2022).

Epstein, Klonimus Kalman. *Sefer Maor Vashemesh* (Jerusalem, 1988).

Eshel, Hanan and John Strugnell, "Alphabetic Acrostics in Pre-Tannaitic Hebrew", *Catholic Biblical Quarterly* 62 (2000): 441–458.

Fackenheim, Emil L. *Metaphysics and History* (Milwaukee: Marquette University Press, 1961).

Fackenheim, Emil L. *To Mend the World: Foundations of Future Jewish Thought* (New York: Schocken, 1982).

Fackenheim, Emil L. *The Jewish Thought of Emil Fackenheim: A Reader* (Michael L. Morgan, ed.) (Detroit: Wayne State University Press, 1987).

Fackenheim, Emil L. *A Political Philosophy for the State of Israel: Fragments* (Jerusalem: Jerusalem Center for Public Affairs, 1988).

Fagenblat, Michael. "Lacking All Interest: Levinas, Leibowitz, and the Pure Practice of Religion", *Harvard Theological Review* 97/1 (2004): 1–32.

Fagenblat, Michael. *A Covenant of Creatures: Levinas's Philosophy of Judaism* (Stanford: Stanford University Press, 2010).

Fagenblat, Michael (ed.). *Negative Theology as Jewish Modernity* (Bloomington: Indiana University Press, 2017).

Falk, Daniel K. and Angela Kim Harkins. "Early Jewish Prayer", in: Matthias Henzeand Rodney A. Werline, *Early Judaism and Its Modern Interpreters*, Second Edition (Atlanta: SBL Press, 2020), 461–486.

Falk, Marcia. "Notes on Composing New Blessings: Toward a Feminist-Jewish Reconstruction of Prayer", *Journal of Feminist Studies in Religion* 3.1 (1987): 39–53.

Farneth, Molly. "Feminist Jewish Thought as Postliberal Theology", *Modern Theology* 33.1 (2017): 31–46.

Faur, José. "Maba Bitzui Umaba Hegedi Bahalakhah", *Dine Israel* 20–21 (2001): 101–121.

Faur, José. *The Horizontal Society: Understanding the Covenant and Alphabetic Society* (Boston: Emunot, 2008).

Feiner, Shmuel. *Haskalah and History: The Emergence of a Modern Jewish Historical Consciousness* (Oxford & Portland: Littman Library of Jewish Civilization, 2002).

Feiner, Shmuel. *Origins of Jewish Secularization in Eighteenth-Century Europe* (Philadelphia: University of Pennsylvania Press, 2010).

Feldmann Kaye, Miriam. *Jewish Theology for a Postmodern Age* (London: Littman Library of Jewish Civilization, 2019).

Fenton, Paul B. "A Meeting with Maimonides", *Bulletin of the School of Oriental and African Studies* 45.1 (1982): 1–4.

Fenves, Peter. *Arresting Language: From Leibniz to Benjamin* (Stanford: Stanford University Press, 2001).

Feuerbach, Ludwig. *The Essence of Christianity* (George Eliot, transl.) (Amherst: Prometheus Books, 1989).

Fidler, Ruth. "A Wife's Vow - The Husband's Woe? The Case of Hannah and Elkanah (I Samuel 1, 21.23)", *Zeitschrift für die alttestamentliche Wissenschaft* 118.3 (2006): 374–388.

Fine, Steven. "How Do You Know A Jew When You See One? Reflections on Jewish Costume in the Roman World", in: Leonard J. Greenspoon (ed.), *Fashioning Jews: Clothing, Culture and Commerce* (West Lafayette: Purdue University Press, 2013), 19–28.

Finkelstein, Israel and Benjamin Sass. "The West Semitic Alphabet Inscriptions, Late Bronze II to Iron IIA: Archaeological Context, Distribution and Chronology", *Hebrew Bible and Ancient* Israel 2.2 (2013): 149–220.

Finkelstein, Israel and Neil Asher Silberman. *David and Solomon: In Search of the Bible's Sacred Kings and the Roots of the Western Tradition* (New York: Free Press, 2006).

Finkelstein, Louis. *The Pharisees: The Sociological Background of Their Faith* (Philadelphia: Jewish Publication Society of America, 1966).

Finkielkraut, Alain. *In The Name of Humanity: Reflections on the Twentieth Century* (Judith Friedlander, transl.) (New York: Columbia University Press, 2000).

Finnegan, Ruth. *Why Do We Quote? The Culture and History of Quotation* (Cambridge: Open Book, 2011).

Fisch, Menachem. "The Tragic Paradox of Political Zionism", *Telos* 192 (2000): 29–39.

Fischer, Elli. "Michael Chabon's Sacred and Profane Cliché Machine", *Jewish Review of Books,* June 13, 2018. https://jewishreviewofbooks.com/articles/3239/michael-chabons-sacred-and-profane-cliche-machine/#.

Fishbane, Michael. *Sacred Attunement: A Jewish Theology* (Chicago: University of Chicago Press, 2008).

Fisher, Cass. *Contemplative Nation: A Philosophical Account of Jewish Theological Language* (Stanford: Stanford University Press, 2012).

Fisher, Cass. "Jewish Philosophy: Living Language at Its Limits", in Hava Tirosh-Samuelson and Aaron Hughes (eds.), *Jewish Philosophy for the Twenty-First Century: Personal Reflections* (Leiden & Boston: Brill, 2014), 81–100.

Fisher, Cass. "Theological Realism and its Alternatives in Contemporary Jewish Theology", in: Steven Kepnes (ed.), *The Cambridge Companion to Jewish Theology* (Cambridge: Cambridge University Press, 2020), 392–422.

Fixler, Ohad. "Hakos Hachamishit", *Torat Har Etzion* (2014). https://etzion.org.il/he/talmud/seder-moed/massekhet-pesachim/%D7%9B%D7%95%D7%A1-%D7%97%D7%9E%D7%99%D7%A9%D7%99%D7%AA.

Fleishacker, Sam. "Words of the Living God – Part II," *The Book of Doctrines and Opinions: Notes on Jewish Theology and Spirituality*, November 3, 2014. https://kavvanah.blog/2014/11/02/sam-fleischacker-words-of-the-living-god-part-ii/.

Flusser, Vilém. *Does Writing Have a Future?* (Nancy Ann Roth, transl.) (Minneapolis: University of Minnesota Press, 2011).

Fonrobert, Charlotte Elisheva. "Regulating the Human Body: Rabbinic Legal Discourse and the Making of Jewish Gender", in: Charlotte Elisheva Fonrobert and Martin S. Jaffee, *The Cambridge Companion to the Talmud and Rabbinic Literature* (Cambridge: Cambridge University Press, 2007), 270–294.

Foster, Hal (ed.). *Vision and Visuality* (Seattle: Bay View Press, 1988).

Foucault, Michel. *The Order of Things: An Archaeology of the Human Sciences* (New York: Pantheon Books, 1970).

Fox, Marvin. "Prayer in the Thought of Maimonides", in: Gabriel H. Cohn and Harold Fisch (eds.), *Prayer in Judaism: Continuity and Change* (Northvale: Jason Aaronson, 1996), 119–141.

Francis Bacon, *The Advancement of Learning and New Atlantis* (Arthur Johnston, ed.) (Oxford, Clarendon Press, 1974).

Franke, William. "Apophasis and the Turn of Philosophy to Religion: From Neoplatonic Negative Theology to Postmodern Negation of Theology", *International Journal for Philosophy of Religion* 60.1/3 (2006): 61–76.

Frankel, David. "What Did God Write on the Tablets of Stone?", *The Torah.com*, 2018. Retrieved August 3, 2023. https://www.thetorah.com/article/what-did-god-write-on-the-tablets-of-stone.

Fredrick, Sharonah. "Disarticulating Lilith: Notions of God's Evil in Jewish Folklore", in: Ian Frederick Moulton (ed.), *Eroticism in the Middle Ages and the Renaissance: Magic, Marriage, and Midwifery* (Turnhout: Brepols, 2016), 59–82.

Freedman, David Noel. "Acrostics and Metrics in Hebrew Poetry", *Harvard Theological Review* 65.3 (1972): 367–92.

Freedman, David Noel. "Acrostic Poems in the Hebrew Bible: Acrostic and Otherwise", *Catholic Biblical Quarterly* 48.3 (1986): 408–431.

Freehof, Solomon B. "Ceremonial Creativity Among the Ashkenazim", *Jewish Quarterly Review* 57 (1967): 210–224.

Freud, Sigmund. *Case Histories 1* (Alix and James Strachey, transl.) (London: Penguin, 1990).

Freud, Sigmund and Lou Andreas-Salomé. *Letters* (New York: Harcourt Brace Jovanovich, 1972).

Freudenthal, Gad. "Stoic Physics in the Writings of R. Sa'adia Ga'on al-Fayyumi and Its Aftermath in Medieval Jewish Mysticism", *Arabic Sciences and Philosophy* 6 (1996): 113–136.

Freudenthal, Gad. "Maimonides' Philosophy of Science", in: Kenneth Seeskin (ed.), *The Cambridge Companion to Maimonides* (New York: Cambridge University Press, 2005), 134–166.

Freudenthal, Gideon. "The Remedy to Linguistic Skepticism. Judaism as a Language of Action'" *Naharaim* 4.1 (2010): 67–76.

Freudenthal, Gideon. "Moses Mendelssohn: Iconoclast", in: Reinier Munk (ed.), *Moses Mendelssohn's Metaphysis and Aesthetics* (Dordrecht: Springer, 2011), 351–372.

Freudenthal, Gideon. *No Religion Without Idolatry* (Notre Dame: University of Notre Dame Press, 2012).

Freudenthal, Gideon. "Idolatry Everywhere, Idolaters Nowhere", in Michah Gottlieb and Charles H. Manekin (eds.), *Moses Mendelssohn: Enlightenment, Religion, Politics, Nationalism* (Bethesda: University Press of Maryland, 2015), 205–235.

Friedland Ben Arza, Sara. *Yehi: Milim Kema'asim* (Jerusalem: Bialik Institute, 2015).
Friedman, Marilyn. "Relational Autonomy and Independence", in: Andrea Veltman and Mark Piper, *Autonomy, Oppression, and Gender* (New York: Oxford University Press, 2014), 42–60.
Friedman, Nathan Zvi. "Din Rodef Lemechablim!", *Shanah BeShanah* (1972). https://www.daat.ac.il/he-il/halacha/modern/fridman-rodef.htm.
Friedmann, Georges. *The End of the Jewish People?* (Eric Mosbacher, transl.) (Garden City: Doubleday, 1968).
Fromm, Erich. *The Revolution of Hope: Toward a Humanized Technology* (New York: Harper & Row, 1968).
Frumkin, Shlomit Cooper. "New Insights Into Yona Wallach's Poem 'Tefillin': *Sefer Or Zaru'a* and Shabbtai Zvi", *Zutot* 17.1 (2019): 37–48.
Frymer-Kensky, Tikva. "Biblical Voices on Chosenness", in: Raphael Jospe, Truman G. Madsen and Seth Ward (eds.), *Covenant and Chosenness in Judaism and Mormonism* (Madison: Fairleigh Dickinson University Press, 2001), 23–32.
Frymer-Kensky, Tikva. "Revelation revealed: The Doubt of Torah", in: Peter Ochs and Nancy Levene (eds.), *Textual Reasonings: Jewish Philosophy and Text Study at the End of the Twentieth Century* (Grand Rapids: Eerdmans, 2003), 68–75.
Funkenstein, Amos. "An Escape from History: Rosenzweig on the Destiny of Judaism", *History and Memory* 2.2 (1990): 117–135.
Gafni, Hanan. *Pshuta Shel Mishnah* (Jerusalem: Hakibbutz Hameuchad, 2011).
Garber, Marjorie. *Quotation Marks* (New York & London: Routledge, 2003).
Geertz, Clifford. *Local Knowledge: Further Essays in Interpretive Anthropology* (New York: Basic Books, 1983).
Geiger, Abraham. *Judaism and Its History* (Maurice Meyer, transl.) (New York: Thalmessinger & Cahn, 1866).
Gelb, Ignace J. *A Study of Writing*, revised edition (Chicago: University of Chicago Press, 1962).
Geller, Jay. "Spinoza's Election of the Jews: The Problem of Jewish Existence", *Jewish Social Studies: History, Culture, Society* 12.1 (2005): 39–63.
Gellman, Jerome. "Theological Realism", *International Journal for Philosophy of Religion* 12.1 (1981): 17–27.
Gellman, Jerome. *God's Kindness Has Overwhelmed Us – A Contemporary Doctrine of the Jews as God's Chosen People* (Boston: Academic Studies Press, 2012).
Gellman, Jerome. *Perfect Goodness and the God of the Jews: A Contemporary Jewish Theology* (Boston: Academic Studies Press, 2018).
Gellman, Jerome. "Jewish Chosenness – A Contemporary Approach", in: Alon Goshen-Gottstein (ed.), *Judaism's Challenge: Election, Divine Love, and Human Enmity* (Boston: Academic Studies Press, 2020), 71–82.
Gershon, Stuart Weinberg. *Kol Nidrei: Its Origin, Development and Significance* (Northvale: Jason Aronson, 1994).

Gesundheit, Benny. "Rav Utalmid She'einam Hagunim", *Tchumin* 21 (2001): 198–206.

Giffone, Benjamin D. "A 'Perfect' Poem: The Use of the Qatal Verbal Form in Biblical Acrostics", *Hebrew Studies* 51 (2010): 49–72.

Ginsburgh, Yitzchak. *The Alef-Beit: Jewish Thought Revealed Though the Hebrew Letters* (Northvale: Jason Aronson, 1995).

Ginzberg, Louis. "Beno shel Samael", *Hagoren* 9 (1913): 38–41.

Ginzberg, Louis. *The Legends of the Jews* (Vol. 3) (Philadelphia: Jewish Publication Society of America, 1968).

Girard, René. *Things Hidden Since the Foundation of the World* (Stephen Bann and Michael Metteer, transl.) (Stanford: Stanford University Press, 1987).

Gisha. "Gaza up Close." June 28, 2023. https://features.gisha.org/gaza-up-close/.

Gitlin, Todd and Liel Leibovitz, *The Chosen Peoples: America, Israel and the Ordeals of Divine Election* (New York: Simon & Schuster, 2010).

Goldenberg, Naomi R. "Anger in the Body: Feminism, Religion and Kleinian Psychoanalytic Theory", *Journal of Feminist Studies in Religion* 2.2 (1986): 39–49.

Goldin, Judah. "Several Sidelights of a Torah Education in Tannaite and Early Amoraic Times", in: Haym Zalman Dimitrovsky (ed.), *Exploring the Talmud* (New York: Ktav, 1976), 176–191.

Goldstein, Jeffrey H. and Paul E. McGhee (ed.). *The Psychology of Humor: Theoretical Perspectives and Empirical Issues* (New York: Academic Press, 1972).

Goldwasser, Orly. "How The Alphabet Was Born from Hieroglyphs", *Biblical Archaeology Review* 36.2 (2010): 40–53.

Goldwasser, Orly. "The Advantage of Cultural Periphery: The Invention of the Alphabet in Sinai (circa 1840 B.C.E.)" in: Rakefet Sela-Sheffy and Gideon Toury (eds.), *Culture Contacts and the Making of Cultures* (Tel Aviv: Tel Aviv University Unit of Culture Research, 2011), 255–321.

Goldwasser, Orly. "The Invention of the Alphabet: On 'Lost Papyri' and the Egyptian 'Alphabet'", in: Christophe Rico and Claudia Attucci (eds.), *Origins of the Alphabet: Proceedings of the First Polis Institute Interdisciplinary Conference* (Newcastle upon Tyne: Cambridge Scholars Press, 2015), 124–140.

Goldy, Robert G. *The Emergence of Jewish Theology in America* (Bloomington & Indianapolis: Indiana University Press, 1990).

Golinkin, David. "Prayers for the Government and the State of Israel", *The Shechter Institutes*, May 13, 2006. https://schechter.edu/prayers-for-the-government-and-the-state-of-israel-yom-haatzmaut-5766/.

Golinkin, David. *The Status of Women in Jewish Law: Responsa* (Jerusalem: Schechter Institute, 2012).

Goodman, Saul L. (ed.). *The Faith of Secular Jews* (New York: Ktav, 1976).

Goody, Jack. *The Interface Between the Written and the Oral* (Cambridge: Cambridge University Press, 1987).

Gordis, Robert. "Quotations in Biblical, Oriental and Rabbinic Literature", *Hebrew Union College Annual* 22 (1949): 157–219.

Gordis, Robert. "Virtual Quotations in Job, Sumer and Qumran", *Vetus Testamentum* 31 (1981): 410–427.

Goshen-Gottstein, Alon. "A Kingdom of Priests and a Holy Nation", in: Alon Goshen-Gottstein (ed.), *Judaism's Challenge: Election, Divine Love, and Human Enmity* (Boston: Academic Studies Press, 2020), 13–49.

Gotlib, Steven. "Theologies of Prayer: Dov Singer and Arthur Green in 'Conversation'", *Lehrhaus*, February 8, 2021: https://thelehrhaus.com/commentary/theologies-of-prayer-dov-singer-and-arthur-green-in-conversation/.

Gottlieb, Jack. *Funny, It Doesn't Sound Jewish: How Yiddish Songs and Synagogue Melodies Influenced Tin Pan Alley, Broadway, and Hollywood* (New York: State University of New York Press, 2004).

Gottlieb, Michah. *The Jewish Reformation: Bible Translation and Middle-Class German Judaism as Spiritual Exercise* (New York: Oxford University Press, 2021).

Gray, Alyssa M. *Charity in Rabbinic Judaism: Atonement, Rewards, and Righteousness* (Abingdon: Routledge, 2019).

Graybill, Rhiannon. "A Child Is Being Eaten: Maternal Cannibalism and the Hebrew Bible in the Company of Fairy Tales", *Journal of Biblical Literature* 141.2 (2022): 235–255.

Green, Arthur. "New Directions in Jewish Theology in America" (Ann Arbor: Jean and Samuel Frankel Center for Judaic Studies, University of Michigan, 1994).

Green, Arthur. *Radical Judaism: Rethinking God and Tradition* (New Haven: Yale University Press, 2010).

Green, Arthur. "A Neo-Hasidic Life: Credo and Reflections", in: William Plevan (ed.), *Personal Theology: Essays in Honor of Neil Gillman* (Boston: Academic Studies Press, 2013), 65–87.

Green, Arthur. *Judaism for the World: Reflections on God, Life, and Love* (New Haven & London: Yale University Press, 2020).

Green, Arthur. *Well of Living Insight: Comments on the Siddur* (Boston & Jerusalem: Paraclete Press, 2023).

Greenberg, Moshe. *Ezekiel 1-20: A New Translation with Introduction and Commentary* (Garden City: Doubleday, 1964).

Greenberg, Moshe. "On the Refinement of the Conception of Prayer in Hebrew Scriptures", *AJS Review* 1 (1976): 57–92.

Greenspoon, Leonard J. (ed.). *Jews and Humor* (West Lafayette: Purdue University Press, 2011).

Greenspoon, Leonard J. (ed.). *Wealth and Poverty in Jewish Tradition* (West Lafayette: Purdue University Press, 2015).
Greenway, William. "Peter Singer, Emmanuel Levinas, Christian Agape, and the Spiritual Heart of Animal Liberation", *Journal of Animal Liberation* 5.2 (2015): 167–180.
Gribetz, Sarit Kattan. *Time and Difference in Rabbinic Judaism* (Princeton: Princeton University Press, 2020).
Gross, Benjamin. *Berit Halashon* (Jerusalem: Reuven Mass, 2004).
Gürkan, S. Leyla. *The Jews as a Chosen People: Tradition and Transformation* (London & New York: Routledge, 2009).
Habel, Norman C. *The Book of Job, A Commentary* (Philadelphia: Westminster Press, 1985).
Hadromi-Allouche, Zohar. "The Death and Life of the Devil's Son: A Literary Analysis of a Neglected Tradition", *Studia Islamica* 107 (2012): 157–183.
Halbertal, Moshe. *Concealment and Revelation: Esotericism in Jewish Thought and its Philosophical Implications* (Princeton: Princeton University Press, 2007).
Halbertal, Moshe. *The Birth of Doubt: Confronting Uncertainty in Early Rabbinic Literature* (Elli Fischer, transl.) (Providence: Brown Judaic Studies, 2020).
Halevi, Judah. *The Kuzari: An Argument for the Faith of Israel* (Hartwig Herschfeld, transl.) (New York: Schocken, 1964).
Halevi, Judah. *Selected Poems of Jehudah Halevi* (Heinrich Brody, ed.) (New York: Arno Press, 1973).
Halivni, David Weiss. *Revelation Restored: Divine Writ and Critical Responses* (Boulder: Westview Press, 1997).
Halivni, David Weiss. *Breaking the Tablets: Jewish Theology After the Shoah* (Lanham: Rowman and Littlefield, 2007).
Halperin, David J. *The Faces of the Chariot: Early Jewish Responses to Ezekiel's Vision* (Tübingen: Mohr Paul Siebeck, 1988).
Hamilton, Gordon J. *The Origins of the West Semitic Alphabet in Egyptian Scripts* (Washington DC: Catholic Biblical Quarterly Monograph Series 40, 2006).
Haralick, Robert M. *The Inner Meaning of the Hebrew Letters* (Northvale: Aronson, 1995).
Haring, Ben. "Ancient Egypt and the Earliest Known Stages of Alphabetic Writing", in: Phillip J. Boyes and Philipa M. Steele (eds.), *Understanding Relations Between Scripts II: Early Alphabets* (Oxford/Philadelphia: Oxbow Books, 2020), 53–67.
Harries, Karsten. *The Antinomy of Being* (Berlin; de Gruyter, 2019).
Hartman, David. "Relationship, Memory are Principles of Jewish Common Destiny, Interdependence." *Shalom Hartman Institute*, May 23, 2019. https://www.hartman.org.il/relationship-memory-are-principles-of-jewish-common-destiny-interdependence/.

Hartman, Donniel. *The Boundaries of Judaism* (London & New York: Continuum, 2007).
Harvey, Warren Zev. "Albo's Discussion of Time", *Jewish Quarterly Review* 70.4 (1980): 210–238.
Harvey, Warren Zev. "Idel on Spinoza", *Journal for the Study of Religions and Ideologies* 18 (2007): 88–94.
Harvey, Warren Zev. "Spinoza's Counterfactual Zionism", *Iyyun: The Jerusalem Philosophical Quarterly* 62 (2013): 235–244.
Harvey, Warren Zev. "Rashi on Creation: Beyond Plato and Derrida", *Aleph* 18.1 (2018): 27–50.
Harvey, Warren Zev. "Buber on False Prophets and Nationalism", *Journal of World Philosophies* 4.2 (2019a): 1–7.
Harvey, Steven. "The Author's Haqdamah as a Literary Form in Jewish Thought", in: Aaron W. Hughes and James T. Robinson (eds.), *Medieval Jewish Philosophy and Its Literary Forms* (Bloomington: Indiana University Press, 2019b), 133–160.
Hason, Nir. *Urshalim: Yisrael Vehapalestinim Biyerushalayim, 1967-2017* (Tel Aviv: Yediot, 2017).
Hauptman, Judith. "Women and the Conservative Synagogue", in: Susan Grossman and Rivka Haut (eds.), *Daughters of the King: Women and the Synagogue* (Philadelphia: Jewish Publication Society, 2010), 159–181.
Hecht, Jennifer Michael. *Doubt: A History* (New York: HarperCollins, 2003).
Heidegger, Martin. *Poetry, Language, Thought* (Alfred Hofstadter, transl.) (New York: Harper & Row, 1971).
Heidegger, Martin. *Schelling's Treatise on the Essence of Human Freedom* (Joan Stambaugh, transl.) (Athens: Ohio University Press, 1985).
Heinemann, Isaac. *The Reasons for the Commandments in Jewish Thought: From the Bible to the Renaissance* (Leonard Levin, transl.) (Boston: Academic Studies Press, 2008).
Heller, Agnes. *Immortal Comedy: The Comic Phenomenon in Art, Literature, and Life* (Lanham: Lexington Books, 2005).
Hellner-Eshed, Melila. *Seekers of the Face: Secrets of the Idra Rabba (The Great Assembly) of the Zohar* (Raphael Dascalu, transl.) (Stanford: Stanford University Press, 2021).
Henderson, Ruth. "Structure and Allusion in the *Apostrophe Zion*", *Dead Sea Discoveries* 20 (2013): 51–70.
Herberg, Will. *Judaism and Modern Man* (New York: Farrar, Straus & Young, 1951).
Herberg, Will. "The 'Chosenness' of Israel and the Jew of Today" in Arthur A. Cohen (ed.) *Arguments and Doctrines: A Reader of Jewish Thinking in the Aftermath of the Holocaust* (New York: Harper & Row, 1970), 267–283.

Herr, Moses David. "Tefisat Hahistoria Etzel Chazal", *Proceedings of the World Congress of Jewish Studies* 3.3 (1973): 129–142.
Heschel, Abraham Joshua. "The Quest for Certainty in Saadia's Philosophy", *Jewish Quarterly Review*, 38.2/3 (1942): 265–313.
Heschel, Abraham Joshua. "The Holy Dimension", *Journal of Religion* 23.2 (1943): 117–124.
Heschel, Abraham Joshua. *Man Is Not Alone: A Philosophy of Religion* (New York: Jewish Publication Society, 1951a).
Heschel, Abraham Joshua. *The Sabbath: Its Meaning for Modern Man* (New York: Farrar, Straus & Young, 1951b).
Heschel, Abraham Joshua. *Man's Quest for God: Studies in Prayer and Symbolism* (New York: Macmillan, 1954).
Heschel, Abraham Joshua. *God in Search of Man: A Philosophy of Judaism* (New York: Farrar, Straus and Giroux: 1955).
Heschel, Abraham Joshua, "Lo Toar Ela Ol", *Ma'ariv*, June 18, 1965: 13.
Heschel, Abraham Joshua. "No Religion Is an Island", *Union Seminary Quarterly Review* 21.2 (1966): 117–134.
Heschel, Abraham Joshua. *Israel: An Echo of Eternity* (New York: Farrar, Straus and Giroux, 1969).
Heschel, Abraham Joshua. *The Insecurity of Freedom* (New York, Schocken, 1972).
Heschel, Abraham Joshua. *A Passion for Truth* (New York: Farrar, Straus & Giroux, 1973).
Heschel, Abraham Joshua. *Moral Grandeur and Spiritual Audacity* (Susannah Heschel, ed.) (New York: Farrar, Straus and Giroux, 1997).
Heschel, Abraham Joshua. *Heavenly Torah As Refracted Through The Generations* (Gordon Tucker, transl.) (New York & London: Continuum, 2006).
Heschel, Susannah. "Jewish and Muslim Feminist Theologies in Dialogue: Discourses of Difference", in: Beth Wegner and Firoozeh Kashani-Sabet (eds.), *Gender in Judaism and Islam: Common Lives, Uncommon Heritage* (Philadelphia: University of Pennsylvania Press, 2015), 17–45.
Hilfritch, Carola. "'Making Writing Readable Again': Sign Praxis Between the Discourse on Idolatry and Cultural Criticism", *Journal of Religion* 85.2 (2005): 267–292.
Himmelfarb, Lea. "The Identity of the First Masoretes", *Sefarad* 67.1 (2007): 37–50.
Himmelfarb, Milton. "Jewish Tradition and the Educated Jew", in: Alfred Jospe [ed.], *Tradition and Contemporary Experience: Essays on Jewish Thought and Life* (New York: B'nai Brith, 1970), 325–335.
Hirsch, Samson Raphael. *Horeb: A Philosophy of Jewish Law and Observances*, I. Grunfeld (transl.), Volume 1 (London: Soncino, 1962).
Hirsch, Samson Raphael. *The Nineteen Letters on Judaism*, Bernard Drachman (transl.) (Jerusalem & New York: Feldheim, 1969).

Ho, Peter C. W. "The Macrostructural Logic of the Alphabetic Poems in the Psalter", *Vetus Testamentum* 69.4-5 (2019): 594–616.
Hoffman, Lawrence A. (ed.). *All These Vows: Kol Nidre* (Woodstock: Jewish Lights, 2011).
Hofstadter, Douglas R. and Daniel C. Dennett. *The Mind's I: Fantasies and Reflections on Self & Soul* (Brighton: Harvester Press, 1981).
Hollander, Dana. *Exemplarity and Chosenness: Rosenzweig and Derrida on the Nation of Philosophy* (Stanford: Stanford University Press, 2008).
Hollander, Dana. "The Significance of Franz Rosenzweig's Retrieval of Chosenness", *Jewish Studies Quarterly*, 16.1 (2009): 146–162.
Holtz, Avraham. "Hatav Hakemutzah Mameta'tea", *Leshonenu* 79.1/2: 180–183.
Horn, Dara. *In The Image* (New York: Norton, 2002).
Horney, Karen. *Our Inner Conflicts: A Constructive Theory of Neurosis* (London: Routledge & Kegan Paul, 1946).
Houston, Stephen (ed.). *The First Writing: Script Invention as History and Process* (Cambridge: Cambridge University Press, 2006a).
Houston, Walter J. *Contending for Justice: Ideologies and Theologies of Social Justice in the Old Testament* (London: T & T Clark, 2006b).
Hudson, Nicholas. *Writing and European Thought 1600-1830* (Cambridge: Cambridge University Press, 1994).
Hughes, Aaron W. "Boundary Maintenance: Religions as Organic-Cultural Flows", in: Michael Stausberg (ed.), *Contemporary Theories of Religion: A Critical Companion* (London & New York: Routledge, 2009), 209–223.
Hughes, Aaron W. *The Art of Dialogue in Jewish Philosophy* (Bloomington: Indiana University Press, 2008).
Hume, David. *A Treatise of Human Nature* (Oxford: Clarendon Press, 1978).
Hurowitz, Victor Avigdor. "An Often Overlooked Alphabetic Acrostic in Proverbs 24:1-22", *Revue Biblique* 107.4 (2000): 526–540.
Ibn Gabirol, Solomon. *Vulture in a Cage* (Raymond P. Scheindlin, transl.) (New York: Archipelago, 2016).
Idel, Moshe. "Tefisat Hatorah Besifrut Hahekhalot Vegilguleha Bakabbalah", *Jerusalem Studies in Jewish Thought* 1 (1981): 23–84.
Idel, Moshe. "The Land of Israel in Medieval Kabbalah", in: Lawrence A. Hoffman (ed.). *The Land of Israel: Jewish Perspectives* (Notre Dame: University of Notre Dame Press, 1986), 170–187.
Idel, Moshe. "Some Concepts of Time and History in Kabbalah", in: Elisheva Carlebach, John M. Efron, and David N. Myers (ed.), *Jewish History and Jewish Memory: Essays in Honor of Yosef Haim Yerushalmi* (Hanover & London: Brandeis University Press, 1998), 153–188.
Idel, Moshe. *Absorbing Perfections: Kabbalah and Interpretation* (New Haven & London: Yale University Press, 2002).

Idel, Moshe. "Sabbath: On Concepts of Time in Jewish Mysticism", in: Gerald J. Blidstein (ed.), *Sabbath – Idea, History, Reality* (Beer Sheva: Ben Gurion University of the Negev Press, 2004), 57–93.

Idel, Moshe. "Modes of Cleaving to the Letters in the Teachings of Israel Baal Shem Tov: A Sample Analysis", *Jewish History* 27 (2013): 299–317.

Idel, Moshe. "Perush Nosaf Le-Alef Bet Shel R. David ben Yehudah HeChasid ve-Sefer Temunah", *Alei Sefer: Studies in Bibliography and the History of the Printed and the Digital Hebrew Book* 26/27 (2017): 237–245.

Idelson-Shein, Iris. "The Monstrous *Mame*: Mapping the Margins of Maternity in Early Modern Jewish Discourse", *Jewish Social Studies* 20.3 (2014): 37–71.

Ilich, Ivan and Barry Sanders. *ABC: The Alphabetization of the Popular Mind* (New York: Vintage Books, 1998).

Inbari, Motti. *Messianic Religious Zionism Confronts Israeli Territorial Compromises* (Cambridge: Cambridge University Press, 2012).

Inbari, Mordechai (Motti). "Psychology in Religion and Politics: The Role of Cognitive Dissonance in Religious Readings of the Israeli Disengagement Plan", in: Simone Raudino and Patricia Sohn (eds.), *Beyond The Death of God: Religion in 21ʰᵗCentury International Politics* (Ann Arbor: University of Michigan Press, 2022), 281–304.

Irigaray, Luce. *This Sex Which Is Not One* (Catherine Porter, transl.) (Ithaca: Cornell University Press, 1985).

Jachter, Haim. "The Great Reishit Tzemichat Geulatenu Debate," *Jewish Link*, May 5, 2002. https://jewishlink.news/the-great-reishit-tzemichat-geulatenu-debate/.

Jackson, Bernard S. "Law in the 9th Century?" The Jehosaphat Tradition in Context", in: H.G.W. Williamson (ed.), *Understanding the History of Ancient Israel* (Oxford: Oxford University Press, 2007), 369–397.

Jacobs, Louis. *We Have Reason to Believe- Some Aspects of Jewish Theology Examined in the Light of Modern Thought* (London: Vallentine, Mitchell, 1957).

Jacobs, Louis. *A Jewish Theology* (London: Darton. Longman & Todd, 1973a).

Jacobs, Louis. *Hasidic Prayer* (New York: Schocken, 1973b).

Jacobs, Louis. *God, Torah, Israel – Traditionalism Without Fundamentalism* (Cincinnati: Hebrew Union College Press, 1990).

Jacobs, Louis. *Judaism and Theology: Essays on the Jewish Religion* (London: Vallentine Mitchell, 2005).

Jacobson, Eric. *Metaphysics of the Profane: The Political Theology of Walter Benjamin and Gershom Scholem* (New York: Columbia University Press, 2010).

Jaeger, Rani. *Avraham Hama'amin Ha'ivri* (Jerusalem: Carmel, 2021).

Jakobovits, Immanuel. *"If Only My People..." :Zionism In My Life* (London: Weidenfeld and Nicolson, 1984).

Jalbert, John E. "Time, Death, and History in Simmel and Heidegger", *Human Studies* 26.2 (2003): 259–283.

James, William. *A Pluralistic Universe* (New York: Longmans, Green and Co., 1916).
James, William. *The Varieties of Religious Experience* (Cambridge: Harvard University Press, 1985).
Janowitz, Naomi. "Good Jews Don't: Historical and Philosophical Constructions of Idolatry", *History of Religions* 47.2/3 (2007–8): 239–252.
Jaspers, Karl. *Philosophical Faith and Revelation* (New York: Harper and Row, 1967).
Jones, Hugh O. "Gordon Kaufman's Perspectival Language", *Religious Studies* 14 (1978): 89–97.
Jordan, Brigitte. "Blurring Boundaries: The 'Real' and the 'Virtual' in Hybrid Spaces", *Human Organization* 68.2 (2009): 181–193.
Jospe, Raphael. "The Superiority of Oral Over Written Communication: Judah Ha-Levi's Kuzari and Modern Jewish Thought", in: Jacob Neusner, Ernest S. Frerichs and Nahum M. Sarna (eds.). *From Ancient Israel to Modern Judaism: Intellect in Quest of Understanding* vol.3 (Atlanta: Scholars Press, 1989), 127–156.
Kadari, Adiel. "Asher Bachar Banu – Al Mashmautan Hatiksit Shel Birkot Hakeriah", *Kenishta* 3 (2007): 257–273.
Kaminsky, Joel S. "Humor and the Theology of Hope: Isaac as a Humorous Figure", *Interpretation* 54.4 (2000): 363–375.
Kaminsky, Joel S. *Yet I Loved Jacob: Reclaiming the Biblical Concept of Election* (Nashville: Abingdon, 2007).
Kaminsky, Joel S. "New Testament and Rabbinic Views of Election", in: Isaac Kalimi (ed.), *Jewish Bible Theology: Perspectives and Case Studies* (Winona Lake: Eisenbrauns, 2012), 119–146.
Kanarfogel, Ephraim. "Rabbinic Attitudes Toward Nonobservance in the Medieval Period", in: Jacob J. Schachter (ed.), *Jewish Tradition and the Nontraditional Jew* (Northvale: Jason Aaronson, 1992), 3–35.
Kant, Immanuel. *The Metaphysics of Morals* (Cambridge: Cambridge University Press, 1996).
Kaplan, Dana Evan (ed.). *The New Reform Judaism: Challenges and Reflections* (Lincoln: University of Nebraska Press, 2013).
Kaplan, Mordecai M. *Judaism as a Civilization: Toward a Reconstruction of American Jewish Life* (New York: Macmillan, 1934).
Kaplan, Mordecai M. *The Future of the American Jew* (New York: Macmillan, 1949).
Kaplan, Mordecai M. *Questions Jews Ask: Reconstructionist Answers* (New York: Reconstructionist Press, 1956).
Kaplan, Mordecai M. *The Greater Judaism in the Making: A Study of the Modern Evolution of Judaism* (New York: Reconstructionist Press, 1960).
Karsenti, Bruno. "'Si Je Me Bats Seulement Pour Moi, Que Suis-Je?': Leo Strauss et l'Élection des Juifs", *Les Études Philosophiques*, 4 (2014): 547–572.

Kasher, Hannah. "On Yeshayahu Leibowitz's Use of Religious Terminology", *Journal of Jewish Thought and Philosophy*, 10 (2000): 27–55.

Kasher, Hannah. *Elyon Al Kol Hagoyim* (Tel Aviv: Idra, 2018).

Kasher, Menachem. *Haggadah Shelemah* (Jerusalem: Torah Shelemah Institute, 1967).

Kasher, Rimon. "The Mythological Figure of Moses in Light of Some Unpublished Midrashic Fragments", *Jewish Quarterly Review*. 88.1/2 (1997): 19–42.

Kashima, Yoshihisa, Aparna Kanakatte Gurumurthy, Lucette Ouschan, Trevor Chong, and Jason Mattingley. "Connectionism and the Self: James, Mead, and the Stream of Enculturated Consciousness", *Psychological Inquiry* 18.2 (2007): 73–96.

Katz, Menachem. "*Aleinu* – A Prayer Common to Jews and Gentile God-Fearers", in: Alon Goshen-Gottstein (ed.), *Judaism's Challenge: Election, Divine Love, and Human Enmity* (Boston: Academic Studies Press, 2020), 83–97.

Katz, Steven B. "Letter as Essence: The Rhetorical (Im)pulse of the Hebrew Alefbet", *Journal of Communication and Religion* 26.2 (2003): 125–160.

Kaufman, William E. *Contemporary Jewish Philosophies* (New York: Reconstructionist Press & Behrman House, 1976).

Kavka, Martin. *Jewish Messianism and the History of Philosophy* (Cambridge: Cambridge University Press, 2004).

Kawashima, Robert S. "Oaths, Vows, and Trust in the Bible", in: Nina Caputo and Mitchell B. Hart (eds.), *On the Word of a Jew: Religion, Reliability and the Dynamics of Trust* (Bloomington: Indiana University Press, 2018), 17–35.

Kaye, Lynn. *Time in the Babylonian Talmud: Natural and Imagined Times in Jewish Law and Narrative* (Cambridge: Cambridge University Press, 2018).

Kellner, Menachem. "Maimonides' 'Thirteen Principles' and the Structure of the Guide for the Perplexed", *Journal of the History of Philosophy* 20.1 (1982): 76–84.

Kellner, Menachem. *Maimonides on Judaism and the Jewish People* (Albany: State University of New York Press, 1991).

Kellner, Menachem. "Chosenness, Not Chauvinism: Maimonides on the Chosen People", in: Daniel H. Frank (ed.), *A People Apart: Chosenness and Ritual in Jewish Philosophical Thought* (Albany: State University of New York Press, 1993), 51–75.

Kellner, Menachem. *Must a Jew Believe Anything?* (Liverpool: Liverpool University Press & Littman Library of Jewish Civilization, 2006).

Kellner, Menachem. *We Are Not Alone: A Maimonidean Theology of the Other* (Boston: Academic Studies Press, 2021).

Kenney, John Peter. "The Critical Value of Negative Theology", *Harvard Theological Review* 86.4 (1993): 439–453.

Kepnes, Steven. "Revelation as Torah: From an Existential to a Postliberal Judaism", *Journal of Jewish Thought and Philosophy* 10.1 (2000): 205–237.

Kermani, Elise. *Sonic Soma: Sound, Body and the Origins of the Alphabet* (New York: Atropos, 2009).

Khalidi, Rashid. *The Hundred Years' War on Palestine: A History of Settler Colonialism and Resistance, 1917-2017* (New York: Metropolitan Books, 2020).

Kierkegaard, Søren. *The Concept of Anxiety – A Simple Psychologically Orienting Deliberation on the Dogmatic Issue of Hereditary Sin*, Reidar Thomte (transl.) (Princeton: Princeton University Press, 1980).

Kimelman, Reuven. "Psalm 145: Theme, Structure and Impact", *Journal of Biblical Literature* 113.1 (1994): 37–58.

King, Clive. *The 22 Letters* (London: Hamish Hamilton, 1966).

Kiperwasser, Reuven and Geoffrey Herman (eds.). *Expressions of Sceptical Topoi in (Late) Antique Judaism* (Berlin: de Gruyter, 2021).

Kneebone, Roger. "Total Internal Reflection: An Essay on Paradigms", *Medical Education* 36 (2002): 514–518.

Knight, John Allan. *Liberalism Versus Postliberalism: The Great Divide in Twentieth-Century Theology* (Oxford: Oxford University Press, 2013).

Knohl, Israel. "The Election and Sanctity of Israel in the Hebrew Bible", in: Alon Goshen-Gottstein (ed.), *Judaism's Challenge: Election, Divine Love, and Human Enmity* (Boston: Academic Studies Press, 2020), 1–12.

Knowlton, Eloise. *Joyce, Joyceans and the Rhetoric of Citation* (Gainesville: University Press of Florida, 1998).

Kogan, Michael S. *Opening the Covenant: A Jewish Theology of Christianity* (Oxford: Oxford University Press, 2008).

Kohler, Kaufmann. *Jewish Theology, Systematically and Historically Considered* (New York: Macmillan, 1918).

Kohn, Hans (ed.). *Nationalism and the Jewish Ethics: Basic Writings of Ahad Ha'am* (New York: Schocken, 1962).

Koltun-Fromm, Ken. *Moses Hess and Modern Jewish Identity*, (Bloomington: Indiana University Press, 2001).

Koppel, Moshe. "Resolving Uncertainty: A Unified Overview of Rabbinic Methods", *Tradition* 37.1 (2003): 27–51.

Koren, Sharon Faye. *Forsaken: The Menstruant in Medieval Jewish Mysticism* (Waltham: Brandeis University Press, 2011).

Kosman, Admiel. "The Cultural Crisis of Contemporary Israel: A Jewish Theological Perspective On Its Causes", *Israel Studies Review* 26.2 (2011): 28–53.

Kotzin, Daniel P. *Judah L. Magnes: An American Jewish Noncomformist* (Syracuse: Syracuse University Press, 2010).

Krasner, Jonathan. "The Place of Tikkun Olam in American Jewish Life", *Jewish Political Studies Review* 25.3/4 (2013): 59–98.

Kreisel, Haim. "'Ilu Yedativ Hayyitiv': Legilgulo Shel Pitgam", *Daat: A Journal of Jewish Philosophy and Kabbalah* 74/75 (2013): 73–103.

Krinis, Ehud. *God's Chosen People: Judah Halevi's* Kuzari *Doctrine and the Shi'i Imam Doctrine* (Turnhout, Brepols, 2014).
Krinis, Ehud. "Cyclical Time in the Isma'ili Circle of Ikhwan al-safa (Tenth Century) and in Early Jewish Kabbalistic Circles (Thirteenth and Fourteenth Centuries)", *Studia Islamica* 3 (2016): 20–108.
Krochmal, Nachman. *Kitvei Rabbi Nachman Krochmal* (Simon Rawidowicz, ed.) (Waltham: Ararat, 1961).
Kuhn, Thomas S. *The Structure of Scientific Revolutions* (Chicago: University of Chicago Press, 1996).
Kulp, Joshua. "The Origins of the Seder and the Haggadah", *Currents in Biblical Research* 4.1 (2005): 109–134.
Kundera, Milan. *Testaments Betrayed: An Essay in Nine Parts* (New York: HarperPerennial, 1996).
Küng, Hans. *Does God Exist? An Answer for Today* (New York: Vintage Books, 1981).
Kushner, Lawrence. *Sefer Otiyot: The Book of Letters – A Mystical Hebrew Alphabet* (Woodstock: Jewish Lights, 1990).
Lafont, Robert. "Relationships Between Speech and Writing Systems in Ancient Alphabets and Syllabaries", in: Derrick de Kerckhove and Charles J. Lumsden (eds.), *The Alphabet and the Brain: The Lateralization of Writing* (Berlin & Heidelberg: Springer, 1988), 92–105.
Lahav, Hagar. "Post-Secular Jewish Feminist Theology? The View From Israel", *Journal of Modern Jewish Studies* 14.3 (2015): 355–372.
Langer, Ruth. "Biblical Texts in Jewish Prayers: Their History and Function", in: Albert Herhards and Clemens Leonhard (eds.), *Jewish and Christian Liturgy and Worship: New Insights Into Its History and Interaction* (Leiden & Boston: Brill, 2007), 63–90.
Langer, Ruth. "The Censorship of Aleinu in Ashkenaz and its Aftermath", in: Debra Reed Blank (ed.), *The Experience of Jewish Liturgy: Studies Dedicated to Menahem Schmelzer* (Leiden & Boston: Brill, 2011), 147–166.
Langer, Ruth. "Jewish Universalism? The Nations in the Rosh Hashanah Liturgy", *Studies in Christian-Jewish Relations* 15.1 (2020): 1–20.
Langermann, Y. Tzvi. *The Jews and the Sciences in the Middle Ages* (Aldershot: Ashgate, 1999).
Langermann, Y. Tzvi. "From My Notebooks: Two Treatises on the Letters of the Hebrew Alphabet", *Aleph* 3 (2003): 293–299.
Lasch, Christopher. *The Culture of Narcissism: American Life in an Age of Diminishing Expectations* (New York: W.W. Norton & Company, 1991).
Lawrence, Beatrice J.W. "Rape Culture and the Rabbinic Construction of Gender", in: Rhiannon Graybill, Meredith Minister, and Beatrice Lawrence (eds.), *Rape Culture and Religious Studies: Critical and Pedagogical Engagements* (Lanham: Lexington, 2019), 137–155.

Lazarus, Moritz. *The Ethics of Judaism* (Henrietta Szold, transl.), volume 1 (Philadelphia: Jewish Publication Society of America, 1900).
Lebens, Samuel. "Is There a Primordial Torah?", *International Journal for Philosophy of Religion* 82.2 (2017): 219–239.
Lebens, Samuel. *The Principles of Judaism* (Oxford: Oxford University Press, 2020).
Lebens, Samuel. *A Guide for the Jewish Undecided* (New Millford: Maggid Books, 2022).
Lederach, John Paul. *The Journey Toward Reconciliation* (Scottsdale & Waterloo: Herald Press, 1999).
Leibowitz, Nehama. *Studies in Shemot* (Aryeh Newman, transl.) (Jerusalem: World Zionist Organization, 1976).
Leibowitz, Yeshayahu. *Judaism, Human Values, and the Jewish State*, edited by Eliezer Goldman (Cambridge & London: Harvard University Press, 1992).
Levenson, Jon D. "The Universal Horizon of Biblical Particularism", in: Mark G. Brett, *Ethnicity and the Bible* (Boston & Leiden: Brill, 2002), 143–169.
Levenson, Jon D. "Chosenness and Its Enemies", *Commentary* (2008): 25–31.
Levenson, Jon D. "Miscategorizing Chosenness", in: Shelly L. Birdsong and Serge Frolov (eds.), *Partners with God: Theological and Critical Reading of the Bible in Honor of Marvin A. Sweeney* (Claremont: Claremont Press, 2017), 327–343.
Levin, Elizabetha. "Various Times in Abraham Ibn Ezra's Works and Their Reflection in Modern Thought", *Kronoscope* 18 (2018): 154–170.
Levinas, Emmanuel. *Totality and Infinity: An Essay on Exteriority*, translated by Alphonso Lingis (Pittsburgh: Duquesne University Press, 1969).
Levinas, Emmanuel. "Language and Proximity", in: *Collected Philosophical Papers* (Dordrecht: Martinus Nijhof, 1987), 109–126.
Levinas, Emmanuel. *Difficult Freedom: Essays on Judaism* (Sean Hand, transl.) (Baltimore: Johns Hopkins University Press, 1990a).
Levinas, Emmanuel. *Nine Talmudic Readings* (Annette Aronowicz, transl.) (Bloomington: Indiana University Press, 1990b).
Levinas, Emmanuel. *Beyond the Verse* (Gary D. Mole transl.) (London: Continuum International, 1994).
Levisohn, John A. "What Work Do the Concepts of 'Language' and 'Literature' Do for Michael Rosenak?", *Journal of Jewish Education* 80.4 (2014): 411–433.
Lévy, Bernard-Henri. *The Genius of Judaism* (New York: Random House, 2017).
Levy, Richard N. *A Vision of Holiness: The Future of Reform Judaism* (New York: URJ Press, 2005).
Lewin, Judith. "'Diving into the Wreck': Binding Oneself to Judaism in Contemporary Jewish Women's Fiction", *Shofar*, 26.3 (2008): 48–67.
Liberman, Alida. "On the Rationality of Vow-Making", *Pacific Philosophical Quarterly* 100.3 (2019): 881–900.
Lichtenstein, Aharon. "Prayer in the Teachings of Rav Soloveitchik" (summarized by Aviad Hacohen), *Torat Har Etzion* April 7, 1996. https://etzion.org.il/

en/philosophy/great-thinkers/rav-soloveitchik/prayer-teachings-rav-soloveitchik-ztl.

Lichtenstein, Aharon. "The Philosophy of the Laws of Vows and Oaths", *Torat Har Etzion* March 22, 2018. https://etzion.org.il/en/philosophy/great-thinkers/harav-aharon-lichtenstein/matot-philosophy-laws-vows-and-oaths.

Lichtman, Maria. "Negative Theology in Marguerite Porete and Jacques Derrida", *Christianity and Literature* 47.2 (1998): 213–227.

Lieber, Laura S. "Confessing from A-Z: Penitential Forms in Early Synagogue Poetry", in: Mark J. Boda, Daniel K. Falk and Rodney Werline (eds.), *Penitential Prayer: Origins, Development and Impact*, vol.3 (Atlanta: Society of Biblical Literature, 2008), 99–125.

Lieberman, Saul. *Greek in Jewish Palestine* (New York, Jewish Theological Seminary, 1942).

Liebreich, Leon J. "Psalms 34 and 145 in Light of Their Key Words", *Hebrew Union College* 27 (1956): 181–192.

Lifschitz, Avi. "A Natural Yet Providential Tongue: Moses Mendelssohn on Hebrew as a Language of Action", in: Sabine Sander (ed.), *Language as Bridge and Border: Linguistic, Cultural and Political Constellations in Eighteenth to Twentieth Century German-Jewish Thought* (Berlin: Hentrich & Hentrich, 2015), 31–50.

Lindberg, David C. *Theories of Vision from Al-Kindi to Kepler* (Chicago: University of Chicago Press, 1976).

Lipiner, Elihu. *Chazon Haotiot – Torat Hadeot Shel Haalef Bet* (Jerusalem: Magnes, 1989).

Lookstein, Haskel. "Tefillin and God's Kingship", *Tradition* 4.1 (1961): 66–78.

Lorberbaum, Yair. "The Rise of Halakhic Religiosity of Mystery and Transcendence", *Diné Israel* 34 (2020): *1–*49.

Löw, Immanuel. *Fauna und Mineralien der Juden* (Hildesheim: Georg Olms, 1969).

Luz, Ehud. *Wrestling with an Angel: Power, Morality and Jewish Identity* (Michael Swirsky, transl.) (New Haven & London: Yale University Press, 2003).

Mackenzie, Catriona. "Three Dimensions of Autonomy", in: Andrea Veltman and Mark Piper, *Autonomy, Oppression, and Gender* (New York: Oxford University Press, 2014), 15–41.

Magid, Shaul. *American Post-Judaism: Identity and Renewal in a Postethnic Society* (Bloomington: Indiana University Press, 2013).

Magid, Shaul. *The Necessity of Exile: Essays from a Distance* (Brooklyn: Ayin Press, 2023).

Magnes, Judah L. *Dissenter in Zion: From the Writings of Judah L. Magnes*, edited by Arthur A. Goren (Cambridge: Harvard University Press, 1982).

Maimin, Rachel M. "Interview with Rabbi Eugene B. Borowitz", in: Lisa Grushcow (ed.), *The Sacred Encounter: Jewish Perspectives on Sexuality* (New York: CCAR Press, 2014), 305–313.

Maimon, Solomon. *The Autobiography of Solomon Maimon*, edited by Yozhak Y. Melamed and Abraham P. Socher and translated by Paul Reitter (Princeton: Princeton University Press, 2018).

Manekin, Michael. *End of Days: Ethics, Tradition, and Power in Israel* (Maya Rosen, transl.) (Boston: Academic Studies Press, 2023).

Mann, Jacob. "Oaths and Vows in the Synoptic Gospels", *American Journal of Theology* 21.2 (1917): 260–274.

Margolin, Ron. *Inner Religion in Jewish Sources: A Phenomenology of Inner Religious Life and Its Manifestation from the Bible to Hasidic Texts* (Edward Levin, transl.) (Boston: Academic Studies Press, 2021).

Marion, Jean-Luc. *God Without Being* (Thomas A. Carlson, transl.) (Chicago: University of Chicago Press, 2012).

Marmur, Dow. *Beyond Survival: Reflections on the Future of Judaism* (London: Darton Longman & Todd, 1982).

Marmur, Dow. *The Star of Return: Judaism After the Holocaust* (Westport: Greenwood Press, 1991).

Marmur, Dow. "The Here and Hereafter," in: Jack Reimer (ed.), *Wrestling With the Angel: Jewish Insights on Death and Mourning* (New York: Schocken, 1995), 335–338.

Marmur, Dow. *Six Lives: A Memoir* (Toronto: Key Porter, 2004).

Marmur, Michael. "Are You My Witnesses? The Use of Sources in Modern Jewish Thought", *Modern Judaism* 32.2 (2012): 155–173.

Marmur, Michael. "Ethical Theories in the Reform Movement", in: Elliot N. Dorff and Jonathan K. Crane (eds.), *The Oxford Handbook of Jewish Ethics and Morality* (Oxford: Oxford University Press, 2013), 206–224.

Marmur, Michael. "Why Jews Quote", *Oral Tradition* 29.1 (2014): 5–46.

Marmur, Michael. *Abraham Joshua Heschel and the Sources of Wonder* (Toronto: University of Toronto Press, 2016a).

Marmur, Michael. "God of Language", in: Leonard Kaplan and Ken Koltun-Fromm (eds.), *Imagining the Jewish God* (Lanham: Lexington Books, 2016b) 267–292.

Marmur, Michael. "The Kaddish as a Speech Act", in: David Birnbaum and Martin S. Cohen (eds.), *Kaddish* (New York: New Paradigm Matrix, 2016c), 475–491.

Marmur, Michael. "Israel, God's Chosen People?", *The Torah.com*, 2020. https://www.thetorah.com/article/israel-gods-chosen-people.

Marmur, Michael. "On Petrification", in: Alon Goshen-Gottstein (ed.), *Idolatry: A Contemporary Jewish Conversation* (Boston: Academic Studies Press, 2023), 232–252.

Marmur, Michael and David Ellenson (eds.). *American Jewish Thought Since 1934: Writings on Identity, Engagement and Belief* (Waltham: Brandeis University Press, 2020).

Marx, Dalia. "The Prayer for the State of Israel: Universalism and Particularism", in: Lawrence Hoffman (ed.), *All The World: Universalism, Particularism and the High Holy Days* (Woodstock: Jewish Lights, 2014), 49–76.

Marx, Dalia and Alona Lisitsa (eds.). *Tefillat Ha'adam: Siddur Reformi Yisraeli* (no city listed: Maram and IMPJ, 2020).

Masson, Robert. *Without Metaphor, No Saving God: Theology After Cognitive Linguistics* (Leuven: Peeters, 2014).

May, Todd. *A Decent Life: Morality for the Rest of Us* (Chicago: University of Chicago Press, 2019).

Maybaum, Ignaz. *The Jewish Mission* (London: J. Clarke, 1951).

Maybaum, Ignaz. *Happiness Outside the State: Judaism, Christianity, Islam: Three Ways to God* (London: Oriel Press, 1980).

Maybaum, Ignaz. *Ignaz Maybaum: A Reader*, edited by Nicholas R.M. de Lange (New York: Berghahn, 2001).

Mayse, Ariel Evan. "The Voices of Moses: Theologies of Revelation in an Early Hasidic Circle", *Harvard Theological Review* 112.1 (2019): 101–125.

Mayse, Ariel Evan. *Speaking Infinities: God and Language in the Teachings of Rabbi Dov Ber of Mezritsh* (Philadelphia: University of Pennsylvania Press, 2020).

McCloskey, Deirdre N. *Bourgeois Dignity: Why Economics Can't Explain the Modern World* (Chicago & London: University of Chicago Press, 2010).

McIntyre, Lee. *Post-Truth* (Cambridge MA: MIT Press, 2018).

Melamed, Yitzhak Y. "Mihu Filosof Yehudi Moderni?", *Mita'am* 21 (2010): 47–59.

Mendelsohn, Barak. "State Authority in the Balance: The Israeli State and the Messianic Settler Movement", *International Studies Review* 16 (2014): 499–521.

Mendelssohn, Moses. *Jerusalem – Or On Religious Power and Judaism* (Allan Arkush, transl.) (Hanover & London: Brandeis University Press, 1983).

Mendes-Flohr, Paul R. "Secular Religiosity: Reflections on Post-Traditional Jewish Spirituality and Community", in: Marc Lee Raphael (ed.), *Approaches to Modern Judaism* (Chico: Scholars Press, 2020), 19–30.

Mertzani, Maria. "Interdisciplinarity in Archaeology and Historical Linguistics: The Case of Alpha", *Cadernos Do Lepaarq (UFPEL)* 12.24 (2015): 270–289.

Mevorach, Yishay. *Aron Ha'edut: Chazarato Shel Hanidchak Ha'acharon* (Tel Aviv: Resling, 2019).

Meyer, Michael A. "Two Persistent Tensions within Wissenschaft des Judentums", in: Andreas Gotzmann and Christian Wiese (eds.), *Modern Judaism and Historical Consciousness: Identities, Encounters, Perspectives* (Leiden: Brill, 2007), 73–89.

Michael, Rosen, *We're Going on a Bear Hunt* (London: Walker Books, 1989).

Milgrom, Jacob. *The Anchor Bible: Leviticus 1-16* (New York: Doubleday, 1991).

Miller, Mordechai. "'Kvar Lo Mavdilim Bein Am Yisrael Legoyim': Milchamto Shel Harav Tau Behashpaot Zarot", *Reshit* 5 (2021): 2–33.
Miner, Earl and Jennifer Brady (eds.). *Literary Transmission and Authority: Dryden and Other Writers* (Cambridge: Cambridge University Press, 1993).
Mintz, Ruth Finer (ed.). *Modern Hebrew Poetry: A Bilingual Anthology* (Berkeley: University of California Press, 1966).
Mirsky, Yehudah. *Rav Kook: Mystic in a Time of Revolution* (New Haven & London: Yale University Press, 2014).
Mittleman, Alan L. *Human Nature & Jewish Thought* (Princeton: Princeton University Press, 2015).
Mizrahi, Noam. "Reconsidering the Semantics of the 'Inclination' (Yeser) in Classical Biblical Hebrew", in: James K. Aitken, Hector M. Patmore, and Ishay Rosen-Zvi (eds.), *The Evil Inclination in Early Judaism and Christianity* (Cambridge: Cambridge University Press, 2021), 13–32.
Molseed, Mari J. "The Problem of Temporality in the Work of Georg Simmel", *Sociological Quarterly* 28.3 (1987): 357–366.
Morell, Samuel. "The Samson Nazirite Vow in the Sixteenth Century", *AJS Review* 14.2 (1989): 223–262.
Moreshet, Menachem. "Tzachak-Sachak; Yitzchak-Yischak", *Bet Mikra* 13 (1968): 127–130.
Morreall, John (ed.). *The Philosophy of Laughter and Humor* (Albany: State University of New York Press, 1987).
Morreall, John. "The Rejection of Humor in Western Thought", *Philosophy East and West* 39.3 (1989): 243–265.
Mosès, Stéphane. *System and Revelation: The Philosophy of Franz Rosenzweig* (Detroit: Wayne State University Press, 1992).
Munk, Michael L. *The Wisdom in the Hebrew Alphabet: The Sacred Letters as a Guide to Jewish Deed and Thought* (Brooklyn: Mesorah Publications, 1983).
Myers, David N. *Resisting History: Historicism and Its Discontents in German-Jewish Thought* (Princeton: Princeton University Press, 2003).
Nadler, Steven. "Why Spinoza Was Excommunicated", *Humanities* 34.5 (2013). https://www.neh.gov/article/why-spinoza-was-excommunicated.
Naeh, Shlomo. "Boreh Niv Sfatayim: Perek Bephenomenologia Shel Hatefillah Al Pi Mishnat Berakhot", *Tarbiz* 63 (1994): 185–218.
Nagel, Thomas. *The View From Nowhere* (New York: Oxford University Press, 1986).
Nahme, Paul E. "God is the Reason: Hermann Cohen's Monotheism and the Liberal Theologico-Political Predicament", *Modern Theology* 33.1 (2017): 116–139.
Naveh, Joseph. *Early History of the Alphabet: An Introduction to West Semitic Epigraphy and Palaeography* (Jerusalem & Leiden: Magnes & E.J. Brill, 1982).

Nehorai, Michael Z. "Halakhah, Metahalakhah, and the Redemption of Israel: Reflections on the Rabbinic Rulings of Rav Kook", in: Lawrence J. Kaplan and David Shatz (eds.), *Rabbi Abraham Isaac Kook and Jewish Spirituality* (New York & London: New York University Press, 1995), 120–156.

Neis, Rafael Rachel. *The Sense of Sight in Rabbinic Culture: Jewish Ways of Seeing in Late Antiquity* (Cambridge: Cambridge University Press, 2013).

Nelson, Robert S. (ed.). *Visuality Before and Beyond the Renaissance: Seeing As Others Saw* (New York: Cambridge University Press, 2000).

Neusner, Jacob. *Torah: From Scroll to Symbol in Formative Judaism* (Philadelphia: Fortress Press, 1985).

Neusner, Jacob. *Recovering Judaism: The Universal Dimension of Jewish Religion* (Minneapolis: Fortress Press, 2001).

Niditch, Susan. *The Responsive Self: Personal Religion in Biblical Literature of the Neo-Babylonian and Persian Periods* (New Haven: Yale University Press, 2015).

Niebuhr, Reinhold. *Discerning the Signs of the Times: Sermons for Today and Tomorrow* (New York: Charles Scribner's Sons, 1946), 111–131.

Niehoff, Maren R. "What Is in a Name? Philo's Mystical Philosophy of Language", *Jewish Studies Quarterly* 2.3 (1995): 220–252.

Niehoff, Maren R. *Philo of Alexandria: An Intellectual Biography* (New Haven & London: Yale University Press, 2018).

Nolan, Edward Peter. *Now Through A Glass Darkly: Specular Images of Being and Knowing from Virgil to Chaucer* (Ann Arbor: The University of Michigan Press, 1990).

Norlian, Allison. "Israeli and Palestinian Women: The Only Way Forward Is Together", *Forbes*, September 3, 2001. https://www.forbes.com/sites/allisonnorlian/2021/09/03/israeli-and-palestinian-women-the-only-way-forward-is-together/?sh=57ee4e895625.

Novak, David. *The Election of Israel: The Idea of the Chosen People* (Cambridge: Cambridge University Press, 1995).

Novak, David. "What Is Jewish Theology?", in: Steven Kepnes, *The Cambridge Companion to Jewish Theology* (Cambridge: Cambridge University Press, 2020), 20–38.

Noyes, Dorothy. "Tradition: Three Traditions", *Journal of Folklore Research* 46.3 (2009): 233–268.

Nussbaum, Martha C. "Judaism and the Love of Reason", in: Ruth E. Groenhout and Maya Bower (eds.), *Philosophy, Feminism and Faith* (Bloomington: Indiana University Press, 2003), 9–39.

Ochs, Peter. "Borowitz and the Postmodern Renewal of Theology", *CrossCurrents* 43.2 (1993): 164–183.

Ohana, David. "The Politics of Political Despair: The Case of Political Theology in Israel", in: Tamar Hermann (ed.), *By The People, For the People, Without the*

People? The Emergence of (Anti) Political Sentiment in Israel and in Western Democracies (Jerusalem: Israel Democracy Institute, 2011), 356–378.

Ohana, David. *Modernism and Zionism* (London: Palgrave Macmillan UK, 2012).

Oliveira, Manuel D. *Humanity Divided: Martin Buber and the Challenges of Being Chosen* (Berlin & Boston: de Gruyter, 2021).

Olyan, Saul M. "The Search for the Elusive Self in Texts of the Hebrew Bible", in: David Brakke, Michael L. Satlow and Stephen P. Weitzman (eds.), *Religion and the Self in Antiquity* (Bloomington & Indianapolis: Indiana University Press, 2005), 40–50.

Oring, Elliott. *The Jokes of Sigmund Freud: A Study in Humor and Jewish Identity* (Philadelphia: University of Pennsylvania Press, 1984).

Orlov, Andrei A. *The Atoning Dyad: The Two Goats of Yom Kippur in the* Apocalypse of Abraham (Leiden & Boston: Brill, 2016).

Oron, Michal. "Sipur Haotiot Umekorotav: Iyun Bemidrash Hazohar Al Otiot Haalefbet", *Jerusalem Studies in Jewish Thought* 3.1/2 (1983): 97–109.

Orr, Mary. *Intertextuality: Debates and Contexts* (Cambridge: Polity, 2003).

Paine, Robert. "Behind the Hebron Massacre, 1994", *Anthropology Today* 11.1 (1995): 8–15.

Pappa, Eleftheria. "The Poster Boys of Antiquity's 'Capitalism' Shunning Money? The Spread of the Alphabet in the Mediterranean as a Function of Credit-Based, Maritime Trade", *Revista do Museu de Arqueologia e Etnologia* 33 (2019): 91–138.

Pardes, Ilana. *Countertraditions in the Bible: A Feminist Approach* (Cambridge: Harvard University Press, 1992).

Pateman, Carole. *The Sexual Contract* (Stanford: Stanford University Press, 1988).

Paynter, Helen. "'Revenge for My Two Eyes': Talion and Mimesis in the Samson Narrative", *Biblical Interpretation* 26 (2018): 133–157.

Pelikan, Jaroslav. *The Vindication of Tradition* (New Haven: Yale University Press, 1984).

Penslar, Derek J. *Zionism: An Emotional State* (New Brunswick: Rutgers University Press, 2023).

Perloff, Marjorie. *Unoriginal Genius: Poetry by Other Means in the New Century* (Chicago: University of Chicago Press, 2010).

Persico, Tomer. *Adam B'Tzelem Elohim: Hara'ayon Sheshinah et Haolam V'et Hayahadut* (Rishon LeZion: Yedioth Ahronoth Books, 2021).

Pessin, Sarah. "Loss, Presence, and Gabirol's Desire: Medieval Jewish Philosophy and the Possibility of a Feminist Ground", in: Hava Tirosh-Samuelson (ed.), *Women and Gender in Jewish Philosophy* (Bloomington: Indiana University Press, 2004), 27–50.

Petuchowski, Jakob Josef. *Heirs of the Pharisees* (New York: Basic Books, 1970).

Pew Center. *A Portrait of Jewish Americans: Findings from a Pew Research Center Survey of U.S. Jews*, October 1, 2013. https://www.pewresearch.org/religion/2013/10/01/jewish-american-beliefs-attitudes-culture-survey/.

Pfenniger, Jennifer. "Speaking of Smouldering Lips in Song of Songs 7:10 (Eng.9)", in: Randall Heskett and Brian Irwin (eds.), *The Bible as a Human Witness to Divine Revelation* (New York: T& T Clark, 2010), 285–301.

Philipson, David. *The Reform Movement in Judaism* (New York: Ktav, 1967).

Pianko, Noam. *Zionism and the Roads Not Taken: Rawidowicz, Kaplan, Kohn* (Bloomington: Indiana University Press, 2010).

Pianko, Noam. *Jewish Peoplehood: An American Innovation* (New Brunswick: Rutgers University Press, 2015).

Pinker, Aron. "A Goat To Go To Azazel", *Journal of Hebrew Scriptures* 7.8 (2009): 2–25.

Pinker, Aron. "The Famous But Difficult Psalm 90:10", *Old Testament Essays* 28.2 (2015): 497–522.

Plantzos, Dimitris. "Crystals and Lenses in the Graeco-Roman World", *American Journal of Archaeology*, 101.3 (1997): 451–464.

Plaskow, Judith. "Jewish Theology in Feminist Perspective", in: Lynn Davidman and Shelly Tenenbaum (eds.), *Feminist Perspectives in Jewish Studies* (New Haven: Yale University Press, 1994), 62–84.

Plaskow, Judith. *Standing Again At Sinai: Judaism from a Feminist Perspective* (San Francisco: Harper & Row, 1990).

Plaut, W. Gunther. *The Case for the Chosen People* (New York: Doubleday, 1965).

Pockett, Susan. "If Free Will Did Not Exist, It Would Be Necessary to Invent It", in: Gregg D. Caruso (ed.), *Exploring the Illusion of Free Will and Moral Responsibility* (Lanham: Lexington, 2013), 265–272.

Poincaré, Lucien. *The New Physics and Its Evolution* (London: Kegan Paul, Trench, Trübner & Co., 1907).

Pollok, Anne. "The Power of Rituals: Mendelssohn and Cassirer on The Religious Dimension of 'Bildung'", *Religious Studies* 50.4 (2014): 445–464.

Popper, Karl. *The Poverty of Historicism* (New York: Harper & Row, 1964).

Porter, James I. "Language as a System in Ancient Rhetoric and Grammar", in: Egbert J. Bakker (ed.), *A Companion to the Ancient Greek Language* (Oxford: Wiley-Blackwell, 2010): 512–523.

Prager, Marcia. *The Path of Blessing: Experiencing the Energy and Abundance of the Divine* (New York: Bell Tower, 1998).

Pressman, Hannah. "The Hebrew Alphabet Gets An Orthodox Feminist Makeover", *Stroum Center for Jewish Studies*, March 23, 2015. https://jewish-studies.washington.edu/israel-hebrew/the-hebrew-alphabet-gets-an-orthodox-feminist-makeover/.

Priel, Joseph. "Kamah Leshonot Geulah Yesh Bakatuv?", *Morashtenu* 18 (2009): 199–209.

Ramon, Einat. "Tziyonut Tarbutit Kechalufa Lareforma Bektvei Ahad Ha'am", in: Yaakov Yadgar, Gideon Katz and Shalom Ratzabi (eds.), *Me'ever Lahalakhah* (Sde Boker: Ben-Gurion University Press, 2014), 108–140.

Ramshaw, Gail. *God Beyond Gender: Feminist Christian God-Language* (Minneapolis: Fortress Press, 1995).

Raphael, Melissa. *Religion, Feminism and Idoloclasm: Being and Becoming in the Women's Liberation Movement* (London: Routledge, 2019).

Raphael, Melissa. *The Female Face of God in Auschwitz: A Jewish Feminist Theology of the Holocaust* (London, Routledge, 2003).

Rappel, Joel. *Hatefillah Lishlom Hamedinah* (Modi'in: Kinneret, Zmora-Bitan, Dvir, 2018).

Raschke, Carl A. *Postmodern Theology: A Biopic* (Eugene: Cascade, 2017).

Ratson, Eshbal. "Counting the Hours", *Segula* 52 (2020): 28–37.

Ratzabi, Shalom. "Religious Thinkers on the Secular State", *Israel Studies* 13.3 (2008): 114–136.

Rauschenbusch, Walter. "The Influence of Historical Studies on Theology", *American Journal of Theology* 11.1 (1907): 111–127.

Ravitzky, Aviezer. "'Hatzivi Lakh Tziyunim' Letziyon: Gilgulo Shel Ra'ayon", in: Moshe Halamish and Aviezer Ravitzky (eds.), *Eretz Yisrael Bahagut Hayehudit Biymei Habeynayim* (Jerusalem: Yad Ben-Zvi, 1991), 1–39.

Rawidowicz, Simon. *Israel, the Ever-Dying People and Other Essays*, edited by Benjamin C.I. Ravid (Rutherford: Fairleigh Dickinson University Press, 1967).

Raz-Krakotzkin, Amnon. "Jewish Memory Between Exile and History", *Jewish Quarterly Review* 97.4 (2007): 530–543.

Rechnitzer, Haim O. *Ars Poetica – Theology in the Poetry of Twentieth-Century Israeli Poets: Avraham Halfi, Shin Shalom, Amir Gilboa, and T. Carmi* (Cincinnati: Hebrew Union College Press, 2023).

Reese, M.R. "Roman Emperor Caligula and the Floating Bridge of Baiae," *Ancient Origins,* December 15, 2014. https://www.ancient-origins.net/history/roman-emperor-caligula-and-floating-bridge-baiae-002452.

Reif, Stefan C. "The Place of Prayer in Early Judaism", in: Stefan C. Reif and Renate Egger-Wenzel, *Ancient Jewish Prayers and Emotions* (Berlin & Boston: de Gruyter, 2015), 1–17.

Reik, Theodor. *Pagan Rites in Judaism – From Sex Initiation, Magic, Moon-Cult, Tattooing, Mutilation, and Other Primitive Rituals to Family Loyalty and Solidarity* (New York: Farrar, Straus, 1964).

Reik, Theodor. *Jewish Wit* (New York: Gamut Press, 1962).

Rembaum, Joel E. "Medieval Jewish Criticism of the Christian Doctrine of Original Sin", *AJS Review* 7/8 (1982/1983): 353–382.

Riley, Jonathan. "Isaiah Berlin's 'Minimum of Common Ground'", *Political Theory* 41.1 (2013): 61–89.

Robb, Kevin. *Literacy and Paideia in Ancient Greece* (New York & Oxford: Oxford University Press, 1994).
Robbins, Jeffrey W. *Radical Theology: A Vision for Change* (Bloomington & Indianapolis: Indiana University Press, 2016).
Robinson, Andrew. *The Story of Writing – Alphabets, Hieroglyphs and Pictograms* (2nd ed.) (London: Thames & Hudson, 2007).
Rorty, Richard. *Philosophy and the Mirror of Nature* (Princeton: Princeton University Press, 1979).
Rorty, Richard. *Philosophy and Social Hope* (London: Penguin, 1999).
Rose, Gillian. "Walter Benjamin – Out of the Sources of Judaism", in: Laura Marcus and Lynda Nead (eds.), *The Actuality of Walter Benjamin* (London: Laurence & Wishart, 1998), 85–117.
Rose, Or, Jo Ellen Green Kaiser, and Margie Klein (eds.). *Righteous Indignation: A Jewish Call for Justice* (Woodstock: Jewish Lights, 2008).
Rose, Sven-Erik. "Lazarus Bendavid's and J.G. Fichte's Kantian Fantasies of Jewish Decapitation in 1793", *Jewish Social Studies* 13.3 (2007): 73–102.
Rosen, Tova. "'Meshal Sechel Alei Ahav': Eros ve-Intelekt Bemachberet Harishonah Shel Yaakov Ben Eliezer", *Teudah* 19 (2002): 191–212.
Rosen-Zvi, Ishay. *Demonic Desires: Yetzer Hara and the Problem of Evil in Late Antiquity* (Philadelphia: University of Pennsylvania Press, 2011).
Rosenak, Avinoam. *Zehuyot Mitnagshot: Nisuei Ta'arovet: Nituach Filosofi, Teologi Umachshevet Chinuch*, vols. 1 & 2 (Jerusalem: Carmel, 2023).
Rosenak, Michael. *Roads to the Palace: Jewish Texts and Teaching* (Providence: Berghahn, 1995).
Rosenberg, Shalom. "Yadot Nedarim", in: Moshe Bar (ed.), *Mechkarim Behalakha Uvemachshevet Yisrael* (Ramat Gan: Bar Ilan University Press, 1994), 193–217.
Rosenberg, Shalom. "Prayer and Jewish Thought: Approaches and Problems (A Survey)", in: Gabriel H. Cohn and Harold Fisch (eds.), *Prayer in Judaism: Continuity and Change* (Northvale: Jason Aaronson, 1996), 69–108.
Rosenblatt, Samuel. "The Relations Between Jewish and Muslim Laws Concerning Oaths and Vows", *Proceedings of the American Academy of Jewish Research* 7 (1935): 229–243.
Rosenstein, Marc J. "A Brief History of Jewish Victimhood Identity", *CrossCurrents* 73.2 (2023): 127–152.
Rosenthal, David. "Al Birkot Hatefillin B'Eretz Yisrael Ubebavel", *Tarbiz*, 79 (2011): 63–86.
Rosenstock, Bruce. *Philosophy and the Jewish Question: Mendelssohn, Rosenzweig, and Beyond* (New York: Fordham University Press, 2020).
Rosenthal, Ruvik. "Gvul im Kol Davar." *Hazira Haleshonit*, February 2, 2007. https://www.ruvik.co.il/%D7%94%D7%98%D7%95%D7%A8-%D7%94%D7%A9%D7%91%D7%95%D7%A2%D7%99/2007/02022007.aspx.

Rosenzweig, Franz. *On Jewish Learning* (Madison: University of Wisconsin Press, 1955).
Rosenzweig, Franz. *The Star of Redemption* (Barbara E. Galli, transl.) (Madison: University of Wisconsin Press, 2005).
Ross, Tamar. *Expanding the Palace of Torah: Orthodoxy and Feminism.* (Hanover: Brandeis University Press, 2024).
Rotman, Brian. "Thinking Dia-Grams: Mathematics, Writing and Virtual Reality", *South Atlantic Quarterly* 94.2 (1995): 389–415.
Rotman, Brian. *Becoming Beside Ourselves: The Alphabet, Ghosts and Distributed Human Being* (Durham & London: Duke University Press, 2008).
Rubenstein, Richard L. *Power Struggle* (New York: Scribner, 1974).
Rubenstein, Richard L. "On Becoming A Radical Theologian", *Journal for Cultural and Religious Theory* 19.1 (2019–20): 208–215.
Rudavsky, Tamar M. *Time Matters: Time, Creation, and Cosmology in Medieval Jewish Philosophy* (Albany: State University of New York Press, 2000).
Rudavsky, Tamar M. *Jewish Philosophy in the Middle Ages: Science, Rationalism and Religion* (New York: Oxford University Press, 2018).
Rudavsky, Tamar M. "Crescas on Time, Space and Infinity", *Journal of Textual Reasoning* 13.1 (2022): 188–212.
Sacks, Elias. *Moses Mendelssohn's Living Script: Philosophy, Practice, History, Judaism* (Bloomington: Indiana University Press, 2017).
Sacks, Jonathan. *Will We Have Jewish Grandchildren? Jewish Continuity and How To Achieve It* (London: Vallentine Mitchell, 1994).
Sacks, Jonathan. *The Dignity of Difference: How To Avoid the Clash of Civilizations* (London & New York: Continuum, 2002).
Sagi, Avi. *Jewish Religion After Theology* (Boston: Academic Studies Press, 2009).
Sagi, Avi. *Prayer After the Death of God: A Phenomenological Study of Hebrew Literature* (Batya Stein, transl.) (Brighton: Academic Studies Press, 2016).
Saiman, Chaim N. *Halakhah: The Rabbinic Idea of Law* (Princeton: Princeton University Press, 2018).
Sandberg, Ruth. "Rethinking the Notion of Universality in Judaism and Its Implications", *Studies in Christian-Jewish Relations,* 12.1 (2017): 1–8.
Sands, Kathleen M. "Ifs, Ands, and Butts: Theological Reflections on Humor", *Journal of the American Academy of Religion* 64.3 (1996): 499–523.
Saperstein, Marc. "The Land of Israel in Pre-Modern Jewish Thought: A History of Two Rabbinic Statements", in: Lawrence A. Hoffman (ed.). *The Land of Israel: Jewish Perspectives* (Notre Dame: University of Notre Dame Press, 1986), 188–209.
Sarason, Richard S. "The Significance of the Land of Israel in the Mishnah", in: Lawrence A. Hoffman (ed.). *The Land of Israel: Jewish Perspectives* (Notre Dame: University of Notre Dame Press, 1986), 109–136.

Sarna, Nahum M. *Songs of the Heart: An Introduction to the Book of Psalms* (New York: Schocken, 1993).

Sartiliot, Claudette. *Citation and Modernity: Derrida, Joyce, and Brecht* (Norman & London: University of Oklahoma Press, 1993).

Sass, Benjamin. *The Alphabet at the Turn of the Millennium: The West Semitic Alphabet CA. 1150-850 BCE – The Antiquity of the Arabian, Greek and Phrygian Alphabets* (Tel Aviv: Emery & Claire Yass Publications in Archaeology, 2005).

Sass, Benjamin. "The Emergence of Monumental West Semitic Alphabetic Writing, with an Emphasis on Byblos", *Semitica* 59 (2017): 109–141.

Sasson, Jack M. "The Genesis of Time", *The Torah.com*, 2019. https://thetorah.com/article/the-genesis-of-time.

Satherley, Tessa. "'The Simple Jew': The 'Price Tag' Phenomenon, Vigilantism, and Rabbi Yitzchak Ginsburgh's Political Kabbalah", *Melilah: Manchester Journal of Jewish Studies* 10.1 (2014): 57–91.

Satherley, Tessa Dawn. *Unity and Opposite in Israel's Settler Movement: Rabbi Tzvi Yisrael Tau and Rabbi Yitzchak Ginsburgh* (Unpublished PhD Thesis, University of Melbourne, 2015).

Savran, George W. *Telling and Retelling: Quotation in Biblical Narrative* (Bloomington & Indianapolis: Indiana University Press, 1988).

Sax, Benjamin E. "Walter Benjamin's Karl Kraus: Negation, Quotation, and Jewish Identity", *Shofar* 32.3 (2014): 1–29.

Sax, Benjamin E. "Judaism, Experience, and the Secularizing of Life: Revisiting Walter Benjamin's Montage of Quotation", *Religions* 13 (2022): 1033.

Scheindlin, Raymond P. *The Gazelle: Medieval Hebrew Poems On God, Israel, and the Soul* (Philadelphia: Jewish Publication Society, 1991).

Schiff, Danny. *Judaism in a Digital Age: An Ancient Tradition Confronts a Transformative Era* (New York: Palgrave Macmillan, 2023).

Schiffman, Lawrence H. "The Pharisees Revisited: Louis Finkelstein on the Second Temple Period", in: Zvia Ginor (ed.). *Yakar Le'Mordecai: Jubilee Volume in Honor of Rabbi Mordecai Waxman* (Hoboken: Ktav & Temple Israel of Great Neck, 1998), 85–101.

Schiffman, Zachary Sayre. "Historicizing History / Contextualizing Context", *New Literary History* 42.3 (2011a): 477–498.

Schiffman, Zachary Sayre. *The Birth of the Past* (Baltimore: Johns Hopkins University, 2011b).

Schirmann, Jefim. "Hebrew Liturgical Poetry and Christian Hymnology", *Jewish Quarterly Review* 44.2 (1953): 123–161.

Schmookler, Andrew Bard. *The Illusion of Choice: How the Market Economy Shapes Our Destiny* (Albany: State University of New York Press, 1993).

Scholem, Gershom. "The Name of God and the Linguistic Theory of the Kabbalah", *Diogenes* 79/80 (1972): 164–194.

Scholem, Gershom. *On Jews and Judaism in Crisis* (Werner J. Dannhauser, ed.) (New York: Schocken, 1976).
Scholem, Gershom. *Kabbalah* (New York: Meridian, 1978).
Scholem, Gershom. *Origins of the Kabbalah* (Philadelphia: Jewish Publication Society, 1987).
Scholem, Gershom. *On the Possibility of Jewish Mysticism in our Time, and Other Essays* (Avraham Shapira, ed.) (Philadelphia: Jewish Publication Society, 1997).
Schonfeld, Eli. "Shichchi Elohim: Moshe Mendelssohn VeRabbi Yaakov Emden Al Nivcharut Veuniversalizm", *Da'at* 81 (2016): 351–368.
Schorsch, Ismar. "Editor's Introduction: Ideology and History in the Age of Emancipation", in: Heinrich Graetz, *The Structure of Jewish History and Other Essays*, edited and translated by Ismar Schorsch (New York: Jewish Theological Seminary of America, 1975), 1–62.
Schorsch, Ismar. *From Text to Context: The Turn to History in Modern Judaism* (Hanover: Brandeis University Press, 1994).
Schorsch, Ismar. *Leopold Zunz: Creativity in Adversity* (Philadelphia: University of Pennsylvania Press, 2016).
Schram, Steven. "Tefillin: An Ancient Acupuncture Point Prescription for Mental Clarity", *Journal of Chinese Medicine* 70 (2008): 5–8.
Schultz, Joseph P. "Angelic Opposition to the Ascension of Moses and the Revelation of the Law", *Jewish Quarterly Review* 61.4 (1971): 282–307.
Schwarzschild, Steven S. *The Pursuit of the Ideal: Jewish Writings of Steven Schwarzschild*, edited by Menachem Kellner (Albany: State University of New York Press, 1990).
Schweid, Eliezer, *Ra'ayon Ha'am Hanivchar Vehaliberaliut Hachadashah* (Tel Aviv: Hakibbutz Hameuchad, 2015).
Seeskin, Kenneth. "Can There Be A Positive Theology?", in: Steven Kepnes (ed.), *Cambridge Companion to Jewish Theology* (Cambridge: Cambridge University Press, 2020), 375–391.
Seigel, Jerrold. *Modernity and Bourgeois Life: Society, Politics, and Culture in England, France and Germany Since 1750* (Cambridge: Cambridge University Press, 2012).
Seltzer, Robert M. and Lance J. Sussman. "What Are the Basic Principles of Reform Judaism?", in: Judisth S. Lewis (ed.), *Thinking Ahead: Toward the Next Generation of Judaism* (Binghamton: Keshet, 2001), 7–16.
Sharkansky, Ira. *Governing Israel: Chosen People, Promised Land and Prophetic Tradition* (New Brunswick & London: Transaction, 2005).
Sharvit, Yosef. "Harav Yehuda Leon Ashkenazi (Manitou): Giyur, Halakhah Vezehut", in: Avinoam Rosenak [ed.], *Hahalakhah* (Jerusalem: Magnes, 2012), 266–282.
Sherwin, Byron L. *Faith Finding Meaning: A Theology of Judaism* (Oxford: Oxford University Press, 2009).

Sherwin, Byron L. "Tikkun Olam: A Case of Semantic Displacement", *Jewish Political Studies Review* 25.3/4 (2013): 43–58.
Shlain, Leonard. *The Alphabet Versus The Goddess: The Conflict Between Word and Image* (New York: Penguin/Compass, 1998).
Shlonsky, Avraham. "Karati Elekha," *Kol Shirei Avraham Shlonsky* (Tel Aviv: Sifriat Poalim, 1968), 54.
Simão, Lívia Mathias. "The Bounded Indeterminacy of Tradition", in: Brady Wagoner, Bo Allesøe Christensen, and Carolin Demuth (eds.), *Culture as Process: A Tribute to Jaan Valsiner* (Cham: Springer Nature, 2021), 105–114.
Simkovich, Malka. *The Making of Jewish Universalism: From Exile to Alexandria* (Lanham: Lexington Books, 2017).
Simmel, Georg. *The View of Life: Four Metaphysical Essays with Journal Aphorisms* (John A. Andrews and Donald N. Levine, transl.) (Chicago & London: University of Chicago Press, 2010).
Singer, Peter. "Famine, Affluence, and Morality", *Philosophy and Public Affairs* 4.1 (1972): 229–243.
Slomp, Gabriella. "The Theory of the Partisan: Carl Schmitt's Neglected Legacy", *History of Political Thought* 26.3 (2005): 502–519.
Smith, John H. "The Infinitesimal as Theological Principle: Representing the Paradoxes of God and Nothing in Cohen, Rosenzweig, Scholem, and Barth", *MLN* 127.3 (2012): 562–588.
Sneed, Mark R. *The Politics of Pessimism in Ecclesiastes: A Social-Science Perspective* (Atlanta: Society of Biblical Literature, 2012).
Soll, William Michael. "Babylonian and Biblical Acrostics", *Biblica* 69.3 (1988): 305–323.
Solomon, Norman. *Torah From Heaven: The Reconstruction of Faith* (Oxford: Littman Library of Jewish Civilization, 2012).
Solomon, Norman. "The Attenuation of God in Modern Jewish Thought", *Melilah: Manchester Journal of Jewish Studies* 12 (2015): 97–109.
Soloveitchik, Joseph B. *Kol Dodi Dofek: Listen – My Beloved Knocks* (David Z. Gordon transl.) (New York: Yeshiva University, 2006).
Soloveichik, Meir. "God's Beloved: A Defense of Chosenness", *Azure* 4 (2005): 59–84.
Stadelmann, Luis I. J. *The Hebrew Conception of the World: A Philological and Literary Study* (Rome: Pontifical Biblical Institute, 1970).
Statman, Daniel. "Negative Theology and the Meaning of the Commandments in Modern Orthodoxy", *Tradition: A Journal of Orthodox Jewish Thought* 39.1 (2005): 58–71.
Stein, Dina. "Linguistic Liaisons: Wives and Vows in the Babylonian Talmud (BT Nedarim 66a-b)", *Nashim* 35 (2019): 176–198.
Steiner, George. *After Babel: Aspects of Language and Translation* (Oxford & London: Oxford University Press, 1975).

Steiner, George. *Grammars of Creation* (New Haven: Yale, 2001).
Stephens, Elizabeth. "Feminism and New Materialism: The Matter of Fluidity", *Interalia: A Journal of Queer Studies* 9 (2014): 186–202.
Stern, David. "The Alphabet of Ben Sira and the Early History of Parody in Jewish Literature", in: Hindy Najman and Judith Newman (eds.), *The Ideal of Biblical Interpretation* (Leiden: Brill, 2004), 423–448.
Stern, Josef. *Quotations as Pictures* (Cambridge: MIT Press, 2022).
Stern, Sacha. *Time and Process in Ancient Judaism* (Oxford: Littman Library of Jewish Civilization, 2007).
Sternberg, Elaine. *Just Business: Business Ethics in Action* (Oxford: Oxford University Press, 2000).
Stone, Geoffrey R. *Perilous Times: Free Speech in Wartime from the Sedition Act of 1798 to the War on Terrorism* (New York: Norton, 2004a).
Stone, Suzanne Last. "Truth and Illusion", *Jewish Quarterly Review* 94.1 (2004b): 19–22.
Stout, Jeffrey. *Democracy and Tradition* (Princeton: Princeton University Press, 2004).
Stout, John C. "Experimenting with Letters: Alphabetical Sequences in Contemporary Innovative Poetry – Bök, Silliman, Mullen and Christensen", *Modern Language Review* 111.3 (2016): 613–632.
Strassfeld, Max K. *Trans Talmud: Androgynes and Eunuchs in Rabbinic Literature* (Oakland: University of California Press, 2022).
Strassfeld, Michael. *Judaism Disrupted – A Spiritual Manifesto for the 21ˢᵗ Century* (Teaneck: Ben Yehuda Press, 2023).
Stratton, Jon. "Sampling and Jewishness: A Short History of Jewish Sampling and its Relationship with Hip-Hop", *Shofar* 34.3 (2016): 50–75.
Strauss, Leo. "Why We Remain Jews", in: Leo Strauss, *Jewish Philosophy and the Crisis of Modernity*, (Kenneth Hart Green, ed.) (Albany: State University of New York Press, 1997), 311–356.
Stroumsa, Sarah. "Masoret Tsitut: 'Al Mekorot Geluyim Umekorot Mutsna'im Besifrut Hafilosofit Be'aravit – Yehudit", in: Joshua Blau and David Doron (eds.), *Masoret Veshinui Betarbut Yehudit-ʿArvit Biymei Habeynayim* (Ramat Gan: Bar-Ilan University Press, 1990), 167–178.
Strugnell, John and Hanan Eshel. "It's Elementary: Psalms 9 and 10 and the Order of the Alphabet", *Bible Review* 17.3 (2001): 41–44.
Summers, Chelsea G. "From Yellowjackets to Dahmer, How Cannibalism Took Over Culture," *British Vogue*, December 4, 2022. https://www.vogue.co.uk/arts-and-lifestyle/article/cannibalism-on-screen.
Swartz, Michael D. *Mystical Prayer in Ancient Judaism: An Analysis of* Ma'aseh Merkavah (Tübingen: Mohr, 1992).

Sviri, Sara. "Words of Power and the Power of Words: Mystical Linguistics in the Works of Al-Ḥakīm Al-Tirmidhī", *Jerusalem Studies in Arabic and Islam* 27 (2002): 204–244.

Tabory, Joseph. *Pesach Dorot: Perakim Betoldot Leil Haseder* (Tel Aviv: Hakibbutz Hameuchad, 1996).

Tabory, Joseph. "The Piety of Politics: Jewish Prayers for the State of Israel", in: Ruth Langer and Steven Fine (eds.), *Liturgy in the Life of the Synagogue: Studies in the History of Jewish Prayer* (Winona Lake: Eisenbrauns, 2005), 225–246.

Tallis, Raymond. *Of Time and Lamentation: Reflections on Transience* (Newcastle: Agenda, 2017).

Tawil, Hayim. "'Azazel The Prince of the Steepe: A Comparative Study", *Zeitschrift für die alttestamentliche Wissenschaft* 92.1 (1980): 43–59.

Taylor, Charles. *Sources of the Self: The Making of the Modern Identity* (Cambridge: Harvard University Press, 1989).

Taylor, Charles. *Modern Social Imaginaries* (Durham & London: Duke University Press, 2004).

Telushkin, Joseph. *Jewish Humor: What the Best Jewish Jokes Say About the Jews* (New York: HarperCollins, 1992).

Thiselton, Anthony C. *Systematic Theology* (Grand Rapids & Cambridge: Eerdmans, 2015).

Thompson, John B. "Tradition and Self in a Mediated World", in: Paul Heelas, Scott Lash, and Paul M. Morris (eds.), *Detraditionalization: Critical Reflection on Authority and Identity* (Cambridge: Blackwell, 1996), 89–108.

Thon, Johannes. "The Power of (Hebrew) Language: Grammar, Cabbalah, Magic and the Emerging Protestant Identity", *European Journal of Jewish Studies* 6.1 (2012): 105–122.

Tiemeyer, Lena-Sofia. "Vocalization and Interpretation in Isaiah 56-66", in: Tommy Wasserman, Greger Anderssen and David Wilgren (eds.), *Studies in Isaiah: History, Theology and Reception* (London & New York: Bloomsbury T & T Clark, 2017), 152–175.

Tillich, Paul. *The Courage to Be* (New Haven: Yale University Press, 1952).

Tirosh-Samuelson, Hava. *Judaism and Ecology: Created World and Revealed World* (Cambridge: Center for the Study of World Religions, 2002).

Tishby, Isaiah (ed.). *The Wisdom of the Zohar: An Anthology of Texts* (David Goldstein, transl.) (Oxford: Oxford University Press, 1989).

Tönnies, Ferdinand. *Community and Society* (Charles P. Loomis, transl.) (East Lansing MI: Michigan State University Press, 1957).

Tsalka, Dan. *Sefer Haalef Bet* (Tel-Aviv: Xargol, 2003).

Tsoffar, Ruth. "Staging Sexuality, Reading Wallach's Poetry", *Hebrew Studies* 43 (2002): 87–117.

Tucker, Ethan. "Gender and Tefillin: Possibilities and Consequences", *Times of Israel* (blog) January 26, 2014. https://blogs.timesofisrael.com/gender-and-tefillin-possibilities-and-consequences.
Turner, Joseph. "A Reading of Psalm 90 in Light of Franz Rosenzweig's Notion of Time", in: Martin Brasser (ed.), *Rosenzweig als Leser: Kontextuelle Kommentare sum "Stern der Erlösung"* (Tübingen: Max Niemeyer, 2004), 499–508.
Tur-Sinai, Naftali Herz. "The Origin of the Alphabet I", *Jewish Quarterly Review*, 41.1 (1950a): 83–109.
Tur-Sinai, Naftali Herz. "The Origin of the Alphabet II", *Jewish Quarterly Review*, 41.2 (1950b): 159–179.
Tur-Sinai, Naftali Herz. "The Origin of the Alphabet: B) The Mnemonic Verses and the Alphabetically Arranged Poems of the Bible", *Jewish Quarterly Review*, 41.3 (1951): 277–301.
Tweed, Thomas A. *Crossing and Dwelling: A Theory of Religion* (Cambridge: Harvard University Press, 2006).
Tworek, Wojciech. *Eternity Now: Rabbi Shneur Zalman of Liady and Temporality* (Albany: State University of New York Press, 2019).
Uffenheimer, Binyamin. "Segula", *Beit Mikra* 4 (1977): 427–434.
Ulmer, Jasmine. "Refocusing the Anthropocenic Gaze: A Photo Essay", *Journal of Posthumanism* 1.2 (2021): 235–243.
United States Bureau of Education. *The Letters of Rabbi Akiba, or, The Jewish Primer As It Was Used in the Public Schools Two Thousand Years Ago* (Washington, DC: Government Printing Office, 1897).
Urbach, Efraim Elimelech. *The Sages, Their Concepts and Beliefs* (Israel Abrahams, transl.) (Jerusalem: Magnes Press, 1979).
Van der Heide, Albert. "'Mem and Samekh' Stood by a Miracle: The Sugya on the Hebrew Script (Shabbat 103a-104a)", *Studia Rosenthaliana* 38/39 (2005-6): 137–143.
Vandaele, Jeroen. "Narrative Humor (I): Enter Perspective", *Poetics Today* 31.4 (2010): 721–785.
Vanhooser, Kevin J. (ed.). *The Cambridge Companion to Postmodern Theology* (Cambridge: Cambridge University Press, 2003).
Vecchione, Patrice (ed.). *Faith and Doubt: An Anthology of Poems* (New York: Henry Holt, 2007).
Walfish, Avraham. "Hatefillah Hashogeret – Al Gvul Hahashra'ah Vehaekztaza", *Tarbiz* 65.2 (1996): 301–314.
Waskow, Arthur (ed.). *Torah of the Earth: Exploring 4,000 Years of Ecology in Jewish Thought*. Vol.2 (Woodstock: Jewish Lights, 2000).
Watts Belser, Julia. "The Bible and Ecotheology", in: Hilary Marloe and Mark Harris (eds.), *The Oxford Handbook of the Bible and Ecology* (Oxford: Oxford University Press, 2022), 355–371.

Wazana, Nili. *All the Boundaries of the Land – The Promised Land in Biblical Thought in Light of the Ancient Near East* (Liat Qeren, transl.) (Winona Lake: Eisenbrauns, 2013).

Weber, Elizabeth. "Fending Off Idolatry: Ceremonial Law in Mendelssohn's *Jerusalem*", *MLN* 122.3 (2007): 522–543.

Weinroth, Avraham. "Tafkid Hamilim Umashmautan", *Sinai* 119 (1997): 199–245.

Weisberg, Dvora E. "On Wearing *Tallit* and *Tefillin*", in: Susan Grossman and Rivka Haut (eds.), *Daughters of the King: Women and the Synagogue* (Philadelphia: Jewish Publication Society, 2010), 282–283.

Weiss, Andrea L. *Figurative Language in Biblical Prose Narrative: Metaphor in the Book of Samuel* (Leiden: Beill, 2006).

Weiss, Shira. *Joseph Albo on Free Choice: Exegetical Innovation in Medieval Jewish Philosophy* (Oxford: Oxford University Press, 2017).

Weiss, Tzahi. "On the Matter of Language: The Creation for the World from Letters and Jacques Lacan's Perception of Letters as Real", *Journal of Jewish Thought and Philosophy* 17.1 (2009): 101–115.

Weiss, Tzahi. *Otiot Shenivrau Bahen Shamayim VaAretz* (Jerusalem: Bialik Institute, 2014).

Weiss, Tzahi. *Sefer Yesirah and Its Contexts: Other Jewish Voices* (Philadelphia: University of Pennsylvania Press, 2018).

West, William C. III, "Learning the Alphabet: Abecederia and the Early Schools in Greece", *Greek, Roman and Byzantine Studies* 55 (2015): 52–71.

Wiener, Max. *Abraham Geiger and Liberal Judaism: The Challenge of the Nineteenth Century* (Ernst J. Schlochauer, transl.) (Philadelphia: Jewish Publication Society, 1962).

Wiener Dow, Leon. *Uvlechtecha Baderech* (Ramat Gan: Bar Ilan University Press, 2017).

Wiese, Christian. "'Most Powerful Comrade in Conviction': David Einhorn and the Debate Concerning Jewish Universalism in the Radical Reform Movement", in: Christian Wiese (ed.), *Redefining Judaism in an Age of Emancipation: Comparative Perspectives on Samuel Holdheim (1806-1860)* (Leiden & Boston: Brill, 2007), 306–373.

Wieseltier, Leon. *Kaddish* (New York: Alfred A. Knopf, 1998).

Wisse, Ruth R. *Jews and Power* (New York: Schocken, 2007).

Wisse, Ruth R. *No Joke – Making Jewish Humor* (Princeton & Oxford: Princeton University Press, 2013).

Wistrich, Robert. "Theodor Herzl: Zionist Icon, Myth-Maker, and Social Utopian", in: Robert Wistrich and David Ohana, *The Shaping of Israel Identity: Myth, Memory and Trauma* (London: Frank Cass, 1995), 1–37.

Witczyk, Henryk. "The Eternal God's Response To Man's Cry In His Passing 'Days' and 'Years' (Ps 90)", *The Biblical Annals* 10.4 (2021): 533–562.

Wolfson, Elliot R. "Mystical Rationalization of the Commandments in 'Sefer ha-Rimmon'", *Hebrew Union College Annual* 59 (1988): 217–251.

Wolfson, Elliot R. *Through a Speculum That Shines: Vision and Imagination in Medieval Jewish Mysticism* (Princeton: Princeton University Press, 1994).

Wolfson, Elliot R. *Language, Eros, Being: Kabbalistic Hermeneutics and Poetic Imagination* (New York: Fordham University Press, 2005).

Wolfson, Elliot R. *Giving Beyond the Gift: Apophasis and Overcoming Theomania* (New York: Fordham University Press, 2014).

Wolfson, Elliot R. *Heidegger and Kabbalah: Hidden Gnosis and the Path of Poiesis* (Bloomington: Indiana University Press, 2019).

Wolfson, Elliot R. *Suffering Time: Philosophical, Kabbalistic, and Hasidic Reflections on Temporality* (Leiden & Boston: Brill, 2021).

Wolosky, Shira. "Gershom Scholem's Linguistic Theory", *Jerusalem Studies in Jewish Thought* 21 (2007): 165*–205*.

Wright, David P. *The Disposal of Impurity: Elimination Rites in the Bible and in Hittite and Mesopotamian Literature* (Atlanta: Scholars Press, 1987).

Wright, Charles D. and Stephen Pelle, "The *Alphabet of Words* in the Durham Collectar – An Edition With Two New Manuscript Witnesses", *Traditio* 72 (2017): 61–108.

Wright, Edmond. *Narrative, Perception, Language, and Faith* (London: Palgrave Macmillan, 2005).

Wyschogrod, Michael. *The Body of Faith: Judaism as Corporeal Election* (New York: Seabury Press, 1983).

Yadgar, Yaakov. "Transcending the 'Secularization vs. Traditionalization' Discourse: Jewish-Israeli Traditionists, the Post-Secular and the Possibilities of Multiculturalism", in: Avi Sagi and Ohad Nachtomy (eds.), *The Multicultural Challenge in Israel* (Boston: Academic Studies Press, 2009), 150–179.

Yadgar, Yaakov. *Secularism and Religion in Jewish-Israeli Politics: Traditionists and Modernity* (Abingdon: Routledge, 2011).

Yadgar, Yaakov. "Tradition", *Human Studies* 36 (2013): 451–470.

Yaffe, Martin D. (ed.). *Judaism and Environmental Ethics* (Lanham: Lexington, 2001).

Yeats, W. B. *Collected Poems* (London: Penguin, 2000).

Yerushalmi, Yosef Haim. "Spinoza on the Survival of the Jews", in: David N. Meyers and Alexander Kaye (eds.), *The Faith of Fallen Jews: Yosef Hayim Yerushalmi and the Writing of Jewish History* (Waltham: Brandeis University Press, 2014), 213–244.

Yisraeli, Oded. "Jewish Medieval Traditions Concerning the Origins of the Kabbalah", *Jewish Quarterly Review* 106.1 (2016): 21–41.

Yisraeli, Oded. "'Taking Precedence Over the Torah': Vows and Oaths, Abstinence and Celibacy in Naḥmanides' Oeuvre", *Journal of Jewish Thought and Philosophy* 28.2 (2020): 121–150.

Yonge, C. D. (transl.). *The Works of Philo, Complete and Unabridged* (Peabody: Hendrickson, 1993).

Yoreh, Tanhum S. *Waste Not: A Jewish Environmental Ethic* (Albany: State University of New York, 2019).

Yovel, Jonathan. "The Creation of Language and Language Without Time", *Biblical Interpretation* 20.3 (2012): 205–225.

Zakovitch, Yair. "Humor and Theology or The Successful Failure of Israelite Intelligence: A Literary-Folkloric Approach to Joshua 2", in: Susan Niditch (ed.), *Text and Tradition: The Hebrew Bible and Folklore* (Atlanta: Scholars Press, 1990), 75–98.

Zatelli, Ida. "The Origin of the Biblical Scapegoat Ritual: The Evidence of Two Eblaite Texts", *Vetus Testamentum* 48.2 (1998): 254–263.

Zeitlin, Solomon. "Did Agrippa Write a Letter to Gaius Caligula?", *Jewish Quarterly Review* 56.1 (1965): 22–31.

Zhong, Yorou. *Chinese Grammatology: Revolution and Chinese Literary Modernity, 1916-1958* (New York: Columbia University Press, 2019).

Zierler, Wendy and Joshua D. Garroway. *These Truths We Hold: Judaism in an Age of Truthiness* (Cincinnati: Hebrew Union College Press, 2022).

Zijlstra, Onno. *Language, Image, and Silence: Kierkegaard and Wittgenstein in Ethics and Aesthetics* (Bern: Peter Lang, 2006).

Zisquit, Linda. "Innovation and Tradition: Translating Yona Wallach & Rivka Miriam (And Me)", *Bridges* 14.2 (2009): 56–74.

Zola, Gary P. "The Common Places of Reform Judaism's Conflicting Platforms", *Hebrew Union College Annual* 72 (2001): 155–191.

Zoloth, Laurie. *Health Care and the Ethics of Encounter: A Jewish Discussion of Social Justice* (Chapel Hill & London: University of North Carolina Press).

Zwick, Martin. "Words and Diagrams about Rosenzweig's *Star*", *Naharaim* 14.1 (2020): 5–33.

Author Index[1]

A
Abarvanel, Isaac, 100
Adler, Rachel, 18, 42n53, 90, 175, 346
Akbar, Kaveh, 347
Albo, Joseph, 21, 40n27, 153
Allen, Woody, 188
Allison, Dorothy, 156
Amichai, Yehuda, 245
Amir, Yigal, 100
Arendt, Hannah, 13, 98
Aristotle, 54, 315

B
Baal, Shem Tov, 48n98, 174
Baeck, Leo, 16, 50n130, 89, 125
Bahya, ben Asher, 35, 285n7
Bahya, ibn Paquda, 72, 76n11, 77n19, 249, 265
Bauman, Zygmunt, 145n32, 212, 219n5, 318, 319
Ben Arza, Sara Friedland, 235n27, 268
Ben Zakkai, Rabban Johanan, 217

Bendavid, Lazarus, 225
Ben-Gurion, David, 331
Benjamin, Walter, 98, 99, 104n22, 269, 274n39
Berger, Peter, 243, 283, 285n6
Berlin, Isaiah, 111, 112, 115
Berlinerblau, Jacques, 230
Beruriah, 281, 282, 286n16, 286n17
Bialik, Haim Nachman, 97, 235n16, 240, 241, 324
Bialik, Hayim Nachman, 97
Bloom, Harold, 97, 98
Blumenthal, David, 15, 20
Borowitz, Eugene, 1–3, 9, 37n2, 37n3, 38n4, 38n5, 41n41, 175, 224, 235n19, 331
Bounds, Elizabeth, 291
Boyarin, Daniel, 118n23, 126, 251, 261n18, 339, 340
Buber, Martin, 127, 158n27, 253, 292, 293, 299n15, 310, 313n20, 344, 348n13, 348n15
Butler, Judith, 74, 84, 118n23

[1] Note: Page numbers followed by 'n' refer to notes.

C

Caligula, 3, 108, 116
Caputo, John, 19, 153, 154, 166, 167
Chabon, Michael, 319–324
Chaucer, Geoffrey, 342
Cohen, Hermann, 124, 132n27, 158n27, 173–175, 179, 191, 269
Comins, Mike, 206
Cypel, Sylvain, 258

D

David (King), 25, 148–151, 156
Deutsch, Gotthard, 138, 139
Douglass, Frederick, 330, 332

E

Eliot, T.S., 217
Ellenson, David, x, 143n9, 235n19, 317
Ellis, Marc, 118n23, 340
Emerson, Ralph Waldo, 93
Eshkol, Levi, 257

F

Fackenheim, Emil, 136, 175, 192, 196n23, 223, 227, 310
Feuerbach, Ludwig, 57, 64n20, 151
Finkielkraut, Alain, 252
Finnegan, Ruth, 93, 102n3
Fisch, Menachem, 308
Fischer, Elli, 321
Fishbane, Michael, 162, 270, 274n42, 294
Freud, Sigmund, 179, 204, 245n3, 278, 285n5
Friedman, Marilyn, 332
Frymer-Kensky, Tikva, 243

G

Geertz, Clifford, 84
Geiger, Abraham, 132n23, 202, 203, 205, 206
Ginzberg, Louis, 176
Goethe, Johann Wolfgang von, 219
Goldstein, Baruch, 99, 104n31, 320
Greenberg, Irving, 118n23, 186
Greenberg, Moshe, 264, 272n5

H

Halbertal, Moshe, 241, 242
Halevi, HayimDavid, 112
Halivni, David Weiss, 169, 171n19
Har-Shefi, Sivan, 26
Heidegger, Martin, 40–41n33, 157n16, 268
Heller, Agnes, 279
Herberg, Will, 181, 318, 325n10
Heschel, Abraham Joshua, 12, 41n44, 58, 63n1, 64n23, 131n22, 135, 142n6, 154, 163, 171n12, 174, 193, 217, 218, 266, 267, 312n8, 337n21, 342, 347n8
Heschel, Susannah, 203–204, 207n17
Hirsch, Samson Raphael, 200, 201, 207n17
Holdheim, Samuel, 83, 130n6, 140
Horney, Karen, 75
Hume, David, 232, 233

I

Idel, Moshe, 94, 144n16, 338n33

J

Jacobs, Louis, 39n22, 265
Jakobovits, Immanuel, 308
James, William, 54, 156
Janowitz, Naomi, 33

K

Kafka, Franz, 194
Kant, Immanuel, 225, 331
Kaplan, Mordechai, 122, 123, 126, 127, 130n12, 267, 293, 299n16
Kipnis, Evyatar Eviatar, 257
Kohler, Kaufmann, 16, 18, 68
Kook, Abraham Isaac Hacohen, 150, 273n11, 301
Koppel, Moshe, 243
Kotzk, Menahem Mendel of, 174
Krochmal, Nachman, 97
Kuhn, Thomas, 185

L

Landauer, Gustav, 293
Lapidoth, Moshe, 266
Lasch, Christopher, 68
Leibowitz, Yeshayahu, 12, 40n31, 43n59, 132n31, 200, 201, 266, 302
Leifer, David, 297
Levinas, Emmanuel, 4, 12, 13, 37, 63n2, 71, 117n2, 118n19, 167, 168, 191, 208n20, 268, 311
Levita, Elijah, 139
Luzzatto, Moses Haim, 76n11
Luzzatto, Moses Hayim, 9

M

Magid, Shaul, 133n39, 244
Magnes, Judah, 252, 253, 309–311, 313n20
Maimon, Solomon, 41n44, 266
Maimonides, 11, 12, 37, 40n31, 44n72, 44n73, 56, 90n1, 110, 124, 141, 143n9, 162, 166, 169, 170n8, 175, 217, 243, 245n7, 263, 272n1, 325n4

Marmur, Dow, x, 42n46, 42n48, 194, 252, 259, 274n25, 296, 302
Marx, Karl, 188, 318
May, Todd, 107
Maybaum, Ignaz, 16, 42n47, 188, 189, 193, 207n19
Mendele, Mocher Seforim, 315
Mendelssohn, Moses, 2, 4, 13, 29–37, 50n120, 50n123, 204, 206n4
Mevorach, Yishai, 175, 193
Moses, 54–57, 61, 62, 64n35, 95, 135, 137, 161–165, 168, 169, 171n15, 171n17, 171n18, 181, 215, 224, 236n33, 238, 261n18, 286n19, 289, 290, 305, 343

N

Nachman, of Bratzlav, 193, 232, 244
Nagel, Thomas, 59
Netanyahu, Benjamin, 104n30
Niebuhr, Reinhold, 283, 286n23
Nussbaum, Martha, 13, 87

P

Pelikan, Jaroslav, 211–213, 219, 219n4, 221n40
Petuchowski, Jakob, 34
Philipson, David, 225
Philo of Alexandria, 3, 268
Plaskow, Judith, 42n53, 88, 122, 123, 127, 211, 293
Plato, 46n78, 54
Posner, Netanel, 290
Prager, Marcia, 190

R

Rabbi, Akiva, 9, 58, 135, 246n10, 286n19, 297
Rabbi, Biri, 282

Rabbi, Ishmael, 58, 246n10
Rabbi Jose, 281, 282
Raphael, Melissa, i, 42n53, 64n20, 88
Rashi (Rabbi Shlomo Yitzhaki), 36, 46n78, 56, 189, 286n19, 328, 329
Rauschenbusch, Walter, 139
Reik, Theodor, 204
Rorty, Richard, 61, 156
Rosenak, Avinoam, 218, 321
Rosenak, Michael, 217, 218
Rosenzweig, Franz, 6, 16, 41n44, 124, 133n40, 145n27, 158n27, 164, 189, 193, 203, 207n19, 208n20, 259, 261n26
Ross, Tamar, 42n53, 163, 170n11
Rubenstein, Richard, 43n59, 186, 188, 194

S
Sacks, Jonathan, 3, 7, 132n33
Sadia Gaon, Saadia Gaon, 4, 124, 175, 245n4, 249, 259n1
Samuel ben Meir, Rabbi, 279
Sandberg, Ruth, 128
Scholem, Gershom, 27, 175, 183n19, 194, 274n39
Schwarzchild, Steven, 255, 260n13
Schweid, Eliezer, 191
Shakespeare, William, 53, 100, 239
Sherwin, Byron, 15, 39n22, 41n36
Shlonsky, Avraham, 147, 148, 157n1
Shneur Zalman, of Liadi, 57
Silver, Vivian, 253–256, 261n16
Simon, Ernst, 253
Simon, Paul, 152
Sofer, Avraham Shmuel Binyamin, 297
Solomon (King), 25, 148, 149, 188

Spinoza, Baruch, 55, 58, 60, 61, 63n12, 121–125, 127, 130n5, 289, 290
Steiner, George, 130n12, 267
Sternberg, Elaine, 107
Stout, Jeffrey, 45n74, 307–309

T
Taylor, Charles, 77n14, 291
Teitelbaum, Moshe, 137, 140, 143n11
Teitelbaum, Yekusiel Yehuda, 266
Thompson, John B., 213
Tirosh-Samuelson, Hava, 335
Tönnies, Ferdinand, 292, 293
Tweed, Thomas, 89

U
Ulmer, Jasmine, 60

W
Wolfson, Elliot, 43n59, 63n3, 143n8, 268

Y
Yadgar, Yaakov, 216, 317
Yehudah Halevi, Judah Halevi, 83, 86, 124, 126
Yerushalmi, Yosef Haim, 141
Yerushalmi, Yosef Hayim, 136
Yoffie, Eric, 228

Z
Zejderveld, Anton, 243
Zunz, Leopold, 140, 201–203, 206, 207n17

Work Index[1]

A

The Alphabet of Ben Sira, 29
Arba'ah Haturim, 284n2
Avodat Yisrael, 246n16

B

Babylonian Talmud
  Avodah Zarah, 73, 104n29
  Baba Metzia, 118n19
  Bava Batra/Baba Batra, 171n14, 183n18, 328
  Berakhot/Berachot, 77n23, 78n26, 143n9, 144n18, 207n5, 246n7
  Eruvin, 281
  Gittin, 110, 118n18
  Hullin, 89
  Ketubot, 246n18
  Menachot, 206n2, 286n19
  Nedarim, 171n14, 224, 231, 234n5, 235n27, 280
  Niddah, 117n9
  Rosh Hashanah, 149, 152, 231, 232
  Sanhedrin, 99, 103n14
  Shabbat, 54, 82, 100, 138, 199, 273n15, 301
  Sotah, 170n7
  Ta'anit, 144n15

H

Haketav Vehakabbalah, 260n3
Hebrew Bible
  Chronicles, 60, 133n45, 148, 234n6
  Daniel, 270
  Deuteronomy, 14, 35, 95, 117n6, 122, 125, 142n6, 183n18, 214, 271, 328
  Esther, 95, 336n1
  Exodus, 14, 36, 77n24, 137, 143n9, 163, 187
  Ezekiel, 54, 72, 215, 218, 220n23, 336n1, 346
  Genesis, 77n23, 77n24, 78n26, 78n27, 109, 133n45, 137, 143–144n14, 176, 178, 234n6, 245n2, 268, 274n27, 279, 285n7, 285n11, 301

[1] Note: Page numbers followed by 'n' refer to notes.

Hebrew Bible (cont.)
  Hosea, 54
  Isaiah, 10, 16, 59, 77n23, 78n26, 114, 115, 125, 217, 218
  Jeremiah, 9, 77n23, 78n26, 114, 241, 270
  Job, 68, 241, 329, 330
  Joshua, 4, 14, 15, 28, 77n24, 309
  Judges, 77n24, 78n27, 230, 261n21
  Kings, 188
  Lamentations, 23, 47n80
  Leviticus, 82, 177, 240, 250
  Micah, 188, 339
  Numbers, 36, 54, 77n24, 78n27, 104n24, 143n9, 231, 235n25
  Proverbs, 23, 29, 95
  Psalms, 10, 47n80, 47n83, 96, 125, 148, 171n18, 272n1, 285n11
  Samuel, 73, 74, 77n24, 100, 230
  Song of Songs, 68, 96, 103n14
  Zechariah, 74, 100

I
Igra Dekala, 219n13

K
Kehillat Ya'akov, 273n13

M
Machberet Menachem, 313n25
Maimonides
  Mishnah Commentary, 64n14, 170n8
Midrash
  Ecclesiastes Rabbah, 241
  Exodus Rabbah, 164, 171n18
  Genesis Rabbah, 109
  Leviticus Rabbah, 54
  Mechilta/Mekhilta, 313n14
  Numbers Rabbah, 171n14
  Otzar Hamidrashim, 246n10
  Pesikta Rabbati, 171n17
  Proverbs, 103n12
  Ruth Rabbah, 47n85
  Sifra, 109
  Sifre, 42n46
  Song of Songs Rabbah, 275n46
  Tanchuma, 103n12
  Tanna debe Eliyahu, 246n9
Midrash Alpha Beta, 337n28
Mishnah
  Avot, 215
  Bava Metzia/Bava Metzia, 118n19
  Berakhot, 104n24, 143n9, 144n15, 246n7, 274n45
  Eruvin, 281
  Kelim, 57
  Ohalot, 91n7
  Pesachim, 195n6, 196n9
  Sanhedrin, 41n39, 170n8
  Yoma, 104n26

N
New Testament, 64n13, 88, 131n21, 339

P
Palestinian Talmud
  Berakhot, 77n18, 103n14
  Kiddushin, 104n26, 117n9, 235n27
  Kilayim, 77n19
  Nazir, 96
  Pesachim, 104n26
  Shabbat, 199, 240
  Shekalim, 171n15
  Sotah, 170n7, 261n17
  Taaniot, 171n26

S

Sefer Hachinuch, 213
Sefer Ikkarim, 21
Sefer Yetzirah, 27, 103n10, 315
*Sheelot Uteshuvot
    Maharil*, 208n21
Shnei Luchot Haberit, 64n16,
    281, 286n17
Shulchan Arukh, 170n1, 227
Sifre, 104n26, 125, 183n18
    Deuteronomy, 42n46, 117n6
Silver, Vivian, 253–256, 261n16
Soferim, 170n1

T

Tikkunei Zohar, 64n35
Toldot Aharon, 220n21
Torat Moshe, 219n13

Y

Yeri'ot Shlomo, 285n13
Yetev Lev, 266

Z

Zohar, 48n93, 190, 206n5, 268

Subject Index[1]

A

Alphabets, 1, 22–34, 44n70, 44–45n74, 45n75, 45n76, 46n77, 46n78, 47n90, 48n93, 48n98, 48n100, 49n103, 49n108, 53, 284, 342–344, 346, 347

Anxiety, 2–10, 37, 38n4, 38n9, 73, 74, 96–98, 249, 339, 343, 346

Armageddon/Megiddo, 1, 3, 339–340

Aspaklaria, 53–62, 67, 70, 71, 88, 90, 94, 116, 129, 135, 153, 158n17, 162, 174, 185, 191, 211, 223, 243, 267, 280, 295, 303, 316, 327, 339, 341, 342, 347

B

Borders and boundaries, 79–90
Buddhism, 278

C

Chosenness, 31, 121–129, 185, 294, 341

Christianity, 11, 17, 189, 285n6

Community, 2, 4, 5, 10, 20, 53, 60, 88, 123, 128, 141, 155, 161, 182, 185, 186, 189–191, 194, 212, 227–229, 233, 234, 252, 264, 267, 269, 284, 289–298, 316, 317, 319, 320, 331, 340, 341

Conservative Judaism, 216

Culture, 22–30, 33, 37, 45n76, 46n77, 53, 59, 72, 81, 87, 94, 97, 98, 101, 110, 167, 189, 202, 206n1, 211, 257, 261n18, 264, 277, 279, 284, 306, 308, 309, 321, 324, 335

[1] Note: Page numbers followed by 'n' refer to notes.

D

Decency, 107–116, 188–189, 239, 251, 259, 302, 307, 311, 341, 344, 345
Dependence, 68, 264, 327–336

E

Education, 7, 27, 61, 80, 93–102, 169, 191, 217, 227, 234
Election/chosenness, 31, 114, 121–129, 130n1, 130n2, 130n6, 130n11, 132n31, 133n36, 134n46, 185, 294, 341
Endogamy, 319
Enlightenment, 67, 81, 148, 176, 212, 249, 301

F

Feminism, 86–88

G

Gaza, 113, 191, 249–259, 302, 339
Gemeinschaft and *Gesellschaft*, 292
God, 2, 54, 57, 67, 81, 95, 121, 137, 147–156, 163, 173, 188, 201, 212, 228, 237, 252, 263, 267–270, 278, 289, 316, 328, 339

H

Halakhah, 79, 88, 91n26, 100, 200, 223, 226–227, 232, 240–242, 244, 317, 318, 331
Hasidism, 27, 48n97, 76n5, 143n8, 174, 265
Hebrew Union College, 16, 34, 138, 149, 301, 319, 339
Hieroglyphics, 31–33, 204

History, 3, 11, 13–15, 17, 18, 23, 34, 41n41, 68, 80, 94, 95, 99, 100, 112, 122, 123, 128, 129, 133n40, 135–141, 150, 156, 166, 167, 173, 177, 178, 185, 188–191, 193, 206n1, 212, 214, 235n23, 249, 256–258, 260n6, 264, 278, 296, 298, 301, 304, 305, 311, 315, 318, 322, 323, 333, 334, 340, 342
Hope, 2–10, 13, 23, 37, 60, 62, 74, 86, 101, 116, 141, 152, 168, 170, 175, 187, 192, 200, 201, 203, 217, 234, 249, 252–254, 259, 296, 302, 305, 306, 335, 339, 343, 345, 346
Humor, 22, 277–284, 341

I

Idolatry, 31
Independence, 182, 290, 292, 305, 309, 327–336
Inequality, 8, 112, 332
Interdependence, 335–336
Islam, 4, 22, 189, 285n6
Israel, 1, 2, 7–8, 61, 81, 99, 108, 122, 149, 161, 178, 180, 187, 216, 226, 243, 249, 266, 283, 297, 302, 316, 331, 339

J

Jerusalem, 3, 25, 62, 100, 110, 113–116, 252, 254, 312n2, 339

K

Kabbalah, 6, 97, 181, 183n19, 220n18
Kaddish, 296, 299n22
Karaites, 4, 83

SUBJECT INDEX

L
Liberalism, 2, 17, 42n51
Liberation, 80, 81, 117n2, 139, 332, 340
Living script, 2, 31–34, 204

M
Masoretes, 2, 34–37, 139, 216
Megiddo, 339–340
Mission, 3, 87, 124, 125, 130n6, 132n31, 133n38, 150, 156, 304
Modernity, 2, 5, 6, 8, 9, 11, 17, 18, 34, 42n59, 55, 60, 61, 69, 80, 83, 84, 86, 97, 98, 118n20, 123, 136, 138–140, 175, 178, 193, 194, 212, 213, 224–226, 232, 238, 255, 266, 268, 283, 286n25, 289, 290, 292, 294, 295, 301, 306, 318, 319, 330, 331, 341

O
Orthodox Judaism, 57, 170n11, 297

P
Palestinians, 1, 8, 28, 114–116, 239, 251–258, 268, 306, 309–312, 313n12, 345
Particularism, 56, 294
Peoplehood, 91n26, 121–129, 341
Pluralism, 53
Postliberal, 1, 2, 17, 18, 42n52, 42n53, 42n54
Postmodern, 5, 18–22, 37n3, 42n56, 43n60, 85, 87, 97–99, 102, 154, 167, 175, 193, 319
Postmodernism, 42n56

Prayer, 7, 71, 72, 75, 77n23, 78n26, 86, 97, 100, 127, 128, 134n47, 138, 143n9, 148, 153, 156, 175, 194, 199, 206, 207n19, 208n26, 263–272, 290, 293, 296, 301, 341, 344

Q
Qumran, 25
Quotation, 21, 40n31, 54, 93–102, 177, 219n4, 325n15, 347n3

R
Redemption, 56, 81, 102, 115, 138, 140, 164, 185, 187, 189, 195, 195n6, 214, 249, 259, 263, 301–312
Reform Judaism, 16, 34, 68, 83, 124, 136, 140, 173, 174, 176, 186, 188, 195n4, 201, 205, 216, 224–227, 331, 346
Responsibility, 2, 41n41, 67–75, 81, 101, 115, 121, 177, 191, 218, 229, 233, 234, 251, 258, 259, 266, 268, 278, 291, 296, 306, 332, 333, 341

S
Samael, 176–179, 181, 182, 183n10, 250
Segulah, 126
Self, 2, 36, 38n9, 59, 67–75, 76n4, 76n5, 76n10, 77n14, 93, 167, 264–266, 273n8, 291
Shoah/Holocaust, 43n59, 192, 193, 196n23, 249, 261n16, 310, 343, 344
Sinai, 29, 30, 58, 80, 135, 164, 167, 181

Soul, 9, 68–75, 76n4, 76n11, 77n17, 77n18, 78n31, 82, 86, 97, 148, 151, 154, 190, 253, 265, 266, 273n16, 299n15, 311, 316, 325n5

Spirituality, 67–75, 101, 141, 194, 291, 341

T

Tefillin (phylacteries), 199–206, 206n1, 206n4, 207n5, 207n9, 207n14, 207n17, 207n19, 208n20, 208n26

Theology
 crunchy, 1, 2, 11–22
 definition, 13, 39n22, 41n43
 feminist, 293
 liberal, 16–18
 orthodox, 17
 radical, 18–22
 smooth, 2, 11–22, 94

Time, 5, 9, 14–16, 19, 24, 29, 31, 35–37, 41n44, 42n59, 49n106, 53, 56, 58, 61, 62, 63n7, 67, 72, 80, 81, 83, 86, 89, 94, 110, 115, 124, 128, 135–141, 142n1, 142n2, 142–143n8, 143n9, 143n11, 143–144n14, 144n15, 144n18, 148, 149, 167, 168, 175–180, 182, 186, 187, 189–191, 196n8, 203, 214, 216, 227, 232, 233, 239, 242, 249, 252–253, 255, 257, 258, 261n14, 264, 266, 270, 274n27, 275n46, 278, 280, 285n7, 286n19, 289, 291, 295, 296, 301, 304–307, 310, 312n8, 316, 318, 319, 322, 324, 325n5, 325n13, 332, 333, 335, 339, 340, 342, 343, 345

Torah, xi, 2, 7, 14, 28, 30, 35, 41n41, 46n78, 47n85, 50n129, 58, 81, 84, 95, 99–101, 104n27, 113, 129, 132n31, 134n46, 135, 136, 141, 142n6, 161–170, 174, 178–182, 183n18, 199, 202, 214, 215, 226, 227, 232–234, 236n33, 237, 244, 255, 280, 281, 286n19, 297, 304, 313n14, 315, 319, 325n13, 334, 338n30, 341

Tradition, xi, 1, 6–11, 17–23, 25, 27, 31, 35, 37, 39n22, 46n78, 48n93, 48n98, 54, 55, 57, 58, 61, 63n9, 64n13, 68, 74, 77n23, 78n26, 83, 84, 88, 89, 94–101, 103n10, 103n14, 113, 125, 129, 142n6, 143n8, 143n10, 145n31, 149, 151, 152, 157n8, 163, 169, 171n12, 171n17, 173, 174, 177, 181, 182, 183n19, 187, 189, 192, 194, 199, 200, 203, 206, 209n29, 211–219, 225–228, 233, 239, 244, 246n10, 252, 256, 258, 260n1, 261n18, 261n20, 263, 264, 267, 268, 270–272, 272n1, 273n21, 278, 282–284, 285n6, 286n16, 291, 294, 307, 308, 311, 315–317, 320, 321, 329, 331, 335, 336, 341, 342

Truth, 4, 17–20, 26, 29, 35, 39n22, 47n90, 49n107, 49n108, 53, 55–60, 62, 63n12, 71, 84, 87, 94, 112, 122, 128, 136, 139, 140, 144n22, 152, 153, 176, 200, 213, 238, 239, 241, 244, 245n5, 251, 256, 258, 259, 263, 280, 283, 289, 290, 296, 303, 315, 324, 329, 332, 340

SUBJECT INDEX 407

U
Universalism, 18, 124, 125, 294, 304

V
Vision, 5, 8, 54–58, 60, 62, 63n2, 63n3, 63n7, 63n8, 79, 94, 97, 100, 128, 188, 243, 256, 280, 302, 305, 306, 308, 311, 331
Vows, 223–234, 280

W
West Bank, 1, 81, 113, 250–252, 254, 311

Z
Zionism, 150, 151, 186, 256, 258, 261n19, 283, 290, 304, 306–309, 313n22, 317, 331, 345

The manufacturer's authorised representative in the EU is Springer Nature Customer Service Centre GmbH, Europaplatz 3, 69115 Heidelberg, Germany. If you have any concerns regarding our products, please contact ProductSafety@springernature.com

Printed and bound by CPI Group (UK) Ltd, Croydon, CR0 4YY

26/03/2026

02078951-0001